Shakespeare *the* Thinker

Yale University Press NEW HAVEN & LONDON

Shakespeare
the Thinker

A. D. NUTTALL

Published with assistance from the Mary Cady Tew Memorial Fund and the
foundation established in memory of Oliver Bay Cunningham of the Class of
1917, Yale College.

Designed by Nancy Ovedovitz and set in Postscript Monotype Bembo by
Keystone Typesetting, Inc. Printed in the United States of America
by Vail-Ballou Press.

Library of Congress Cataloging-in-Publication Data
Nuttall, A. D. (Anthony David)
Shakespeare the thinker / A. D. Nuttall.
    p.   cm.
Includes bibliographical references and index.
ISBN-13: 978-0-300-11928-2 (alk. paper)
1. Shakespeare, William, 1564–1616—Knowledge and learning. 2. England—
Intellectual life—16th century. 3. England—Intellectual life—17th century.
I. Title.
PR3000.N88 2007
822.3'3—dc22   2006035179

A catalogue record for this book is available from the British Library.

10 9 8 7 6 5 4 3 2 1

To Will Poole, Richard Scholar, and Noël Sugimura

Triton de he dianoia, "And third comes thought"
—Aristotle, *Poetics,* 1450b4

It must puzzle us to know what thinking is if Shakespeare and
Dante did not do it—Lionel Trilling, *The Liberal Imagination*

Ockham's razor: "The scientific principle that in explaining a
thing no more assumptions should be made than are necessary"
—*The Oxford English Dictionary*

Contents

Preface

About ten years ago Robin Lane Fox urged me to write an expansive book on Shakespeare. I was unwilling to do this. I had in mind a short, tightly organized book on certain points of philosophic interest in Shakespeare. Then John Kulka, in words that echoed those of Robin Lane Fox, again urged me to write a larger book, about the distinctiveness of Shakespeare's genius. I agreed and am now happy that I did so. The new plan forced me to read again play after play, and so to watch the playwright's thought as it grew and changed shape in successive dramatic essays. I ended by writing about almost all the plays (I say virtually nothing about *King John* and *The Merry Wives of Windsor*, nor do I discuss such cases of doubtful attribution as *The Two Noble Kinsmen* or *Edward III*, but all the rest are there). I became vividly aware of the importance of the notion of process to any understanding of Shakespeare as a creative intellect. To watch him or to read him becomes a kind of hunt, an everlasting pursuit of something glancingly wild, where the elusiveness of the prize is part of its essence.

I owe a special debt of gratitude to the three people to whom this book is dedicated. Noël Sugimura (N. K. Sugimura), Richard Scholar, and William Poole were all, at one time or another, pupils of mine (but of course the relationship was swiftly reversed—they were soon teaching me). In 2004 they organized a one-day conference on "Shakespeare and Philosophy" to mark my retirement. That memorable day, crowded as it was with more ideas and insights than I can ever fully assimilate, was a vital stimulus for the writing of this book. All three took the trouble to read through a typed draft, spotted mistakes, and made immensely useful comments. I have a similar debt to the admirable readers who acted for Yale University Press. Others have helped by answering queries and reading sections: Eric Christiansen, Stephen Medcalf, Julie Maxwell, Patrick Gray, Ann Jefferson, Robin Lane Fox, Erik Tonning, Graham Bradshaw, Christopher Tyerman, Katherine Duncan-Jones, Mark Griffith, Patrick Grant, Richard Proudfoot, Laurence Lerner. Behind and beyond these stand the hosts of those with whom I have talked about Shakespeare, in lecture-rooms, in tutorials, and less formally, down the years. The errors and absurdities that remain are all mine.

Almost all of the section on *Measure for Measure* was published earlier, as "*Measure for Measure:* Shakespeare's Essay on Heresy" in *The Glass*, 16 (2003). There are many points of contact, of a more diffuse nature, with earlier writings. What I say here about the two parts of *Henry IV, Henry V, The Merchant of Venice, Othello, Julius Caesar,* and *Coriolanus* develops from an argument begun in my *New Mimesis* (1983). Some of what I say about *The Winter's Tale* harks back to a little book I published in 1966. The account of *Timon of Athens* is similarly related to my book of that name (1989). The discussion of *The Tempest* near the end of the present volume recalls, but also radically transforms, things I said in my *Two Concepts of Allegory* (1967). Earlier articles in which some degree of overlap with the present book may be discerned are: "*Measure for Measure:* Quid Pro Quo?" *Shakespeare Studies,* 4 (1968); "Shakespeare's Richard II and Ovid's Narcissus," in *Ovid Renewed,* edited by Charles Martindale (1988); "*Hamlet:* Conversations with the Dead," in *Proceedings of the British Academy,* 74 (1988); "Freud and Shakespeare," in *Shakespearean Continuities: Essays in Honour of E. A. J. Honigman,* edited by John Batchelor, Tom Cain, and Claire Lamont (1997); "*A Midsummer Night's Dream:* Comedy as Apotrope of Myth," *Shakespeare Survey,* 53 (2000); "*The Winter's Tale:* Ovid Transformed," in *Shakespeare's Ovid,* edited by A. B. Taylor (2000); and "Action at a Distance: Shakespeare and the Greeks," in *Shakespeare and the Classics,* edited by Charles Martindale and A. B. Taylor (2004). The text of Shakespeare referred to is always (unless otherwise explained) that of *The Riverside Shakespeare,* 2nd ed. (Boston, 1997).

When I was well into the writing of this book I happened to meet an old friend in the street. We exchanged civilities and he asked how I was occupying my time. I said, "I'm writing an unforgivably long book on Shakespeare," and then added, "You know how there's a tradition whereby formerly lively minds produce in old age unduly mellow books on Shakespeare." This was his cue to say, "Oh, yours won't be like that." Instead, he looked gravely at me and said, "When you find yourself writing about his essential Englishness, you must stop." The persistent reader will find that there is a point in this book where I come perilously close to what my friend darkly predicted. But I stop, as instructed, at that point.

Shakespeare *the* Thinker

Introduction: Time-bound Shakespeare, Timeless Shakespeare

We know what Milton thought about many things. He didn't believe in the doctrine of the Trinity; he thought the execution of Charles I was morally right; he believed that married couples who didn't get on should be allowed to divorce. But we have no idea what Shakespeare thought, finally, about any major question. The man is elusive—one might almost say, systematically elusive. There is something eerie about a figure that can write so much and give so little away.

On a certain summer evening in Stratford-on-Avon in the 1960s I remember breaking free from the clotted discussion in the lecture-room (the International Shakespeare Conference was in full spate) and breathing the fresher air in the street. The author of the best plays ever written must often have walked in the street in which I was standing. The recurrent "must have" employed by biographers is rightly regarded with suspicion by all reasonable persons. But this was as safe a "must have" as one could hope to find. I struggled to imagine him, there in the street. What was he actually like? What was it like to *be* William Shakespeare, walking through Stratford in the later sixteenth century? Everyone knows the bald, bland head that appears at the opening of the First Folio of Shakespeare's dramatic works. But it is a poor drawing; if Shakespeare had "happened," around the same date, in Italy rather than England we might have done rather better. Even the baldness may be a distraction. Presumably Shakespeare in his younger days had hair on his head.

I began to guess wildly. He certainly had no toothpaste, so his teeth were perhaps unpleasing. He was probably, by our standards, short. If however we shift from the perspective of the 1960s time-traveller to "How did it seem, *then?*" the grey teeth (if true) and the low stature in any case vanish. In the country where most men are five feet, five inches tall, five feet, five inches will not "feel short." Similar strictures apply to the town, Stratford itself. "I must cut out," I said to myself, "the Shakespearean Disneyland of the twentieth-century tourist; I must see this street with the same slight curve but without shop windows, the road surface rough and marked with dung of horses and cattle, all the houses or almost all timber-framed, malodorous." It is an error to suppose that a real Elizabethan town would have been uniformly Elizabethan in its architecture. Many medieval buildings would have been mingled with the newer constructions. The centre of a typical English town in the mid-twentieth century included a fair amount of Victorian architecture. Of course there are surviving Elizabethan buildings in Stratford, lovingly preserved, aggressively presented. These are the same as the buildings Shakespeare undoubtedly saw. But this "same" covers a more-than-Copernican revolution in perception. Their primary characteristic for us is, precisely, their "Elizabethan-ness." For Shakespeare they would have been just houses.

In 1582 Shakespeare, still in his teens, married Anne Hathaway. She was eight years older and three months pregnant. We know, as certainly as we know anything, that she lived in a substantial farm house at Shottery, a few miles outside Stratford, and the house is still there. It is now known as "Anne Hathaway's cottage." It sits coyly in an improbable profusion of flowers and is on the tourist schedule of places to visit. I decided to walk to Shottery as Shakespeare must often have done ("must have" again!). I crossed the road when the traffic lights allowed me to do so, walked past many nondescript brick houses, late nineteenth century, early twentieth, offering bed and breakfast, crossed the track of the old branch line (now obliterated), continued by way of a hedged back-alley into a new housing estate, where toy cars and bikes lay scattered, came to a large grassy area crossed by an asphalt path, and so on to Shottery. As it grew darker the idea of re-enacting Shakespeare's walk became gradually less fatuous. Of course my actual route would not have been identical to that taken by the young Shakespeare. The differences, any way, were legion, and clamorous. But as the shadows gathered the "visual noise" of my own century was diminishing. The accidents of a particular time were gradually effaced. As I was leaving the suburbs behind I became aware of great shadowy tree-shapes, Warwickshire oaks. These were not the same trees that stood there when Shakespeare walked at dusk, but they were *just such* as he must have looked at, as I looked at now.

Philosophers distinguish "qualitative" from "numerical" identity. Two photographs of Bill Clinton, one taken when he was sixteen, the other when he was forty-five, certainly show the same person. This use of "same" is called "numerical." But Bill Clinton at forty-five is not the same as he was when he was sixteen. This use is called "qualitative." Shakespeare's birthplace, on view in Stratford, is numerically the same as the house Shakespeare knew. Qualitatively, however, it is different. The oak trees I saw in the gathering darkness were numerically different from the trees Shakespeare saw but qualitatively they were the same—or nearly so. Soon all I could make out distinctly was the horizon, the line marking the range of low hills in the distance, where some light lingered in the sky. This really was exactly what he saw. For a spooky second I felt as if we were standing side by side. "In such a night," I thought, "he might have stood just here."

The words, "In such a night," are Shakespeare's:

> In such a night
> Stood Dido with a willow in her hand
> Upon the wild sea-banks.   (*The Merchant of Venice,* V.i.9–11)

Why did Shakespeare not write "In such a morning" or "In such a day"? It will be said, "Because the scene in which the line occurs is a night scene." But that is not an answer. Why does a night scene prompt this thought where a day scene would not have done so? It is because night cancels the temporary accidents of history, erases difference. Matthew Arnold on the darkening shore of Dover Beach felt the same power of the night to unite us with a remote past, but came a cropper when he added that Sophocles on his tideless Mediterranean beach would have heard, precisely, the noise made by waves breaking on shingle, in Kent. So let us be careful. Let me not claim, for example, that the air smelled exactly as it did then. But that line of distant hills was identical, numerically and qualitatively. I felt, sentimentalist that I am, momentarily close to the dead poet.

It was as if I had reached the object, Shakespeare, by eliminating, successively, all the intervening differences. The result is a sense of exciting immediacy followed at once by utter frustration, as Narcissus in the myth was frustrated by the very compliance of the image in the pool. The moment of sensed contact, half exciting, half absurd, could tell me nothing, could not add a particle to my understanding of Shakespeare, the writer of plays. Perhaps—awful thought—they were actually getting closer to him in the airless lecture-room I had left.

The only way back is after all by verbally loaded records and monuments. What do we know about the early years in Stratford? The paucity of information on Shakespeare's life has become a commonplace of rhetorical criticism, though in fact we know quite a lot. Occasionally the records throw up an item that really does connect with the work. In December 1579 a young woman was drowned in the Avon at Tiddington, near Stratford. It seemed that she slipped in the mud on the river-bank but some thought of suicide. An inquest was held and ruled that the death was accidental. Already words from a play Shakespeare was to write years later arise in the mind: "Her death was doubtful," for this is a real-life pre-echo of the "muddy death" of Ophelia (*Hamlet*, V.i.227, IV.vii.183). When we add that the young woman's name was Katherine Hamlett the association is simply inescapable.

The year 1579 was perhaps a formative one for Shakespeare. In this year his sister Anne died. In July 1579 at Balsall, nine miles from Stratford, one John Shakespeare was found dead, hanging from a beam. He was a poor man, having at the time of his death goods to the value of three pounds, fourteen shillings, and fourpence.[1] In this case the verdict was criminal suicide. So now we have a Warwickshire Shakespeare, bearing the same Christian name as Shakespeare's own father, killing himself. The deaths of Anne Shakespeare, John Shakespeare, and Katherine Hamlett, coming one after another, have the effect of a tolling bell presaging things to come, the death of Hamnet, Shakespeare's son, in 1596, and then the play itself, written around 1600 when the other John Shakespeare, the poet's father, was nearing his end (he died in 1601). The tragedy, *Hamlet,* is a prolonged meditation on self-destruction, haunted by the shade of a dead father, transfixed by the image of a drowned, innocent woman.

I first came across the story of Katherine Hamlett in a footnote in E. A.

Armstrong's *Shakespeare's Imagination,* which appeared in 1946. Armstrong is a curious figure in the history of Shakespeare criticism. It rather looks as if he set out to write what would have been a very boring book on "birds in Shakespeare" (he had written earlier on birdsong and avian plumage) but then noticed something: if Shakespeare mentioned kites (a kind of bird) within a few lines, for no evident reason, he would mention sheets and death. Armstrong had happened upon one of the "image-clusters" that were to become famous. Others soon appeared. Shakespeare, it seems, could not think of dogs without thinking, within a few lines, of sweetmeats. These loose clusters and skeins, the Lucretian linked atoms of his poetry, are oddly persistent. Caliban's cluster, "berries," "cave," "pinch," "feeding," strong in Shakespeare's last play, *The Tempest,* can be glimpsed in the early *Titus Andronicus,* where it is attached to Aaron the Moor. Between these two plays it surfaces at intervals: it is associated with Thersites in *Troilus and Cressida* and, most oddly, with the melancholy Jaques in *As You Like It.* It is a law of Shakespeare's art that he endlessly recycles ideas and never repeats himself. Caliban "grew from" Aaron the Moor and is at the same time profoundly new. Armstrong's book still fascinates—far more than the more famous book by Caroline Spurgeon, *Shakespeare's Imagery and What It Tells Us* (1935). Armstrong had the livelier mind.

Perhaps too lively. In his footnote on Katherine Hamlett he wrote, "When Shakespeare was sixteen a girl was found drowned after an unfortunate love affair, and at the inquest which was held at Stratford her parents, endeavouring to prevent a verdict of *felo de se,* pleaded that their daughter was drowned by accident and that she slipped from a great slanting willow while dipping flowers she had gathered in the stream."[2] The story has grown, illicitly, in Armstrong's fertile imagination. The first inaccuracy is trivial: Shakespeare was fifteen, not sixteen, in December 1579. But the "unfortunate love affair," the protective parents, the slanting willow,[3] and the gathered flowers all bring the event into closer accord with Ophelia's death and are all added by Armstrong. The dog Latin of the original Stratford minute is less lyrical. Katherine went to the river not to dip flowers (it was mid-December) but to fill her bucket with water. The parents do not figure in the story, nor is there any evidence for an unhappy love affair. The minute certainly implies directly that, as in the case of Ophelia, there was an eye-witness to the death. She was seen to draw water, to slip, and to fall. Moreover the carefully emphatic wording, *non aliter nec alio modo ad mortem suam devenit,* "not otherwise nor in any other way did she meet her death," strongly suggests that an alternative hypothesis—suicide—is being excluded.[4]

The strange, independent growth of this story in early-twentieth-century criticism is a curiosity in itself. In effect the myth grows because it is nourished by the subsequent tragedy. Armstrong, as we saw, imported the willows and the unhappy love affair, both of which appear in the play. He seems to have drawn his version from Clara Longworth de Chambrun's *Shakespeare: Actor-Poet.* Armstrong's plain assertion of the affair is presented in a more guarded form in Chambrun: "There was evidently some reason to think that the girl had been crossed in love." She speaks of a claim put in by the family and adds, "But the coroner's jury were inclined to pronounce *felo de se*" and says nothing about the fact that they settled on "accidental death." Chambrun brings in the willow and writes as if she knows the very tree: "where . . . the knotted roots of an ancient willow formed a deep pool."[5] It is as if Chambrun and Armstrong are the exact opposite of the modern Historicist. Instead of permitting historical events to determine and limit the meaning of the text, they allow the later fiction to modify the earlier history. And this is of course crazy.

This wretched, unglamorous accident-or-worse is something that really happened, in a cold month in rural England more than four hundred years ago. It happened near a town where a certain remarkable boy lived, although no one knew yet how remarkable. In those days long before television, gossip flourished. Everyone in Stratford would have talked about the case and the fifteen-year-old Shakespeare would have listened and absorbed. Poor Katherine Hamlett with her water pail stayed in his mind and was gradually changed until she was at last projected on the huge screen of the most famous of all tragedies:

There is a willow grows askaunt the brook,
That shows his hoary leaves in the glassy stream,
Therewith fantastic garlands she did make
Of crow-flowers, nettles, daisies, and long purples
That liberal shepherds give a grosser name,

But our cull-cold maids do dead men's fingers call them.
There on the pendant boughs her crownet weeds
Clamb'ring to hang, an envious sliver broke,
When down her weedy trophies and herself
Fell in the weeping brook. Her clothes spread wide,
And mermaid-like awhile they bore her up,
Which time she chaunted snatches of old lauds,
As one incapable of her own distress,
Or like a creature native and indued
Unto that element. But long it could not be
Till that her garments, heavy with their drink,
Pull'd the poor wretch from her melodious lay
To muddy death.   (*Hamlet*, IV.vii.166–83)

What has happened? It used to be fashionable to make fun of those who detached "beauties from Shakespeare" to be read in isolation from the plays. Yet Shakespeare seems sometimes to write "anthology pieces" as if he had such future treatment in mind. This sudden lyric ascent, "the Death of Ophelia," is such a case. It is like an aria or, still more, like a great painting, and, in due course, John Everett Millais will paint it. It might seem then that the original, low-life incident has been wholly erased by this exercise in "heightening."

But certain continuities, linking Katherine and Ophelia, persist. If, as is likely, the inquest on Katherine Hamlett considered the possibility of suicide, they would also have had to think about the fact that a verdict of suicide would mean that there could be no Christian burial for the dead woman. In the play, immediately after the great speech describing the drowning, Act V opens with a low-life discussion between two rustics of "crowner's" ("coroner's") law in connection with Ophelia. One says that if she had not been a great lady she would have been denied Christian burial. Katherine Hamlett was no "great lady." Later we learn that even though Gertrude's elaborate description makes it clear, first, that Ophelia's death was accidental ("a sliver broke") and, second, that the balance of her mind was disturbed, Ophelia is buried with "maimed rites" because the death was "doubtful" (V.i.219, 227).[6] The "Doctor of Divinity" says that she would in fact have been given an unsanctified burial, but "great command" overruled this with a charitable compromise (V.i.228). The narrative in the Stratford minute exonerates Katherine Hamlett much as the Queen exonerates Ophelia. The gritty legal questioning that is likely to have surrounded the death of 1579 is still working, in a slightly odd sequence, in the accomplished tragedy.

Indeed, a near-obsession with law has long been discerned in *Hamlet*. At Act I, Scene i, lines 84 and following, Horatio, in the middle of a heroic narrative of old Hamlet's victory over the Norwegians, suddenly enters eagerly into technical detail on how forfeiture of lands to the victor is to be ratified. In the next scene, Claudius discloses that the son of the defeated Norwegian king has raised the same legal point (I.ii.22–25). In the most famous of all soliloquies, "To be or not to be," Hamlet, listing the calamities of life, includes "the law's delay" (III.i.71). The same preoccupation shows recurrently in minor tricks of phrasing: "give in evidence" (III.iii.64), "hear and judge 'twixt you and me" (IV.v.206), "acquittance seal" (IV.vii.1), and the like.

Shakespeare, we begin to see, is aiming at a complex effect. He does not *simply* transform the fate of Katherine Hamlett. The end of his thought remembers its beginning. He plays the lyrical elegy off against a thorny subtext of harsh law. Even the rusticity of the original case makes itself felt in the complex music of the tragedy. The Queen tells us of the low, rustically obscene names given by country people to the flowers Ophelia gathered (IV.vii.170). And her very last words, "Pull'd the poor wretch from her melodious lay / To muddy death" (IV.vii.182–83), are not just an oxymoron, setting elevation against "lowness," the word "melodious" abruptly confronted by "muddy." Brilliant, meta-poetic self-reference is also involved. The Queen's own speech, no less than the songs of Ophelia, has been melodious but must admit at the close the muddy reality of the death. In their ending Katherine and Ophelia are merely identical. There is something eerie about Shakespeare's ability to anticipate our thoughts. It is something one meets again and again in his work. I, a critic writing in the twenty-first century, was groping towards understanding how Shakespeare transformed, through the exalting agency of high poetry, an almost squalid rural death, and suddenly I find that he has thematized *my* thoughts. It may be said that Shakespeare has merely betrayed, in passing, a trace of the original case and that there is nothing uncanny in this. But that is not what we have here. The narrated death of Ophelia in *Hamlet* is, intelligently, *about* the tension between lyric exaltation and cold, muddy water.

When I wrote *A New Mimesis* in the 1980s I was concerned to save Shakespeare from formalist theory. It was the time summed up in Jacques Derrida's famous phrase, "Il n'y a pas de hors-texte," "There is nothing beyond the text."[7] Of course these words were variously construed within the world of Deconstruction, but there was a palpable drive to suggest that what we call "nature"—a notion varying from age to age—is always a tissue of conventions; there was, in short, a move to resolve substance into form. The word *reality* was always placed in inverted commas, that had to mean, "Not *really* real, of course—'so-called reality.' " Christopher Norris, at the moment in his career when he was beginning to emerge from such "foundationless" thinking (his word) had an admirable epithet for this use of inverted commas: "queasy."[8] Norris was himself moving into what has now assumed centre stage: New Historicism. The real world, including real poets and dramatists, had in a manner been erased by Post-Structuralists and Deconstructionists (remember "the death of the author"). With the sudden ascent of New Historicism the entire scheme flipped, turned inside out. The real world in all its rebarbative factual detail returned and virtually obliterated the fictive universe of poetry. *Naturam expellas furca, tamen usque recurrit,* "You can drive out nature with a pitchfork, but she always comes running back."[9] The author was restored to life, and so too were the author's friends and relations. These were real people in a real setting, pressed by real politics and brutally exigent power struggles. The meaning of a given play is suddenly no longer a matter of endlessly receding differentiations within a formal system; instead, the meaning of *Coriolanus* is determined by corn riots in the Midland counties in 1607.

Perhaps we should feel grateful. The new regime is certainly better than its predecessor. In its narrowest, most doctrinaire form, however, it is disabled from the start by two assumptions. First, reality is conceived nominalistically[10] as a series of idiosyncratic facts or events, and, second, although these events *cause* and account for the content of a poem or play, the poet cannot, so to speak, turn round and comment on or criticize the now sovereign environment. Although I have said that New Historicism is a turning inside out of earlier Theory, the two movements are united in their hostility to the idea of cognitive intelligence in the work of art discussed. The writer is a mere effect, at the mercy of the prior causal scheme. The true import of a play is now something betrayed rather than asserted by the words of the text. And this is absurd. *Coriolanus* obviously does not mean "There were corn riots last year." It is about the irony of a Stoic integrity essayed by one who has in fact been thoroughly conditioned by an evil mother; it is about the moment in *Roman* history when co-operative civic institutions were beginning to displace an older warrior ethic; it is about the anxieties of popular power where the populace is not, as in the writings of Karl Marx, economically productive but is instead parasitic upon the wealth-production of a still warlike aristocracy; it is about femaleness distorted and love crushed—and now I will grant, the audience will certainly be thinking of those corn riots.

There have been earlier phases of historicist criticism ("Mr. Ramsay in *To the Lighthouse* IS the author's father" and the like), but these early "embeddings" of literary fiction in its context commonly allowed the correspondence between the feigned person and the real to be something artfully managed by the writer; the clear correspondence in Edmund Spenser's *Faerie Queene* of Artegall with the real-life Lord Grey is something proposed, articulated, and worked by the poet as part of a consciously allegorical scheme, and Virginia Woolf is similarly in charge of the Ramsay/Stephen implied correspondence. Today the common assumption, especially in the field of Renaissance literature, is that such correspondences with real persons are not the product of intelligent art on the part of the author but are rather produced by the historical process itself. *It* plants the code, and the code propels the poet's pen. When I say that *Coriolanus* deals with "love crushed" I intend the phrase as description of a possible reality. This would not be well received by a doctrinaire "Nominalist" Historicist. "Love" applies to millions of persons, to innumerable contexts, to successions of centuries. The mere use of this highly general word does not commit the user to the thesis that love is the same at all times; it allows us to notice that falling in love in 1384 is not the same as falling in love in 1943, while in 2006 it is different again, but it does imply an insistence on a strong analogy underlying the variable instances. It is an "elastic universal."

Of course there are among the Historicists many with a less restrictive mindset. Pierre Bourdieu has championed a mode of criticism that "far from annihilating the creator by the reconstruction of the universe of social determinants that exert pressure on him, and reducing the work to the pure product of a milieu instead of seeing in it the sign that the author has known how to emancipate himself from it . . . . sociological analysis allows us to . . . understand the specific labour the writer had to accomplish, both against these determinations and thanks to them, to produce himself as creator, that is, as the subject of his own creation."[11]

To this I can at once give general assent. But if anyone thinks that it shows that my earlier picture of theorists who make the work the pure inert product of its context is a gross caricature—"straw men"—it must be pointed out that Bourdieu indeed is himself an altogether subtler theorist yet that meanwhile he is quite clearly as convinced as I am of the existence of the "art as mere product" party. Stephen Greenblatt is a Historicist (indeed he is one of the founding fathers of Historicism) who, like Bourdieu, escapes my stricture. He always sees causation as two-way street; writers do not only reflect or betray the pressures of the milieu; they "negotiate" with them. But a sense that meaning is being in some degree confined persists even in Bourdieu's formulation: the writer can now write against the milieu; but can the writer write about *something else?*

I am suggesting that as soon as we allow the poet cognitive or referential power, we enter a world of analogy in which the social conditions of composition or, for that matter, the psychological genesis remain palpably distinct from the achieved work. The root is not the flower.

It may be said, however, that my own assertion of the relevance of the death of Katherine Hamlett to Shakespeare's play works against me. There it turned out that the "flower," that is, the exalted lyrical narrative, *included,* in a kind of counterpoint, a recurrent reference to nit-picking law, rusticity, and, finally, mere mud that stemmed directly, without any artistic metamorphosis, from the case at Tiddington in 1579. Obviously historical investigation can make a contribution to critical understanding. But, note, to grant this is not to grant that meaning is determined or exhausted by immediate context. The action of *Hamlet* is set in motion by the ghost of a dead king. The play itself is haunted, *ab extra,* by the ghost of a dead woman. I have said that the lyric exaltation is crushed at the end of Gertrude's speech, but the high poetry is there, before it is crushed. It remains a powerful element in the poetic economy of the whole. Shakespeare *needs* the lyric beauty because without it he cannot effect his startling final reduction. If we flatten the sequence so that it is, so to speak, reduced from the start, we falsify. The death of Ophelia really was beautiful before it was squalid.

I chose the example of Katherine Hamlett because it shows vividly how detailed historical knowledge can play a part, *but only a part,* in enhancing our critical understanding. The transforming, extending power of Shakespeare's fictive interpretation is, inescapably, also part of the picture. Mimesis, or representation of the world, is not confined to the strand of implicit reference to Katherine. As Shakespeare enlarges the scope of the episode we have the mimesis of a broader field of human possibility, the trauma of rejection and the rest. The final twist, in which Shakespeare himself *makes a point* of the shift in register, can easily assume the character of ironic admonition, directed at the too-confident tunnel-vision Historicist.

I have said that we do not know what Shakespeare thought about any major question, in the sense that we have no settled judgements of which we can be sure. The major question of the years through which he lived was religious. This is the period of the splitting of Christendom into Roman Catholics on one hand and Protestants on the other. Has Shakespeare nothing to say on the Reformation?

There has been a strong move recently to argue that Shakespeare was either a crypto-Catholic or else sympathetic to the Catholic side. Again we begin from material external to the plays. This is basically gossip. Richard Davies, chaplain of Corpus Christi College, Oxford, added to some notes on Shakespeare the sentence, "He dyed a Papist."[12] These words were written more than fifty years after Shakespeare's death. The "red and jolly," hard-drinking Davies makes mistakes elsewhere.[13] While Shakespeare was still alive, John Speed in *The Theatre of the Empire of Great Britain* (1611) attacked the British Jesuit Robert Parsons and Shakespeare in one and the same breath: "This Papist and his Poet, of like conscience for lies, the one ever faining, the other ever falsifying the truth."[14] In 1757, according to report, labourers retiling a roof in Stratford found, hidden in the rafters, a document that has come to be known as "John Shakespeare's Spiritual Testament." Shakespeare's father was called John. The document is plainly Catholic, strewn with references to Purgatory, to "Mary mother of god," ending on an *Ave Maria*. At times it strays into lush language that may remind the reader of the papist poet Crashaw: "The sweet and amorous coffin of the side of jesus Christ."[15] The document itself is lost. We rely on a transcription made in the eighteenth century by the great Shakespearean scholar Edmond Malone. Malone himself came to doubt its authenticity, but many recent scholars have taken it to be genuine.

The writer of the document hopes that his "parents" will pray for him, and this, since both the parents of John Shakespeare were dead at the time, is not easily explained by believers (they suggest that "parents," like the Latin *parentes,* is used loosely to refer to relations). The writer of the "testament" is following a form set down by Cardinal Carlo Borromeo, archbishop of Milan in the plague years. We are told that the British Jesuit missionaries Edmund Campion and Robert Parsons brought copies of Borromeo's testament to England in the 1580s. This is the same Robert Parsons—sometimes spelled "Persons"—that John Speed had in mind when he wrote of "this Papist and his Poet." The fact that the document was carefully concealed suggests that the writer knew how dangerous it was to commit such thoughts to paper. It was the time of the anti-Catholic terror when popish priests and those who harboured them were tortured, strung up, cut down while still conscious, and disembowelled. This is heady stuff. But "John Shakespeare's Spiritual Testament" was blown out of the water in 2003 by Robert Bearman. Bearman demonstrated in meticulous detail that there is no basis for the assertion that Campion and Parsons brought the Borromean document to England at this time. English versions did appear, but far too late—in the 1630s. Bearman can see only one explanation: in the 1770s someone came across a defective copy of the printed English version of the testament, lacking the first page or two, and conspired to turn it into a "Shakespeare document."[16]

Here one central prop of the "Catholic Shakespeare" theory, the secretly Catholic father, falls away. But other, fainter indications remain in place. Shakespeare's mother was an Arden, and Edward Arden, head of the family and a strong recusant, turned his house, Park Hall, into a seminary for Catholic boys, persons "hungry," as John Donne put it, "of an imagin'd Martyrdome."[17] William Shakespeare's favourite daughter, Susanna, got into trouble in 1606 for failing to attend Easter Communion.[18] This was the time of national panic following Guy Fawkes's popish plot to blow up the Houses of Parliament (the wild celebrations that followed the detection of the plot are themselves eloquent of an underlying fear). The supposition is that Susanna stayed away because she was "Popishly affected."

Setting aside the "Spiritual Testament" we have, so far, a stray remark, made long after the event, that Shakespeare died a Catholic, a jibe from a Puritan historian calling Shakespeare a lapdog of the Jesuits, his mother's Catholic connections, and the guess that Susanna missed Easter Communion because of loyalty to Rome. The last may be the weakest. Susanna later married John Hall, a strong Protestant with Huguenot connections. We really do not know why she missed church on that day in 1606. It is all, at best, mildly suggestive. Can we learn anything from Shakespeare's education? Stratford itself is said to have been a hotbed of secret Catholic activity at this period. Samuel Schoenbaum, however, is bluffly confident that, whatever was going on behind closed doors in the town, "the religious training . . . provided by his community was orthodox and Protestant."[19] When he wrote this Schoenbaum was thinking of church instruction. If, however, we extend the notion of training to include the education Shakespeare received at Stratford Grammar School, the "Protestant orthodoxy" case begins to look a little less firm.

T. W. Baldwin in his magisterial study, *William Shakspere's Small Latine and Lesse Greeke,* noted that Stratford Grammar School in the 1580s employed a succession of masters who were committedly Catholic in the cold war. For example, Thomas Jenkins, "Shakespeare's principal schoolmaster," was at Campion's college, St. John's, Oxford, and was an associate of Campion. John Cottom, who was succeeded as master at the school by Alexander Aspinall in 1582, may be the brother of the Catholic priest Thomas Cottom (or Cottam) arraigned along with Campion in 1581 and executed in 1582. Baldwin notes that Cottom must have passed for Protestant with the bishop of Worcester or he would not have got the job, but sums up, "It is not likely that any of these Stratford masters was at the time a known or suspected extremist . . . but there is a great deal to show that . . . their sympathies were Catholic rather than Puritan."[20] School, it seems, may have echoed home.

There is notoriously a large hole in the record of Shakespeare's life, from 1582 to 1592. This decade has come to be known as "the lost years" and has been variously filled by speculative biographers, in line with the dominant interest of the writer. Those fascinated by law think Shakespeare spent this time working for a lawyer and can point to his intricate and knowing allusions to legal niceties. Others, led by Duff Cooper, think he must have served in the army. Yet others think, remembering Holofernes in *Love's Labour's Lost,* that he was obviously, as his contemporary William Beeston said, a schoolmaster in the country.[21] Clearly we need a Catholic story to contend with the others and there is a fairly good one. It was in the 1930s that it was first noticed that a certain William Shakeshafte, perhaps a player, was in service with the Hoghton family in Lancashire at the time of the "lost years."[22] Was "Shakeshafte" our William Shakespeare? Roman Catholic resistance was strong in Lancashire, and the Hoghtons were at the centre of this resistance. The name "Shakeshafte" is not "Shakespeare" of course, but in these years of persecution it might well have been prudent to dissemble one's name. It has been suggested that "Shakeshafte" as an alternative ingeniously combines evasion with backward-looking family piety, since the poet's grandfather Richard Shakespeare used Shakeshafte as his form of the surname. But this rests on a mistake; Richard in fact wrote "Shakestaff," not "Shakeshafte."[23]

It is the kind of speculative theory hard-headed scholars are quick to dismiss. There were many Shakeshaftes around in Lancashire, and the complex terms of Hoghton's will make it probable that "Shakeshafte" was considerably older than the poet would have been at this date.[24] Schoenbaum acidly observes that if Shakespeare was in Lancashire working for Sir Thomas Hoghton when he was seventeen, he would have had to get himself back to Stratford by the time he was nineteen in order to impregnate Anne Hathaway—"not the most plausible of scenarios."[25] Schoenbaum's scorn is perhaps premature. Ernst Honigmann, the ablest of the proponents of the Shakeshafte theory, pointed out that the stay in Lancashire was perfectly compatible with the impregnation of Anne, since the poet probably spent only a few months with the Hoghtons.[26] In 1985 Honigmann showed that John Cottom (Cottam), the Stratford schoolmaster we noticed earlier, belonged to a social circle based in Lancashire, intimately connected with the Hoghtons. The "John Cotham" named as legatee in the 1581 will of Alexander Hoghton, head of the family, is likely to be identical with John Cottom, the Stratford schoolmaster. The testator bequeaths theatre costumes to his brother and immediately afterwards asks his friend Sir Thomas Hesketh of Rufford to look after "William Shakeshafte now dwelling with me."[27] It is clear that both Stratford and Lancashire were sites of intense Catholic activity. What is not clear, still, is that Shakeshafte was Shakespeare.

We are looking at a period of ideological crisis—perhaps the most intense in British history. I have written lightly about young Catholics imagining martyrdom, but it was no light matter then. We must endeavour seriously to understand what made men like Campion risk and undergo hideous torture; we must try, with the same obstinacy I brought to my evening walk to Shottery, to comprehend what it was like for these young people, in dark country houses with hiding places for priests—how by candlelight they would have talked: "Could you withstand the Scavenger's Daughter? I *think* I could, if I could keep my thoughts fixed on my saviour and Mary the mother of God . . . I *think* I could . . . ." The Scavenger's Daughter was a device in the form of an iron hoop that so compressed the body that blood was forced from the nose and ears.[28] When John Carey published his *John Donne: Life, Mind and Art* in 1983 he painted a vivid picture of the anti-Catholic terror. Some historians thought he overplayed the *grand guignol*. One said, "John is like the fat boy in *Pickwick*—'I wants to make your flesh creep.' " But a certain distinguished historian of the reign of Elizabeth said to me, "I was shaken by Carey's book. We historians are fond of saying that the persecution of Catholics was fitful and inefficient, but Carey makes one see the real horror. Perhaps the very variability added to the fear-factor?" Franz Kafka knew how uncertainty exacerbates fear; both *The Trial* and *The Castle* turn on the psychological truth that an accused person will pass from pleading innocence to actively seeking conviction, if the nature of the charge is kept hidden; unclarity is itself felt to be worse than the imagined sentence. In Elizabethan England, indeed, the punishment was so horrible that the full Kafkaesque paradox was unlikely to find realisation, but the circumambient uncertainty must, nevertheless, have made things worse—much worse. These were the years of "the bloody question": "If the pope sent an army to invade England, would you obey pope or queen?" Senator Joseph McCarthy's question, "Are you or have you ever been a communist?" destroyed lives but seems faint when set beside the bloody question of Shakespeare's time. McCarthy never disembowelled a communist, making sure that the victim remained alive until the process was complete.

It will be the argument of this book that Shakespeare was not only a master of imaginative and emotional effects but that he was also very intelligent. He can hardly have failed to notice what was happening around him. He grew up in a place where awareness was sharpened, where the Reformation itself was rejected by people of influence. Yet his plays are eloquent of nothing so much as a rosy unconsciousness of division. Neither the Reformation nor the shock waves it produced in the counter-culture of Catholicism—the Council of Trent—make any palpable impression on the plays. In *Romeo and Juliet,* Juliet speaks of attending evening Mass (IV.i.38). Evening Mass was forbidden by the Council of Trent in 1566, and some bridle at what they see as a mistake on Shakespeare's part (although it appears that Verona was one of several places where the practice was in fact continued).[29] Of course Shakespeare would have known that in any case Juliet lived long before the Council of Trent, but that, somehow, is not the point. The Christianity is strangely timeless.

Some think the absence of a "politically correct" Protestant ferocity from the plays is itself evidence of not-so-crypto-Catholicism. The young dramatist, it is conceded, temporarily toes the party line in order to establish himself. Joan of Arc is portrayed in *Henry VI, Part 1* as the vile witch of Protestant propaganda; Beauford in *Henry VI, Part 2* and Pandulph in *King John* are stereotypically wicked cardinals. But thereafter, it is suggested, his Warwickshire and Lancashire background reasserts itself. The Protestants had abolished the Roman Catholic Purgatory, the place, neither heaven nor hell, where persons are purged of their sins after death, but the ghost in *Hamlet* comes to us from an unsatirized Purgatory (I.v.13); Friar Lawrence in *Romeo and Juliet* is a luminously benevolent figure, a sweet old man who picks flowers and medicinal herbs. The comedies are full of benign Catholic minor clergy: the friar who met Silvia in the forest in *Two Gentlemen of Verona* (V.ii.38), Friar Patrick in the same play at whose cell "she did intend confession" (V.ii.41, cf. IV.iii.44), Friar Francis in *Much Ado about Nothing,* the priest in *Twelfth Night,* the "old religious man" in the "wild wood" who had so startling an effect on Duke Frederic in *As You Like It* (V.iv.159–61). There is no sign in *Two Gentlemen of Verona* of implied criticism of the practice of confession; it is seen as ordinary virtue. We could add the religious "convertites" to whom the melancholy Jaques is dispatched (not to join, but to watch) in *As You Like It*. These moments bear no charge of anti-papal feeling, nor does the hermitage that is to receive the King of Navarre at the end of *Love's Labour's Lost* (V.ii.795). Schoenbaum writes, "Theologically minded readers ask 'Does not the dramatist treat his lesser Romanist clergy, a Friar Lawrence or an Abbess Aemilia, more respectfully than his Protestant vicars of the villages, the Martexts and the Nathaniels?' "[30] This, it is said, is a dramatist who, after a few early wobbles, refused to play the Protestant game, to join the chorus of denunciation, and in such an environment, to refuse in this way is to espouse the old religion. "He that is not with me is against me." Shakespeare is *against* the Reformation.

But this will hardly do. There are committed Catholics in England at this period, and they do not write in this way. Perhaps the most brilliant of the Shakespearean Historicists is Richard Wilson. In his *Secret Shakespeare,* Wilson makes a cumulative case for Shakespeare's early association with dangerous Catholics in both Stratford and Lancashire with an array of detailed support that is almost overwhelming.[31] At the same time, however, he notes a persistent hostility in the plays to Jesuit extremists. It is as if the intense religious experiences of his early years were gradually cocooned in a benign Montaignian scepticism. Like Stephen Greenblatt,[32] he suggests that the secrecy that must have become second nature in ordinary Catholic families (who were not eager to be tortured and wished brave priests like Campion could simply shut up for a while) became the central habit of his mind—and so the source of his famous elusiveness. Shakespeare's work is a huge vanishing act. This copious body of superlative dramatic writing is accompanied by no letters, no evidence of attendance at any church, no professional accounts: "a chronicle of immaculate absenteeism."[33] The driving idea of the book is that Shakespeare took care to hide any hint of specific allegiance—and this is itself the political and religious import of his work.

But, if Shakespeare wanted to hide, why did he not avoid mentioning Purgatory in *Hamlet?* It would have been simple to do. Why does he actively fill his plays with friars, abbesses, private chapels, and the like? Greenblatt wrote in his *Shakespearean Negotiations* of the way in which a

Shakespearean text may be "haunted by a sense of rituals and beliefs that are no longer efficacious, that have been *emptied out*."[34] "Haunted" implies "ghost," and "ghost" means "dead person." If the Catholic apparatus of Shakespearean drama is a dance of ghosts, the Reformation is after all clearly implied; the old religion is dead, a thing of the past. Greenblatt argued that in transposing such material to the stage Shakespeare was emptying it of religious significance. This Wilson rightly resists. The ethical resonance of such things will not be stilled, or emptied away. Strongly Protestant Spenser in the huge neo-Gothic literary sham castle called *The Faerie Queene* likewise filled his allegorical landscape with Catholic paraphernalia—beadsmen, hermits, and the like. But there the rationale, at least initially, is tolerably clear. Protestantism internalized Christianity. The physical whip of "penaunce" became an inwardly smarting contrition. This means that when a Protestant poet allegorizes the interior life, giving it an imagined body, we shall be returned to a field of images in ironic coincidence with the rejected physicalities of Catholicism.[35] Spenser developed a special style, "golden" yet oddly repellent to the reader seeking intimate engagement, so that we never forget that the physical adventures recounted are mere metaphor, the images mere pasteboard. Even in Spenser, however, the old images retain a problematic moral force of their own. In Shakespeare, meanwhile, there is in any case no such scheme of conscious differentiation on offer.

A hermit and a mossy cell find their way into ultra-Protestant John Milton's *Il Penseroso,* and again, they are obviously picturesque—mock-Gothic. A real Gothic church is "just the way you make a church," but mock-Gothic is like the picture of a building, or like a stage set. So in both Spenser and Milton later there is a clear sense of aesthetic and ideological distance, separating us from this seemingly popish material. But none of this applies to Shakespeare's friars and abbesses. They are simply there, as if they were an ordinary part of a world we all straightforwardly know.

So in Shakespeare we have not a strenuously asserted innocence of change but an innocence lightly assumed, as if there were no problem. Take fairies. To polemical writers of the period fairies went with Catholic mumbo-jumbo, hocus-pocus (*hoc est corpus*). Indeed, the association was not confined to controversialists. A certain Mrs. Parry told Goodwin Wharton that the fairies served God "much in the manner of Roman

Catholics, believing in transubstantiation, and having a Pope who resides here in England."[36] Wharton himself, rather like Bottom the weaver, believed that he had actually married the queen of the fairies.[37] Thomas Hobbes said that Oberon was the fairies' pope.[38] He was joking, but the association is there. Puritans were for stamping out such benighted stuff, along with the imagery carved on old churches. Keith Thomas tells how one Henry Barrow "came near despair at the magnitude of the task; it seemed to him that the idolatrous shapes of Papist religion were so involved with the very fabric of churches that 'this fretting leprosy' could perhaps never be cleaned."[39] Shakespeare, in the England of Stephen Gosson and Philip Stubbes, would have been aware of course that Puritan Protestants were automatically opposed to anything he could put on the London stage. Drama readily admits stretches of topical argument. Yet Shakespeare never engages in explicit argument with Puritans. When he uses the word "Puritan," as he does of Malvolio in *Twelfth Night* (II.iii.140) and again in *The Winter's Tale* (IV.iii.44), it means "kill-joy." Richard Corbett (1582–1635), bishop of Norwich, wrote,

> By which we note the *Faries*
> Were of the old Profession;
> They're Songs were *Ave Maryes,*
> They're Daunces were Procession.[40]

When Corbett wrote these doggerel lines he was remembering Shakespeare, but what is thoroughly un-Shakespearean is their ideological explicitness. For Shakespeare the un-Puritan character of his medium is a simple given, and he chooses not to defend its propriety but instead to assume that it will elicit a warm response in the auditor. The fairies are old England and old England was a world of friars and chapels and holy rites, but Shakespeare will never say, "So fairies are Catholics," as Corbett does. He does not write as if he needs to hide his pre-Reformation materials; he writes as if the Reformation hasn't even happened—and we are all friends. This is not the missionary Catholicism of a Campion, nor is it strenuous evasiveness. It is something else. Of course the ramifying secrecy of the recusant families among which he grew up does reappear, transposed from practical religious politics to comedic plotting, to indefinite interiority of character—to an immense aesthetic success. At this point Greenblatt's thesis, the emptying out of *specifically* religious significance, holds.

Gary Taylor, surveying recent Historicist criticism of Shakespeare, was assailed, like Prendergast in Evelyn Waugh's *Decline and Fall,* by doubts: "As scholars we pounce triumphantly upon each little glimpse of religious allegiance, in the way that committed believers pounce upon each little glimpse of God's intervention in a seemingly Godless world. . . . And we are right to insist that any purely secular representation of Shakespeare's life or world, any account of the Renaissance which ignores the religious passions of the Reformation, is a falsification. But that falsification, that misrepresentation, begins with Shakespeare himself. If Shakespeare has been the god of our idolatry for four centuries, it is because he created the scripture for an emerging secular world."[41] These words come at the close of a book of essays that opened with a piece by Richard Wilson. Wilson in his elegant essay has fun with a certain hapless contributor to the *Edinburgh Review* in 1866. Wilson quotes his description of Shakespeare: "As a man of true nobility of soul, to take up a strong position was incompatible with his temperament which had nothing in common with that of the martyr. So he kept to the even tenor of his way, presenting in his works opinions which no system-monger can squeeze into a formula . . . . Above the narrow janglings and bickerings in which he lived, his 'easy numbers' rise to a full diapason of more than earthly music."[42] This, Wilson says, is vacuous. But if we remove the transcendental element ("more than earthly"), the picture is uncannily close to that presented by the weary sophisticate Gary Taylor.

If Shakespeare has really contrived a world disengaged from the local shocks and collisions of his own time—if *that* is what he has done, as an artist, should we not attend to the thing he has made, in all its strange independence of historical circumstance? Not so long ago it was generally agreed that the good critic should look at the *telos,* the end or aim of a work of art, rather than at its *arche,* or genesis, a variously accidental, imperfectly recoverable affair. In the 1960s the University of Sussex set up a series of "interdisciplinary" seminars, taught jointly by historians and literary scholars. One was called "Poetry, Science and Religion in the Seventeenth Century." The historians were quick to assert that England in the early years of the seventeenth century subscribed to a Calvinist theology. The literary people were baffled by this. They were baffled because these early years were to them represented, overwhelmingly, by Shakespeare. Where is the Calvinism in Shakespeare? As with Calvinism, so with missionary Catholicism. Where in Shakespeare is there anyone resembling Edmund Campion, that dazzling, suffering figure who must have been the subject of innumerable remembered conversations? Shakespeare's liberal art in which every nuance of feeling is registered seems to forget rather than actively to suppress the real extremists of his world.

Gary Taylor's concession that Shakespeare himself may be the source of the "timeless," a-historical criticism Taylor himself abjures is spectacular. It is as if he has said, "Shakespeare decided to produce a body of work expressly designed for reading across centuries." I suppose the strong Historicist could say, "No one can ever really escape the historical determinants of his or her time; if a writer tries to do this in the early modern period the result will inevitably be an *early modern* essay in (pseudo-)universalization, easily distinguishable from, say, a nineteenth-century essay in the same vein." But what if Shakespeare succeeded in his enterprise? Has no one noticed how, while the scholars increasingly seek to confine the meaning of a play to its immediate historical context, directors and actors are playing Shakespeare in seventeenth-, eighteenth-, nineteenth-, twentieth-, and twenty-first-century dress, and even, on occasion, in "mixed period" settings? On stage *Antony and Cleopatra* is freely permitted to allude to the palace of King Farouk and *Coriolanus* to the French Revolution. Such productions seem not to destroy or even diminish the force of the plays presented. It is as if we are being propelled by the scholars into a mode of criticism that makes silence and omission stronger clues than what is actually said to the meaning of a work.

I am not saying that Shakespeare's plays are absolutely unaffected by their historical context. Early Shakespeare is obviously Elizabethan as late Shakespeare is Jacobean. More narrowly, Shakespeare's keen interest in subjectivity is itself a highly intelligent response to the rise of Protestantism. But it is noteworthy that the great explorations of interiority— *Richard II, Hamlet*—do not feel remote or antiquated when they are played to present-day audiences. This is because Shakespeare's response is, precisely, intelligent rather than a mere cultural reflex. He thinks fundamentally, and this makes him a natural time-traveller. Moreover, I willingly grant that silence and suppression can figure in a critical assessment. *A*

Midsummer Night's Dream suppresses the violent elements in the myths it draws on—Theseus the womanizer, sex with animals, *The Golden Ass* of Apuleius, the coarse tale of Pasiphae, who coupled with the bull. All this is turned "to favour and to prettiness." By the anti-Historicist logic that says, "The root is not the flower," the mythic origins of *A Midsummer Night's Dream* ought to be discarded just as the immediate social matrix is to be discarded. But when we know about these origins we notice things we never saw before, starting with the edge of male brutalism in Theseus's words to Hippolyta at the beginning: "Hippolyta, I won thee with my sword" (I.i.16). The war against the women, the Amazons, is in the background. The question is: Should we read *A Midsummer Night's Dream* as a play in which "dark" implications have been banished before the play begins, or should we, more subtly, read it as a play in which the banishment takes place within the drama? Knowledge of the mythic roots of the design may now cause us to notice things that are actually there and to opt for the second alternative. Shakespeare's smiling duke has in fact ravished Perigenia (II.i.78). There is a fear that Bottom's scratchy hide after his transformation may hurt the lady he lies beside, echoing a far grosser anxiety in *The Golden Ass*.[43]

As with myth, so with the historical matrix. Knowledge of the context may alert us to things that really are there. But this in no way implies that the brilliantly centrifugal movement of Shakespeare's mind can properly be ignored. Shakespeare probably did think of corn riots in the Midlands when he wrote *Coriolanus* (and the audience would have made the connection). But he was also thinking hard about Roman politics. Meanwhile, although there is a clear analogy between mythic and sociohistorical contexts, there is also an interesting difference. Mythology is itself already instinct with live imaginative force, as social fact, qua fact, can never be.

New Historicism now holds sway in universities in Britain and North America (though there are signs that its grip is weakening). Where "Historicism" means expending all one's attention on the immediate historical circumstances of composition and seeking to explicate the work in terms of those circumstances, I am opposed. The argument of this book is that, although knowledge of the historical genesis can on occasion illuminate a given work, the greater part of the artistic achievement of our best playwright is *internally* generated. It is the product, not of his time, but of his own, unresting, creative intelligence. Historical circumstance supplies matter, but the major thing, always, is the use the writer makes of that which is given him. The whole point of the biblical parable of the talents (Matt. 25:14–30) is that the good recipient is the one who makes the gift grow, who actively transforms what was given in the first place. The etymological development whereby the word "talent" came to mean "artistic gift" is a proper reflection of this inner dynamism.

This book, therefore, will follow where Shakespeare leads, will range freely in the zodiac of *his* wit. He thinks about causes and motives, identity and relation, about how pretence can convey truth, or language (by becoming conscious of its own formal character) can actually impede communication. He meditates on the reality in dreams and the unreality in hard politics. He sees through and then forgives the Stoic philosopher. He celebrates and then disquietingly interrogates the Christian assumption that mercy transcends justice. His thought is never still. No sooner has one identified a philosophical "position" than one is forced, by the succeeding play, to modify or extend one's account. This Protean quality in Shakespeare is the reason for one curious feature of this book. I begin by treating the plays in the order in which they are likely to have been written. But as the book proceeds, increasingly, I depart from chronological sequence in order to set up thematic comparisons. I have avoided thematic grouping as an overall principle because I want the reader to watch as the thoughts form and re-form in successive plays. Each play, for a while at least, had to be allowed to assert itself, without premature "labelling." Only after certain themes have begun to disengage themselves in a properly gradual manner have I felt free to loosen my grip on the sequence in time.

If ever there was a poet who was not confined by tunnel vision it is Shakespeare. He more than any other writer conducts us from the narrow passage of immediate causation into the vertiginous world of overdetermination, of simultaneously operating causes and mysterious "action at a distance." It all begins at once in his apprentice work, the apparently primitive three-part play on the reign of Henry VI, scornfully dismissed by Maurice Morgann in the eighteenth century as "that drum and trumpet thing."[44]

I To the Death of Marlowe

How Causes Work: The Three Parts of *Henry VI*

We began with Milton, once thought of as the natural counterweight to Shakespeare in the history of English literature. Within Shakespeare's lifetime, meanwhile, there was one figure in the landscape that Shakespeare had reason to fear. Christopher Marlowe was the man to beat. As long as Marlowe lived, and for some time after, Shakespeare's writing is marked by special energy, an almost desperate assertion of brilliance. Later, after Marlowe has been dead for several years, the spring uncoils, and larger, slower effects are essayed.

The three parts of *Henry VI* may be the earliest Shakespearean drama we possess.[1] If we turn immediately from a work of Shakespeare's maturity, such as *Julius Caesar*, to this procession of baronial biffing and bashing, summed up perhaps in the old stage direction, "They fight, severally, about the stage," we shall easily conclude as Maurice Morgann did that the work is simply primitive. In the first act of *1 Henry VI* we have what is called "split-focus staging": the English on one side, doubtless with cardboard battlements to protect them, and the French, similarly guarded, on the other.[2] The few yards of planking between may represent the field of battle. This, I submit, really is primitive in the way it treats space, as crowded medieval pictures in which out-of-scale helmeted heads show over the battlements that box them in are primitive. I am aware as I write this that "primitive" is now almost a taboo word. It will be said that the organization of space in a medieval picture is conceptually highly sophisticated, that meaning is allowed to dominate the banal requirements of perspectival visual data, and that in such work the imagination of both artist and viewer is far more active than in inertly photographic painting. Yet when all this has been said, such medieval painting remains primitive in the sense that it manifestly belongs to an earlier rather than a later phase. These painters did not deliberately over-ride ordinary perspective for conceptual reasons; they did not yet know how to paint using perspective. Children, as E. H. Gombrich pointed out, draw conceptually before they learn to present the phenomenal appearance of a thing.[3] A house will be a rectangle and people will be drawn within the rectangle. If we say, "But you couldn't see the people through the wall," the child answers, "The people are *in* the house!" It is perfectly clear meanwhile that Shakespeare himself felt the force of the term "primitive" in application to such staging. In *Henry V,* written some eight or nine years after *Henry VI,* he frets at the almost comic inadequacy (in the sense, "un-realism") of his stage presentation. He notes, exactly as I did a moment ago, the painful contrast between the cramped wooden box of the theatre and the space it has to represent: "Can this cockpit hold / The vasty fields of France?" (Prologue, 11–12). He also smells out in advance the defence-through-activating-the-imagination: "Piece out our imperfections with your thoughts . . . / Think, when we talk of horses, that you see them" (Prologue, 23, 26).

Equally clearly, however, he is embarrassed by the sheer crudity of the theatrical apparatus. Even if we do not think (or feel that it is not permissible to think) *Henry VI* dramaturgically primitive, it looks as if Shakespeare, within a few years, came to think exactly that. Are we then, as Morgann supposed, confronted, in this first offering from one later acknowledged to be a supreme genius, by an undeveloped, undeveloping affair?

Well, hardly. The three parts of *Henry VI* compose a complex English history, and the history play seems to be a Shakespearean invention. Here it is being invented before our eyes. John Bale's *King John* is indeed earlier, but Bale's play is a strange hybrid, part incipient history, part morality. The anonymous *Troublesome Reign of John, King of England,* once thought to be the source of Shakespeare's *King John,* is now thought to be later than Shakespeare's play.[4] The old play of *Gorboduc* has some claim to be considered as a history, but it is really a Senecan tragedy. Its Shakespearean affinities are with *King Lear,* another chronicle play that we refuse to classify as anything but tragedy. We know that there was an early non-Shakespearean play on the reign of Henry V. Thomas Nashe alludes to it in *Pierce Pennilesse his Supplication to the Divell* (1592). After an admiring reference to Talbot, the hammer of the French, in Shakespeare's *Henry VI,* he goes on to observe that Henry V has cut a similarly triumphant figure on the stage, "leading the French King prisoner."[5] Whether, if we had the text, we should consider this a real history play is a question that cannot be answered. The young Shakespeare is certainly doing something new. Marlowe's *Edward II* is a real history play, but it is later than the *Henry VI* plays. The generic move is so important, so fundamental, that it produced the well-known triple division in the grand folio published after the poet's death, in 1623. Instead of the expected binary scheme, "Comedies and Tragedies," we have "Comedies, *Histories,* and Tragedies." There is indeed a certain awkwardness in the newly intruded category. *Richard II* is obviously a history, but one wishes to be allowed to point out that it is also the purest tragedy, generically, that Shakespeare ever wrote. What is inescapable, however, is that he has made the idea of a history play part of the well-worn furniture of the literary mind.

What is less clear is the priority in time of the first part of *Henry VI.* Some think it was written after parts 2 and 3 and that, in any case, within part 1, only Act II, Scene iv, and Act IV are from Shakespeare's hand.[6] If most of *1 Henry VI* is by someone other than Shakespeare and in fact came before parts 2 and 3, then Shakespeare certainly is not the originator of the history play. Even without Act II, Scene iv, and Act IV, *1 Henry VI* is already forming a real history. Note that, according to this reconstruction of the process of composition, the most strikingly primitive stagings of spaces (they occur in Act I) are no longer Shakespearean, although he is working with them on the table, so to speak. And Act II, Scene iv, is simply astonishing in its subtlety, by any standard of dramatic sophistication.

The play is about a war with France and an emerging conflict between the Houses of York and Lancaster. It begins with the funeral of Henry V, the great warrior king who had subdued France. His successor, Henry VI, is, we soon learn, a man of very different temper: mild, devout, notably devoid of the killer instinct. Meanwhile his wife, Margaret of Anjou, is a fighter, frustrated by her husband's passivity. All this, note, will be re-run later, with added power, in certain conversations of Macbeth with his lady. The dynamic of the opening scene looks forward to the beginning of *King Lear* in that a grand processional display is swiftly splintered in a discordant play of individual personalities. The disintegrators could be wrong—the whole play could quite easily be Shakespearean. Gloucester, the Lord Protector of the King, who came to the throne when he was a child, is at odds, we learn, with the churchman, Winchester. The rising quarrel is then interrupted in its turn by the entry of a breathless messenger, with news that great tracts of France have been lost through disputes among the English military leaders. Act I, Scene ii, shows the fighting before the gates of Orleans. Here the twenty-first-century reader gets his or her first shock, with the entry of Joan de Pucelle. Slowly we realize, "This is Joan of Arc, the Maid of Orleans." Shakespeare's Joan is, as we say, demonized, almost literally (we see her surrounded by actual fiends who have done her bidding in Act V, Scene iii). For Shakespeare as for Edward Hall, the chronicler (his principal source), Joan was an evil witch, assisting the French. Led by Joan de Pucelle the French beat back the English and raise the siege of Orleans.

Act I, Scene iii, is set in London. The good Duke Humphrey of Gloucester, the Lord Protector, is refused admission to the Tower on the orders of the Bishop of Winchester. The insult is extreme and causes street fighting among the followers of both parties. Gloucester's men have the upper hand, but the Mayor arrives suddenly and sends them all home. This too will be re-run later—in the opening of *Romeo and Juliet*. As he watches them depart the Mayor observes, "I myself fight not once in forty year" (I.iii.91). This pause in the action, with the glimpse it gives of a human individual and another mode of life, looks very Shakespearean. Throughout his career he had this power to endow an individual with autonomous identity, amid the hurly-burly of the play's action. The Mayor is *bürgerlich,* civil not martial. The feudal belligerents he quiets and sends home seem for a second to belong to the childhood of the world, he to its maturity. A grown-up comes and order is restored. But because the dominant ethos of the play remains feudal, the Mayor is not especially impressive. We smile in something close to contempt when he tells us that he scarcely ever fights. Yet again we are looking at something that will grow later. In *Coriolanus* the "co-operative values" of the guild-hall and the marketplace will be set in opposition to the "competitive values" of the battle-field.

The rest of Act I and the first three scenes of Act II are taken up with the progress of the war with France. Talbot fights like a tiger but shows that he has brains as well as brawn by evading a trap laid for him by the oily-tongued Countess of Auvergne. This is a thoroughly enjoyable, dance-like sequence that ends with the lady herself applauding. And then we come to Act II, Scene iv.

We have already seen, together with the coarsely schematic presentation of war at the level of staging and props, a very different suppleness at the level of plot-progression—personality clashes interwoven expertly with larger political antagonisms, one action interrupting, overlapping, reinforcing, or retarding another. We become aware that history has a multiple momentum and is imperfectly controlled by the most powerful persons concerned. The lines describing the discussions that led to the loss of large parts of France are in a somewhat stilted style, but they are also politically expert in their effortless analysis of a complex field:

One would have ling'ring wars with little cost;
Another would fly swift, but wanteth wings;
A third thinks, without expense at all,
By guileful fair words peace may be obtain'd.   (I.i.74–77)

Before the American army entered Iraq some said, "Let us go in with a large force and save money in the long run," others said, "Let us go in with few soldiers but in a spectacular manner," and yet others said, "Let us see what the United Nations can do." Shakespeare's language here is intelligently faithful to the real to-and-fro of high-level political discussion. This means that before we reach the crucial scene, Act II, Scene iv, we have already acquired a sense of historical process as something both violent and mysterious.

The scene itself shows the quarrel among noblemen from which the long Wars of the Roses sprang. The dynamic is supplied by a kind of contradiction. The scene presents the origin of the Wars of the Roses, how it all began, and, simultaneously, withholds the reason. It is an aetiology without an *aitia,* or "cause." The essence of the scene is proleptically summed up in the very first line: "Great lords and gentlemen, what means this silence?"

The speaker is Richard Plantagenet, late Duke of York. He is asking angrily why no one will speak openly "in a case of truth." In response his interlocutor Suffolk says, in effect, "Hush. We need privacy for this. Let us go into the garden." We follow them into the private garden but learn only that Plantagenet and Somerset are disputing "sharp quillets of the law" (II.iv.17), that is to say, legal niceties. As the play unfolds it becomes apparent that the Duke of York is asserting a claim to the throne, presently held by a descendant of the House of Lancaster. The best critical account known to me of what follows is Tania Demetriou's.[7]

She points out that in Hall's chronicle York's claim emerges later, after the death of Gloucester. Hall's earlier references to York, when he was still Richard Plantagenet, simply recount his actions and then add, with editorial hindsight, that this is the man who *will* claim the throne.[8] Shakespeare could have managed his earlier placing of the claim by a straight change in the sequence of public events, as he does elsewhere. Instead he does something very subtle. He cuts off Hall's clear, explanatory hindsight, for obviously this cannot have been available to persons at the time, and the drama is technically confined to their perceptions, has no over-riding narrative or editorial voice. Then he turns the space between origin and visible action into a tantalizing mystery. Commentators on the play tend to say that the "sharp quillets of the law" must have something to do with the succession, but they, like Hall, are comforting themselves with hindsight.

Each party to the dispute thunderously affirms the self-evidence of his cause, but the audience is kept guessing. Then, suddenly, Plantagenet proposes that, since no one will speak out, any man who believes him to be right should pluck a white rose—and as he speaks he plucks a white rose. Somerset responds by inviting *his* supporters to pluck red roses. As with the picking of the apple in Milton's Eden, the picking of the roses is felt by the audience as a point of origin. This is it, the beginning of all that killing. But as with the apple, so with the roses: the apparent clarity of the event is involved in a spider's web of indefinite presuppositions that drain away the promised explanatory power. "Why did Eve pick the apple? This cannot be the point at which sin entered the world, she must have been bad already to disobey God in this way," and so on and so forth.

The moment of the rose-picking is simultaneously chivalric (backward-looking) in its resonance and politically sophisticated. It hovers between "Here I plant my standard!" and "Let's take a straw vote."

But that is not all. There is a further sense that each man's case is mysteriously crystallized by the physical roses, bravely worn. Richard's words as he suggests the device, "Since you are tongue-tied and so loath to speak, / In dumb significants proclaim your thoughts" (II.iv.24–25), seem to say that the rose can properly fill a vacuum in the articulation of reasons. It is as if concrete things have a self-evidence, an un-answerable truth-bearing power often absent from words. Juries can be suddenly convinced, quite irrationally, by a blood-stained handkerchief, produced in court. Seeing is believing. Othello, whom we shall meet later, was like one of those jurors; "Give me the ocular proof!" he cried (III.iii.360). And he too, irrationally and tragically, was satisfied by the production of a handkerchief.[9]

Of course a rose cannot set out legal arguments. It can, however, affect behaviour and increase belief, commitment, allegiance, confidence. As the roses are picked, the juggernaut of history picks up speed. Honour rather than reason is now engaged. As Tania Demetriou says, there is something "uncannily real" about the scene.[10] I know that in committee meetings, after a show of hands in which I have declared a view, I warm to that view, begin to set aside counter-arguments that until then had solicited my attention. Group motivation is partly a matter of wearing the colours of one's side, as football supporters do. Shakespeare has hit on something very close to the "James-Lange" theory of motivation. The "James" here is William, Henry's philosopher brother. The theory calls into question the assumption that actions are determined by pre-existing emotions. Instead of striking because we feel angry, in fact, "We feel angry because we strike."[11] The extreme forms of this reversal seem to crop up in military contexts. The sweet-smelling roses, red and white, conduct us to blood and death:

> this brawl today
> Grown to this faction in the Temple Garden,
> Shall send between the Red Rose and the White
> A thousand souls to death and deadly night.   (II.iv.124–27)

Shakespeare understands the vertiginous transformation of reason to honour. When the un-named lawyer picks a white rose, Plantagenet asks, "Now, Somerset, where is your argument?" And Somerset answers, "Here in my scabbard, meditating that / Shall dye your white rose in a bloody red" (II.iv.59–61). Sixteen lines earlier Somerset had agreed, on the straw-poll logic, that if he got fewer votes he would yield. That is now forgotten as mere symbols harden into governing realities. A rose is a more potent thing than an argument, and a sword is more potent still. The recurrent use of the word "maintain" (II.iv.73, 88) is the language of trial by combat, as in the opening of *Richard II*. The intimate texture of the poetry reveals how Shakespeare has the whole development of the scene in his mind from the beginning. When he gave the phrase "sharp quillets of the law" to Warwick he was saying under his breath, "Careful! You could cut yourselves!"

In this scene Shakespeare moves to and fro between latent and avowed motives in a way that is true to the real movement of politics. It could be said that what I take for subtlety could be mere confusion, that Shakespeare simply forgot to explain the occasion of the quarrel and slipped in the necessary genealogical information later. But the language of the scene *makes a point of* silence and inarticulacy that is inescapable.

Shakespeare returns to the enigmatic, all-powerful rose in Act IV, Scene i. White rose Vernon and red rose Basset are clamouring for the right of formal combat. Basset says,

This fellow here, with envious carping tongue,
Upbraided me about the rose I wear,
Saying the sanguine color of the leaves
Did represent my master's blushing cheeks,
When stubbornly he did repugn the truth
About a certain question in the law
Argu'd betwixt the Duke of York and him.   (IV. i.90–96)

Note that nothing is said here about York's claim to the throne. The legal difference is alluded to, but we seem further than ever from knowing what it was. Basset is obviously not interested. What fills his mind is the roses themselves and their force as badges of allegiance, importing or endangering the wearer's honour.

The fascinating thing in this revisiting of the rose theme is the behaviour of the sweetly reasonable King. He shows no sign of any awareness of York's ambition, lurking in the background. He seeks, but far less
effectively than the unwarlike Mayor in the earlier scene, to defuse the
quarrel. He identifies the immediate cause and pronounces it "slight and
frivolous" (IV.i.112): they are fighting over roses. To show the silliness of
the affair he takes a rose himself, observing as he does so how meaningless
the action is—there is no earthly reason why the mere picking of a red rose
should mean that he prefers Somerset to York! It was Samuel Johnson
who inserted the stage direction, "Pulling a red rose," in his edition.
There is no stage direction in the Folio, but Johnson is obviously correct.
The King may have picked a rose at random. He notices perhaps only as
he is fixing the rose on his breast that this might cause a foolish person to
infer that he favoured Lancastrian Somerset. The King assures us that this
is not the case, and the King is not a liar. Yet the rose is stronger than he. It
proclaims—visually—the right of Lancaster more loudly than any eirenic
words from the sovereign's mouth. To seal the effect we must add that
Henry himself is of the House of Lancaster. He has made a huge mistake.
When he thought he was pouring water on the fire he was pouring petrol.

Henry is neither stupid nor immoral, but he is an ineffective king. If
we ask, "How should Henry behave, confronted by these bloodthirsty
lords?" the natural answer might be that he ought to try to calm them,
should remind his subjects of the obligations of charity and forgiveness.
Henry does both of these things. His sceptical response to roses as badges
feels strong, intellectually. But such brisk scepticism, offered as realism,
has always been disconnected from the real. The old scorn for gold that
finds expression in Thomas More's *Utopia*—"Why revere a chunk of
metal?"—sounds like earthy common sense but is in fact wilfully obtuse.
People who live in the real world know that a gold coin will buy bread for
a child. Thus signifiers, after an initially vacuous *fiat*—"Let this mean
that"—acquire purchase upon real events. The movement of the King's
hand as he puts on the rose is the most mysterious thing of all. Does the
hand know that it is a Lancastrian hand, and must therefore take a red rose,
not a white? Or was it simply chance, a truly random act, instantly my-
thologized and rendered politically operative by context? Did the King
himself become half aware that he was caught in a web of meanings and so
assumed a tunnel vision to avoid confronting the frightening implica-

tions, as school-teachers avert their eyes from misbehaviour they cannot easily correct?

No one before had come close to the subtlety of *1 Henry VI*, Act II, Scene iv, and Act IV, Scene i. How, it might be asked, can this subtlety co-exist with the coarseness of sensibility we see in the treatment of Joan of Arc? If ever there were a case of mindless abuse, this surely is it. How could that Shakespeare who was taught by brave Roman Catholics and grew up amid the ugly persecution of such Catholics lend his pen to this gross cartoon? The answer is: this is what his history books told him, as firmly as our history books tell us that Adolf Hitler was evil. It will be said, "But Hitler *was* evil!" and I assent. But Shakespeare had no reason to doubt the received account of Joan, embedded as it is in grittily factual narrative. So we should start from the supposed fact that she was a witch. Shakespeare then, working within that tradition, makes her interesting: intelligent, sexy, and a formidable fighter. In early modern drama disguises and altered identities are conventionally impenetrable; one is not allowed to say, "But surely someone would have noticed that the beard was false?" Joan, however, instantly sees through the Dolphin's (Dauphin's) pretence that he is a mere onlooker, although she has never seen him before, at I.ii.66–67. Of course it may be that what I take for intelligence is supernatural—magic. Where ladies are supposed to win men by their softness, by the appeal weakness makes to strength, Joan wins the Dolphin's love by beating him, woman to man, in fair fight. He says, "Impatiently I burn with thy desire; / My heart and hands thou hast at once subdu'd" (I.ii.108–9).

What saves the episode from being a knock-about exercise in topsy-turvydom is an utterly unexpected tremor of hesitation in Joan, as she beats her lover down. When he cries out, "Thou art an Amazon," she answers, "Christ's Mother helps me, else I were too weak" (I.ii.106). The words are like a blush. They show that Joan is attracted to the Dolphin. This figure of plated steel has the sudden thought, "O gosh—I'll lose him if I can't make him think of me as a weak woman!" After all, the male ego is a notoriously fragile thing. Meanwhile her prowess in battle is undoubted. When Talbot says, "Our English troops retire, I cannot stay them; / A woman clad in armour chaseth them" (I.v.2–3), the laugh is on the English, not Joan, who is made splendid by the line.

Later in the scene Talbot darkens the picture. Joan is now indeed a witch. She drives back the troops by fear, not force, as smoke sends bees flying from their hives (I.v.21–24). When the English capture Joan, they prepare to burn her. Warwick suggests that because of her spotless purity, barrels of pitch be set round the stake to make the flames burn more strongly, shortening the victim's agony (V.iv.55–58). Joan, however, abruptly reveals that she, "the maid," is pregnant. She thinks they cannot kill an unborn child. I believe the audience then as now would be pulled up short by the strength of this moral appeal. But it is instantly involved in the coarsest comedy. Joan desperately names as father first one man and then another. No one draws the conclusion that she is *pretending* to be pregnant. Instead the cruel mirth is all at the expense of her suddenly revealed promiscuity.

Is the attack on Joan of Arc necessarily an attack on Roman Catholicism, or could it be, rather, an attack on the French? Joan on her first appearance refers repeatedly to the Virgin Mary (I.ii.74, 78, 106), and Mariolatry is a charge levelled at Catholics by Protestants. This false piety is thrown back at her at the end when she is unmasked as a sexual adventuress, with a joke on the virgin birth:

> the holy maid with child?
> WARWICK The greatest miracle that e'er ye wrought!   (V.iv.65–66)

What is the comic logic here? If Joan's iniquity consists in the falsity of her claim to be a virgin, the cult of virginity is not itself under attack. We are not within range of Parolles's "virginity is peevish, proud, idle, made of self-love" (*All's Well That Ends Well,* I.i.144). The same considerations apply perhaps to Alanson's (Alençon's) words: "We'll set thy statue in some holy place, / And have thee reverenc'd like a blessed saint" (III.iii.14–15).

Deeply committed Protestants, it may be supposed, would have stayed away from the theatre. If there were nevertheless a few in the audience, they would probably have thought at this point, "Ugh! These papists!" Most, I would guess, did not. Earlier, when Joan was professing her devotion to the Virgin, Alanson saw her as "Venus" (I.ii.144). Alanson's piety, like Joan's, is erotically compromised. This, not Mariolatry, is his offence.

The exchanges between Gloucester and the Bishop of Winchester, afterwards Cardinal, look more directly anti-papal. Looking back on the glorious reign of Henry V, Winchester intones, "The battles of the Lord of hosts he fought; / The Church's prayers made him so prosperous" (I.i.31–32). The good Duke Humphrey answers, "The Church? where is it? Had not churchmen pray'd, /His thread of life had not so soon decay'd." This looks like *general* scepticism, from an admired person, directed at the prayers of priests and so at the Church itself. Later when Winchester says, "Rome shall remedy this," Gloucester answers, punning, "Roam thither then" (III.i.51). This looks like straight anti-Catholic popular rhetoric. It goes with the earlier picture of Winchester as a wicked cardinal, giving indulgences to whores (I.iii.35). Gloucester threatens to stamp on the Cardinal's hat "in spite of Pope" and calls the Cardinal himself a "scarlet hypocrite!" (I.iii.49–50, 56). "Scarlet" takes us to "scarlet sins" (Isa. 1:18) and to the "scarlet woman" of Revelation (17:4), identified by Protestants with the Church of Rome. The word burns still with a sectarian flame some twenty years later in John Webster's *The White Devil:* "O poor charity, / Thou art seldom seen in scarlet" (III.ii.70–71). Even here, however, if we listen hard, another thread in the discourse can be discerned. There is something momentarily disorienting in Gloucester's question, "The Church? Where is it?" It half-implies that all these corrupt priests are not the true Catholic Church, which, perhaps, is far away and yet still there, a little like the communist polity as seen in the later thought of Terry Eagleton: a great idea that hasn't actually been tried yet. Just as Joan is condemned not for her cult of virginity but for her unchastity, so Winchester is condemned not for his priestly power but for the abuse of that power, and also, like Joan, for unchastity. One's ears prick up at the word "indulgences." Protestants saw the very notion of an indulgence— the remission of punishment in Purgatory, often in return for money—as corrupt. The power of granting indulgences was passed by the pope to bishops and was scandalously exercised by dodgy professional "pardoners" in the later Middle Ages. Once more, however, Winchester is condemned not for purveying indulgences per se but for granting them to whores (he is supposed to have derived a comfortable income from brothels in Southwark).[12] This, we suddenly realize, could be good old anti-clericalism, which began long before the Reformation. The picture of hell drawn by the Limbourg brothers for the *Très Riches Heures du duc de Berry* shows many tonsured friars being dragged to everlasting torment, as does the *Inferno* of Buonamico Buffalmacco (1350) in the Campo Santo at Pisa. Catholic Dante's bête noire was Boniface—a pope. The Pardoner is one of the nastiest characters in Chaucer's *Canterbury Tales*. Of course the play, *Henry VI*, though written towards the end of the *sixteenth* century is *set* in pre-Reformation England. Shakespeare is clearly conscious of this, though he, so to speak, keeps his consciousness to himself. At one point the King says that there should be no quarrel between the nations of England and France, professing as they do "one faith" (V.i.14). In part 2 Henry, that ineffective but undoubtedly Christian king, is mocked by his unpleasant wife because he is addicted to "holiness, / To number Ave-Maries on his beads" (I.iii.55–56). Good King Henry is clearly a Catholic. Strong Protestants, I have granted, would hear this material in one way, the ordinarily confused auditor in another. It could all be received without difficulty by an Old Catholic. The "Rome/roam" crack on the other hand remains obstinately anti-papist. Shakespeare with his antennae for likely audience-response would have foreseen all this. Perhaps we must allow that the young dramatist, eager to make his mark, was not above giving *all* the sections of the audience what they wanted.

What remains remarkable is the co-existence of conventional dance-like sequences such as Talbot's defeat of the wily Countess of Auvergne (loved by Victorian audiences) or the scenes of antiphonal exchanges between castled generals on one hand and, on the other, a subtle reflex of attention to underlying or simultaneous causes and counter-causes—creating a catch in the rhythm of the dance. This is distinctively Shakespearean, and because it is found throughout, I am inclined to think, with Michael Hattaway, that the whole of *1 Henry VI* is by Shakespeare (the resemblance to Nashe detected by Gary Taylor's stylistic analysis can be accounted for by the readiness of a young dramatist to adopt the style of available models).[13] The most vivid instance of this "catch in the rhythm" is Suffolk's almost Freudian slip at in Act V:

I'll undertake to make thee Henry's queen,
To put a golden sceptre in thy hand,
And set a precious crown upon thy head,
If thou wilt condescend to be my—

MARGARET   What?

SUFFOLK His love.   (V.iii.117–21)

Suffolk is speaking of the splendid match he can make for Margaret, but the secret thought, that Margaret might be his, not Henry's, breaks through. The model is Ovid, with his glancingly mobile Latin. Pygmalion, the man who fell in love with a statue he had devised, is made to stumble in his speech: " 'Sit coniunx opto' non ausus 'eburnea virgo' / Dicere, Pygmalion, 'similis mea' dixit 'eburnae.' " ("I wish my wife could be"— Pygmalion dared not say "my ivory maiden," but said "one like my ivory maiden"; *Metamorphoses,* x.275–76). Ovid was Shakespeare's favourite poet, the writer to whom he most often refers. He will later use the Ovidian hesitation to brilliant effect in *The Merchant of Venice:*

One half of me is yours, the other half yours—
Mine own, I would say; but if mine, then yours,
And so all yours.   (III.ii.16–18)

Here the effect is especially delicious because the speaker is the normally queenly, all-controlling Portia, now trapped in a momentary mental stammer by love. Suffolk's line is Shakespeare's first shot at amorous parapraxis. Freud's notion of a latent real intention or desire disturbing the surface utterance is clearly applicable to both Suffolk and Portia.[14]

The scene in the rose garden, which all allow to be Shakespeare's, remains the astonishing thing. I return to Tania Demetriou's phrase, "uncannily real." Of course Shakespeare is not giving a factually accurate account of the origin of the Wars of the Roses; he is giving an accurate account of the way such things can come about. All this was sorted out long ago by Aristotle when he said that poetry does not tell us "what Alcibiades did" but rather "the kinds of things that would happen" (*Poetics,* 1451b11, 1451a37). Shakespeare is true to the kinds of things that happen in times of political change. This, as Aristotle at once allows, lets in the kind of universality that present-day Historicists dislike. Perhaps Shakespeare is actually truer to the general character of such movements than the academic historians are. Historians are pre-set to find the causes of events and are perhaps too little prepared to recognize where movements are not so much the product of precedent conditions as self-energizing. Shakespeare knows how the hindsight that gives Edward Gibbon's great history its majestic sweep was unavailable to the original participants. Think of the difference between sober historical accounts of the start of the First World War and Bertrand Russell's observation that his compatriots had become irrational, as if they wanted to die.[15] Russell was remembering what it was like to be there. The closer one comes to the human material, the more it shimmers.

The "shimmer effect" is there again in *2 Henry VI*. Suffolk's slip in addressing Margaret of Anjou betrayed his desire for her, and this hint is gradually developed. Part 2 opens with what appears to be a blandly public report by Suffolk of his negotiation to cement a marriage between Margaret and the King of England:

As by your high imperial Majesty
I had in charge at my depart for France,
As procurator to your Excellence,
To marry Princess Margaret for your Grace;
So, in the famous ancient city Tours,

. . . .

I have perform'd my task, and was espous'd.   (I.i.1–9)

We suppose at first that we are listening to unproblematic, sonorous, official stuff. But a fleeting puzzle is planted in the sequence of the phrases. We believe for a fraction of a second that Suffolk is calmly announcing that *he* has married Margaret. Of course we correct ourselves. "Procurator," not so very different from the low term "procurer," obviously means that Suffolk has obtained Margaret for someone else, and "for" in "for your Grace" must mean "on behalf of." Moreover the Elizabethans were more accustomed than we are to "proxy wooings." At the same time, however, "to marry Princess Margaret" and "I have perform'd my task, and was espous'd" naturally convey the simple meaning, "I am married to Margaret." Still stranger, as the speech continues, it is suggested that there is in any case a technical sense in which Suffolk really has married—or taken to himself—Margaret of France. At lines 11–12 Suffolk proclaims that he will now "deliver up" his "title in the queen" to Henry. If there were no sexual rapport evident elsewhere in the drama between Suffolk and Margaret we might be justified in setting aside these "subauditions" as accidental or irrelevant. As it is we cannot. Ordinary dramatists often confuse the audience inadvertently. Shakespeare knows when he is confusing people and manages the confusion.

The story of 2 Henry VI is the story of the rising star of York and the descending star of Lancastrian Henry. While the dramatist works to undermine clarity of motive, he simultaneously keeps certain obstinate facts before our minds, as that York's claim to the throne is strong whereas the King's own claim is frail. Admittedly, this not made completely explicit until we get to the third part. The essence of York's case is that things went wrong after Richard II. Richard, the legitimate heir of Edward III, via the Black Prince, Edward's first-born son, was forced from his throne by Lancastrian Bolingbroke, who thereupon made himself king (Henry IV). Richard had left no issue. Henry IV could claim descent from Edward III's son John of Gaunt. But John of Gaunt was Edward's fourth son. York meanwhile could show descent from Edward's third son, Lionel, Duke of Clarence. Since both the earlier lines, that of the Black Prince and that of the second son, William of Hatfield, had petered out, this left the dispute between York, descended from the third son, and Henry VI, descended from the fourth son and on the throne only as a result of an act of violent usurpation. Legally, things look black for Henry.

But—and we shall have to get used to bewildering complications of this kind—the paradox of the legal rebel and the illegal governor is not the full story. Henry, the dubious figure (in York's terms, "the usurper," 3 Henry VI, I.i.114), is virtuous, sweet-natured, and fair-minded. He knows what the job requires and at first attempts thunder from the throne:

Think'st thou that I will leave my kingly throne,
Wherein my grandsire and my father sat?
No; first shall war unpeople this my realm;
Ay, and their colors, often borne in France,
And now in England to our heart's great sorrow,
Shall be my winding-sheet. Why faint you, lords?
My title's good, and better far than his.   (I.i.124–30)

The speech that begins as proud defiance turns into an image of the land wasted, the speaker dead. The faintness Henry sees in the faces of the lords is reflected from his own words with their vision of catastrophic defeat. The last sentence is once more defiant, but the defiance now sounds shrill, almost childish. And it has made the question of succession explicit, designated it a matter of debate. Pandora's box is opened, just as it will be opened some eighty years after this by John Milton, when he confidently undertook at the beginning of *Paradise Lost* to justify the ways of God to men. When pressed, Henry swiftly described Henry IV's take-over (which, he knows, is the crucial moment) as "conquest." York stolidly insists that "rebellion" is the right word. In a wonderful momentary acceleration of tempo, as if everything were over before it had properly begun, the King mutters, "I know not what to say, my title's weak" (I.i.134). This, however, is an aside, and so history can unfold at its own slow pace. Henry then argues, not unskilfully, that Richard voluntarily resigned the crown to Bolingbroke; since this act has legal status, Henry IV, his son Henry V, and his grandson Henry VI are all legitimate kings. York replies that the resignation was not truly voluntary because it was constrained. One is reminded of the notion of constructive dismissal in modern British employment law. Typically the employer, who has long wished that Mr. X would leave the firm and has hinted as much, is delighted when Mr. X actually resigns, only to be thrown off balance three months later when Mr. X sues the firm on the ground that he was intimidated by the boss's nasty hints into signing the fatal letter; in short, he pleads constructive dismissal. Richard, York is saying, was clearly frightened into compliance. Exeter, a Lancastrian supporter, then chips in, happily fascinated by legal technicalities, to say that even if Richard's resignation had been unconstrained it could not legitimize the descendants of Henry IV. The King, who is having enough trouble with his own fairness of mind, is understandably nettled and asks, in effect, "Damn it, whose side are you on?" (I.i.147). Disquietingly, Exeter thinks and answers, "Not yours."

In *1 Henry VI* the start of the Wars of the Roses was, in Demetriou's admirable if polysyllabic formulation, "aetiologized as an *aposiopesis*,"[16] that is, the origin was given in the frustrating form of a breaking off of speech, a falling-silent. So here, at a moment of crisis, we have instead of audible speech, an infinitely sinister susurration, as the Lancastrian nobles whisper among themselves (I.i.149). The supporters no longer support. Those who like to talk easily of the contemptible character of Henry VI should now ask themselves, "What could I have done in such a situation that is better than what Henry does next?" He does a deal. York can have the throne after his, Henry's, death. Till then Henry is to remain king. York agrees to abide by this agreement and steps down from the throne on which he has been sitting, pre-emptively, all this time. There is an uncanny echo here of what happened long before (and will soon be dramatized by Shakespeare) to Richard II. Is Henry's resignation of the throne to York after his death tainted by the same flaw the Yorkists found in Richard's resignation? Are we watching, here and now, a fair deal or one made under constraint? Yet Henry, I submit, has made a good move. His most tough-minded critics will continue to say, no doubt, that a really good king would have had York rubbed out long before matters reached this pass. Shakespeare is less quick with contempt than are his readers (Polonius is a case in point). The real Henry VI composed a prayer, still used at Eton College: *Domine, Jesu Christe, qui me creasti, redemisti, et preordinasti ad hoc quod sum, tu scis quid de me facere vis; fac de me secundum voluntatem tuam cum misericordia,* "Lord Jesus Christ, who hast made me, redeemed me, and preordained me to this thing I am, thou knowest what thou wishest to do with me; do with me, according to thy will." It may be said that this is simply the common language of prayer. But the sad, helpless, good man of Shakespeare's trilogy comes through clearly.

Of course the deal comes to pieces. York's son, Richard "Crookback," later to become Richard III, works upon his father with Machiavellian arguments of *Realpolitik* to renege on his oath (I.ii.22–27). Yet again motivation becomes complex. York, clearly, wishes to keep his oath, is an honourable man. Equally clearly there is that in York which wishes to break free. This element in the personality is something Crookback can "trigger." As events unfold we can begin to feel that York's belligerence is justified by the fact that Queen Margaret, Henry's wife, has herself taken up arms against York. But then we remember that he broke his oath before she did this. But then—again!—we remember that he thought it likely that she would do some such thing and has been proved right by the event. Long afterwards York's son, Edward, now King, says to Margaret,

Hadst thou been meek, our title still had slept,
And we, in pity of the gentle king,
Had slipp'd our claim until another age.   (*3 Henry VI*, II.ii.160–62)

And so the subtleties recede from our understanding, into obscurity.

What else in this apprentice work is distinctively Shakespearean? I answer, the use of dramaturgical "islands," small or large, set in the action. We have already met one in the person of the bourgeois Mayor who quells the riot near the beginning of *1 Henry VI*. In part 2 we have, straight from John Foxe's *Book of Martyrs,* the rumbustious late medieval comedy of Simpcox and the bogus miracle. Simpcox is a beggar who claims to have been blind all his life until his sight was miraculously restored at a shrine in St. Albans. The King questions him, asking him to name the colours of various things. Simpcox unhesitatingly gives the correct replies to exhibit the glorious fact of his newly restored sight. The King then observes that a blind man would have no way of knowing that a particular colour, set before him, is the colour sighted people call "red." Simpcox is fairly caught, amid much merriment, and he and his wife are dispatched to be whipped through every market town between St. Albans and Berwick. It still plays well on stage to uproarious laughter from modern audiences, yet we in the twenty-first century cannot easily stomach all this merry whacking and flogging. Shakespeare knew that even then someone in the audience would be troubled about the beating of Mrs. Simpcox, and for that person he created one of his "islands." "Alas, sir," Mrs. Simpcox says simply, "we did it for pure need" (*2 Henry VI*, II.i.154). Suddenly the scene is turned inside out. The egregious rogue Simpcox becomes a man who is hungry, ingenious, and has a wife to support. But then the comedy roars on. Later Shakespeare will modulate the effect to new uses, perhaps most wonderfully in the strikingly dignified words of the dotty schoolmaster, Holofernes, standing isolated amid the wreckage of the entertainment he has put together for grand persons who do nothing but laugh at him (*Love's Labour's Lost,* V.ii.628). This alertness to the possibility of a *completely* different view of things is one of the features that has enabled Shakespeare to survive beyond his immediate ideological context. The person in a corner of the auditorium whom we imagined sympathizing with Mrs. Simpcox can become that other person, some four hundred years later, who has the extraordinary idea that a Jewish moneylender who wants to carve open the chest of a Christian could have something to be said on his side.

Another "island," equally brief, can be found in the sequence of Jack Cade's rebellion. Jack Cade is a communist in the basic sense of the word: he believes in the abolition of private property (2 Henry VI, IV.vii.18–19). Again the dominant logic is clear, and perhaps not to our taste: Cade is a grotesque, half-comic threat to all around him and deserves to be crushed. His henchman's line, "The first thing we do, let's kill all the lawyers" (IV.ii.6–7), must always, I suspect, have got a laugh and a sputtering of applause from some in the audience. Yet there is no serious doubt that a society without law is a kind of horror, a jungle of random suffering and unchecked aggression. We are all now pre-set, culturally, to warm to terms like "subversion" and to recoil from terms like "repression." This automatic response may be a function of our luxurious security, as compared with earlier times in history. Michel Foucault can rely on a similarly automatic charge of condemnation attaching to the word "policing." I respond as others do to these signals. Yet I can remember a time when I was in a dangerous part of the world and surprised myself with the sudden, unbidden thought, "If only they had a proper police force!" A basic fact about the England of Elizabeth—one we should never forget—is that the sovereign had no effective police force and no standing army.

Cade's uprising fails, and we now see him on the run, in rural Kent. In a change of register we have a sudden domesticity; an English garden with a high brick wall, over which comes the desperate Cade. The garden belongs to one Alexander Iden, no aristocratic warlord of the kind to which we have become accustomed in the histories but a substantial country squire. Cade offers a shrill challenge; Iden, who seems to embody a kindlier, post-feudal England, answers in effect, "Come now, I'm not going to fight a poor starving man—look at the thickness of my arm; I could finish you in a second!" Cade makes a fight of it nevertheless and falls. All the sympathy so far has lain with Iden. But then Cade says, "Famine and no other hath slain me" (IV.x.60). Once more the scene is, for a moment only, turned inside out. Karl Marx, in a remote corner of the auditorium of time, finds his own thought expressed for him.

"Islands" are not always so brief. In 3 Henry VI we have the poignant meditative idyll amid the killing and this too is an "island," or a time out of war, a suspension of the hammering engine of the play's action. In "another part of the field," the King enters, alone. This "island" is not like the others a moment of naturalism. Instead it is given its own formal music in counterpoint to the main theme of the play. It is pastoral. The King sits on a molehill to muse on the unattainable happiness of the simple shepherd:

Ah! what a life were this! how sweet! how lovely!
Gives not the hawthorn bush a sweeter shade
To shepherds looking on their silly sheep
Than doth a rich embroider'd canopy
To kings that fear their subjects' treachery? (*3 Henry VI,* II.v.41–45)

I have been stressing, as distinctively Shakespearean, counter-formal moments of naturalist mobility and ambiguity. Here, however, the cadenced language running contrary to the bellicose drama shows how the distinctively Shakespearean tic of opposition can itself assume a stately formal character. This has happened before. When Henry made his grand speech of defiance, the measured curses he laid upon himself and his country, even as we shivered at his weakness, had prophetic authority. "First shall war unpeople this my realm" (*3 Henry VI,* I.i.126). Just so. It will. Even in the strange lull of the intruded pastoral scene we have the stage directions "Enter a Son that hath kill'd his father" and "Enter a Father that hath kill'd his son . . . bearing of his son" (II.v.54, 78). No subtlety now, no clever intricacy. This, if you like, is primitive. But "primitive" is now no term of abuse, as it began to be earlier. For this is the truth of civil wars. The Greek historian Herodotus makes Croesus tell Cyrus that the terrible thing about war is that we see, not sons burying fathers, but fathers burying sons (*History,* I.lxxxvii.4). Civil war, we now see, is even worse. The wordless sequence is symmetrically patterned in the form of a chiasmus, son: father, father: son. Here it would be a critical error to associate the patterned with the vacuous or platitudinous.

Isolating a Monster: *Richard III*

The next history Shakespeare wrote was a barnstormer. For my generation Olivier's Richard III is the one stamped on the memory. It was a performance of sinister power, including sexual power, and it lent itself readily to parody in the years that followed. In a way the potential comedy was there from the start in Shakespeare's writing. As usual, he saw it first. His Richard is a figure hovering between comedy and horror. The deformed murderer of the princes in the Tower, the terrifying seducer of the widowed Lady Anne, is a jovial fellow. He has gripped the popular imagination ever since.

In the mid-twentieth century it was generally agreed that it was a mistake to apply the notion of "characterization" to Shakespeare's plays. Characters, it was said, belong in novels; early modern drama is a dance of images or, at best, stereotypes. L. C. Knights in his immensely influential essay, "How Many Children Had Lady Macbeth?" said that it was logically absurd to make inferences about the previous lives of such poetic constructions. In fact audiences guess and hypothesize all the time, and good dramatists rely on the fact. The earlier critic A. C. Bradley, predictably derided by Knights, felt no such restraint. Now that the dust has settled it is clear that Bradley was a better critic of Shakespeare than Knights. Shakespeare excels at characterization.

In the three parts of *Henry VI,* however, this is not obvious. The barons with their similar-sounding county names easily blur in the mind; only the racy career of the plot keeps them distinct. Even the dynastic factions are not strongly characterized. The audience needs those red and white roses to keep the political parties distinct. Henry himself is an interesting character if one attends carefully, but he is so, *quietly.* His goodness and piety feel genuine and are played off against a weakness that is now, because our sympathy has been engaged, troubling to watch. He is unable to stand his ground and defend the good Duke of Gloucester, whom he knows to be innocent of the charge brought against him, because he is so overwhelmed, emotionally, to find that humankind can be so wicked (*2 Henry VI,* II.i.181). His evident fear of his wife (*3 Henry VI,* I.i.219) is similarly embarrassing. When categories are crossed and mismatched in this way, the mind is drawn to speculate on the likely nature of an individual who could be like that. Thus we guess that this king will probably *not* be troubled by his wife's threat of sexual strike-action (*3 Henry VI,* I.i.248). But all this is faint compared with "Richard Crookback."

Richard is a stunted figure and at the same time a giant of the stage. If characters belong naturally to the novel, is there a later novelist who is relevant here? There is: Charles Dickens. Quilp in *The Old Curiosity Shop* is physically a giant dwarf, having a huge torso and tiny arms and legs. He is a figure of potency, including sexual potency, and he is jolly with it. The Richard of tradition "was born at Fotheringhay in Northamptonshire, retained within his mother's womb for two years, emerging with teeth and hair to his shoulders."[17] The incongruous teeth become in legend the tusks of a wild boar, Richard's emblem. In his *Chronicles of England, Scotland, and Ireland,* Raphael Holinshed preserves the doggerel couplet of William Collingbourne, who was beheaded and chopped into four pieces in 1484: "The Cat the Rat and Lovell our dog / Rule all England under an Hog."[18] The jingle has the queer primal authority possessed by nursery rhymes. The Cat, Catesby, and the Rat, Ratcliffe, we shall meet in the course of the play. The Hog is Richard. In the popular collection of blood-freezing tales of the falls of princes, *The Mirror for Magistrates,* the Duke of Clarence is made to say, "He knew my brother Richard was the Bore / Whose tuskes should tear my brothers boyes and me."[19] The hairy, toothed baby has grown into a beast-man. It is important to forget the sleepy pink pigs of modern farming and remember the great fighting boars of the forests. The image recurs. In an anonymous poem, "The Rose of England," we read, "There came a beast men call a bore / And he rooted this garden up and downe."[20] All this is brought together in Shakespeare's line, "Thou elvish-mark'd, abortive, rooting hog!" (I.iii.227). The image of the boar permeates the play.

The opening soliloquy—very much an address, meanwhile, to the audience—is both self-description and an announcement of self-determination. Richard dwells relishingly on his own unattractiveness, his unfitness for love or sex:

But I, that am not shap'd for sportive tricks,
Nor made to court an amorous looking-glass;

. . . .

therefore, since I cannot prove a lover
To entertain these fair well-spoken days,
I am determined to prove a villain.   (I.i.14–15, 28–30)

The allusion to a looking-glass is a brilliant touch with its insinuation that there is something weakly narcissistic about the benevolent mass of humankind—everyone else; these lovers of the opposite sex are really lovers of themselves, and fools. The conscious decision to be a villain gives a curious depth to all Richard's subsequent actions. Because of this prior decision he can never *be* the simple pantomime Rumpelstiltskin figure we might otherwise have taken him to be. He thematizes himself from the start and cannot be fully identified with the theme any more than the actor can be identified with the role.

But he is wrong about the unattractiveness. In the same opening scene Richard's brother is brought on stage, under guard, on his way to the Tower. All this is in line with Richard's secret plan. The dialogue is startling:

RICHARD Brother, good day. What means this armed guard
   That waits upon your Grace?
CLARENCE   His Majesty,
   Tend'ring my person's safety, hath appointed
   This conduct to convey me to the Tower.
RICHARD Upon what cause?
CLARENCE   Because my name is George.
RICHARD Alack, my lord, that fault is none of yours;
   He should for that commit your godfathers.
   O, belike his Majesty hath some intent
   That you should be new christn'd in the Tower.
   But what's the matter, Clarence, may I know?   (I.i.42–51)

The first thing to register is the grimness of Clarence's situation. The next is Richard's wilfully inapposite good humour (all the crueller since Clarence is himself making an effort to be brave, to make light of what is happening). "Waits upon" is a joke. These men are emphatically not at Clarence's beck and call. Clarence, with an effort, tries to joke back. "Tend'ring my person's safety" is 30 percent hope and 70 percent irony. "Because my name is George" is a reference to a prophecy that the King will be succeeded by one whose name begins with G.[21] Richard with antic gravity takes him at his word and gleefully explores the possibility of suing the godparents. Richard's genial overriding of the human pain before him is like Petruchio's bland ignoring of Kate's distress in *The Taming of the Shrew,* written about the same time. In either case, where the reader shudders, the watcher in the theatre laughs. Richard, we learn, is attractive. His last, comradely, "But what's the matter, Clarence, may I know?" is incongruously charming. All this is to prepare us for the greatest scene in the play, the scene in which the supposedly un-erotic hunchback shows his real power over women, the seduction of Lady Anne, the widow of Prince Edward.[22]

Lady Anne enters at the beginning of Act I, Scene ii, following the corpse of Henry VI as it is carried to burial. She is given a magnificent formal lament in which she expresses her grief at the death of the King, at the death of her husband, and curses Richard, the man who killed them both. As she ends Richard appears and effortlessly takes command. One of the gentlemen guards asks him to stand aside and let the coffin pass. Richard answers,

Unmanner'd dog, stand thou when I command.
Advance thy halberd higher than my breast,
Or by Saint Paul I'll strike thee to my foot,
And spurn upon thee, beggar, for thy boldness.   (I.ii.39–42)

Anne says, "What do you tremble? Are you all afraid?" Somehow this little black creature has terrified the tall halberdiers. Anne orders Richard from her presence. He replies, with a swift mingling of courtliness, Christian ethics, and familiarity, "Sweet saint, for charity, be not so curst." "Curst," meaning "perversely cross," was commonly applied to annoyingly sour, unresponding females and, once more, takes us straight to *The Taming of the Shrew*. Anne answers with a stream of passionate hatred. Richard meets it with bland abstraction: according to Christ's teaching, if he, Richard, is evil, she should return good for evil. She indignantly replies that he knows nothing of the law of God—even beasts show pity. Richard counters again with impeccable logic: since he feels no pity, by her reasoning he cannot be a beast. Of course Richard knows how unreal his arguments seem even when they correctly reproduce New Testament doctrine. This is part of the game. He shows mastery as he beats her, easily, on her own, theological ground (as Angelo will later easily defeat the less intelligent Isabel in *Measure for Measure*). Richard's victory is merely formal but Anne is unable to fault it, logically. He is playing her as an angler plays a fish and at line 86 she is drawn into the word-game, telling Richard that if he hanged himself he could indeed be excused, because an appropriate punishment would have been exacted. Richard, we sense, is pleased by this strange shift of register from Anne and refers to the death of her husband: "Say that I slew him not." "Say" is interesting. It is like "Suppose" or, still more, like a lawyer's "Put the case that . . . ." Anne fires up and rejects the hypothesis directly. Richard then lies, equally directly: "I did not kill your husband" (I.ii.91). Within a few lines, however, he concedes that, all right, he did.

This is a puzzling response because it is the one moment of faltering in an otherwise uniformly powerful assault. I cannot decide whether Shakespeare is deliberately giving Richard a glimmer of humanizing weakness in order to suggest that at some level he is falling in love with Anne and cannot bear that she should think him wholly wicked, or whether it is simply a false note, a patch of *foolish* devilry quite out of place in the mouth of a figure of devilish cunning. Shakespeare's audience would remember from the end of *3 Henry VI* how all three brothers, Edward (the other Edward, who became King), Richard, and Clarence, stabbed the prince. Strictly, where three stab it is hard to be sure that all three are murderers. Which was (or were) the fatal wound(s)? This is enough to give a certain intellectual status to Richard's first response, "Say that I slew him not," though not to his subsequent flat denial of guilt. The last to strike in *3 Henry VI* was Clarence; Richard struck second. The presumption so far is that Clarence finished him off and is therefore the murderer. But when cool-headed Richard strikes, he says, "to end thy agony" (V.v.38); the third blow, delivered by Clarence, may have fallen on one already dead. Shakespeare has expertly contrived a situation that is technically ambiguous but morally unambiguous. Of the wickedness of Richard there is no doubt.

Anne then speaks of the virtue of the murdered King Henry, and Richard, reverting to the game of formal debate, answers that if Henry was bound for heaven then surely the person who helped him on his way to so good a place deserves thanks. Feste, the fool in *Twelfth Night,* "proves" his mistress a fool for first wearing black and then affirming that her brother is happy in heaven (I.v.66–72). The logic is fool's logic but it is good logic. There really is a profound inconsistency in the behaviour of the devout in the face of death. It is as if both Richard and Feste are saying from outside, "You Christians can't mean what you say. See what happens when I take you seriously!" Anne answers that if Henry belongs in heaven, no place is so fitting for Richard as hell. It is here that Richard makes his move. There is *one* other place that is right for him, he muses—Lady Anne's bedchamber. It may be thought that this is bad writing, that Richard ought to have softened up his victim with honeyed words before making any direct sexual suggestion. I have no doubt that the sequence is right as it stands. Richard knows what he is doing. He suddenly hits a woman in shock with sex. It is a kind of mental rape, and it is psychologically credible that it could be done. Anne's reply is dazed and ineffective. Richard then employs his casuistry in a more exalted manner, offering a lover's argument: the real cause of everything was Anne's own beauty (I.ii.121). Anne, having been bewildered by the openly sexual suggestion, now knows where she is again and recovers her spirit, indignantly spurning the courtship offered. At line 144 she spits at him and wishes him dead. Now Richard makes use again of his ploy of "taking the Christian literally" and, choosing his moment with care, passes his sword to Anne and bares his breast. It is a gamble but a safe gamble. He is thinking, "She will not be able to do this, and, after that, she is mine," and he is right. The 1623 Folio text gives a stage direction at this point: "She offers at [it] with his sword." The Folio and the earlier quarto texts all say that five lines later (I.ii.182) she lets the sword drop. Clearly Anne makes a real effort to kill Richard and finds, with a strange shock, that she cannot. Richard is on his knees. This is the posture of the suppliant Petrarchan lover, but never was wooing further removed from such courtly devotion than is Richard's. As the sword falls from her hand he rises and exults in his power, urging her again and again to do the thing she cannot do. Anne is broken, and at the same time her prostrate emotions are mysteriously engaged. Richard is left alone on the stage. He turns to the audience, with a question: "Was ever woman in this humor woo'd? / Was ever woman in this humor won?" (I.ii.227–28). It is, as Latin grammarians used to say, "a question inviting the answer, 'No.' " And Richard's smile is saying, "Of course it seems impossible. But, look, I have done it." Richard's position is secure, but the same security does not extend to the dramatist. Addressing Shakespeare we may continue to insist that the sequence is utterly implausible, absurd. Indeed a common modern response is to see the episode as wholly removed from realism, as an enjoyable, palpably theatrical romp.

There is, however, another way to take the scene. What if Shakespeare chose to dramatize, in all its weirdness, an extremely improbable but just possible sequence of events? Aristotle in his *Poetics* famously observed that plausible impossibilities (supernatural events, say, or "double time-schemes") were allowable in drama—the audience being perfectly happy—but implausible possibilities were not to be countenanced (1460a26–27, 1461b11–12). Shakespeare, whether or not he knew Aristotle's dictum, here flouts it, at least initially, in a spectacular manner. To see the sequence as a theatrical romp is to drain it of its extraordinary power. Well acted it actually convinces, against the grain of expectation. Of course, the scene must be called unnatural, as long as "natural" means "what most people do, most of the time." The whole point of the episode is that it is a marvel. When Aristotle spoke of implausible possibilities, he is likely to have had in mind grotesquely convenient coincidences. But the wooing of Anne is not like that. The audience in the theatre is not entertained by a diverting formal sequence, a "ballet of bloodless categories," to borrow F. H. Brad-ley's phrase. Rather it is gripped by a case of human interaction that is at first implausible but at last (just) credible. Of course if we think in very general terms and simply ask, "Would a woman say yes to a man she hates?" we must answer, "Of course not." But if we ask, "Would just such a woman, so circumstanced, say yes to just such a man?" we may find ourselves answering, "Well, yes, perhaps she would." It is *unexpectedly believable.*

In Ian McEwan's novel *Atonement* the love between Cecilia and Robbie is precipitated by an obscenity.[23] It is grosser than Richard's sudden refer-ence to the bedchamber, but Richard's words are in context more shock-ing. Both are psychologically grounded. More difficult is the contention —a contention I am backing—that Anne is compliant not so much in spite of her bereavement as because of it. Although in the scene Shakespeare gives us she is following the bier of the King, not that of her dead husband, it is fair to see her as a woman in shock. It is clear from her words that the memory of her husband's death is intricately entwined with her grief for the dead king. The actor David Niven said that in his desperate grief at the death of his beloved wife, he suddenly became sexually voracious. It will be said, "But men are different." I am not sure. Anne is reeling, and Richard is overwhelmingly dominant. At the most basic level—biologically—she is in need of a male protector. Looking back later she sees what happened as something inherent in her own sexuality, as coarsely irrational: "My woman's heart / Grossly grew captive to his honey words" (IV.i.78–79). The very occurrence of this retrospective line, so much later in the play, is a sign that the dramatist is fretting, still thinking about how such a thing might have happened. Had the episode been a wantonly unrealistic formal ballet such afterthoughts would not persist.

I am suggesting that there is psychological subtlety in this early work and that this makes the play a good play. It does not follow that the obviously formal passages are to be disparaged. The lamentation of the queens in Act IV, Scene iv, is unanswerably superb. But in Richard the vigour of the late medieval "Vice" gives place to the mystery of the wicked individual, lost to pity, goodness, and humanity. This is *character*.

Near the end, when Richard having waded through blood is losing, he is given a soliloquy. Where before, in the manner of the old morality, he used his soliloquies to talk to us, the audience, now he is talking to himself. We become eavesdroppers on a new species of privacy. It is the night before the battle. Richard, who cannot sleep, is visited by a succession of ghosts, the people he has wronged and violated in the course of his dreadful life. This may be thought to be so much late medieval flummery, but I am told that when Dame Helen Gardner, famous for her academic ferocity, lay dying, she too was visited by the figures of those whose theses she had failed, whose careers she had marred; they stood round her bed. Richard tries to rally: "What do I fear? Myself? There's none else by. / Richard loves Richard, that is I and I" (V.iii.182–83).[24] This is the same strong, clever, twisted little man we saw in dialogue with Lady Anne. Richard the rationalist is quick with his scepticism: ghosts are not real, there is nothing here to be afraid of, I am by myself . . . . The idiom "by myself" is instructive, although Richard does not employ it in his speech. The common locution for solitude implicitly divides the isolated party in two. With no one else to look at one looks within, and instantly a splitting of looker from looked-at follows. Richard's thought is rapid. The self is no sooner objectified than it is eagerly dismissed as un-frightening (we are not convinced and neither is Richard). He struggles to close the gap, first with self-love, then with mere identity. As James Lull says, the dialogue with Anne comes back to haunt him here.[25] Harold Bloom thinks the speech inept.[26] But its strange *staccato* rhythm springs from playing off Richard's earlier logic-chopping against a new kind of terror. The interweaving of stylistic registers is fine.

Richard, alone with himself, is closeted with one who is not lovable. That is why the attempt at self-love fails. In the opening speech of the play Richard, exulting in his own unlovable ugliness, implicitly dismissed the rest of humankind as narcissists, lovers of themselves. When he said this he was referring to his own unfitness for sexual dalliance—and Shakespeare moved swiftly to show us how wrong Richard was on this single point. But at a deeper level he was right. Ordinary people can—must—love themselves. Richard cannot. The later quartos change "I and I" to "I am I," and the editors of the Folio accept this, as have most editions since. Edmond Malone in the eighteenth century said he was not sure that the reading in the First Quarto was wrong. If we accept "I am I" we must say that Richard momentarily closes the gap by an assertion of identity. If we stay with "I and I" we have bleak division returning more swiftly to defeat the warmth of self-love—a grim juxtaposition of unlovely selves. It is an old principle of textual criticism that, other things being equal, the more difficult reading is to be preferred. The usual tendency of textual corruption is to replace unexpected expressions with more ordinary phrases. One can easily see both how Shakespeare might have written "I and I" and how inevitably this would fall prey to the copyist later. Somewhere in the background is the line from the Roman comic dramatist Terence, *Proximus sum egomet mihi,* "I am the closest person to myself" (*Andria,* IV.i.12). Shakespeare would have known the line, if not from his Stratford schooldays, then from its appearance, slightly misquoted, in Marlowe's *Jew of Malta* (I.i.188). There the Jew Barabas, an initially genial, grotesque villain like Richard, cites the line early in the story, when his star is still in the ascendant. The Terentian tag there expresses cat-like self-satisfaction. In giving the line to Barabas Marlowe made it into a Machiavellian theorem. It is after all in *The Jew of Malta* that Machiavelli himself is brought on stage, as Prologue to what comes later. Stemming from this moment, in the centuries that followed, is a line of hard Machiavellian jokes: "If you want a friend, get a dog," "Sure, I cried all the way to the bank," "What's the use of happiness? You can't buy money with it." The younger Richard, "Dicky your boy" in Margaret's rasping phrase, overrode the laws of decency in a manner that at once stamps him as Machiavellian, when he persuaded York to renege on his oath to let Henry live (*3 Henry VI,* I.ii.22–34).[27] If Shakespeare is re-applying the Marlovian thought in a context not of rising fortune but of failure and isolation, this would accord with his similar re-application of the confident humorous rationalism he had directed at Lady Anne. There, in order to prove her weakness and his strength, he offered to kill himself with the hand that had murdered her husband, so now he finds himself alone with Richard the killer:

Is there a murtherer here? No. Yes, I am.
Then fly. What, from myself? Great reason why—
Lest I revenge. What, myself upon myself?
Alack, I love myself. Wherefore? For any good
That I myself have done unto myself?
O no! Alas, I rather hate myself
For hateful deeds committed by myself.
I am a villain; yet I lie, I am not.
Fool, of thyself speak well; fool, do not flatter:
My conscience hath a thousand several tongues,
And every tongue brings in a several tale,
And every tale condemns me for a villain.
Perjury, perjury, in the highest degree;
Murther, stern murther, in the direst degree;
Throng to the bar, crying all, "Guilty! guilty!"
I shall despair; there is no creature loves me,
And if I die no soul will pity me.
And wherefore should they, since that I myself
Find in myself no pity to myself?   (V.iii.184–203)

At the beginning of the play Richard determined himself as a villain. Now, like Milton's Sin looking at her child Death, he shrinks in horror from the thing he has made. Even the egoistic self-love of a Barabas—"I am my own best friend"—is a kind of love, and Richard's loss of that self-love propels him simultaneously into a just appraisal of his real wickedness and a self-hatred that is not, as it might have been in another, the beginning of contrition but is instead stony, frozen despair. True, the speech seemed to open with a prayer, "Have mercy, Jesu!" (V.iii.178). But all that follows cancels any hope that might have begun to form. James Lull is right to detect something Faustian in this re-run of the Machiavellian theorem.[28] Curiously, "conscience," invoked in the speech, is closer to our "consciousness" than to "reforming moral insight" (the two meanings were not firmly differentiated in Shakespeare's time). What might have been a third, redeeming self is somehow objectified, made remote, like an accusing mob heard shouting in the distance. The abrupt movements of Richard's mind, oscillating between smart denial and horror, derive, with a coherence that is frightening, from the smiling sexual bully of Act I, Scene ii.

When at last Richard says, "no creature loves me," he is like a frightened child. Marlowe's homosexual king, Edward II, was a childish figure who desired only an obscure corner in which he could play with his beloved Gaveston (I.iv.72–73). When he was asked why he loved this man whom all the world hated, he replied, unanswerably, "Because he loves me more than all the world" (I.iv.77). Edward, at least for a time, can withdraw into an *égoïsme à deux* that is simultaneously sexual and somehow infantile. When Richard says that no one loves him, he now includes among his "nearest and dearest" his own watching self. The frightened child obtains no pity, from mother, lover, self—or even from us, as we watch. There is only fear.

The Early Comedies: *The Comedy of Errors, Two Gentlemen of Verona, The Taming of the Shrew*

So far we have watched Shakespeare as he virtually invented the history play. His glamorous rival, Christopher Marlowe, was obviously paying close attention. Marlowe's *Edward II*, though hard to date with precision, was composed after, and in response to, Shakespeare's first essays in this genre.[29] The more obvious genres, tragedy and comedy, were meanwhile clamouring for Shakespeare's attention. So he wrote, perhaps immediately after *Richard III, The Comedy of Errors*. Those who think of Shakespeare as Ben Jonson would have us think, as an unlettered child of nature, may be surprised that one of the first things he wrote is the product of his reading in Latin. For his plot Shakespeare draws on a Roman comedy, the *Menaechmi* of Plautus. William Warner's English translation did not appear until 1595. It is just possible that Shakespeare read it in manuscript before publication, but in general scholars are agreed that the play is based on Plautus's Latin. T. W. Baldwin in *William Shakspere's Small Latine and Lesse Greeke* demonstrated that Shakespeare read far more Latin than is covered by persons who describe themselves as classicists in universities today; he can be tracked consulting Thomas Cooper's *Thesaurus* (a Latin dictionary) in preference to available English versions. What is striking is that this play, an immensely clever essay in a classical mode by a rising dramatist, makes no attempt to parade its learning. Thomas Kyd, like Shakespeare, never received a university education. Unlike Shakespeare, he strenuously compensated for the defect by interlarding the English dialogue of his *Spanish Tragedy* (1590) with scraps of Latin (and perhaps in a lost version with Greek also). Shakespeare writes like one who can afford not to show off. His academic exercise retains no smell of the schoolroom. It is pure fun.

For Shakespeare Plautus's play with its twists of plot and its mistakings was simply a marvellous contraption, the complexity of which he immediately doubled mathematically by inserting a second pair of twins, this time twin servants, from another Plautine play, the *Amphitryo* (in which the god Mercury turns himself into the double of the slave Sosia). Although the *Amphitryo* was perhaps Plautus's best-loved play, there was no English version available to Shakespeare. His first action then, to multiply two by two, is an utterly formalist move. It was once observed that on a planet where the number of sexes is two the inhabitants will speak of "the eternal triangle," but on a planet where, say, six sexes are needed for successful procreation, a much more complex geometry of adultery will emerge in the sensational literature of that world. The intricate action of the play, which needs to be performed, like a Goldoni farce, at breakneck speed, is like a glittering dance. The fun at this level is great and has more to do with music (*allegro vivace*) than with insight into human nature.

That said, Shakespeare does go on to add human depth to this immediate delight in kinetic patterning. In the *Menaechmi* a traveller, who has a twin brother he does not know, arrives in Epidamnus, a place of swindlers and courtesans (Plautus plays upon *damnum* in the sense of "loss" at line

267). Shakespeare changes Epidamnus to Ephesus. This lets in St. Paul's Epistle to the Ephesians with its doctrine of wifely subjection and its picture of a city seething not just with trickery but with witchcraft (5:22–33, cf. Acts 19:13). At the same time Shakespeare seems to scent, behind the coarse Roman comedy, a more mythically resonant Greek story. The *Menaechmi* is based on a lost comedy by the Greek dramatist Menander. The tale of Apollonius of Tyre (again, originally Greek) relayed by John Gower gets in, and the moving "children-lost-and-found" pattern from Greek romance grows bright again, under Shakespeare's hand. Thomas Underdowne's translation of the romance *Aethiopica* of Heliodorus had appeared in 1569. Where the newly arrived traveller in Plautus is simply amazed to find himself in a place where all his wishes are met, Shakespeare's Antipholus of Syracuse meets a lady who (believing him to be her husband) addresses him in the language of profound, deeply possessive married love (II.ii.113–46).

Suddenly the human tensions I excluded earlier are upon us, complicated and clamorous. In the popular television program *Wife Swap* real persons are moved around and manipulated as fictional persons are in comedy. The wife of an authoritarian Scottish Calvinist, say, is made to live for a couple of weeks with the feckless husband of an ageing hippie and the lady hippie meanwhile is sent to live with the Calvinist. Despite the titillating name of the program there is a rule: no sex. This "law of the game" is very like a hidden literary law of comedy: nothing irreversibly dreadful must be allowed to occur. The main pleasure of the program lies in the often hilarious incongruity of the temporary matches set up, but what is more interesting is the sexual subtext. Here, in spite of the rule, we become uneasily aware on occasion that there might have been—could now *be*—love between these temporary mates, or we catch a whiff of wistfulness at the supposedly joyful point of going home. This scary discomfort energizes comedy. The greatest of all operatic comedies, Mozart's *Così fan tutte,* is built on the troubling truth that affections—even the affections of the nicest girls—are transferable. The director who makes Antipholus pause before his baffled reply to Adriana's loving speech is not perverse. It means, "How can a woman like this be talking like this, to me?"

As always in Shakespearean comedy there are moments of disquiet, places where we feel, "This is getting out of hand." Yet all, even the violent, knock-about farce, is held in a harmonious synthesis. The play is a *concordia discors,* not a *discordia concors.* "Knock-about" applies literally here. The beating of a servant with a stick would be, were it to occur in our society, an extraordinary act of violation. Imagine boxing the ears of a slow waiter in your favourite restaurant. Yet two hundred years ago you or your uncle would readily have done this. It is said that all the taboos have gone, but the beating of a servant is a very strong taboo indeed and may still be growing. The really odd thing is the way modern audiences adapt to the practice when they are watching *The Comedy of Errors.* This is, finally, a happy play. Greek and Christian, Catholic abbesses, a grieving father and errant children co-exist in an ultimate felicity. Most delicious of all is the pairing at the end of the Abbess with old Egeon, the merchant who had lost his sons. How can an abbess be sexually matched? There are people in the late comedies who are carefully denied mates by the dramatist, such as Antonio in *The Merchant of Venice.* Surely, if Antonio is not the marrying kind, the same logic must apply with greater force to an abbess —unless Shakespeare is satirizing Catholicism? It might be thought that in an age of intense conflict between Catholics and Protestants a sense of violation would be unavoidable here. Martin Luther married a nun and that was, precisely, scandalous. But none of the above applies. The Abbess was married to Egeon long before. She entered the convent because she thought her husband was dead. She can therefore, with happy propriety, embrace him when he reappears. The quiet joining of the Abbess and the old man at the end is the second-most moving thing in the play. This world of the play, so different from the fiercely divided land in which Shakespeare actually lived, the England of Campion and the torturer Richard Topcliffe, is an ideological Illyria. It may be said, however, that, simply because it is a comedy, the play makes marriage the highest good, and this is profoundly opposed to the Catholic exaltation of the monastic life. The Abbess herself describes what has happened as a birth. Without anxiety, she uses the religious word "nativity" (V.i.407). The nuance of incongruity in the word is enough to make the audience smile, but this is not satire. Shakespeare is not making fun of the Abbess. The overwhelming effect is one of joy.

I have called this moment the second-most moving thing in the play. The most moving thing comes later still, in the last seconds of the drama.

The two identical servant-brothers, Dromio and Dromio, are left staring at each other in affectionate wonder:

E. DROMIO Methinks you are my glass, and not my brother:
  I see by you I am a sweet-fac'd youth.
  Will you walk in to see their gossiping?
S. DROMIO Not I, sir, you are my elder.
E. DROMIO That's a question; how shall we try it?
S. DROMIO We'll draw cuts for the senior, till then, lead thou first.
E. DROMIO Nay then thus:
  We came into the world like brother and brother;
  And now let's go hand in hand, not one before another.
Exeunt
                                                              (V.i.418–26)

If *Wife Swap* can be allowed to illustrate the transposition of spouses, popular television programs on separated siblings who find one another after many years testify to a similar strength of feeling in the field of the two Dromios. It is all the stronger when, as here, it is understated. A nice, almost legal question of precedence is reviewed with mock gravity, and then they run off together. The best line of all is "I see by you I am a sweet-fac'd youth." In any other context "I am a sweet-fac'd youth" would be odious self-admiration. Here it is suddenly and mysteriously cleansed. To say it of one's brother is all right. The description can pass as both affectionate and objectively true. Dromio of Ephesus is speaking of his brother and of himself *at the same time*. Dromio calls his brother his glass, but we all know how subtly we learn to *use* mirrors—to select in advance the aspect which, reflected, will please most. The image that catches one unawares, the figure inadvertently glimpsed in a shop-window as one crosses the road, is entirely different. It is as if, wonderfully, that second, unmanaged image were to be entirely pleasing. Dromio loves his brother and, because they are exactly alike, must therefore love himself. Because this self-love flows from the prior love of the brother, it is nothing like the self-love of Barabas in *The Jew of Malta*. Richard III was left alone with a hateful self, and his ending was despair. Dromio finds Dromio and all is joy. The passage is a version of Ovid's Narcissus, who, it will be remembered, saw and loved his own face when he saw it reflected in a pool. Yet here there is no narcissism, no aesthetic pride. After all the shouting and beating we have another Shakespearean "island," a pause. When Dromio, the stripes fast healing on his back, says "I am a sweet-fac'd youth," it is simply true.

The Comedy of Errors is the play to which Shakespeare returned at the end of his working life. The four late "Romances," Pericles, Cymbeline, The Winter's Tale and The Tempest, with their suddenly intensified mythic resonance, all derive from this early comedy. They are all about children lost and found, and they are all sea-plays. In The Comedy of Errors we have, twice, the image of the sea as a place where identity is lost. Near the beginning Antipholus of Syracuse, newly arrived in Ephesus, says lightly as he takes his leave of the merchant, "I will go lose myself, / And wander up and down to view the city" (I.ii.30–31). He is exactly like a modern tourist. The reader who thinks this anachronistic in any work before the eighteenth century should look at Euripides' Ion, 219–33. Euripidean "happy-ending tragedies," of which the Ion is one, are the root from which both Greek romance (Heliodorus) and Menandrian new comedy sprang. Menander begat Plautus and Plautus begat The Comedy of Errors. The atmosphere at this point in Shakespeare's play is sociable and easy, but we are made aware of some great sadness in the background. As soon as Antipholus is alone the thought of losing himself grows much stronger, and this is where we meet the water imagery:

He that commends me to mine own content,
Commends me to the thing I cannot get:
I to the world am like a drop of water,
That in the ocean seeks another drop,
Who, falling there to find his fellow forth
(Unseen, inquisitive), confounds himself.
So I, to find a mother and a brother,
In quest of them (unhappy), ah, lose myself.   (I.ii.32–40)

The hypermetrical "ah" in the last line marks the sudden violence of the emotion. The play itself depends for its comic effect on crystal-clear identification (for the audience) of, as it might be, Dromio 1 as distinct from Dromio 2. Indeed, we, in the audience, are never lost. But behind the comic action we hear the sea-music of dissolved identity. A drop of water is an individuated thing, but perilously so, held together as it is by so frail a thing as surface-tension. As soon as it falls into the ocean, reunion with the lost sibling-drop is impossible, because all is now union, *simpliciter.* The image recurs at Act II, Scene ii, line 120, when Adriana cannot understand why her husband, Antipholus, does not know her (she has the wrong Antipholus, of course):

> O, how comes it,
> That thou art then estranged from thyself?
> Thyself I call it, being strange to me,
> That, undividable incorporate,
> Am better than thy dear self's better part.
> Ah, do not tear thyself away from me;
> For know, my love, as easy mayst thou fall
> A drop of water in the breaking gulf,
> And take unmingled thence that drop again,
> Without addition or diminishing,
> As take from me thyself and not me too. (II.ii.119–29)

Antipholus of Syracuse in wonder hears his own image of the water-drop lost in ocean played back to him (by one who loves the "second self" *he* has lost). Adriana with complete sincerity affirms the essential identity of man and wife—"one flesh"—and when he looks "strange" (that is our "odd," "cold," and "like a stranger" all rolled into one), his behaviour simply makes no sense to her. They have become one, she says, just as two drops, once they have fallen into the sea of marital union, become one. The sea that in its formlessness frustrated Antipholus's quest for an identifiable other self, his twin bother, is evoked by Adriana as a protective unifier. In the background, meanwhile, there may lie the inglorious thought that the drop, her husband, may at any moment trickle away down some Ephesian back alley to visit a prostitute. For Shakespeare the sea is initially an agent of separation, then an emblem of bewilderment and lost identity, and last, most strangely, a source of healing. It was by water that Antipholus was brought from Sicily to see his own face in his brother's. When Narcissus in Ovid tried in vain to kiss his image in the pool, his tears broke the surface and he lost himself (*Metamorphoses*, iii.475–76). We are brought back to the final lines of the play. When that sweet-faced youth Dromio saw his own face and loved it, there were no tears to shatter the image. Joined in brotherly love, joyously distinct, they ran from the stage, hand in hand.

No one knows if *Two Gentlemen of Verona* was written just before or just after *The Comedy of Errors*. It is Shakespeare's weakest play, and it would be nice for those who like to think of their favourite dramatist as steadily improving to think that *Two Gentlemen* is the earlier play. How bad is a bad Shakespeare play? The answer is, "Not very." Even when Shakespeare is palpably off form one can never relax; something remarkable will happen, somewhere. In *Two Gentlemen of Verona* there are two great things. The first is a dog, Crab. In the days when Caroline Spurgeon was poring over the patterns of imagery in Shakespeare it was discovered that the poet associated dogs with sweetmeats and slobbering. With dismay readers faced the fact that the national bard probably did not like dogs! But Crab is glorious. He apparently belongs to Proteus's clownish servant, Launce —but really he is his own dog. Launce comes from an emotional family; they cry easily. Not so Crab. Naturally Launce finds this hard to bear: "I think Crab my dog to be the sourest-natur'd dog that lives: my mother weeping, my father wailing, my sister crying, our maid howling, our cat wringing her hands, and all our house in a great perplexity, yet did not this cruel-hearted cur shed one tear" (II.iii.5–10). "Our cat wringing her hands" is especially fine. But Crab, we know, will not be shamed by any of this. Later Launce tells us how Crab once, showing unwonted energy, thrust himself under a table when a feast was in progress "into the company of three or four gentleman-dogs" (IV.iv.17). Some minutes pass and then Launce, who—a good touch, this—*recognizes* the smell, sniffs the air, and realizes that Crab has urinated under the table. The Duke and his grand friends demand that Crab be ejected at once. Launce, having ascertained that they plan to whip Crab, with Christian virtue takes the offence upon himself, gravely asserting that it was he, not his dog, who urinated under the table. We begin to see who is master here. "I have sat in the stocks," says Launce, "for puddings he hath stol'n" (IV.iv.30–31). Launce in the face of this magnificent indifference maintains his dignity: "When didst thou," he asks, confident of the justice of his cause, "see me heave up my leg and make water against a gentlewoman's farthingale?" (IV.iv.37–39). One senses, behind the strong claim, a possible concession: "Under the table? Well, yes, perhaps, occasionally—but against a lady's skirt, never!" This is very funny, it might be said, but it has nothing to do with the subject: the dramatist as thinker. But, as will appear in a moment, in this early play Shakespeare is thinking hard about the psychology of self-less love and how, in extreme instances, it can border on absurdity. The devotion of Launce to Crab is an accelerated parody of another act of devotion, only a little less ludicrous.

The second great thing is something loved by the author of this book but considered embarrassingly bad by many—perhaps most—Shakespeareans. It is the rapid sequence at the end of the play, in which Proteus attempts to rape his best friend's lady and is forgiven by that friend (Valentine), after which Valentine offers his lady-love to the would-be rapist, in order to show that there are no hard feelings. This is the climax of a plot that sets male friendship in conflict with heterosexual love, a plot described by Harold Bloom as a mere farrago of Monty Python absurdity.[30]

The Elizabethan audience would probably have been quicker than its modern counterpart to pick up the signals given by the names Valentine and Proteus. Valentine, because of St. Valentine's Day, suggests a lover. Proteus evokes "Protean," "mutable" (for the myth, see Ovid, *Metamorphoses*, ii.9, viii.731, xiii.918). They are splendid young men, well-mannered, well-born, well-dressed, but while Valentine is good, Proteus is bad. The play opens with Valentine's farewell to his friend. Valentine is setting out to see the world. Proteus, meanwhile, is tied to Verona by his love for one Julia. We see Proteus prosecute his suit and be accepted. His father, however, orders him to join his friend Valentine at the Milanese court. Proteus swears solemnly that he will be true to Julia, gives her his hand, and receives from her a ring (II.ii.5–8). Valentine meanwhile has reached Milan and fallen in love with the Duke's daughter, Silvia. The Duke is eager to marry Silvia off to one Thurio, an absurd figure. So Valentine and Silvia plan to elope, using a rope ladder. Proteus arrives and immediately breaks his oath to Julia by falling in love with Silvia. This makes him the secret rival of his best friend. So, without any disquiet, he betrays Valentine. He tells the Duke about the planned elopement, and as a result Valentine is banished from Milan. The field is left clear for Proteus. The banished Valentine meets with a band of cheerful outlaws, on the pattern of Robin Hood's Merry Men. Instead of mugging him they make him their leader.

Julia meanwhile has dressed herself in male attire and set out in search of her beloved Proteus. Reaching Milan, she finds him but, like Rosalind in *As You Like It,* remains in disguise. Proteus, failing to see through the disguise, takes her on as his page. Silvia, perhaps predictably, is unimpressed by Proteus and, fearing the marriage to Thurio, takes off into the wilderness to find Valentine. She too is on the point of being captured by the merry men when Proteus turns up, accompanied by his "page," and rescues her. Having done so he points out exactly how grateful she should be (V.iv.19–25). Silvia is simply appalled, so Proteus decides to rape her (V.iv.59). Now Valentine steps forward from the shadows and Silvia is saved for the second time. This time it is a real rescue. This is where the crazy stuff begins. Valentine has stumbled upon his friend's treachery:

> now I dare not say
> I have one friend alive; thou wouldst disprove me.
> Who should be trusted, when one's right hand
> Is perjured to the bosom? Proteus,
> I am sorry I must never trust thee more,
> But count the world a stranger for thy sake.
> The private wound is deepest.   (V.iv.65–71)

Proteus answers simply,

> My shame and guilt confounds me.
> Forgive me, Valentine; if hearty sorrow
> Be a sufficient ransom for offense,
> I tender't here: I do as truly suffer
> As e'er I did commit.   (V.iv.73–77)

Valentine instantly gives the forgiveness requested and joyfully adds, "And that my love may appear plain and free, / All that was mine in Silvia I give thee" (V.iv.82–83). This is either glib incompetence on the dramatist's part or something quite remarkable. Proteus, notice, repents only after he is caught. Valentine's "Thou wouldst disprove me" is as good as a stage direction. Proteus, it seems, was about to say something but is prevented by the fact that his beloved interlocutor presses on with his speech.[31] What was he going to say? Valentine assumed that he was about to exculpate himself, but he could be wrong. When Proteus is free to speak he offers no excuses. Valentine has just said he has no friend in the world. Perhaps Proteus, the squalid liar and traitor, wants to say with perfect truth, "I love you still." The sequence is very fast but responsive at all points to moral nuance and to character. Proteus's repentance is not a simple reversal of the plot-line, imposed *ab extra* in compliance with the need for a happy ending.

We need to go back as far as Silvia's rejection of Proteus, after the first rescue. There she tells him to respect the true love of Julia and ends with the words, "Thou counterfeit to thy true friend!" (V.iv.53). It looks as if by "friend" she means Julia. I think but cannot prove that Proteus hears the word as a reference to Valentine. He urges sophistically that love erases all other obligations, including loyalty to friends. But the dart of guilt has lodged in his flesh. He is no coolly competent erotic Machiavel, like Richard III. Silvia, after all, has known his nature all along. Proteus had not sufficient skill to prevent this. For this the politic Italian would surely have awarded a very low mark. He is a vain young man, used to getting what he wants. He really loved Julia, in his shallow way, really fell for Silvia, and, most important of all, really loved his friend Valentine from first to last, even, conceivably, at the moment when he betrayed him to the Duke. That this is not careless writing in inert conformity to an unmotivated twist in the plot is proved by the anticipations and echoes built into the larger fabric of the play.

When Proteus was told to leave town he compared his love with "the uncertain glory of an April day" (I.iii.85). He meant as he said it that things can go wrong for the lover. But the dramatist meanwhile plants an image of a love that is both beautiful and unreliable (the play may be set in Italy, but this is an English April). When the word "friend" turns in Proteus's mind to "Valentine" something intolerable (to his love for Valentine, to his self-esteem) is gathering at the back of his mind. This he blots out with the sudden move to force Silvia sexually. When Valentine himself appears within his field of vision, it is all over and he truly repents.

This account is rosy—some will say, too rosy, and in a way I agree. Proteus's repentance is completely sincere and at the same time opportunistic, egoistically hungry for results. Proteus repentant is still Proteus. How can we account for Valentine's immediate acceptance of the apology? It is explained by his love for Proteus. This must be taken seriously. I suspect that today gay men can understand the scene more readily than others, not because Valentine and Proteus are involved sexually, but simply because gay men are obviously ready to believe that love between men can be real. There was that in Valentine that desired reconciliation, always. Proteus's speech of contrition releases a Christian generosity natural, in any case, to the good Valentine. On the page, for the reader in the study, the coldly printed lines can seem absurd. In the theatre the effect is electrifying. At David Thacker's brittle, 1930s-style production at Stratford in 1994 I heard a woman say, in the interval, that the play was "full of Shakespearean clichés," and I was sadly inclined to agree. But any such complacent superiority was blown away by the end of the performance. We emerged from the theatre moved, confused, and joyful.

Of course Valentine's offer of Silvia to Proteus is crazy. In saying this we are not telling Shakespeare anything he does not already know. That is why he makes poor Julia swoon away on the spot. Within the story she swoons, indeed, because she sees Proteus receding from her, but in the accelerated comic tempo of the scene the swoon also expresses *audience* excitement and bewilderment so precisely that we almost laugh, even as we wonder whether Valentine has gone completely mad. M. C. Bradbrook thought that Silvia, the lady who, unconsulted, has been so generously re-assigned, should have no reaction at all.[32] I think she should stand stock still with her mouth open, aghast. In the hands of any other dramatist such extravagant action would tip over into satire at the expense of the agents. It is characteristic of Shakespeare that he should refuse to be satirical, should choose to maintain sympathy. We shall see him do this again with the cad Bertram at the end of *All's Well That Ends Well,* with Bassanio (almost a vulgar fortune-hunter) in *The Merchant of Venice,* and with Claudio in *Much Ado about Nothing,* and we shall see Angelo actually forgiven at the end of *Measure for Measure.* Harold Brooks in a letter to Clifford Leech said that the antitheses of *Two Gentlemen of Verona* were "lightning conductors," drawing off excess laughter in the audience, allowing some sympathy to persist.[33] The scattering of laughter in the auditorium when Valentine makes his offer is exactly like that.

What finally sticks in the throat is not so much the unbalanced affection of Valentine for his friend as Shakespeare's affection for both Valentine and Proteus. Shakespeare feels the love that Valentine feels and, at the same time, knows that it is half-mad. These appalling, good-looking young men, Proteus, Claudio, Bassanio, Bertram (and, some might want to add, Prince Hal and the cold young gentleman addressed in the Sonnets), are almost embarrassingly indulged by the dramatist. They all generate light without warmth and Shakespeare—clear-eyed Shakespeare—seems spell-bound by the light.

There is absolutely no blurring of the nastiness of Proteus. The curious thing is that although his unpleasant nature is clearly shown, it is *faintly* shown. For Dante treachery was the worst sin of all. It would have been easy, given Proteus's behaviour, to present him as a half-devil. This the poetry absolutely refuses to do. Again, in saying this I am saying nothing that the dramatist does not already know. As Launce says, "I am but a fool, look you, and yet I have the wit to think my master is a kind of knave" (III.i.263—64). That is, "I am supposed to be the mutt around here, but even I can see that this man is a complete swine." Launce is right, but without efficacy. Later in the play Shakespeare inserts some comic dialogue. One of the outlaws explains that he had to take refuge in the forest "for a gentleman, / Who, in my mood, I stabb'd unto the heart." His companion answers, "And I for such like petty crimes as these" (IV.i.48—50). The humour turns on the minimizing of serious offences, which is what the play as a whole also does.

I have no doubt that the accelerated sequence of rescue from the outlaws, followed by the attempted rape, followed by the second rescue, repentance, forgiveness, and Valentine's amazing offer, is brilliant dramatically. They work in the theatre far better than they do when read. In saying this I do not concede that the reader picks up absurdities that the dazed spectator is prevented from noticing. On the contrary, because we are built, biologically, to respond swiftly to minimal hints from another human being within the field of vision, the spectator gets everything, the absurdity, the touching-ness, the unbroken psychological truth. Far more difficult are the words of Proteus at the end, after Julia has revealed her identity: "What is in Silvia's face, but I may spy / More fresh in Julia's with a constant eye?" And "Bear witness, heaven, I have my wish for ever" (V.iv.114–15, 119). This is supposed to be the happy part, where everything comes right. But we simply cannot, now, trust him. Does this mean that Shakespeare, in choosing to make one of the heroes of his comedy a cad, has fatally disabled his happy ending? Certainly it laces the final happiness with disquiet. But nothing here is inadvertent. Shakespeare's comedies are like fairy tales, but fairy tales notoriously end with the words, "And they lived happily ever after." Shakespeare avoids endorsing the "happily ever after" part. *Two Gentlemen of Verona* ends resoundingly with the line, "One feast, one house, one mutual happiness," but not with "One feast, one house, and everlasting joy." In *As You Like It* Touchstone and Audrey figure in the joyful pairing-off at the end and are actually promised a life of sour quarrelling (V.iv.191). If we listen we know that even when Proteus is joined to the right lady he remains the same dubious character. There is something less than paradisal about his remarking that Julia has as much to offer him in terms of feminine beauty as Silvia; there is something short of true love, something of unsubdued ego, in the half-sinister word "spy" and in his complacent discovery of "something more fresh," after which "constant" is inescapably ironized, not by the speaker but by the dramatist. His last words juxtapose piety with a continuing egoism: "Bear witness, heaven, I have my wish for ever" (V.iv.119). It may be said that "for ever" contradicts everything I have just said about Shakespeare's avoidance of the "happily ever after" formula. But this is Proteus speaking and we simply do not believe him.

The lady at Stratford who complained that the play was all clichés was half-right. The play is full of patterns that we can find in other comedies, where they are more powerful. When, however, these things happen in *Two Gentlemen of Verona* they are not the tired repetition of worn-out ideas. They are not decaying but growing, the pale shoots of what will become vivid later. Julia setting off in disguise is Shakespeare's first essay in the dramatic presentation of woman as the clever, loving suitor, actively taking the inadequate man (Rosalind in *As You Like It,* Helena in *All's Well That Ends Well*). Her disguising as male page to the man she loves will turn into Viola/Cesario in *Twelfth Night.* The brief warning satire on the dangers of heterosexual love addressed by Valentine to Proteus at Act

I, Scene i, lines 39–52, will reappear, greatly intensified, on the lips of Mercutio, Romeo's friend, in *Romeo and Juliet*. The tense play of same-sex bonds against the overmastering claim of heterosexual love is to become a major preoccupation of Shakespearean drama. This theme reaches its greatest intensity in *The Merchant of Venice* and *Much Ado about Nothing*, and as I have suggested, it spills over into tragedy in *Romeo and Juliet*.

There is one more comedy written before Marlowe fell bleeding in the inn at Deptford, and it is a bombshell. *The Taming of the Shrew*, a dazzling, funny, enjoyable play about a man breaking the spirit of a woman. Ouch. Shakespeare's word, to be sure, is "taming," but what is our other word for taming, say, a horse? It is "breaking." Within the play Shakespeare is thinking all the time not of horse-breaking but of falconry, the training of a hawk. The classic modern text on this subject is T. H. White's *The Goshawk* (1951). White explains the training of a hawk as a protracted battle of wills; the hawk is systematically deprived of sleep (but the falconer must also stay awake) until the bird's resistance cracks.[34] Sleep deprivation figures prominently in the breaking of Katherina (also called Kate) in this play.

This is obviously shocking to us, but was it shocking then? Certainly not in anything like the same degree. This was a society that thought real dwarves and idiots hilarious, where we confine our laughter to the more mildly impaired (but still impaired). Plays like *Tom Tyler and His Wife* (about 1551) are far more violent than Shakespeare's play and clearly expect nothing but happy laughter from the audience. Of course, when writers are good they know that laughter is commonly involved with fear as well as relief (Aristotle's theory of *catharsis*, or emotion purged, works better perhaps for comedy than it does for tragedy). Even today jokes are often about the most serious things—death, for example. I once thought some subjects were too horrible ever to be treated comically—Nazism in Hitler's Germany, for instance—until I saw Mel Brooks's *The Producers*. Ben Jonson obviously knew when he wrote *Volpone* that the protagonist's "private zoo" of maimed and distorted persons, though the audience could be relied upon to laugh, was a dreadful thing. Shakespeare, who could sympathize with the socially disabled Malvolio in *Twelfth Night* against the bias of immediate audience-response, could certainly feel the inner horror of what is being done to Katherina in this play. If we are not nervous about what we are watching, our very laughter will be less intense. Meanwhile, however, the cultural difference between the early modern period and our own is equally real. The shock element that Shakespeare could only have seen as obscurely potential in the material has been actualized by developing ideology. This means that *The Taming of the Shrew* is now, what it was not in the 1590s, a black comedy. Yet even today it is somehow not as black as it should be. The audience comes out smiling.

This may be because the audience becomes aware, as does Kate herself, that Petruchio, the tamer, is good news, not bad, for Kate. She is leaving the suffocating world so deviously exploited by her intriguing sister and the absolute rule of a feeble father for a man who can blow her away, can make her laugh, and, most important, is very like her. Kate's father, for all his feebleness, has great power over the women in his house and uses it with repellent entrepreneurial skill. The seemingly submissive Bianca is attractive to suitors, Kate not. So the father raises the stakes by making marriage to Bianca hinge on Kate's getting married first. Life with Petruchio will never be like this. Petruchio is, first, an effortlessly dominant male like Richard III and, second, very funny. It is a winning combination. He is the hilarious opposite of the humble lover on his knees, deviously seeking a gratification conferred by the lady out of pure pity. It is not hard to find women in the present century who say that they respond more readily to the sweep-you-off-your-feet kind of man than to the wheedling lover of courtly tradition—that is, they find him sexier. Also, before Petruchio bursts into her world, Katherina is psychologically in a bad way. Her unremitting fury is a kind of illness. We hear much today of pathological depression and much less of pathological anger, yet such anger exists.

If one asks a reasonably literate person, "Who in the plays of Shakespeare binds a woman, strikes her, and makes her cry?" the chances are that you will get the answer, "Petruchio." The correct answer is "Katherina." She does all this to Bianca at Act II, Scene i, lines 1–24. It is often observed that Petruchio presents himself as a mirror to Katherina—retorts her own violence back on her. It is less often noticed that she is the more violent of the two. Petruchio never strikes Katherina. There is one moment when *she* hits *him* and he responds, "I swear I'll cuff you, if you strike again" (II.i.220). She does not put the matter to the test but instead tells him that he would be no gentleman if he did such a thing. There is a certain irony in this sudden recourse to social convention. Katherina, after all, has not been behaving as a lady should. Petruchio's words are shocking, but lurking within them is a strange assumption of eye-to-eye equality—"If you hit me, I'll hit you"—that can feel like fresh air to one who has left a stuffy room. Were the atmosphere less sexually charged I would call the tone of this "man to man." But he does not strike her, either here or later.

When I first read Germaine Greer's *The Female Eunuch* in the 1970s I remember expecting that the feminist author would roundly despise *The Taming of the Shrew* and Petruchio in particular. Instead I met this: "[Katherina] has the uncommon good fortune to find Petruchio, who is man enough to know what he wants and how to get it. He wants her spirit and her energy because he wants a wife worth keeping."[35]

There is a passing hint of something sinister in the concession that Petruchio wants to *take* Katherina's spirit and energy, but this thought is swallowed up at once in the writer's own warm responsiveness, itself very like Katherina's, to Petruchio. Germaine Greer in those days was herself a brilliant shrew, much given to verbal violence against others. In her discussion of *The Taming of the Shrew* she is obviously itching to box Bianca's ears exactly as Katherina does in the play. And she is really keen on Petruchio. He is a real man. He is exciting. Katherina's big speech in favour of wifely submission is not taken by Greer to be ironic. Of course she disagrees with the speech, seriously and rationally, but she calls it "the greatest defence of Christian monogamy ever written." "It rests," she explains, "upon the role of the husband as protector and friend, and it is valid because Kate has a man who is capable of being both, for Petruchio is both gentle and strong."[36]

I am suggesting that an element working in the play, operating on Katherina and Germaine Greer alike, is a sheerly sexual power fused with Petruchio's overmastering strength. It is only one element in a complex whole, but it is there. Strong sexual reference begins in the Induction, when the vagrant Sly is made to believe that he is a gentleman; he is offered pornography, "wanton pictures" (Ind.i.47), and

a couch,
Softer and sweeter than the lustful bed
On purpose trimm'd up for Semiramis.   (Ind.ii.37–39)

Semiramis, founder of Babylon, was the daughter of Dercetis (a sex goddess). She avoided matrimony but like a black widow had sexual relations with one after another of her courtiers, killing each afterwards.[37] Sly is offered a picture of Venus hiding in bushes that respond excitedly to her presence (they "wanton with her breath," Ind.ii.52) and another of Io "surprised" (that is, raped),[38] "as lively painted as the deed was done" (Ind.ii.54–55), and—a hint here perhaps of sadism—the scratched legs of Daphne as she fled her lustful pursuer (Ind.ii.58). When the page enters in drag as Sly's "wife" we have another early version of Viola/Cesario and Rosalind as Ganymede in *As You Like It*, both more fully developed than the present passage, but the sexuality is strongest in *The Taming of the Shrew*. The page, who has been instructed to give "tempting kisses," says how sad he is to be "abandon'd from your bed" (Ind.i.118, ii.115), and Sly, unlike Bottom the weaver in *A Midsummer Night's Dream*, who is hilariously indifferent to the blandishments of the Fairy Queen, responds with "undress you, and come now to bed" (Ind.ii.117). That is almost exactly what Petruchio says to Kate at the end of the play. When Petruchio promises "rough wooing" at Act II, Scene I, line 137, he means primarily that he is not going to put on smart clothes and behave in the approved manner, but there is an implicit sexual subtext. Entirely explicit is the startlingly indecent "tongue in your tail" (Petruchio to Katherina, II.i.217). First Katherina says that the wasp has his sting in his tongue, not his tail. "Whose tongue?" says Petruchio, meaning, "Are you still talking about the wasp or do you mean something else?" Katherina answers, "Yours, if you talk of tales" (so Petruchio was right, she was thinking of something—or someone—else). His delight at this generates the obscenity: "What, with my tongue in your tail?" which he brilliantly covers by suggesting, what in a way is true, that the thought came from her, while he as a modest gentleman is surprised: "Nay, come again, / Good Kate, I am a gentleman" (II.i.217–18). This interestingly is the moment at which Kate actually strikes Petruchio. It may be that she explodes because he has got inside her head.

The play is also a love story. The love *happens*, between strong Kate and stronger Petruchio. At the beginning Petruchio's motives are entirely financial (though it is made clear that he is not poor). He wants a decent settlement. This is mildly repellent in itself, but it is not obviously worse than the pretended love from equally mercenary suitors elsewhere in Shakespearean drama. Before the play is over Petruchio loves Kate.

In Act II, Scene i, there is a sudden change of register. After the knock-about wit-combats, all won by the man (which is not at all what happens in the later comedies), Petruchio looks directly at Katherina and says,

> Kate like the hazel-twig
> Is straight and slender, and as brown in hue
> As hazel-nuts, and sweeter than the kernels.
> O, let me see thee walk. (II.i.253–56)

To describe this I am obliged to use a word that is almost taboo in current critical discourse. It is "beautiful." Its special force lies in the way it combines sudden beauty with a complete rejection of Petrarchan lovers' idiom. He does not tell her that she has eyes like stars or teeth like pearls. She is straight, slender, and brown as a nut. In his Sonnets Shakespeare dealt with Petrarchan tradition by a simple technique of violent inversion: "My mistress' eyes are nothing like the sun" (Sonnet 130). Here he does something more difficult. He produces a new species of beauty and a new kind of poetry. Something similar happens at the end of Love's Labour's Lost with the songs of Winter and Spring. We become aware as we listen that Petruchio has begun to love Kate. So far, so sweet. But it is followed at line 272 by the superb, imperious, and, to us, finally unacceptable (?)

> Now, Kate, I am a husband for your turn,
> For by this light whereby I see thy beauty,
> Thy beauty that doth make me like thee well,
> Thou must be married to no man but me;
> *For I am he am born to tame you, Kate.*

In a manner of which Freud would have approved, Katherina's behaviour betrays the real movement of her heart before her words assent. Later in the same scene Petruchio says, without any verbal hint of prior agreement from Katherina, "And to conclude, we have 'greed so well together / That upon Sunday is the wedding-day" (II.i.297–98). He knows perfectly well that there is no such agreement; that makes the speech funny. At the same time his words are instinct with performative force (a "performative" expression is one that *does* what it says—"I name this ship the *Baby Spice,*" "I do" in the marriage service). We think of jokes as frivolous extravagance, moving naturally away from serious reality, but Petruchio's wild humour is making something happen. Kate fights back at once with the words, "I'll see thee hang'd on Sunday first." Petruchio then complacently explains to Gremio and Tranio how they have been making furious love in private but have a plot that Katherina should behave like a shrew in public. To this Katherina makes no reply. Petruchio's monstrous lie about the plot may actually shadow, in the contrast it draws between latent love and public aggression, an emotional truth. Her father then claps their hands together in his: " 'Tis a match" (II.i.319). We are once more in the alarming field of the quasi-performative. What we are watching cannot in fact be, what some scholars have suggested,[39] an actual contract (*sponsalia de futuro,* roughly equivalent to our "formal engagement") because Katherina does not speak. But she does join hands. Either she is completely dazed or she is ceasing to resist.

In Act III, Scene ii, straight after the slapstick wedding, Petruchio announces that he must leave at once because of business pressures. Immediately we sense the special tension of the "delayed consummation" motif that will later permeate *Othello.* The audience is appalled, and so, interestingly, is Katherina. Tranio and Gremio entreat him to stay, in vain. Then Katherina speaks from the heart, "Let me entreat you," and Petruchio answers enigmatically, "I am content" (III.ii.200–201). Katherina, having virtually declared her love, thinks he means to stay and is furious when he declares that he is going in any case. The old anger returns, but it is now differently fuelled. Petruchio's immediate response shows a sudden gentleness, quite unlike his earlier manner: "O Kate, content thee, prithee be not angry" (III.ii.215). The knot is cut when Petruchio explains that Katherina is to go with him. Although Katherina may not yet be clear that this is what she wants, it is what she needs. It is escape from the dark house and the detested family.

The story is punctuated by kisses, and each kiss is different from the last. The first is at Act II, Scene i, line 324, after the hand-clasping: "Then kiss me Kate, we will be married a' Sunday." There is no stage direction but a kiss surely follows. It could be delivered by Petruchio at lightning speed, before Kate could dodge. The next kiss appears in the narrative of the crazy church ceremony. Petruchio, we are told,

> took the bride about the neck,
> And kiss'd her lips with such a clamorous smack
> That at the parting all the church did echo. (III.ii.177–79)

This sounds like force majeure, as if Katherina is hardly given the chance to *meet* the embrace, but by this time we know that, contrary to the convention by which the eager bridegroom is on time and the bride late, Katherina was in church on time and it is Petruchio who had everyone worried. The next kiss comes in Act V. It precedes Katherina's long speech on wifely submission and tells us that her words, make of them what we will, come from a loving heart.

KATHERINA Husband, let's follow, to see the end of this ado.
PETRUCHIO First kiss me, Kate, and we will.
KATHERINA What, in the midst of the street?
PETRUCHIO What, art thou asham'd of me?
KATHERINA No, sir, God forbid, but asham'd to kiss.
PETRUCHIO Why then let's home again. (V.i.142–47)

This is no exchange between a bully and a broken spirit. These are like-minded happy people. Kate's vocative, "Husband," is easy, domestic. Petruchio's "First kiss me" is impulsive but not domineering, as is proved by the sequel. Kate, understandably, is embarrassed by kissing in public, the more so perhaps because the kiss if it happened would probably be rather more than a friendly peck on the cheek. When Petruchio asks if she is ashamed of him, the question is painfully pertinent. By all the conventions she has every reason to be ashamed of a husband who turned up for his wedding so badly dressed. It is plain, however, that she is far from being ashamed of him, is worried only by the thought of onlookers. This is touching in its ordinariness. This time Petruchio does not force the issue but says, "Let's go home." In reply Kate spontaneously—after all—kisses Petruchio. The suggestion that the best thing might be to go home alerts the audience to the necessary contrast between what can be done in public and what in private. This returns in a stronger form at the end. There Petruchio, almost embarrassed by Katherina's speech of submission, raises her from her posture of humility and says, "Why, there's a wench! Come on, and kiss me, Kate," and then, a couple of lines later, "Come, Kate, we'll to bed" (V.ii.180, 184). It is probably about seven o'clock in the evening.

Love is sweet but submission leaves a different taste.

PETRUCHIO Come on a' God's name, once more toward our father's.
    Good Lord, how bright and goodly shines the moon!
KATHERINA The moon! the sun—it is not moonlight now.
PETRUCHIO I say it is the moon that shines so bright.
KATHERINA I know it is the sun that shines so bright.
PETRUCHIO Now by my mother's son, and that's myself,
    It shall be moon, or star, or what I list,
    Or ere I journey to your father's house.—
    Go on, and fetch our horses back again.—
    Ever more cross'd and cross'd, nothing but cross'd!
HORTENSIO Say as he says, or we shall never go.
KATHERINA Forward, I pray, since we have come so far,
    And be it moon, or sun, or what you please;
    And if you please to call it a rush-candle,
    Henceforth I vow it shall be so for me.
PETRUCHIO I say it is the moon.
KATHERINA   I know it is the moon.
PETRUCHIO Nay then you lie; it is the blessed sun.
KATHERINA Then God be blest, it is the blessed sun,
    But sun it is not, when you say it is not;
    And the moon changes even as your mind.
    What you will have it nam'd, even that it is,
    And so it shall be so for Katherine.
HORTENSIO Petruchio, go thy ways, the field is won.   (IV.v.1–23)

In the *Satyricon* of Petronius, one Fortunata exercises absolute dominion over her multi-millionaire husband, Trimalchio, to such an extent that "if she tells him it's dark at mid-day he'll believe her."[40] Fortunata is an untamed, uncontested shrew (*est malae linguae,* "she has a wicked tongue"). Trimalchio's abject condition is summed up in the one word, *credet,* "He'll believe her." *The Taming of the Shrew* is not a simple reversal of the Petronian set-up. It is obvious that Katherina does not *believe* for a moment that the moon is shining. Her mind therefore is intact (*mens intacta,* like *virgo intacta,* "un-raped"). But, like the threatened Catholics of Shakespeare's boyhood, she is required to make a public profession that is contrary to her deepest convictions. The passage is almost saved by its crazy extremism. We are watching something closer to the humouring of a lunatic or grown-ups temporarily colluding to prevent a childish tantrum than to the crushing of Katherina. This is caught exactly when Hortensio says, in effect, "Oh, say what he wants or we'll never get there!" Of course Petruchio is not a child. He knows that what he is saying is absurd and Katherina knows that he knows. This *almost* (that word again!) turns the affair into a game. When Petruchio growls, "I say it is the moon," Katherina spontaneously goes further than he and solemnly avers, "I *know* it is the moon." She is having fun. Turning his non-committal "say" into "know" exposes the lunacy of all this moonshine with solar clarity. "Ever more cross'd and cross'd, nothing but cross'd" is the funniest line in a very funny play. Its note of adult exasperation at the petty obstacles interposed by the childish persons around him is *precisely* off-beam, given what we have all witnessed. Katherina's interpolated joke on Petruchio's mind being as changeable as the moon herself again shows a spirit far from abject.

So is all well? No. I said, "almost saved," "almost a game." Almost but not quite. The "game" is, first, part of the therapy for Katherina's pathological anger and, second and more sinisterly, a technique of practical subjection—not of taking the wife's mind away (it is not as bad as that) but of taking away her freedom of behaviour. I know that when I first read this scene in my teens I was profoundly shocked, but that was because I thought it obscene that a husband should require his wife to crush the evidence of her senses in deference to his will. I now think that no such crushing is in question but that nevertheless the degree of control that *is* being seriously imposed is sufficiently disquieting.

As the scene continues we have the hilarious sequence in which Kate is prompted by Petruchio to salute a dazed old gentleman as "young, budding virgin." Here she is so clearly playing along—she enters into the charade with creative zest—that we might begin to think that we can stop worrying about what Petruchio is doing to Katherina, to see this as the after-echo of some sex-game, between consenting parties; "It's a fantasy!" is what the parties to such practices always say when confronted by worried outsiders. But then we have the big speech, admired by Germaine Greer, Katherina to the Widow:

Thy husband is thy lord, thy life, thy keeper,
Thy head, thy sovereign; one that cares for thee,
And for thy maintenance; commits his body
To painful labor, both by sea and land;
To watch the night in storms, the day in cold,
Whilst thou li'st warm at home, secure and safe;
And craves no other tribute at thy hands
But love, fair looks, and true obedience—
Such duty as the subject owes the prince,
Even such a woman oweth to her husband;
And when she's froward, peevish, sullen, sour,
And not obedient to his honest will,
What is she but a foul contending rebel,
And graceless traitor to her loving lord?
I am asham'd that women are so simple
To offer war where they should kneel for peace,
Or seek for rule, supremacy, and sway,
When they are bound to serve, love, and obey.
Why are our bodies soft, and weak, and smooth,
Unapt to toil and trouble in the world,
But that our soft conditions, and our hearts,
Should well agree with our external parts?   (V.ii.146–68)

Today the actor is virtually compelled to deliver these lines ironically, if the audience is not to break out in its own open rebellion. Harold C. Goddard thought such irony no modern imposition but entirely true to Shakespeare's original meaning: Katherina, he felt, is clearly the person controlling Petruchio at the end, and it is part of the fun that she should keep up the public pretence that it is he who is in charge.⁴¹ I said earlier that even modern audiences come out smiling at the end of *The Taming of the Shrew*. It may be that this would not happen if the speech of submission were delivered unironically. But in fact it is entirely unironic. That said, I would add that I suspect that the speech must always have been edged with obscure discomfort for the listeners. But Katherina and Shakespeare mean every word. To turn Katherina into a sly manipulator of her husband, as Goddard did, is to turn Katherina into Bianca. There could be no greater insult.

Things are being said that we do not wish to hear. Most of us now believe that men and women are equal, while conceding as unimportant the fact that the average male is taller than the average female. The harder, the more elementary life is, the more that physical difference will translate into clearly differentiated social functions. I am told that when coal-mining was harder than it is today, the working-class wives of miners treated the breadwinner as king; prepared his bath, waited on him at table, and thought it was right to behave in this way. Petruchio shows no sign of enduring toil and danger to protect Katherina: instead we are given a vivid picture of developing bourgeois affluence; bride and bridegroom are both comfortably off. All the conditions are in place, we might think, for feminism to blossom. If, however, we pause and think what it must have been like to lack a male protector in a society with no effective police force, and further reflect that women of Katherina's class have no option but marriage and will be utterly dependent on whatever husband they can get, her suggestion that men are the protectors of weak women may cease to seem wholly absurd.

Perhaps the most interesting word in her speech is "honest"—"obedient to his honest will." She has said that the relation of the wife to her husband is like that of the subject to the prince. All now hinges on the nature of that subject's duty. If Shakespeare were a Renaissance absolutist, holding that the prince's authority is divinely given and in principle never to be opposed, this part of the speech could be very sinister in its implications. But if he thought that a wicked king was a tyrant, not to be obeyed, everything is different. "Fit to govern? / No, not to live," cries Macduff, when tested on exactly this point (*Macbeth*, IV.iii.102–3). Here the good subject, confronted as he thinks by a wicked ruler, withdraws his service.

So with Katherina. She reserves a place for honourable disobedience. If the husband's will is dishonest—that is, immoral—the wife is no longer under any obligation to obey.

The central doctrine, however, remains hierarchical, and the speech in which the doctrine is stated follows a practical demonstration of obedience. When Lucentio and Hortensio send messages to their wives asking them to come, the wives make excuses. Katherina, summoned, simply appears at once. Then, when her husband tells her that her cap doesn't suit her, she removes it instantly (V.ii.121–23). Of course the context is important. There is here an alliance of Katherina and Petruchio against the rest. He was always the anti-type of her father and of the world her father ruled, so now they work together. In so far as the removal of the cap is a strategic performance, something agreed upon to defeat a shared enemy, it is acceptable. But it is much more than that. Once more we hit real hierarchy. The principle that lower obeys higher is here in force, and in application to something as personal as the choice of a cap. To me it is the ugliest moment in the play. The fact that she obeys out of love makes it worse, not better. It is unacceptable.

Almost always Shakespeare, even when he differs ideologically from his twenty-first-century readers, shows an uncanny ability to anticipate almost every kind of counter-feeling. He knows perfectly well, for example, how shocking Valentine's offer of his mistress to Proteus in *Two Gentlemen of Verona* might be. I believe that even early modern audiences would have gasped, momentarily, at the cap episode, before—swiftly, no doubt—laughing again. But the overwhelming endorsement of hierarchy from the dramatist who will later give us such autonomous female figures as Rosalind and Viola is hard to take. Let us pause—a final hesitation—on the word "hierarchy." Clearly, even today, it is not automatically evil. Everyone I know would agree that a child's death is worse than the death of a fish, which means that we all place human beings above fish, hierarchically. What is now taboo is the application of the term *within* the field of humanity. It may be salutary to imagine at this point what it would be like to explain to John Milton that all human beings are equal. He would answer, "Whatever makes you think that? It's obvious that some human beings are superior to others." Republican Milton, who could see no reason why kings should tell other people what to do, was a firm believer in what is now called "meritocracy," not in equality. "All people are equal" is a benevolent legal fiction designed to cover a real field of intractably fluctuating hierarchies. In truth Mr. and Mrs. Jones are *never* equal. He is better at making toast, she at map-reading, and so on, endlessly. So hierarchy is a fact. But this in no way licenses the *blanket* assertion that husbands should rule their wives. "All are equal" will serve us better. Perhaps we must confess that we have encountered a genuine point of ethical disagreement.

We have reached 1593. In May of that year Marlowe was killed in a scuffle in a tavern. He and Shakespeare were born in the same year, 1564. Before his death Marlowe had written *Dido, Tamburlaine,* parts 1 and 2, *The Jew of Malta, Edward II, The Massacre at Paris,* and *Doctor Faustus.* Shakespeare has written *Henry VI,* parts 1, 2, and 3, *Richard III, The Comedy of Errors, Two Gentlemen of Verona,* and *The Taming of the Shrew.* Seven plays each. Some place Shakespeare's *Titus Andronicus* (a play that, unlike *The Taming of the Shrew,* really is about rape) before the death of Marlowe, but I agree with Jonathan Bate and the Stationer's Register that this disgusting, brilliant work was "new" in 1594.[42] Shakespeare is today the most famous dramatist in the world. Knowledge of Marlowe is virtually confined to the academy. We are all clear that *Hamlet* and *King Lear* outstrip any work by Marlowe, but these come later. Is it so clear, if we restrict our attention to Shakespeare's output up to 1593, that he is the greater dramatist? It is a primitive question—a schoolboy's question (small boys love to speculate about "who would win" in oddly assorted fights—a Tasmanian devil, say, versus a sheep).

If we think in terms of power, Marlowe has the edge. The slow crescendo of violence that makes the life of *Tamburlaine*—in blank defiance of the "Pride-must-have-a-fall" pattern pre-established in the minds of the spectators—is unmatched in early Shakespeare. One suspects that this kind of drama—a sort of protracted roar—would have seemed boring to Shakespeare, though, when Marlowe does it, it is far from boring and is technically of great interest. *Dido* is a camp version of Virgil's *Aeneid,* iv, with some pretty homo-erotic touches, but it is not in this area that Marlowe can challenge Shakespeare, who from the start is an absolute master of verbal grace, irony, and word-play. The entrance of Lightborn, the killer at the end of Marlowe's *Edward II,* is terrifying. I have seen a modern audience, brutalized, one might suppose, by a diet of video-nasties, shake with fear at this moment. Again, it is a matter of Marlovian power. There is nothing in the early Shakespeare to compare with the death of Doctor Faustus. Cardinal Beauford, dying mad in *2 Henry VI,* has the blood-freezing line, "He hath no eyes, the dust hath blinded them" (III.iii.14). But it is as nothing compared with Faustus's anguished "See, see where Christ's blood streams in the firmament, / One drop would save my soul."[43]

If, however, we look not for sheer power but for humanity, humour, and continuous vitality, Shakespeare is ahead. There are tedious scenes in *Edward II.* Shakespeare's Richard III is readily comparable with Marlowe's Jew of Malta, and Richard is the finer creation because the humour is sharper and the complex involvement of deformity with sexual prowess a sheer bonus. The thing that distinguishes Shakespeare from Marlowe is intelligence. This will seem absurd to those who retain the old "naive genius" view of Shakespeare. Marlowe after all is the university man, Shakespeare the Stratford Grammar School boy. If we separately consider the *mind* of either dramatist, an immediate contrast presents itself. Marlowe is a great reductionist, forever asking, "What does it all come down to?" Shakespeare, conversely, loves to ask, "What else could be going on?" Ockham's razor is the principle of economy in explanation: "Entities are not to be multiplied beyond necessity"; that is, "Keep the explanation as simple as possible." It has served science well. Shakespeare, contrariwise, is enamoured of over-determination. Ockham's principle is sometimes referred to as "the law of parsimony." Parsimony, certainly, is not the most obvious characteristic of Shakespeare's genius. That is why, many years ago, I described his work as "Ockham's beard, golden, luxuriant, happily unsubdued by the famous razor."[44] I do not mean to imply that reductionism is automatically inferior, intellectually, to its opposite. David Hume, one of the most intelligent men who ever lived, is rightly famous for his "nothing-buttery."

Philosophers and political theorists have long debated whether economic or military strength is the ultimate basis of power. In the winter of 1607 Francis Bacon addressed the House of Commons. He posed the question put by Croesus to Solon, which is the mightier, gold or iron? Bacon gives Solon's answer, "Why, Sir, if another comes that hath better iron than you, he will be lord of all your gold."[45] With his iron sword the poor man can take the rich man's money and be rich himself. In *The Jew of Malta* Marlowe backs gold as primary (after all, with my purse full of gold I might have bought up all the swords in advance). *Tamburlaine,* on the other hand, is the work in which iron cuts through everything: men, women, children, innocence, justice, fate. Shakespeare will never write in this manner, and so one species of dramatic power, the power consisting in the strange concentration of causes in one, is unavailable to him.

But Shakespeare's dramatic use of over-determination is very skilful. The treatment of the beginning of the Wars of the Roses in the rose-picking scene (*1 Henry VI,* II.iv), in which persons take sides half-arbitrarily and find their motives strengthened, retroactively, by the coarsely physical badges they have assumed, is more penetrating, philosophically and psychologically, than anything in Marlowe. The best thinkers I know have to run to keep up with Shakespeare.

I am saying, then, that Shakespeare is not just a master of emotive imagery; he excels at thinking—a virtue too easily deemed inseparable from an academic education. It is curious that, possessed as he is of this mind and at the same time socially deprived, he does not show off more. Kyd as we saw was similarly placed and strenuously interlarded *The Spanish Tragedy* with Latin. The young Shakespeare uses the Latin at his command with the nonchalance, the *sprezzatura,* of the insider. There is a fascinating moment of unasserted erudition in *The Taming of the Shrew.* Lucentio, disguised as a tutor, is wooing Bianca. He first shows her a couple of lines of Latin: "Hic ibat Simois; hic est Sigeia tellus; / Hic steterat Priami regia celsa senis" (III.i.27–28). Bianca asks him to translate, but instead of translating, Lucentio tells her his real name and explains that he is seeking her love. The lines actually mean, "Here the river Simois ran, here lay the Sigeian land, here stood the lofty palace of old Priam." A few lines later, in an apparently unconnected manner, Lucentio says, "Mistrust it not, for sure Aeacides / Was Ajax" (III.i.52–53). Where has Aeacides appeared from? To get the answer you must be able to place the lines Lucentio quoted earlier. They are from the first of Ovid's *Heroides* (33–34). The next line begins, "Illic Aeacides . . . ," "There was Aeacides . . . ." Shakespeare, who says nothing to help the audience, evidently has the original before *his* mind, with complete clarity. Never was learning more lightly worn. The real subtlety of the exchange (once it is understood!) is great. Bianca is uncertain whether to believe Lucentio when he explains that he is of good lineage, the son of Vincentio of Pisa. "Aeacides," "the descendant of Aeacus," is explained by some as a reference to Ajax. This is what Lucentio says. Others, including George Turberville of New College, Oxford, in 1567, take it to be a reference to Achilles ("There fierce Achilles pight his tents").[46] In fact Achilles is the better bet.[47] If Lucentio is taking a dubious line on a classical lineage at the precise moment when his trustworthiness is being doubted by the lady to whom he is selling his own high birth, the comedy is sharp indeed—but entirely hidden, surely, from 99 percent of the audience.

The use made in *Two Gentlemen of Verona* of John Lyly's *Euphues* is similarly sharp, beyond the capacities of most modern readers, who usually think of *Euphues,* if they think of it at all, as a work of vacuous rhetorical display. In fact it is an intensely moral story about male friendship and the importance of education. At the end Lyly writes penitentially of "the fine and filed phrases of Cicero," to which he bids farewell, choosing instead the Bible.[48] The story is of Philautus and Euphues, best friends who, like Valentine and Proteus, both fall for the same lady. Before it begins Lyly offers an "anti-Sidneian" account of his own art (Philip Sidney in the *Apology for Poetry* urges writers to provide positive role models). Idealization is not the way, says Lyly; faults should be included; Euphues is a far-from-perfect young man.[49] It is correct to call *Two Gentlemen of Verona* a Euphuistic play but an error to think that in consequence it is a mere tissue of trivial felicities. Shakespeare has read Lyly better than most university-educated moderns read him. Therefore his play is all about moral obliquity coexisting with social and rhetorical grace. Here he "of the native wood-notes wild" is the better *reader,* the more intricately informed mind.

In the last soliloquy of Richard III Shakespeare joins the despair of Faustus damned to a psychological exploration of consciousness entirely beyond the reach of Marlowe. This is the beginning of a protracted process of thought, an investigation of the nature of consciousness and identity that will develop strongly in the later work. Again it is a factor of *intellectual* force that makes the difference between the two men.

So who wins? Pitting the seven extant plays against Marlowe's seven, I am still not sure. I have granted the greater power to Marlowe, and surely to grant power is to grant much. But if one changes the question from "Which one produces the better body of dramatic work by 1593?" to "Which shows the greater promise?" I am sure the answer is Shakespeare. It is not just that more complex operations of the imaginative intelligence can be seen; one can watch those operations, always in motion, beginning to cohere and develop. And of course one has the suspicion that Marlowe the daring atheist spy, mad, bad, and dangerous to know, was in any case going to burn out soon. Shakespeare, who watched his pennies, got himself a coat of arms, and bought the best house in Stratford, is one of nature's survivors. The crucial thing, however, is that Shakespeare's early work is instinct with ramifying potentialities. Reductive Marlowe does not foster "the green shoots" within his own mind any more than he countenances simultaneous explanations of human behaviour. There is finally something coarse in his spectacular feats of reduction. To put the matter at its simplest, Shakespeare is more interested in people. If Marlowe had lived on, Shakespeare would still have "won."

2 Learning Not to Run

Love's Labour's Lost and the Problem of Style

After 30 May 1593 the field was clear. Marlowe was the only serious rival and Marlowe was dead. If I am right to date *Titus Andronicus* to January 1594, it is Shakespeare's next venture, but from this play I flinch. The eighteenth century, by and large, saw it as grotesquely horrific and was unwilling to believe it was Shakespeare's. The twentieth century disagreed and increasingly stressed the artistic sophistication of the work. The test case is Marcus's long speech as he gazes at the mutilated Lavinia (II.iv.11–57). The speech is certainly elegant, full of mannered word-play and mythological allusion. What is upsetting is the application of such elegant language to physical horror. Ovid is the evil genius of this mode. The myth of Tereus and Philomel (*Metamorphoses,* vi) is a chillingly playful narrative of rape and dismemberment. At lines 559 to 560 Ovid describes, in dapper hexameters, how Philomel's severed tongue skipped like a tail cut from a snake and tried, pathetically, to rejoin its bleeding mistress. When bad taste is as extreme as this it becomes something else, something strangely impressive. An explosion happens in the mind and the usual values somehow no longer apply. The incongruity of horror and aestheticism is clearly deliberate. But how does the incongruity function? It could have produced "black farce," "horrid laughter." It is said that in these days of comic-tempo blood-bath films like Martin Scorsese's *Goodfellas* (1990) we are better placed than eighteenth-century audiences to understand and enjoy *Titus Andronicus*. But it is not black farce. We are far removed from the cackling zest of the bloodthirsty Ithamore in Marlowe's *Jew of Malta*. Rather, Shakespeare invites us to consider and to experience a special kind of alienation, the mind recoiling from the intolerable into pattern and form. When Richard II asked John of Gaunt how he, a dying man, could bear to pun on his own name, Gaunt answered, "Misery makes sport to mock itself" (II.i.85). Shakespeare has noticed that in real situations humour is not blankly incompatible with suffering but can have a defensive function. "Trench humour," clearly, is one form of this. But Marcus is not joking. Rather the emphasis is on the sheer fact of alienation into beauty. Nearer in spirit than Marlowe but further off in time is Richard Crashaw. Crashaw mingles milk with blood in "Upon the Infant Martyrs" and writes of Christ's wounds, "Thee with Thyself they have too richly clad, / Opening the purple wardrobe of Thy side," in "On Our Crucified Lord, Naked and Bloody." Such alienation can work on two levels. Thematically, the articulate richness of the speech is in contrast with the tongue-less condition of Lavinia herself.[1] Psychologically, Marcus himself is in a curious state of garrulous shock. Indeed the play is saved morally by its compassionate psychological reference. Anne Calder-Marshall, who played Lavinia in a television production in the 1980s, wrote to Jonathan Bate, "It's just like a video nasty, isn't it?" but added, "Somehow we've found—or I think we have—that the characters through their suffering get closer. Titus has committed the most appalling deeds and it isn't until he's maimed and his daughter's maimed that he learns anything about love."[2] Yet the play is still disgusting. "Enter LAVINIA, her hand cut off and her tongue cut out, ravish'd," is a stage direction from which, very simply, I wish at once to avert my mind.

Love's Labour's Lost is so different from Titus Andronicus that it might seem hard to believe that the same person wrote both. But the man who wrote Titus Andronicus is fascinated by a hysteria of style, seen, academically, as classical in tone. Love's Labour's Lost is likewise about another kind of hysteria of style, a feast of languages that at one point becomes classical again, on the lips of Holofernes, the sweet-natured, mildly deranged schoolmaster. The comedy, however, is finally more serious than the Roman tragedy, because in it Shakespeare repents of his own brilliance. Four young men, one of whom is a king (but seems to have slender governmental responsibilities), decide to give up chasing young women, to turn down all party invitations, and to become, collectively, a miniature university, "a little academe, / Still and contemplative in living art" (I.i.13–14). Stillness is to replace motion, art nature. The body, Longaville chimes in, is to give way to mind, and Dumaine, the third member of the group, adds that love and riches are to give way to philosophy. One gets the picture. The fourth man, Berowne, has doubts. He has signed up to three years of study, he agrees, but he doesn't see why he should also undertake to sleep only three hours a night and never see any ladies. Here at the very beginning of the play Berowne puts his finger on a curious feature of the scheme. The planned academy is clearly non-religious. It is a thoroughly Renaissance affair, humanist in the old, technical sense— that is, committed to "humane letters," the study of Greek and Latin texts. Yet as the King conceives it, the scheme is swathed in spectral garments, the burden of an imperfectly shed monastic past. It may seem strange to a modern reader that such bright, switched-on young fellows should assume (Berowne excepted) that academic study must entail celibacy. Historically it is not strange at all. Oxford and Cambridge colleges were from the first firmly distinct from monasteries as places devoted primarily to teaching and research, and yet it was not until quite late in the nineteenth century that fellows of colleges were allowed to marry. A. E. Housman remembered how in his youth it was "not done" to ask colleagues where they had been during the long vacation, because they had secret love-nests in anonymous places like Birmingham.[3] Berowne is ahead of his time in querying the major premise. All is thrown into confusion when a party of ladies arrives.

E. M. Forster's *The Longest Journey* (1907) gives us an analogous moment at a later period in history. Cambridge—the academy—is first established in the novel as a site of innocence and intelligence, where men love one another. Then "ladies" invade. The bubble bursts and nothing can ever be the same again. It may be that Forster's homosexuality gives the story a special intensity. Forster's invading female is evil; in Shakespeare the invading ladies are entirely good. We are dealing with profound, simple antinomies: action and contemplation, nature and art, body and mind, and by an elementary logic it would seem to follow that, if sex is an affair of the body, the life of the mind must be asexual. This Berowne denies.

Love's Labour's Lost is as much a play about education as is *The Taming of the Shrew,* but instead of the husband teaching the wife, the ladies now teach the gentlemen. The difference could hardly be greater. "To teach a teacher ill beseemeth me," says the Princess to the young King at the beginning of the educative process she conducts so skilfully (II.i.108). The situation is simultaneously paradoxical and warmly recognizable. The paradox lies in the fact that education, usually thought of as the province of the academy, is here anti-academic. The warm immediacy, meanwhile, springs from the fact that the counter-argument put by the ladies is not logically intricate; it is the mere fact that they are marriageable young women and the young men have blood in their veins. Nature is herself the answer to art and needs neither words nor wit to make her fundamental point.

The opening scene is all about the solemn plans for abstemious study, but it ends with a comic episode. Costard the clown has been caught copulating with Jaquenetta, a country wench. The formal penalty is a year's imprisonment (I.i.287), but the King is content to sentence Costard to a week on bran and water (I.i.300–301). Costard is left alone with Berowne, his natural ally. "I suffer for the truth," he says ruefully. The phrase is funny because of a slippage in the sense of "truth" from "conceptual veracity" to "truth of nature, reality." This slippage encapsulates the argument of the whole play. By the time we reach Act I, Scene ii, line 128, the punishment seems to have been reduced again, to bran and water for three days out of the seven. The laws devised by the King to protect his miniature academy are subjected to an even more rapid diminuendo:

BEROWNE "*Item,* If any man be seen to talk with a woman within the
   term of three years, he shall endure such public shame as the rest of the
   court can possible devise."
This article, my liege, yourself must break,
For well you know here comes in embassy
The French king's daughter with yourself to speak—
A maid of grace and complete majesty—
About surrender up of Aquitaine
To her decrepit, sick, and bedred father;
Therefore the article is made in vain,
Or vainly comes th' admired Princess hither.

KING What say you, lords? Why, this was quite forgot.
BEROWNE So study evermore is overshot.   (I.i.129–42)

Theory is error, overtaken and displaced by fact. The speech homes in on oaths. Oaths are, as the philosopher J. L. Austin taught us, "performatives," and performatives are found at a point of intersection, where language becomes practice and so meshes with the extra-linguistic world. As we saw earlier, if I say, "I name this ship the *Baby Spice*," what I *say* is, simultaneously, *done; the ship *is* so named. Oaths admittedly are not quite so securely "enmeshed." They "perform" a commitment, certainly, but that does not make them reliable as predictors. In this play they evaporate instantly on contact with the real. Words and natural reality are suddenly dismayingly disjunct.

The "natural fact," meanwhile, of the arrival of the ladies is itself a *social* occasion, swathed in rich vestments of formal obligation, etiquette, and courtesy. In the mirror world of *Love's Labour's Lost* importunate women harass retreating men. The harassment, to be sure, is polite and not directly sexual. But the sexual tension inherent in such a reversal is not wholly absent. Long before *Love's Labour's Lost*, in *Gawain and the Green Knight*, Sir Gawain, visited as he lies in bed by the wife of his host, is impelled by the obligations of hospitality to shrink back but is at the same time pressed by the ethic of gallantry to respond positively. The underlying notion is that because it is unusual for a woman to initiate a relationship she risks far more in doing so than a man would. In consequence, a man refusing a woman gives a far harder slap in the face, figuratively, than would a woman refusing a man. Long after *Love's Labour's Lost,* Henry Fielding's Tom Jones, who is remorselessly pestered by love-hungry women, feels obliged by gallantry to say yes. Fielding writes that "it was as much incumbent on him to accept a challenge to love, as if it had been a challenge to fight."[4] The analogy reminds us that such conventions have their roots in elementary physical circumstances. A man, propositioned, is on his mettle as a woman is not. His manhood is in question. The physiological fact that men cannot always perform sexually is part of the picture. It will be said, and truly, that the ladies in *Love's Labour's Lost* are not pressing for a sexual response and that the Princess's motive in coming is a matter of territorial politics. I have already said that the situation is not directly sexual. This, note, reserves the possibility that it may meanwhile be indirectly sexual. The embarrassment, the red faces that greet the arrival of the ladies, are caused by the conflict, within the male, of austerity and gallantry. Shakespeare makes the sexual element in the situation evident when he makes the ladies swap starry-eyed descriptions of the dashing young men ahead of the actual meeting (II.i.37–76). Before the negotiation the courtier Boyet urges the Princess to use all her powers of persuasion, and she in reply shows that she knows he is talking about her beauty, her attractiveness as a woman (II.i.1–14). After the meeting the Princess exclaims, "God bless my ladies! are they all in love?" (II.i.77).

I coined the phrase *mens intacta* (by analogy with *virgo intacta*), "mind virginally intact," for Katherina in *The Taming of the Shrew*. In this mirror-play the phrase is applicable to the King. To keep his intellectual program intact, safe from sexual interference, he must cloister himself in his quasi-monastic academe. Like men excluded from a nunnery the ladies are asked to remain outside in the open fields. But to ask them to do this—even if they are given, as they no doubt are, pretty tents and pavilions—is monstrously discourteous. The hapless King greets his guest with the words, "Fair Princess!" (II.i.90). She in her turn with lethal accuracy picks up the gallant innuendo in "fair" and knocks it straight back over the net, pointing out that the welcome is cold indeed. The King switches at once to the more coolly formal "Madam" (II.i.95). He seeks to cut the knot by agreeing at once to the Princess's political request, saying in effect, "I'll sign now if you like." This entirely fails to resolve the situation, which means that we were right earlier to guess that sexual politics are as important here as political politics. The minor figures meanwhile are swiftly establishing contact: "Did not I dance with you in Brabant once?" says Berowne to Rosaline (II.i.115). She responds with a brittle put-down, but we are not deceived; we know already (from II.i.66–76) that she is disposed to fall in love with him. Rosaline's witty replies are the flimsiest of screens, mere words to be shattered by ensuing love.

We have then, in *Love's Labour's Lost,* a play with a message. Theory is nothing, practice is all; words are no match for things; art is vain, nature is supreme. And at the same time we have a play that explodes at every point with wit, verbal intricacy, joyous art. A full analysis of the word-play of this comedy would fill several volumes. More than forty years ago I took part in a summer school, also attended by a very strong personality, who genially suggested a play-reading of *Love's Labour's Lost*. We met and read the play aloud, different persons taking different parts, and it was quite amusing. As the meeting broke up our convener said, to my absolute amazement, "Tomorrow we meet again and read the play again." I thought, "This is going to be unpleasant; he is presuming too far on the good will of these nice people." By sheer strength of will he succeeded, and the following evening we repeated the reading—but faster. It was pure joy. Suddenly the jokes became not arcane intricacies to be laboriously disentangled but explosions of humour. There is a line in *Love's Labour's Lost* that uses the word "light" four times and in four distinct senses: "Light, seeking light, doth light of light beguile" (I.i.77). The immediate context differentiates these chiming sounds, for those who listen:

> all delights are vain, but that most vain
> Which, with pain purchas'd, doth inherit pain:
> As, painfully to pore upon a book
> To seek the light of truth, while truth the while
> Doth falsely blind the eyesight of his look.
> *Light, seeking light, doth light of light beguile;*
> So ere you find where light in darkness lies
> Your light grows dark by losing of your eyes.   (I.i.72–79)

Berowne is speaking against the extremist program of study set out by the King, and his actual meaning, amid the glittering cleverness, is down-to-earth: too much reading makes you go blind, and where's your dream of study then? So, of the four "light"s in the line, the first means "mind," the second "enlightenment," or "knowledge," the third "eye," and the fourth "sight."[5] The fun of such writing is utterly formal. It is like a dance.

Yet there is something sinister in this juxtaposition of verbal gymnastics and an anti-verbal message. Berowne is trapped in a bright bubble of art, and so is everyone else. Even the ladies, beautiful emissaries of Nature herself, teachers of the men in the field of unpretentious loving, are not exempt from the fatal tic of style. Very near the end of the play Berowne says to Rosaline,

Henceforth my wooing mind shall be express'd
In russet yeas and honest kersey noes.
And to begin, wench, so God help me law!
My love to thee is sound, sans crack or flaw. (V.ii.412–15)

Rosaline, his tutor in the difficult subject called "reality," catches him,
predictably, on the mannered Gallicism "sans," scarcely the homespun
language he is vowing at this very moment to stick to. "Sans 'sans' I pray
you," says she, and Berowne hangs his head in shame:

Yet I have a trick
Of the old rage. Bear with me, I am sick;
I'll leave it by degrees. (V.ii.416–18)

The imagery is suddenly very strong. Cleverness is a disease, a plague
(V.ii.421). This almost turns Rosaline from tutor into doctor. If so, however, we must confess that the doctor is herself infected. For "Sans 'sans' I
pray you" is itself artfully cadenced, wittily equivocating on the repeated
word. We begin to sense that the pestilence has spread beyond the circle of
the fiction and has seized the writer. Shakespeare himself seems to be
imprisoned in the glassy prison of art he notionally condemns. It is indeed
a kind of hysteria. The chattering ingenuity cannot be stilled. It is commonly said that one great difference between mental imagery and perceptions lies in the fact that imagery is freely manipulable; we can stop it, start
it, change it at will. There is, however, an exception to this rule. If one
imagines a spinning wheel it is curiously difficult to stop it spinning as one
continues to "watch." The reader is invited to try the experiment. If one
tries really hard (*experto crede*) one can feel slightly sick. So here the spinning Catherine-wheel of wit-that-cannot-be-arrested becomes a source
of fear, of desperation—or even of pain.

Such are the difficulties encountered by the young Shakespeare. Where
others learning their craft struggle to find felicitous expressions, Shakespeare, conversely, is oppressed by his own verbal facility. Effortlessly he
hits every nail on the head, finds the stirring image, lights upon the
undermining parody, and, amid all this, hears in the distance a voice that
says, "Slow down." A friend of mine and I once saw three small boys

(choristers) moving across an open space in a peculiar lurching manner. "Why are they moving like that?" my friend asked, and then answered himself, "I know! They've been told they mustn't run, and this is the result." Small bodies, crackling with natural energy, eager to reach the destination, experience the requirement that they must walk (not run) as a grotesque impediment. Shakespeare's youthful genius is a runner, a dancer. He has to learn to move at the more temperate pace that comes naturally to the rest of us. He has to learn not to run.

Desperation breeds desperate remedies. The extraordinary ending of *Love's Labour's Lost* may be the result of a rising terror in the dramatist. He mortifies the comic conclusion proper to the play. Just as the lovers are about to fall into one another's arms and run off to church to be joined he brings on a man in black, bearing news of a death. Whether or not the theatre is equipped with manipulable lighting, we feel that the stage has grown dark. These young lords and ladies, pretty gilded butterflies, are suddenly hushed and draw apart: "Our wooing doth not end like an old play: / Jack hath not Gill" (V.ii.874–75). Everything has suddenly gone horribly wrong. It may be said that the comedic happy ending is still there—that it is merely postponed, because after a year the lovers will meet again. But Shakespeare lets in (at V.ii.832) the thought that these splendid young men who have already broken one promise—the one made to learning—may break another: "Yet swear not, lest ye be forsworn again."

The only way to stop the spinning is to smash the wheel. Perhaps the sinister dominance of bloodless language is really broken with this convulsive disruption of genre, but notice the shift that has occurred at the level of the play's "message." From the beginning Berowne, seemingly with the full backing of the playwright, was preaching that real love triumphs by natural right over verbal forms. But at the end verbal facility is silenced not as we might have expected by a warm, wordless embrace but by the great negation of death. Nothing but nothingness itself is strong enough to shut them up.

It might be supposed the "black hole" at the end of *Love's Labour's Lost* entails the destruction of all poetry. The underlying logic is anti-art and poetry is an art. What we are given last of all, however, is the pair of songs, one sung by Spring, the other by Winter. They are poetry, but poetry freed from the self-consciousness of everything that has gone before. They are transparent. We are removed from the erotic adventure playground of silken aristocrats to a demotic, Brueghelesque world where milk is frozen in the bucket and—a matchless description of an English parish church in January—people are coughing so much that one cannot hear the parson's sermon. "Marian's nose looks red and raw" (V.ii.924) may not seem to be a line worth pausing on—low matter, expressed in low language, devoid of "point." But its very oppositeness to the preceding bravura gives it a healing power. It is a window opening to admit cold, fresh air. We must not call these songs pastoral because "pastoral" became, quintessentially, the genre that confessed the final impossibility of escaping from art into that green nature it sought to celebrate. The poignancy of pastoral lies in its sad emphasis on its own disabling grace; no form is so literary as that which preaches the superiority of artless simplicity. *As You Like It* is proof that Shakespeare understood this very well. But the songs of Spring and Winter seem miraculously to have burst the glassy bubble, if only because Marian is called Marian, and not Amaryllis.

I have said that the sudden news of a death at the end either destroys or almost fatally postpones the expected happy ending. Yet there is a sense in which this sudden silence really is instinct with the only hope they have. The Princess, guessing the message before she hears it, says, "Dead, for my life!" (V.ii.720). In the words "for my life" she is merely using a common expletive. But the poet, standing behind the character, may hope to catch something more: the life of the young coming out of the death of the old. The joking stops. Shakespeare is very sharp on the way brittle cerebral badinage is both natural to the early stages of courtship and can impede congress. Later he will write a play about two good young people who love each other but are eerily trapped in a running wit-combat and cannot show their love—*Much Ado about Nothing.* The ladies repeatedly say what is reasonable and practical, that they cannot trust the oaths of the young men. So the ladies give tasks to the gentlemen. The King is told by the Princess that he must live out the year in a hermitage and that, if he does, she will be his. The academic celibacy he proudly opted for at the beginning is to be temporarily exchanged for full (pre-Reformation) monasticism. This ordeal is a penance for, of all things, the sin of being a bright young man. Berowne, who saw his own wit finally as a sickness, is sent off by Rosaline to do social work. He is to cheer up the people in a hospital by telling them jokes. Rosaline's requirement is interestingly different from the Princess's. She does not tell him to fast and pray. With part of her mind she wants him to go on being himself, to go on being funny, because, we may guess, she loves him so. Nevertheless, modern audiences can miss the grimness of the "hospital." She is referring to a place of horror, where people die. That is why Berowne at first protests—

To move wild laughter in the throat of death?
It cannot be, it is impossible:
Mirth cannot move a soul in agony.   (V.ii.855–57)

Rosaline answers severely that if the jokes fall flat so that he stops making such jokes, that will be so much ground gained. But then she softens and says that if some of the jokes survive he should keep them in and that she will in the end take both the jokes and their maker. Berowne, perhaps because he was from the first unwilling to swear to what he thought he could not perform, is perhaps the one most likely to get his lady in that strange happy ending, so far off as to be invisible to us, watching in the theatre.

The effect of the ending is to daze the spectator, who had until now been comfortable with the virtual Nominalist philosophy intermittently projected by the play: words are mere breath, physical reality is all. I want to say that the spectator is *philosophically* dazed. The simple antithesis, words versus things, begins to shimmer and break down into a far more complex array. Verbal dancing may be a form of art and so opposed to nature, but verbal dancing comes *naturally* to young people. The simple scheme "Eloquence is antithetical to true love" is replaced by a much more complex suggestion: "Eloquence can spring naturally from love arising in a social context, but can then prove a temporary impediment to consummation." Meanwhile words can be used in other ways, for example to attack merely verbal frivolity. Words may frolic, but they can also express apology and humble self-doubt. And language *in itself* is *something* —perhaps something rich. The delight taken by the dotty old schoolmaster Holofernes in scraps of Latin is loved, not depised, by the dramatist.

There is something vernal about this unquenched fount of joy in so old a man.

Ernst Cassirer believed that Shakespeare virtually invented kindly comedy; before Shakespeare laughter was assumed to be derisive.[6] For Thomas Hobbes laughter is still "sudden glory," which sounds delightful until we realize that Hobbes means *our* glory, at the expense of the person laughed at.[7] Perhaps Shakespeare taught us how to laugh with rather than at others. But the phrase "laugh with" occurs in Paul Turner's admirable translation of More's *Utopia,* a work written long before Shakespeare was born. If, however, one looks up More's original Latin one finds that, where Turner gives the sentence, "His efforts to raise a laugh were usually so feeble that one tended to laugh at him rather than with him,"[8] More's Latin, literally rendered, is "He himself was laughed at more often than his words were."[9] More is not thinking about *affectionate* laughter. W. H. Auden once remarked that at the end of a Ben Jonson (Roman) comedy those on stage are weeping and those in the audience are laughing, but at the end of a Shakespearean (Christian) comedy both audience and players are wreathed in smiles.[10] Holofernes puts on a play within the comedy, and the grand audience indeed sees him as an object of derision. But Cassirer and Auden, though they simplify, are basically right. We do not laugh as the King and his friends laugh. We feel an affection that Shakespeare has planted in us but not in them.

So what are we to make of Holofernes' jubilant linguistic pedantry? It is in him that language assumes its most completely abstracted character, and yet even here we find life. In the songs of Spring and Winter language is at its least abstract, is not aware that it is language, admits us at once to things we know. Some mathematicians are ontological dualists in that they see the sphere of mathematics not as an arbitrary human construct but as separately real (a kind of objectivist idealism). They are "Platonists at heart," seeing their work as a process of discovery rather than as a free play of hypothesis. For Holofernes language itself has this kind of substance; it is a glittering world, autonomous and, to him, wonderful. But the play also shows us, not only language in disjunction, but also intricate, playful language *functioning* socially, in complex situations. The automatic critical reflex today is to say that emphasis within the work on language betrays or confesses the fact that the work itself is a purely formal structure. Shakespeare can certainly contrive this effect—he does it with Duke Senior's verbally elegant praise of preverbal nature in *As You Like It* (II.i.1f.). But the impulse, clear in *Love's Labour's Lost,* to explore the complex intersection of linguistic pattern and social (erotic) life is the very opposite of a confessed formalism; it is a move to engage nature, even here. Of course it remains true that language, before it is applied or used, *is* a formal system, and this makes possible flights of verbal ingenuity that can make us forget material reality. This is the thought that haunts the effortlessly witty Berowne and it haunted Shakespeare, too. I will not say that Shakespeare worked out a complex philosophy of language involving not only (mis)representation but also linguistic agency, because I do not suppose that he would recognize any of these terms, but his play has laid the groundwork for such a philosophy, through its responsiveness to the real variety of human interaction.

The fear of premature articulateness, the sense of an obscure blasphemy in dealing too easily with love, grief, death, remains very strong. The pluralism of the play, with its knowing variation of registers, is radiantly sane, but the note of desperation at the end, the smashing of the spinning wheel, with the entry of the man in black and the sudden harshness of the penances imposed by the ladies, can make us feel that things are running out of control, that the dramatist himself is seriously disturbed. I think that indeed he was. His fear is not the Nominalist fear that verbal abstractions refer to nothing at all. Shakespeare's worry is ethical. He grasps the psychological truth that even if words are variously engaged with the extra-verbal world, we can, by a trick of the mind, focus on the formal expression and so lose full engagement, even while we are still applauding our own cleverness. Of this he is ashamed.

Words, Love, Death: *Romeo and Juliet*

It is impossible to be sure whether *Romeo and Juliet* was written just before or just after *A Midsummer Night's Dream,* but most scholars make the tragedy the earlier play. About the same time, Shakespeare was pushing ahead with his English histories *King John* and *Richard II.* The switches of tone have been violent—from the bloody horror of *Titus Andronicus* to the tinsel elegance of *Love's Labour's Lost*—but these can be ascribed in part to genre. *Titus Andronicus* is a tragedy, *Love's Labour's Lost* a comedy. But *Romeo and Juliet* is another tragedy, and yet it differs deeply from *Titus Andronicus*. We want to ask, "Can one mind have seen the world and formed his art in such profoundly different ways?" There is, however, no serious doubt but that Shakespeare wrote all these plays. There are links as well as ruptures.

Titus Andronicus and *Love's Labour's Lost* are both about a certain hysteria lurking in verbal formalism and death. Because in *Love's Labour's Lost* death breaks the dramatic sequence so radically, it is felt as a more serious reality in the comedy than it is in the Roman tragedy. In *Romeo and Juliet* he turns again to tragedy, but to a form of tragedy that can negotiate with comic expectations. Young lovers who get together despite parental opposition, the solidarity of the all-male group split and transcended by heterosexual love, friars as holy intermediaries in the intrigue, an upper-middle-class rather than a royal or aristocratic milieu—all these are characteristic of comedy but are found here, with the dreadful ending we all know. Most important of all, the tempo is that of comedy, not tragedy. That the same story can be comic if told fast and tragic if told slowly is a familiar proposition. Most jokes narrate a *peripeteia,* a turning of the tables in which the agent is hoist on his or her own petard. Tragedy, as Aristotle observed, thrives on *peripeteia*. Ribald rugby players on the way home from a match used to chant a comic dialogue involving a deep and a shrill voice; the deep voice kept saying, "To the woods! To the woods!" while the shrill voice protested, until at last the shrill voice cried, "But the vicar wouldn't like it!" and the deep voice answered, "I *am* the vicar!" A slow version might run as follows (but constraints of space prevent me from being as slow as I should be, so this may still be funny): A lady is lost in a dark wood, hears the footfall of a lustful, powerful pursuer; this is stretched out through various, inconclusive episodes until at last, desperate and trembling, she sees among the trees the temple of Diana, protector of virgins; she falls across the threshold, crying, "Help me, Priest of Diana!" The figure standing in the shadow of the temple moves into the light; it is the man who has been pursuing her; he smiles and says, "I am the Priest of Diana." We have reached "I *am* the vicar." Tempo, then, is of fundamental importance. To be sure *Romeo and Juliet* has an inescapably tragic conclusion, but the problem of pace remains. Shakespeare still cannot slow down, cannot help running.

Consider the Prologue to the play:

Two households, both alike in dignity,
In fair Verona, where we lay our scene,
From ancient grudge break to new mutiny,
Where civil blood makes civil hands unclean.
From forth the fatal loins of these two foes
A pair of star-cross'd lovers take their life;
Whose misadventur'd piteous overthrows
Doth with their death bury their parents' strife.
The fearful passage of their death-mark'd love,
And the continuance of their parents' rage,
Which, but their children's end, nought could remove,
Is now the two hours' traffic of our stage.

It is as if Berowne, unbroken by his year in the hospital, has stepped in from *Love's Labour's Lost* to lend a hand with the Prologue. It is remorselessly witty. As Thomas De Quincey said of Alexander Pope's coruscating verse, "The eye aches at it."[11] "Fair Verona" sounds like a city on a picture postcard, but it contains something ugly; two households, evenly balanced, generate, from their very likeness, difference, a conflict that is itself both old and new. The antitheses are effortlessly multiplied. "Civil blood" is itself an oxymoron, and the word "Civil" is made to chime in the line in a thoroughly Berownean manner. The clash of civility and blood then turns into a darker conjunction, sex with death. The two opposed houses generate sexually ("loins") not enemies but lovers, but the marriage of the lovers is in its turn opposed by the stars. The life-giving "loins" are called "fatal"—another oxymoron—because they beget death. The death of the lovers is matter for grief, but at the same time it brings about the death of enmity between the two houses and is therefore matter for joy. So the last death image is potentially comedic—the burial of the strife between the Montagues and the Capulets. The sheer cleverness and grace of this interlacing of images is astonishing. This is something Marlowe could never have learned to do, however long he lived. But the demon of *Love's Labour's Lost* is still at work. This dapper stuff about love and death is to grow in the drama that follows into the greatest *Liebestod* in English, but the tempo and the elegance mysteriously exclude serious engagement, for the time at least. *Love's Labour's Lost,* as we saw, ends with a death that might prove healing, for those who live after; now we are promised a healing death before the play has begun. We are also told, however, that in this play it is the young, not the old, who are to die.

Shakespeare's strategy in dealing with the demon of comic facility is to give him what he wants, a preliminary flourish or, say, a conventional-erotic episode pre-echoing the main action as "a sop to Cerberus," something to keep the beast occupied, in such a way that when the real action begins it will be felt as crucially distinct from all that has been said or done till now, as the actual is stronger than the merely hypothetical or notional. Act I, Scene i, therefore, is a straightforwardly comic scene in which the strife between the two houses is enacted by low-life persons in a street brawl. The scene assumes the status of mock-heroic as the more elevated persons come on stage. Benvolio, one of the masters, enters and stops the fight. At this moment we could easily think the whole quarrel trivial. But not for long. The Capulet Tybalt enters and instantly tries to provoke Benvolio (a Montague) to fight. Benvolio tries to carry the light atmosphere of the comic brawl over into the negotiation with Tybalt: in modern terms, "Don't be crazy, man! Help me pacify these impossible servants." In *1 Henry VI* we saw the "causes" of an inter-dynastic feud forming mysteriously in the air, in the scene in the Temple Garden. Tybalt is deliberately presented as one without rational motive. As soon as he sees Benvolio with his sword drawn, he sees a chance to kill somebody: "Turn thee, Benvolio, look upon thy death" (I.i.67). The effect is of fact replacing a picture of fact.

The other example is subtler still. Shakespeare gives Romeo a no-tional love affair before the real one that arrives with the appearance of Juliet. It might be thought that to show the hero to be so easily susceptible might weaken the effect of the main story. In fact the opposite happens.

First we have a narrative of Romeo's behaviour, given by Benvolio to Romeo's mother:

an hour before the worshipp'd Sun
Peer'd forth the golden window of the east,
A troubled mind drive me to walk abroad,
Where, underneath the grove of sycamore
That westward rooteth from this city side,
So early walking did I see your son.
Towards him I made, but he was ware of me,
And stole into the covert of the wood.   (I.i.118–25)

This is a curiously precise anticipation of English Romanticism, as it will later develop. A line runs from this passage through Milton's *Il Penseroso* to the aesthetic solitaries of William Wordsworth, walking on the northern fells. The naturally crowded scenes of earlier dramatic literature are replaced by a new composition, a single figure, not in a town but in an empty landscape. Certainly pastoral poetry long before this exchanged the urban environment for a country setting, but the point holds. Pastoral typically depicts not a figure in a landscape but a landscape dotted with figures (Nicolas Poussin, not Caspar David Friedrich). Romanticism, when it comes, will be strenuously a-social. Jean-Jacques Rousseau's proto-Romantic "state of nature," unlike that of Thomas Hobbes or John Locke, shows not a society but an individual wandering through forests.[12] When Romeo returns to his friends after his brush with love Mercutio cries out happily, "Now art thou sociable, now art thou Romeo!" (II.iv.88–89). Shakespeare senses a deep literary topos before it is fully formed.

After Benvolio has told his tale Romeo himself appears. He asks if the person who has just gone is his father and then confesses that he is sad. So far we have the pattern proper to the opening of a Shakespearean comedy: sadness that appears for a moment to be associated with a parent but then proves to be the result of unrequited love. At the beginning of *As You Like It* Rosalind is thought to be grieving for her banished father but is really pining for the young wrestler she saw (I.iii.1–11 and I.ii.22). So here Benvolio immediately guesses the cause of Romeo's sadness: "In love?" (I.i.165). Romeo in response explodes in a burst of eloquence:

Here's much to do with hate, but more with love.
Why then, O brawling love! O loving hate!

O any thing, of nothing first create!
O heavy lightness, serious vanity,
Misshapen chaos of well-seeming forms,
Feather of lead, bright smoke, cold fire, sick health.   (I.i.175–80)

Romeo sounds like Berowne. He speaks of a profound confusion, but his speech easily masters the confusion with style, with a bravura display of oxymoron. We are once more in the world of comedy, and of one particular comedy, *Love's Labour's Lost*. If *Romeo and Juliet* had remained a comedy there would perhaps have been no need to smash the initial love, here reported, of Romeo for Rosaline. Notice that she has the same name as Berowne's lady. Shakespeare is again wrestling with the problem of brilliant articulateness, with its implicit substitution of form for matter. In *Love's Labour's Lost* this led to the breaking, before our eyes, of the comic happy ending with a narrated death and the strange appearance of a demotic poetry of the seasons that seemed wholly other than the play we had just watched. Here in *Romeo and Juliet* comedy will again be broken, for this play that certainly begins like a comedy will end with a death, not narrated but acted, and so the normal comedic progression from sadness about the inaccessible loved one to eventual union with that same loved one will be aborted. Once more Shakespeare will have to produce from somewhere a new species of dramatic poetry that is not, so to speak, merely brilliant but will convey a feeling of substance. In *Love's Labour's Lost* he performed the operation extraneously, with the song of Winter, un-integrated into the play. In *Romeo and Juliet* he essays the more difficult task of an *integrated* answer to the glitteringly unreal poetry of love offered in the early part of the play. The strong drama that is to transcend the earlier verse is to deal, again, with love. Hence the strange sequence of this tragedy. Instead of suggesting a young man easily infatuated, the erasure of love (1) by love (2) persuades the audience at once that the second love must be real.

There is a curiously similar ploy in E. M. Forster's novel about English people on holiday in Italy, *A Room with a View* (1908). In a way the book is the record of a love affair the author had with a country, with Italy itself. Within the story the characters are made aware of a marvellously different, beautiful world. Near the opening Forster plants Miss Lavish, a garrulous intellectual who chatters insufferably about how important it is to find "the true Italy." As she steers her charge through the narrow streets she cries out joyously, "A smell! A true Florentine smell!" and a moment later eagerly explains that "one doesn't come to Italy for niceness, one comes for life!" Miss Lavish is a figure of fun. But her opinions are Forster's. *He* is hungry to find "the true Italy," *he* thinks "niceness" an inadequate word, *he* loves the very smelliness of Florence and sees it as life. The very rightness of Miss Lavish's views makes it all the clearer in the end that any formal expression of opinion, however accurate, falls hopelessly short of the reality. If Miss Lavish had been guyed in a slightly different way—if, for example, she had said that Florence (with its great austere *palazzi*) was "pretty," the reader would have remained in the comfortable formal world, in which opinion is compared with opinion. As it is Miss Lavish's *rightness,* together with an overwhelming sense of difference when Italy really impinges on the events of the story, leaves the elementary ontological distinctness of reality itself as the only possible ground of the shift we experience.

So with Romeo at the beginning of the play. Like Berowne he is no fool. On the contrary, he speaks brilliantly about the fire and ice of love. His oxymorons, like those employed by Shakespeare in the Prologue, accurately describe the love of Romeo and Juliet, itself an acted oxymoron like lightning in the collied night. Yet Romeo's fine language is blown away like cobwebs, not by a superior analysis of love from a better thinker, but by the actual encounter with Juliet. Shakespeare interestingly makes sure that we never meet Rosaline. Actuality must be reserved for Juliet. This time Shakespeare solves his problem dramaturgically, rather than by the intrusion of a palpably "other" (style-less) style. "Drama" comes from a Greek word meaning "doing" or "action." Shakespeare the dramatist finds that he can answer a verbal description with an actual entrance, can eclipse all previous talk of love by allowing us to see the great love-object of the play. This could be seen as a way of dodging rather than solving the problem of style. The simple dramaturgical move is followed, however, by a successful de-celeration and deepening of poetic style.

Just as mysterious-sadness-in-the-temporarily-frustrated is a mark of Shakespearean comedy, so also is same-sex-solidarity-transcended-by-heterosexual-love. Of all the twentieth century performances of the play it was an Italian production that caught this side of the play more readily than English directors had, perhaps because Italian same-sex camaraderie is played out in the sun-warmed streets while the English experience, above a certain social level, is frigidly confined to memories of sexually segregated boarding schools (but, note, the King in *Love's Labour's Lost* is inventing the English public school system as we watch, with his little celibate academy). Certainly the Italian model is closer to the world of *Romeo and Juliet*. Franco Zeffirelli's 1968 film showed groups of combustible young men, all with a strong sense of style, hanging around on street corners, and this was dead right. The street scene itself is properly comic and goes back to Roman comedy and to Greek new comedy, earlier still.

It was Mercutio who cried out, "Now art thou sociable, now art thou Romeo!" Note the second clause: "Now you are yourself." It is a little stronger, I think, than "Now you are the Romeo we all know—your old self again." The suggestion, pressed by Mercutio, is that the fullest identity is that nourished and perhaps constituted by relationship. Mercutio is Romeo's closest male friend. He is a good fellow and remorselessly opposed, not just humorously we guess, to romantic love. The intensity of his antagonism is so great that it is difficult in the present age to play the part without suggesting homosexual feeling in the background. I believe that this is a mistake, but not a grievous mistake (it will emerge later that I do not exclude the possibility of homosexual feeling in Antonio, in *The Merchant of Venice*). Mercutio is the wittiest person in the play as Berowne was in his, but where Berowne deployed his wit in the service of love and procreation, Mercutio uses his to divide sex from love, disparaging the former and annexing the later as the natural medium of happy male badinage. The incidence of bawdry is higher in the speeches of Mercutio than in those of any other Shakespearean character. This means that by the logic of the plot Mercutio is the antagonist of Juliet. But the play loves them both and they do not hate each other. Although the love of Juliet falls across the adolescent social life of Romeo like a spear of light, it does not destroy Mercutio. Someone else does that: Tybalt.

Tybalt is the strangely frightening figure that interrupted the farcical quarrel of the servants at the beginning of the play. Mercutio calls him "Prince of Cats" and "King of Cats" and "rat-catcher" (II.iv.19, III.i.77, III.i.75), and the language of the play elsewhere reinforces this. Cats scratch, and Tybalt fights "as you sing *prick*-song," with a fencer's sword.

The first syllable of his name suggests "cat."[13] In Act III, Scene i, Tybalt happens upon Mercutio and his friends. Romeo is not present. We already know from his first appearance that Tybalt does not need a reason to kill others. Here he requests a moment of conversation. Mercutio, who can smell evil, asks him why he does not make it "a word and a blow" (III.i.40). Tybalt in reply pretends with savage humour to be like other people to the extent that he needs a reason for striking: "You shall find me apt enough to that, sir, and you will give me occasion" (III.i.41–42). Mercutio rises to the bait, but before the fight can develop Romeo enters, and Tybalt at once loses interest in Mercutio as he concentrates on the new arrival: "Here comes my man" (III.i.56). This time there is no dallying. Instead of seeking an occasion to fight, Tybalt at once provides the standard provocation: "Thou art a villain" (III.i.61). With Mercutio, we may surmise, this would have been enough. Romeo, however, is by this point in the play in love with Juliet, a member of the opposing family, and is eager to make peace. His tameness is too much for Mercutio, who acts according to the same-sex solidarity code: stand by your friend in a fight—even if he won't fight himself. Mercutio and Tybalt cross swords; Romeo intervenes clumsily, and Mercutio is stabbed. He dies joking. Asked if the wound is deep, he answers, " 'Tis not so deep as a well, nor so wide as a church-door, but 'tis enough, 'twill serve" (III. I.96–97). Mercutio as he dies gives us the best of the cat images for Tybalt: "To scratch a man to death!" (III.i.101). With Mercutio there dies a world of youth, spirit, courage, gaiety. When Hotspur (who has something in common with Mercutio) dies in 1 *Henry IV* he says, "O Harry, thou hast robb'd me of my youth!" (V.iv.77). The last words to fall from the mouth of Mercutio are a curse on the two houses, Montague and Capulet. He dies attacking not romantic love but the circumambient a-sexual society of power relations and rivalry. There are two social spaces in the play, that of young male friends gate-crashing parties and that of inter-dynastic rivalry. The spheres intersect of course like circles in a Venn diagram. The feast at which Romeo and Juliet meet is at such a point of overlap; the clash between Mercutio and Tybalt at another. Indeed the tragedy lies in the intersections. Male camaraderie is one counterpoise in the play to the private love-world of Romeo and Juliet, but the sphere of dynastic hatred is the more important, darker counterpoise.

Everything I have said so far is anticipated in the smart verse of the Prologue. The two households have made civility uncivil. But the Prologue also says that, somehow, these same unlovable, unloving families produced two good, naturally loving people who will die before the play is over.

Before the encounter with Tybalt, Mercutio is allowed to imagine the as yet unwritten *Midsummer Night's Dream,* in a long speech that halts the drama in its tracks exactly as an aria halts the action of an opera. We return to the point I raised earlier, in connection with Gertrude's lyrical narrative of the death of Ophelia. It has long been thought proper to sneer at those who in earlier centuries compiled anthologies with titles like "Beauties from Shakespeare" (a fashion started in 1752 by the forger William Dodd). "How crass," it was said, "not to see that speeches in Shakespeare depend at every point upon context and cannot be excerpted without falsification." Yet Mercutio's Queen Mab speech (I.iv.53–94) seems to invite excerption. It is an obvious anthology piece, before anyone has reached for scissors and paste. Of course it does have a context. Romeo has told Mercutio that he has been dreaming, and Mercutio is eager to make fun of the dream, which he fears will be a love dream. His speech is an exercise in minimizing, in making small. One reason why J. R. R. Tolkien used to find *A Midsummer Night's Dream* annoying was its minuscule fairies, untypical of the period.[14] The fairy knights in Spenser's huge poem are as big as the human knights. *A Midsummer Night's Dream* is the play of Peaseblossom, Mustardseed, Cobweb, Moth, and, above all, Moonshine. In Mercutio's speech we find "hazel-nut," "spider web," "gnat," "dream," and "moonshine's wat'ry beams." Berowne in his aria in praise of love found his way to the miniature world when he said, "Love's feeling is more soft and sensible / Than are the tender horns of cockled snails" (*Love's Labour's Lost,* IV.iii.334–35). You must—ever so gently— touch a snail's boneless horn to know what he means. But a chasm yawns between Berowne and Mercutio. Berowne is intent upon the cognitive power of love, its tender sensitivity to what is there. Mercutio is conversely intent on showing the absurdity of love, that it is all illusion. Like Duke Theseus in *A Midsummer Night's Dream* he is a sceptic, but the sudden grossness at the end of his gossamer fantasy when he says that the fairy hag lays maids on their backs to receive lustful men betrays a hostility to the act itself that would never have occurred to Theseus the ravisher of Perigenia, the conqueror of the Amazons.

Yet in the course of the speech Mercutio becomes rapt by beauty, as does the audience. It is as if poetry (which he probably despises) is stronger than he. It is one of the places in Shakespeare that will feed the future, not our time indeed, but the nineteenth century, with its amazing array of fairy painting, reaching its zenith perhaps in the work of the homicidal lunatic Richard Dadd (1817–1886). In the play Mercutio fathers, *A Midsummer Night's Dream,* the question whether the experience of love and of dreams can be considered real is explored more fully. Already the scoffer seems to be falling under the spell of that which, ostensibly, he scorns. As the dramatic action is arrested by the "aria," so Mercutio himself is held in a suspension, immobilized as surely as the Lady is immobilized by the enchantment of Comus in Milton's *Masque.* "Such tricks hath strong imagination," says Theseus (V.i.18). Let us rather say, "Such force hath strong imagination," enough to impinge on the mind with palpable violence even when that mind is hostile.

As the plays succeed one another a certain fluid antinomy keeps forming and re-forming: on one hand glittering, vacuous formalism, on the other reality. Reality, however, has variable paradigms. If one is deluded by academic pretension, like the young men at the beginning of *Love's Labour's Lost,* the appropriate countervailing reality will be sexual love. If one is trapped in a convention of restless badinage so that one is never able to look steadily at anything, the appropriate reality will be perhaps the great negative fact of death; this alone can stop the witticisms. As long as sexual love is seen in physical terms it works unproblematically as an antidote to formalism. If however we decide that the strongest *experience* will provide the most effective antidote, we may think the ecstasy of exalted romantic love a better paradigm of maximal reality than physical coupling. But ecstasy is so special, so momentary, so isolated and isolating from the rest of our experiences (which elsewhere support one another ontologically in a sustaining web of quiet corroboration), that it is open to the charge of being an aberration or a delusion, like a a dream. At the same time the internal character of ecstasy seems to oscillate alarmingly between maximum intensity of experience and an extinction of experience. One feels as one has never felt before and at the same time the experiencing mind is blotted out, one drops into nothingness. That is why "die" became a slang word for "orgasm."

This is the scheme that will grow under Shakespeare's hand as he moves from *Love's Labour's Lost* to *Romeo and Juliet*. Wit will be silenced first by love and then by death as in the comedy, yet the death will no longer be an off-stage reported affair but will be made central to the action, turning the play into a tragedy. Meanwhile love, still the antidote of formalism as it was in *Love's Labour's Lost,* will become an ecstasy that can actually *ally itself with death.*

First Shakespeare must contrive a kind of poetry to express a love that breaks through those conventional patternings he does so well. When Romeo first sees Juliet he is given a speech that expresses not his verbal mastery (though the speech is masterly) but the fact that he is dazzled: "O, she doth teach the torches to burn bright!" (I.v.44). After this they begin to talk and Shakespeare has them play "a set of wit," as lovers do in comedies. But now the epigrammatic surface of the exchange seems fragile and thin. The words are charged with unacknowledged energies. This is done technically by importing religious vocabulary, "shrine," "saint," "pilgrim," "palmer." The dramatist gives us an after-echo of the medieval fusion and confusion of religious language and exalted erotic love. The lover in Chrétien de Troyes kneels outside his lady's room as if before a shrine.[15] Such a description expresses simultaneously profound devotion and hell-brink blasphemy. Thomas Aquinas thought passionate love was a "binding up" of reason, like drunkenness, something that rendered the subject incapable of seeing that God is the primary love-object.[16] Romantic love is thus more dangerous spiritually than cool fornication. Andreas Capellanus, author of a medieval treatise on love, having explained at length how love ennobles the lover, abruptly recants at the end. Chaucer's narrator, at the end of the greatest medieval love story in English, scorns worldly love,[17] and Paolo and Francesca, Dante's courtly lovers, are in hell forever. The great medieval lovers we still remember, Lancelot and Guinevere, Tristan and Isolde, are adulterous, and doomed. By the 1590s the tension has eased, but Shakespeare taps into it here. I have written about the curious innocence of Shakespeare's pre-Reformation imagery, but here the surviving medieval material is itself still laced with a terror that has nothing to do with Elizabethan suppression of Catholicism. When Romeo says, "If I profane . . . this holy shrine," and when the words "saint," "pilgrim," and "holy palmer" turn up in the ensuing dialogue, the simultaneous charge of exalted devotion and extreme danger is still present. The good reader or the good listener knows from these words alone that Romeo and Juliet are doomed. The metaphor from tennis applied to the initial exchanges of lovers in *Love's Labour's Lost* (V.ii.29) works here. Juliet plays back the ball served by Romeo, telling him, modestly, that he does wrong to join talk of palmers who kiss by touching hands to kissing with the lips. Romeo tries weakly to argue, in the manner of Berowne, from warm physical reality: even saints *have* lips, but Juliet's reply sharpens our sense of the obstinate difference between religion and romantic love: saints have lips indeed but use them to pray, not to kiss and flirt. It is as if Juliet understands the dread behind the language Romeo would use lightly. His assumed modern nonchalance is in any case false to the strength of what he now feels. Juliet is suddenly still and allows the kiss. Romeo says urgently, "From my lips, by thine, my sin is purg'd" (I.v.107), and she says, with a completeness of submission he cannot yet comprehend, "Then have my lips the sin that they have took." Romeo sounds still like a Renaissance suitor; Juliet sounds like Guinevere or Isolde. When Romeo kisses her again, too casually, she says (it is like Rosaline to Berowne, but charged now with imminent tragedy), "You kiss by th' book" (I.v.110). Shakespeare has interwoven Renaissance lovers' raillery with a darker, more intense register, medieval in origin. The second more and more displaces the first as the conversation develops, Juliet being the one to revive the ancient fear. We know by the end of the exchange that we are no longer in the world of elegant flirtation. Juliet has led Romeo into the otherness of real love.

We must grant that the play does not keep up the medieval idea of love as inextricably entwined with sin and hell. The love of Romeo and Juliet is not adulterous; on the contrary, they marry, validly. The two people named in the title of the play are clearly good, though those named in Shakespeare's other two-person titles, *Antony and Cleopatra* and *Troilus and Cressida,* may not be. But the elementary fusion of ecstasy with terror immanent in the older literature works on in all that follows, for die they must.

There is a marvellous moment in the balcony scene when Juliet says,

Fain would I *dwell on form,* fain, fain deny
What I have spoke, but farewell compliment!
Dost thou love me?   (II.ii.88–90)

This is a poignant valediction to form, made by one overwhelmed by form's opposite, reality. There is a pathos in the loss of adolescent flirtation, and there is fear in the movement from acceptable convention to truth, but with all this there is great joy and wonder. The immense simplicity of "Dost thou love me?"—what she actually wants to know—contrasts absolutely with the earlier tropes of persuasion. Juliet knows the full reality of love sooner than Romeo and, more realistic than he as to its place in the world, senses that it will all go wrong. Their love is too like lightning by night, gone before it can be named (II.ii.119).

I have said that Shakespeare, like Forster centuries later, makes reality succeed and transcend the formal description of that reality, that the only difference between love as it is described by Romeo when he talks of Rosaline and love as it happens afterwards with Juliet is that the second is actual, real. It will be said that the whole play, not just the early witty part, is made of words and words are formal entities; the songs of Spring and Winter in *Love's Labour's Lost* are themselves poetic exercises in real-*ism*, not extra-verbal reality. The love dialogue of Romeo and Juliet from beginning to end is made of words, and yet we do not want to say that it is "merely verbal." Because language can engage a reality other than itself, it can send the mind directly to the object. The person who asks, "Where is the post office?" hears a series of formal expressions a result of which, five minutes later, she arrives at the post office. The Post-Structuralist urge to suggest that we are somehow *confined* within an insulated world of pure form or textuality rested often on a naive appeal to the fact, long familiar, that words are not things. The underlying simple error can be illustrated by the following dialogue (where *A* is a Post-Structuralist):

A. How many things have you in your right trouser pocket?
B. Three, a key, a telephone, and a handkerchief.
A. *(triumphantly)* But "key," "telephone," and "handkerchief" are words, not things; you have nothing in your pocket!

It remains true, however, that both Shakespeare and Forster are purveyors of fiction. Neither can ever, as long as we continue to watch the play, read the novel, give us an "extra-verbal reality" in the literal sense. It is within the circumambient fiction that the love of Romeo and Juliet is presented as actual. But this *is* something that fiction can do. It is not a con or a cheat. It is indeed a "reality-effect," but such effects are adequately produced only by artists who are willing and able to attend closely to the real world. Such attention enables them to present not indeed specific persons or things but real possibilities, things that in Aristotle's phrase, "would happen" (*Poetics*, 1451a37). At the level of language, for language persists of course throughout the play, what happens is an over-riding of linguistic self-consciousness by an urgency of reference so great that we no longer notice the elegance of the expression, though literary analysis may afterwards reveal great complexity in the material. That is why I used the terms "transparent" and "window" of the songs at the end of *Love's Labour's Lost*. It might be supposed that the only way to make sure of this reality-effect would be to write in the plainest of plain prose. Later Daniel Defoe will lodge his huge reality-effect, the start of the modern novel, by writing apparently without "point," without figurative brilliance. Shakespeare instead moves into heightened lyric poetry at exactly this point. Complex poetic utterance is not fundamentally at odds with experience but can take us unawares, have force, because of its unusually close involvement with experience. When Juliet thinks that Romeo has gone she says,

> O, for a falc'ner's voice,
> To lure this tassel-gentle back again!
> Bondage is hoarse, and may not speak aloud,
> Else would I tear the cave where Echo lies,
> And make her airy tongue more hoarse than mine,
> With repetition of my Romeo's name.   (II.ii.158–63)

This is Shakespearean lyric poetry at its height, and it is certainly not simple. The fierce imagery of taming a hawk that lurks behind Petruchio's breaking of Katherina in *The Taming of the Shrew* is reversed. Juliet is the falconer, Romeo the bird to be caged. The hint of a clash of wills is one of the things that prevents this love story from becoming too saccharine-sweet. Elsewhere we find more "gender-reversal": impatience for the wedding night belongs conventionally to the male lover, but in this play it is given to Juliet (II.v.1–78, III.ii.1–13). Meanwhile her speech is actually about not being able to speak. Juliet desires a huge voice to proclaim

Romeo's name but is gagged by the politics of Verona, the mutual hatred of Montagues and Capulets. As she expresses the pain of being reduced at such a time to a hoarse whisper, the inner splendour of metaphoric utterance suddenly breaks free, with language adequate to the magnitude of the love expressed. If Ovid was the evil genius of *Titus Andronicus,* he is the good genius of these lines. Juliet's words recall the third book of the *Metamorphoses,* in which Narcissus falls in love with a reflection of himself and the nymph Echo, who loved Narcissus, becomes in her turn a mere auditory reflection, a bodiless voice, "echo" with a small "e": *solis ex illo vivit in antris,* "From that time on she lived in lonely caves" (iii.394). The movement of Juliet's thought is audacious. As she longs for a great voice to burst forth, the cave where Echo dwells seems to turn into the human throat, which, with the violence we glimpsed in the imagery from falconry ("kill thee with much cherishing," II.ii.183), she would tear open to release the loved name clamorously to the winds, over and over. There is an obstinate incongruity meanwhile in the idea of tearing rock, an incongruity eloquent of that frustration that is the theme of the speech. Frustration is the running theme in Ovid's story of Narcissus and Echo. One tears fabric or human flesh more easily than one tears stone. Yet Juliet's love is so great she feels she might do even this. The bondage of Verona is played against the freedom of air, the dark constriction of the dramatic action against the liberty of myth, with extraordinary poignancy. The sense that the cave where Echo lies is far away exerts its own strange force in the speech. It is formally admirable, but we are not detained by the formal beauty. The expression is both complex and powerfully human. I know no writing better than this.

Act III, Scene ii, opens with Juliet's soliloquy: "Gallop apace, ye fiery-footed steeds." Remember, in Marlowe's *Doctor Faustus,* the line, *O lente, lente, currite noctis equi* ("Oh slowly, slowly run, ye horses of the night"). Faustus wants time to stand still because he stands on the brink of hell. The words he uses come from another world, one full of delight, from Ovid's *Amores* (I.xiii.40). The man who said this first wished to stop time for a very different reason; he wanted his night of love to be prolonged indefinitely. The effect in Marlowe of the wrenching of the line to a new meaning is marvellous. In *Romeo and Juliet* we have a second wrenching, less violent but equally marvellous. Juliet reverses the usual lovers' logic; instead of asking time to stand still she asks him to hurry—but for a lover's reason, to bring Romeo to her the sooner. Nevertheless, as in Marlowe but less obviously, the thought is darkened by the idea of imminent death, hinted rather than expressed. Juliet was from the first the realist; she saw that their love was dangerous and likely to end dreadfully. Her fear now finds expression not at the rational level of inference and hypothesis but inadvertently, through her imagery.

Earlier Romeo had cried out that Juliet taught the torches to burn bright. There it is the love that blazes and the surrounding cruel world is alone dark. Now, in this speech of initially joyful desire, the absolute contrast between shining love and its murky opposition gives place to a strange intertwining:

Spread thy close curtain, love-performing night,
That th' runaway's eyes may wink, and Romeo
Leap to these arms untalk'd of and unseen!
Lovers can see to do their amorous rites
By their own beauties, or, if love be blind,
It best agrees with night. Come, civil night,
Thou sober-suited matron all in black,
And learn me how to lose a winning match,
Play'd for a pair of stainless maidenhoods.
Hood my un-mann'd blood, bating in my cheeks,
With thy black mantle, till strange love grow bold,
Think true love acted simple modesty.
Come, night, come, Romeo, come, thou day in night,
For thou wilt lie upon the wings of night,
Whiter than new snow upon a raven's back.
Come, gentle night, come, loving, black-brow'd night,
Give me my Romeo, and, when I shall die,
Take him and cut him out in little stars,
And he will make the face of heaven so fine
That all the world will be in love with night,
And pay no worship to the garish sun.   (III.ii.5–25)

She asks first for darkness, to favour their secret amorous enterprise. "Runaways" is notoriously unexplained. I suspect that thought has been telescoped: "That-those-on-the-lookout-for-fugitives may shut their eyes and miss what is going on." I can offer no Elizabethan parallel for "runaways" in the sense needed, "runaway police" (we have the idiom, "the vice" for "vice squad"). Then we have the lovers as light against dark, though here a furtive light, shining as it were under the bed-clothes. This, the standard contrast, melts at once, on an "or" conjunction, into a strange allying of love with darkness; "It best agrees with night." "Come, night, come, Romeo, come, thou day in night" performs the same operation in reverse. The sentence begins by suggesting that Romeo and the night are not opposites but identical, but then the original contrast is reasserted with "day in night." Romeo is white snow, contrasting with the black plumage of the raven, but the imagery of snow on a beating wing propels the mind into the thought of that snow blowing away or melting into the feathers. When Romeo is re-imagined as star-light the original contrast may seem to have been recovered, but it is now subtly qualified; star-light is not ordinary light; it is a kind of counter-light, itself contrasted with the sun. *A Midsummer Night's Dream,* a play closely linked to *Romeo and Juliet,* is lit for much of its length by a counter-light, the moon. When Juliet calls softly, "come, loving, black-brow'd night" we may shiver; here night is addressed as the lover, as if he has somehow displaced Romeo. This slow, lyrical entangling of the initially opposed terms is prophetic, for this is a tragedy of love in death and death in love.

I have said that Juliet, the realist, knows that their love is dangerous because of the society in which they live. Here, however, the danger seems to be different, as if it were internal to the very intensity of the love itself. The hawk imagery returns (you "hood" a hawk, and in protest, it "bates"—that is, "beats" its wings), but it is now applied not to the male lover but to Juliet's desire. "Blood" means "sexual desire" and "unmann'd" means "lacking a man to satisfy it." When Juliet speaks of the blood fluttering in her cheeks she echoes the language of the almost bawdy nurse who said, when Juliet told her that Romeo was waiting for her at Friar Lawrence's cell, "Now comes the wanton blood up in your cheeks" (II.v.70). Juliet imagines winning by yielding, unfamiliar love becoming erotically adventurous. There is a streak of humour here as there was earlier when she imagined night as a "sober-suited matron" (chaperone, or bawd?), but there is I think no irony in "true love acted simple modesty." The physical reference of these lines is startling. Juliet is as earthy as Mercutio, but what is matter for satire to him is serious to her.

It may be said that "loving, black-brow'd night" need not imply that darkness is seen as a lover; it may mean only that darkness favours their love. But there is no doubt that the full, black meaning is present when Juliet reacts to the news of Tybalt's death and Romeo's banishment: "Death, not Romeo, take my maidenhead!" (III.ii.137). The idea goes on growing. In Act III, Scene v, lines 55–57, Juliet's clairvoyant imagination conjures a picture of her lover as himself a bloodless dead man. When Romeo is told (falsely) that Juliet is dead we have the grim necrophilia of "Well, Juliet, I will lie with thee to-night" (V.i.34). When he enters the tomb and finds Juliet, as he thinks, dead, her beautiful face seems flushed, as by sexual fulfilment (orgasm as death). The nurse's words about blood wantoning in Juliet's cheek live on and acquire tragic power:

> beauty's ensign yet
> Is crimson in thy lips and in thy cheeks
> .   .   .   .
> Shall I believe
> That unsubstantial Death is amorous,
> And that the lean abhorred monster keeps
> Thee here in dark to be his paramour?   (V.iii.94–95, 101–5)

Romeo and death have changed places in the dark. In later comedies (*All's Well That Ends Well, Measure for Measure*) we have the device known as "the bed-trick" whereby one person takes the place of another in bed, as part of an erotic intrigue. In *Measure for Measure* the substitution is arranged by a duke disguised as a friar, and in *Romeo and Juliet* Friar Lawrence plays a similar role. Here, before the comedies, Death works his own bed-trick on Romeo and Juliet. His is the eucatastrophe—he gets the girl—ours the tragedy. Romeo kills himself, which is as much as to say, Death takes him too. Juliet, whose apparent death by a stratagem of the pharmaceutically skilled Friar Lawrence has begun to loosen its grip, sees Romeo dead and determines to turn her pretence into fact; she too will really die. Now we are moving rapidly towards the tragic conclusion of this potential comedy. She dies by thrusting Romeo's dagger into her heart. Her language is sexual: "O happy dagger, / This is thy sheath; there rust, and let me die" (V.iii.169–70). The Latin for "sheath" is *vagina*.

Perhaps in this play imagination outruns intellect. The apparent wildness of the love-death intertwining may be empirically rooted in the poet's attentiveness to the psychology of ecstasy, to its mysterious fusion of consciousness heightened with consciousness eclipsed. But as the play unfolds this paradox assumes a nightmare, active form. The figurative becomes actual. The happy "death" of orgasm becomes Juliet bleeding on Romeo's dagger in an underground room. The play dramatizes a shocking instability. Shakespeare had good reason to start his play in the manner of a comedy, because this is a story that ought to end in happiness. The properly comedic structure swings dizzily out of control. The texture of real historical causation was brilliantly analysed as subject to irrational acceleration in the garden scene in *I Henry VI*; in *Romeo and Juliet* causation seems instead to be supernaturally threatened. It is a firm law of drama and story that predictions are fulfilled. In *Romeo and Juliet* the predictions are left in suspension, strangely at odds with the event. Romeo's presentiment of an evil "consequence yet hanging in the stars" (I.iv.107) is followed by the joyful meeting with Juliet. In Act V, Scene i, lines 1–10, Romeo tells how he dreamed that Juliet came and found him dead but then revived him with a kiss (the "Sleeping Beauty," with the sexes transposed). This vision of joy is immediately followed by the horrible death of both lovers. It is not so much that the predictions are pathetically wrong as that they combine rightness and wrongness in a way that is deeply disturbing. Romeo was wrong if he thought that gate-crashing the Capulets' party would prove a disaster, but he was right about the remoter consequence. In Act V he is wrong when he says he will be brought back to life by Juliet and made an emperor of love, but the mental picture of Juliet finding him dead is uncannily accurate. We sense that he is seeing something real, but it belongs in one of those almost-but-not-quite-parallel universes postulated by speculative physicists like David Deutsch. Or else Romeo can see, what we will never see, the romance comedy of Romeo and Juliet, the other, unwritten play.

This, then, is a wild play, a fantasia on the thought: "It might have been different." The fire and ice of the climax has never been matched, not even by the ecstasy poems of the dying Keats, not even by Richard Wagner's *Tristan und Isolde*. Yet this wildness is joined to human sympathy. The most heart-rending moment in the play is not the ending but Juliet's words in Act III:

Wilt thou be gone? it is not yet near day.
It was the nightingale, and not the lark,
That pierc'd the fearful hollow of thine ear;
Nightly she sings on yond pomegranate tree.
Believe me, love, it was the nightingale.   (III.v.1–5)

This scene is Shakespeare's aubade, his poem of dawn breaking on lovers after their night together. We saw earlier how Ovid's line *O lente, lente currite noctis equi* set in motion the trope of the lover asking time to stand still and how Marlowe made it tragic by placing it in the mouth of one going down into hell, and then how Shakespeare changed it again in "Gallop apace, ye fiery-footed steeds" to a lover's wish that, after all, time could run faster. Now the central, original idea is restored. Juliet wants the night to go on forever. Meanwhile the ordinary realism of the scene is strong. One can almost smell the air at the open window, see the lightening sky. They both know by this time that Romeo is a banished man and must leave Verona. What makes the lines so touching is that they are given to Juliet, the *realist*. Juliet was always the one whose feet were on the ground, who saw things steadily. Here in an excess of love she reels. This wilful false presentiment, the nightingale replacing the lark, has nothing of the spooky quality of the other mis-predictions in the play. It is luminously human, wholly understandable. This is the saddest play of them all.

The Ontology of Moonshine: *A Midsummer Night's Dream*

If we have the chronology right, *Love's Labour's Lost* fed into *Romeo and Juliet* and *Romeo and Juliet* feeds into *A Midsummer Night's Dream*. Both *Romeo and Juliet* and *A Midsummer Night's Dream* seem to belong to the period 1595–96, and I have admitted that it is impossible to prove that either play preceded the other. That certain strands link the two plays is indisputable. It has long been noticed that the play of Pyramus and Thisby put on by the mechanicals is a parody of *Romeo and Juliet*. I have described this as the saddest of his plays. Shakespeare saw that it has its funny side. It would surely be very odd indeed if the parody came before the tragedy. It by no means follows that Shakespeare came to despise *Romeo and Juliet*, as coarse reasoners infer. Lysander's lines on love-choices,

Brief as the lightning in the collied night
That, in a spleen, unfolds both heaven and earth;
And ere a man hath power to say "Behold!"
The jaws of darkness do devour it up:
So quick bright things come to confusion (I.i.145–49)

are as good a description of *Romeo and Juliet* as could well be done in five
lines. As the character discourses on love the playwright seizes on the
problem of celerity in the earlier tragedy, the difficulty felt first and most
acutely in *Love's Labour's Lost* of being able only to run, never to walk. In
Romeo and Juliet he turned a naturally comedic swiftness into a dark
urgency: "Gallop apace, ye fiery-footed steeds" becomes the proper emblem for a tragedy of brief luminescence. The word "dream" occurs
frequently in *Romeo and Juliet*. Mercutio used the word seven times in his
Queen Mab speech, and the speech itself was a response to Romeo's
phrase, "*Dream* things true" (I.iv.52). Mercutio pours scorn on love, but
that need not mean that the tragedy is satirizing the comedy it evokes.
This, if true, would provide a counter-argument in favour of the priority
in time of *A Midsummer Night's Dream*: if the satiric force of "Pyramus and
Thisby" suggests that the comedy is the later work, by exactly the same
reasoning the satiric force of Mercutio's speech suggests contrariwise that
the comedy must be the earlier of the two plays. The case is weaker than it
sounds. Mercutio may be against love, but when his imagination carries
him over the threshold of the fairy world, the tone ceases to be satirical.
Enchantment prevails. All this makes excellent sense if Shakespeare was at
the time working towards rather than away from the comedy of magic
and moonlight.

   If we set the two plays side by side it might be thought that *Romeo and
Juliet,* dealing as it does with the unpalatable truth of death, is intellectually the heavy-weight work, while *A Midsummer Night's Dream* is an
escapist, gossamer affair. In fact the opposite is true. It is in *Romeo and Juliet*
that wild imagination outruns intellect. *A Midsummer Night's Dream* is not
escapist; it is about escapism. The problematic status of ecstatic love as a
reality counter to formalism is lost when we are drawn into the black
vertigo at the end of *Romeo and Juliet*. In *A Midsummer Night's Dream* the
philosophic scrutiny of the status of love-experience is maintained to the

end of the comedy. Intellect is never eclipsed, though it may be led into strange places. It is important to listen when women are talking. But it is hard to do this when the men make so much noise. Everyone knows Duke Theseus's speech on imagination:

> I never may believe
> These antic fables, nor these fairy toys.
> Lovers and madmen have such seething brains,
> Such shaping fantasies, that apprehend
> More than cool reason ever comprehends.
> The lunatic, the lover, and the poet
> Are of imagination all compact.
> One sees more devils than vast hell can hold;
> That is the madman. The lover, all as frantic,
> Sees Helen's beauty in a brow of Egypt.
> The poet's eye, in a fine frenzy rolling,
> Doth glance from heaven to earth, from earth to heaven;
> And as imagination bodies forth
> The forms of things unknown, the poet's pen
> Turns them to shapes, and gives to aery nothing
> A local habitation and a name.
> Such tricks hath strong imagination,
> That if it would but apprehend some joy,
> It comprehends some bringer of that joy;
> Or in the night, imagining some fear,
> How easy is a bush suppos'd a bear! (V.i.2–22)

Like Mercutio's Queen Mab speech, this is natural game for the anthologist and has indeed been endlessly excerpted. Although I grant that the speech actively invites such treatment, this time, I want to resist the invitation, to insist on the modifying effect of its context, within the action of the play. Who is Theseus? He is, mythically, the same man we meet in Racine's black tragedy *Phèdre,* the brutal womanizer Thésée. I suggested in chapter 1 that it is a mistake to suppose that the darker side of the mythical material has been excluded from the play. Rather, the comedy makes us aware of the process of exclusion. I drew attention to

Shakespeare's retaining in his happy comedy reference to Theseus's rape of Perigenia (II.i.78), and I found a surviving touch of the sexual bully of the myth in his opening line to his new lady love: "Hippolyta, I woo'd thee with my sword" (I.i.16). The speech continues, "And won thy love doing thee injuries," where the reference is to the war against the Amazon women. This is followed swiftly of course by the switch into a happier key, but what is interesting is the way the domineering tone continues, in the supposedly antithetical second half of the speech. Where we might have expected "But I will wed thee in another key, / And humbly sue to earn thy love at last," we actually get "But I will wed thee in another key, / With pomp, with triumph, and with revelling." Theseus can't stop strutting. He is characterized from the beginning as owning a sort of insensitivity that is perhaps peculiar to males. That is why it is important to listen carefully to any woman who is present when he speaks, even if that woman doesn't make it into the anthologies.

Here, when Theseus airs his views on imagination, the woman present is Hippolyta, and it soon appears that she is at least twice as intelligent as he. Before Theseus launches himself into his eloquent diatribe, Hippolyta, looking back on the adventures of the night that we have all been watching, says, very reasonably, " 'Tis strange, my Theseus, that these lovers speak of" (V.i.1). Theseus at once cuts her down to size: "More strange than true." He takes charge of her mind with "true," a teacher's word, or supposes that he has done so. The first thing to say is that there is a sense in which Theseus is absolutely wrong. He says that the account Hippolyta has heard of magic and transformation in the night is all illusion; they have imagined all this, and imagination is the mother of error. We meanwhile have *seen* Puck drop the love-juice, by mistake, on Lysander's eyes, and we have seen how well it worked. We have also *seen* Bottom turned into an ass. We understand these things as firmly as we understand that Theseus is a great man, about to marry Hippolyta. Of course if Theseus were to step out of the fiction and sit beside us in the theatre, the status of his observations would be higher. He would then be saying, with some plausibility, that plays like *A Midsummer Night's Dream* are idle fantasies, utterly unreal. In fact I am sure that some such overspill into the extra-dramatic realm is foreseen by Shakespeare, and he relies upon its giving a general force to Theseus's words. But, equally, there is a sense in which the play makes a fool of him. He is ill-attuned to the situation in which he finds himself and quite unable to deal with it. Graham Bradshaw observes that Theseus's disparagement of lovers is un-gallant, given the circumstance of his impending marriage to Hippolyta.[18] It may be said that audiences never notice this, but a good director can make sure that they do. All that is needed is a pause in the flow of the speech, something to make us look at Hippolyta, and a wry smile from her. Theseus is gauche, and *gaucherie* is a form of stupidity. Hippolyta's reply is far from stupid:

But all the story of the night told over,
And all their minds transfigur'd so together,
More witnesseth than fancy's images
And grows to something of great constancy;
But howsoever, strange and admirable. (V.i.23–27)

Hippolyta's mind is focused on the question, "What makes us decide that an account is true?" At one level she thinks like a police detective (a role Theseus might have relished); if the witnesses separately tell stories that form a consistent whole, they are likely to be telling the truth. She is also thinking philosophically: we disparage something as mere fancy when it is unsupported by other elements in our experience or common discourse. Its isolation proclaims it "merely subjective." Things count as true, on the other hand, when they interlock with innumerable other elements. The important word in Hippolyta's speech is "constancy." It means "consistency" or "coherence." Indeed she is on the brink of articulating what will be known in the twentieth century as "the coherence theory of truth." The twentieth century saw an extended intellectual war between two theories of truth, the correspondence theory, which says a statement is true if it corresponds with a certain fact, and the coherence theory, which says a statement is true if it can be "verified"—in the sense, "shown to be harmonious"—with the larger belief system (in practice, the other statements we make). The present state of play seems to be that the correspondence theory is in deep trouble because of the difficulty of giving an account of the "fact" to which the true sentence is supposed to correspond without simply repeating the original sentence; the postulated isomorphic relation between fact and statement cannot be demonstrated. The coherence theory, however, is not without its own troubles. Even if we give a strong sense to "verify," the theory founders on the fact that we can all see how a statement that none of us, as it happens, can verify *could* be true. Clearly there is unfinished business here. I ought to come clean here and admit that I think the correspondence theory as stated by Aristotle and Alfred Tarski the better of the two. "The cow is in the meadow" is true if the cow *is* in the meadow—never mind verification, "the right to know," or harmony with the world-view of the human species; it is as elementary as that.[19] It may be said that I have done the absurd thing; I have merely repeated the original sentence, "The cow is in the meadow." But in this version no attempt is made to trace the intricacies of correspondence, the connection of the cog-wheels. Instead, the inverted commas are simply removed and the truth is what is then asserted, seamlessly and immediately. Hippolyta is leaning in the other direction, towards coherence theory. She is thinking about the way, in practice, we do trust propositions that cohere with other propositions. What is remarkable is how, having effortlessly outdistanced her stick of a fiancé, she checks her own thought: "But howsoever, strange and admirable." She is saying, "Although I have stressed the consistency of these accounts and urged that this consistency could ripen into truth status, I don't want to deny that the events of the night, seen now not as internally related to one another but as a whole, are utterly strange, a matter for wonder." Her alpha brain seizes first the factor of coherence and then, with regard to the larger context, incoherence (as if she were kindly sketching a possible reply for Theseus, within coherence theory). Once more we sense unfinished business. But philosophy is like that. Gilbert Ryle once observed that it is a fiction encouraged by historians of ideas that philosophers have certain doctrines or tenets; real philosophers think continuously, and the "tenets" in the history books are obtained by artificially arresting the process of their thought.[20]

The word "imagination" was normally a pejorative term when Shakespeare wrote *A Midsummer Night's Dream*. The word "imaginary" even today is the natural antithesis of "true." As late as 1759 Samuel Johnson could entitle a chapter of *Rasselas*, "The Dangerous Prevalence of Imagination." Yet for the Romantics it is a term to be revered. The curious thing is that it is this play that gives the Romantics the notion they need: imagination as a glowing reality. Theseus is given star billing and his speech is a stylistic fanfare, but his reductive doctrine is swept away by the play itself.

Note that Hippolyta is willing to give low status to what she calls "fancy's images." There is a possible defence of the reality of these that is in a way trivial. Dorothy Emmett points out briskly that dreams and mental images are unreal in terms of their content—that is, if I dream that there is a badger in the refrigerator this is unreal because there is nothing in the refrigerator but stale croissants—but real in that people actually have fancies, do dream: I really did have that vivid dream about the badger.[21] By this simple argument "fancy's images" are obviously real; lies and misleading testimony are also real in exactly the same sense. But that is not what Hippolyta is after. She is seeking a reality of *content* in dream, poetry, and love-experience. In the eighteenth century the empiricist David Hume thought perceptions could be distinguished from mere mental images by their "vivacity." One might add, "And by their consistency with other perceptions." It is not wholly absurd to consider Hippolyta as addressing the unborn Hume, across the centuries, empiricist to empiricist. The strong Historicist will explode at this point and say, "Damn it, it *is* absurd!" But conceptual affinity is not the same thing as immediate influence. Hippolyta and Hume are thinking about the same problem in oddly similar terms. She says to him, "What are we to do when by *your* criterion, vivacity, the dream suddenly registers a high score—especially when that dream is shared by several persons? It is still palpably distinct, I grant, from the grey world of perceptions as generally accepted, but by empirical criteria could it be assuming the status of a secondary reality?" Hippolyta has sketched a dual (not a dualist) ontology: two real worlds, one of the day, the other of the night. This is symbolized in the imagery of the play as two great light-bearing bodies, the sun and the moon. The fluid, feminine moon with her menstrual phases will never dominate as the sun does, but she is there. She may seem weak: she "looks with a wat'ry eye" (III.i.198), but she is to be feared: "Therefore the moon (the governess of floods) /Pale in her anger, washes all the air" (II.i.103–4).

Throughout the dialogue of Theseus and Hippolyta Shakespeare is still worrying about *Romeo and Juliet*. There love experienced was the first principal counter to the formalism that began to frighten him in *Love's Labour's Lost*. But if love is made of illusion, as Theseus maintains, can that structure stand? Convention should be opposed by reality, not delusion. In *Romeo and Juliet* Shakespeare chose, as we saw, to answer formal eloquence not with plain prose but with a more powerful, deeper lyricism. Poetry, like love-experience, is made to bear the weight of a corrective truth. The poetry and the love of Romeo and Juliet are fused; there is a sense in which such heightened experience cannot be conveyed in plain prose; it just isn't up to the job. We might still wish to say, in the manner of Dorothy Emmett, "All we need grant is that young people have these feelings and poetic language describes them most effectively." Again, however, Emmett's terms fail to meet the case. Her formulation brushes aside the intuition—or creation—of *value* in the story of the lovers. They by the end have known (strong, cognitive word) a kind of goodness that others are the poorer for never having known. Take away the love of Romeo and Juliet from the sum of things and the world is less than it was before, *absolutely* reduced. Or are we kidding ourselves? Shakespeare, I submit, is *thinking*.

Theseus and Hippolyta are the up-market, upper-class, obviously well-educated figures of the play. Facing them are the mechanicals, Bottom the weaver and his friends, who put on the play of Pyramus and Thisby (itself as we saw an accelerated parody of *Romeo and Juliet*) to entertain the grand persons and perhaps make a bob or two. It is odd that the epithet "literal-minded" seems to apply to Theseus and then, having flipped over, to the mechanicals. Theseus is literal-minded in the sense that he restricts reality to ordinary language and experience and absolutely denies it to lyric poetry and heightened love-experience. The mechanicals are literal-minded because they, contrariwise, extend full reality status to the most absurd fictions. There is great anxiety among them that Snug the joiner should explain to the ladies that he is Snug the joiner, because, if he doesn't, the ladies will be terrified by the lion he presents (III.i.27). These "hard-handed men" (V.i.72) are worrying about the ladies because *they* find the lion seriously scary. Of the two modes of literal-mindedness, that of the mechanicals is the more lovable. Their error is generous, Theseus's ungenerous. It is clear, however, that some dividing line must be drawn between the poetic experience and the un-poetic, as Hippolyta saw.

Bottom himself is loved by all. When he turns up for the rehearsal, his companions greet him with unfeigned joy. Harold Bloom admirably observes that if Bottom were turned into a beetle like Franz Kafka's Gregor Samsa, his good humour would be unbroken. He is unthinkingly, happily fearless. His being changed into an ass doesn't faze him in the slightest degree. His best friend, however, could not describe Bottom as clever. Yet Shakespeare gives him the most profound speech in the play:[22]

I have had a most rare vision. I have had a dream, past the wit of man to say what dream it was. Man is but an ass, if he go about t' expound this dream. Methought I was—there is no man can tell what. Methought I was, and methought I had—but man is but a patch'd fool, if he will offer to say what methought I had. The eye of man hath not heard, the ear of man hath not seen, man's hand is not able to taste, his tongue to conceive, nor his heart to report, what my dream was. I will get Peter Quince to write a ballet of this dream. It shall be call'd "Bottom's Dream," because it hath no bottom.

(IV.i.204–19)

We laugh at Bottom's "misplacings," yet they have a resonance that is not ridiculous but haunting. The sentence beginning "The eye of man" is an echo of 1 Corinthians 2:9: "The things which eye hath not seen, neither ear hath heard, neither came into man's heart, are, which God hath prepared for them that love him" (Geneva Bible). In the preceding chapter St. Paul has said that the wisdom of the world is foolishness and that the foolish things of the world confound the wise—and that God is behind this work of confounding. Erasmus cites the words Bottom so happily mangles, at the end of his *Praise of Folly*. This is a work that makes the reader dizzy by placing the praise of folly in the mouth of a figure called Folly. This may be thought a paradox easily resolved, since if Folly praises folly obviously the wise will despise folly—and we are back to common sense. This brisk resolution of the problem loses its force when we encounter Paul's huge scorn of worldly values and intellection. At one level Bottom's hilarious confusion of ear and heart makes nonsense of the Pauline thesis; at another level it deepens it. Paul is striving to lead our minds to a place where the ordinary categories no longer apply. Bottom's wild synaesthesia enforces the idea of a reality beyond categories.

Scholars have long been aware that when Bottom says, "It shall be call'd 'Bottom's Dream,' because it hath no bottom," Shakespeare is playing ingeniously upon an old chestnut of the grammarians, *lucus a non lucendo,* "A *lucus* ('wood') is so called because it has no *lux* ('light')."[23] The simplicity of Bottom is set in counterpoint with the dotty ingenuity of people as different from Bottom as anyone can be, the learned pedants. The schoolmaster Holofernes' eye would brighten as heard the phrase, for the *lucus a non lucendo* point is made by Priscian, a favourite of his (*Love's Labour's Lost,* V.i.27–28).[24] The latent Latin phrase is more potently relevant than is generally realized. *A Midsummer Night's Dream* is a "transposed pastoral." It is pastoral because, like *As You Like It,* it sends its courtly persons to a wild place where they can be re-educated before returning to the court. It is "transposed" because this green world has itself been subjected to a transformation. Shakespeare, in this lunar comedy, has darkened pastoral. Instead of the sunny forest of Arden we have, precisely, a wood without light, a *lucus a non lucendo.* With the last sentence of Bottom's speech many things happen at once. First, he crazily names his experience according to the one thing it lacks—bottom, bedrock. Second, as he does so, the very craziness evokes a parallel craziness joyously discerned in language by dusty grammarians. Third, Bottom knows, better even than Hippolyta, that his dream is unfathomable. His speech is indeed the most profound in the play.

I suggested earlier that *A Midsummer Night's Dream* poses a question. Is this a play in which the demons of myth have been charmed out of existence, a work of pure innocence and felicity, or is it a play in which the exorcism is still perceptible as a process within the drama we watch? The mythological groundwork of the play led us back to the story of Theseus the brutal womanizer. It also takes us back to Pasiphae, who coupled with a bull. Pasiphae is never mentioned by Shakespeare, but she is, so to speak, within earshot. In Greek legend she is the mother of Theseus's bride. She became enamoured of Zeus when he assumed the form of a bull, and she asked Hephaestus to make a wooden cow. The cow deceived the bull-god, who eagerly mounted it and unknowingly impregnated Pasiphae, straddling inside. It is the grossest of the Greek myths. Even Ovid shrank from telling the story explicitly (*Metamorphoses,* viii.132). As a result of this bestial-divine lust Pasiphae gave birth to a monster, the Minotaur, part beast, part man, who lived at the centre of the Cretan Labyrinth. In

Shakespeare's play the bride of Theseus appears on stage and so does Bottom the weaver. Bottom is turned not into a bull but into an ass. Here Shakespeare is drawing not on Greek myth but on a classical "novel," *The Golden Ass* of Apuleius, and it may be supposed that the atmosphere lightens accordingly. Indeed it lightens, but not so much as we might expect. In Apuleius we meet a matron who lusts after the main character, Lucius, *after* he has been turned into an ass. I referred earlier to the fear of physical violation expressed by Lucius. It is time to look more closely at the way all this shows still in the play. When Lucius fears that his huge member will hurt the matron, *he* alludes to the story of Pasiphae.[25] The profound innocence of Bottom the weaver defuses this material. Although he has been transformed into a beast and Titania is in love with him, Bottom, like a small boy, seems hardly to notice that a beautiful woman is climbing all over him and is more interested in the cakes and sweets (and in hay, as he proceeds more deeply into donkeyhood). So has the murky classical story no place in this happy play? I have granted that Shakespeare entirely suppresses the bestial coupling. Yet he makes us feel the contrast between the creamy softness of Titania and the harsh, hirsute ass, in the image of the "female ivy" encircling the "barky fingers of the elm" (IV.i.43–44) and when Bottom says, "I am marvail's hairy about the face" (IV.i.24–25). Our laughter at the innocence of Bottom is partly relief, as a fleeting Apuleian anxiety about beast mating with woman is successfully dispelled. The Minotaur is nowhere in the play, but the Labyrinth surrounds us. The darkened pastoral of the tangled wood is an Athenian Labyrinth having a beast-man at its centre as the Cretan Labyrinth had a beast-man at *its*.

Even the fairies who might seem to supply a simple joyous antithesis to the murky ancient myth have their darker side. They are "the good folk" and Puck is "Robin Goodfellow," but these names are more conciliatory than descriptive. Robert Kirk, writing in the seventeenth century, explained that these names are used because people "use to blesse all they fear harme of."[26] We are reminded of what fairies *might* do when Oberon benevolently promises, at the end of the play, that no baby with a hare-lip will be born to any of the couples (V.i.410). Shakespeare's miniaturizing of the fairies, his turning them into creatures of minuscule prettiness, is itself another "apotrope," that is a "turning-away," of evil.[27]

Perhaps the notion of apotrope can be traced back into the tragedy from which *A Midsummer Night's Dream* was born. In *Romeo and Juliet,* when Mercutio prophetically imagined the world of *A Midsummer Night's Dream,* he too perhaps was seeking to turn aside or fend off something he felt as a threat: heterosexual love. *Romeo and Juliet,* meanwhile, grew out of *Love's Labour's Lost.* Wit and word-play belong to Mercutio, who represents the same-sex bonding of pre-maturity, a world less substantial than that of marriage. In *Love's Labour's Lost,* as we saw, the supervening reality of heterosexual love is itself subjected to a lateral assault, through a reported death, the only way to arrest the rattling wit of the young people. In *Romeo and Juliet,* as heterosexual love is explored in terms of ecstasy, it becomes entwined with death, the dark opposite of substance. Mercutio in miniaturizing the world of love-dreamers is, we sense, attempting an apotrope of the kind of growing up that will separate him from Romeo (this thought reaches back to *Two Gentlemen of Verona*). He has no inkling, however, that by the same act of reduction he is averting, for a time, a far more dangerous darkness. He knows enough to fear love but does not know that love in this play is fused with death. In *A Midsummer Night's Dream* the strange alliance of love, dream, magic, and violence is presupposed from the start—and is turned to joy.

Although Hippolyta with her "dual ontology" outdistances the slow-thinking Theseus, the Epilogue to the play is more Thesean than Hippolytan.

If we shadows have offended,
Think but this, and all is mended,
That you have but slumbr'd here
While these visions did appear.
And this weak and idle theme,
No more yielding but a dream,
Gentles, do not reprehend.
If you pardon, we will mend,
And, as I am an honest Puck,
If we have unearned luck
Now to scape the serpent's tongue,
We will make amends ere long;

Else the Puck a liar call.
So, good night unto you all.
Give me your hands, if we be friends,
And Robin shall restore amends.   (V.i.423–38)

"Ontological comfort" may seem, as a mere phrase, both pretentious and absurd, but it accurately describes what Puck here provides. He tells the audience that what they have been watching is a flimsy tissue of illusion, and when the requested applause comes, those applauding feel the warm physicality of their own hands as contrast and depart happily sure of their own reality. Duke Theseus would benignly agree.

But Shakespeare is Shakespeare, and so there is more. If we listen carefully we discover that some of this comfort is implicitly withdrawn. The opening imperative is interesting: "*Think* but this." If you are upset, the speaker suggests, "you'll feel better if you think . . . kid yourselves (?) . . ." The use of "think" here is a little like the use of "deem" in law, to cover a threatened chasm in due sequence: "If we deem that the payment was made before 1 July, none of the above applies." Puck hints that we may decide to adopt the dismissive ontology of Theseus not because it is clearly true but because any alternative is disturbing. Then there is the fact that Puck presents himself throughout the speech as Puck. This violates Thesean logic, the absolute division between imagination and reality. If the play, an airy fiction, is now over and one of the actors is reassuring a dazed audience, that actor should remove his mask, step forward, and say, "Look, I'm Joe; I was playing Puck, but that's all nonsense. Hope you enjoyed the show. This is where you clap." Instead, the person who tells us that the illusion is over is Puck, who actually belongs not to our world but to the wild wood. It is a little like Erasmus's making Folly utter the praise of folly. Fiction spills over into the world of fact at the crucial moment of reassurance. That Shakespeare is conscious of the paradox is signalled by the poker-faced "honest Puck" at line 431 and by "Else the Puck a liar call" at line 435. The humour is delicious: "You wouldn't want to call *me* a liar, would you? Especially when I'm being sensible!"

In Act IV, Scene i, the lovers emerge from their magical experience, blinking uncertainly. Demetrius says how good it is to return to one's senses, to recover one's "natural taste" (IV.i.174). Again the thought is

Thesean, with one small snag. Demetrius now loves Helena, but he loves her because of the magic love philtre administered by Puck. When he entered the wood he loved not Helena but Hermia. Just as Puck by remaining "in character" in the Epilogue represents an overspill of fiction into fact, so Demetrius's love of Helena is a haunting overspill, from the moonlit night into the plain ensuing day. Demetrius himself—"an honest Demetrius"—is contentedly sure that the love is natural. Even now, however, we have not finished. The dominant plot line unquestionably gives us a Demetrius who scorned Helena when he was in his right mind but magically loves her in the end. Early in the play, however, Shakespeare gives Helena a brief reminiscence of a yet earlier time when Demetrius *had* courted her assiduously—before he fell in love with Hermia (I.i.243). We can now begin to wonder whether the daylit infatuation with Hermia was itself a temporary madness, so that his natural taste, originally and fundamentally, really was for Helena. But this early love for Helena registers far less strongly than the passionate pursuit of Hermia. We are left not with a resolution but with a "shimmer effect."

A Midsummer Night's Dream is a happy comedy. It performs its apotrope of the violent mythology it draws on. Yet the apotrope is never quite complete. Theseus indeed enunciates the philosophy of triumphant apotrope. In his big speech the spirits are exorcised and lose their potency. But the philosophy of the play, if one may speak of such a thing, is less confident, remaining always in process, questioning. Demetrius himself, who may sound like Theseus when he talks about his natural taste, sounds more like the doubtful Hippolyta a few lines later: "These things seem small and undistinguishable, / Like far-off mountains turned into clouds" (IV.i.186–87). Hermia answers, "Methinks I see these things with parted eye, / When everything seems double." Helena, watching, having got her love in the reeling double ontology Hippolyta glimpsed, says, "I have found Demetrius like a jewel / Mine own, and not mine own (IV.i.191–92). Happiness flawed by uncertainty, but happiness still.

3 The Major Histories

"Be yourself": *Richard II*

Shakespeare began his writing career with histories and then branched
out into comedy and tragedy. In the first part of *Henry VI* he probed the
nature of historical causation. He presented the origin of the Wars of the
Roses as mysterious. Starting in an inchoate sense of genealogical wrong
the play progresses swiftly and incrementally; the mere fact of taking sides,
the adoption of badges, adds irrationally to the momentum. If this is
psychology entering historiography it is very much a psychology socially
conceived, in terms of the interaction of persons and groups. In *Richard III*
the strongest psychological interest was in the isolated individual, in a
king who seems to become two persons when he introspects. In *The
Comedy of Errors* the idea of a doubled self is allowed to dance free from
individual psychology into a fairyland of twins, objectively coexisting
doubles. If *The Comedy of Errors* is earlier than *Richard III* we must say that
Shakespeare played with the idea of split identity before he worked with
it, in the history play. Psychological tension, as we saw, did get into *The
Comedy of Errors,* but the play was primarily social. The comedic interest
in the tension between same-sex solidarity and heterosexual love may be
called psychological but is, again, social in its reference. The characters in
the four comedies, *The Comedy of Errors, Two Gentlemen of Verona, The
Taming of the Shrew,* and *A Midsummer Night's Dream,* are in comparison
with those in the history plays slight and schematic. Lysander and Demetrius are hard to keep distinct in the mind, but no one ever forgets
Richard III, alone at the end. At the same time, however, comedy allowed

an excursion from concrete into abstract thinking, from "What caused what in the history of England?" to metaphysical questions: "What is real? What is imagination? What is role-playing?"

In *Richard II* Shakespeare marries the comedic worry about role-playing and pretence to the analysis of introspection begun in *Richard III*. Richard II, as everyone knows, is Shakespeare's player-king—at least until Act V, where he turns into the poet-king. Like Jean-Paul Sartre's waiter in *L'Être et le néant* who can be watched playing the part of a waiter, Richard histrionically struts as—what he in fact is—king.

At the beginning of the play Richard has to deal with a dangerous dispute between two noblemen. Bullingbrook accuses Mowbray of murdering the Duke of Gloucester. Mowbray was involved in the murder but cannot allude openly to the fact that King Richard himself had wanted Gloucester dead. Mowbray can claim truthfully that his hand did not actually kill the Duke, but he is in a difficult position because of the obligation to observe secrecy. As he proclaims his innocence to his accuser, he tries as it were to catch the King's eye and to apologize, preposterously enough, for not having moved more swiftly against Gloucester. Hence the curious, choking speech:

For Gloucester's death,
I slew him not, but to my own disgrace
Neglected my sworn duty in that case.   (I.i.132–34)

How is the audience to understand this? There was an anonymous play, *Thomas of Woodstock,* that told the story of Gloucester's murder, and A. P. Rossiter thought that Shakespeare was relying on the fact that the audience had seen this recently,[1] but it is by no means clear that *Woodstock* was staged before *Richard II.* Mowbray's speech is best explained by the account given in Holinshed's Chronicles. There we are told that Richard secretly ordered the death of Gloucester and Mowbray temporized. But Shakespeare could not assume knowledge of Holinshed in his audience. There was no such thing as "program notes" in the Elizabethan theatre. In the following scene, however, Richard's complicity in the murder is made explicit. John of Gaunt says,

God's is the quarrel, for God's substitute,
His deputy appointed in His sight,
Hath caus'd his death, the which if wrongfully,
Let heaven revenge, for I may never lift
An angry arm against His minister.   (I.ii.37–41)

This, however, leaves us still with the question, "How did the audience understand Mowbray's earlier speech, *before* they had the information now provided by Gaunt?" It is likely that the first audience of the play, as it listened to Mowbray's contorted sentence, was sharp enough to see that something lay in the background, that Mowbray was for some reason unable to speak directly. No film of archaism was imposed for them, as it is for us, between thought and expression. Also, they were attuned, in a general way, to the manner in which significant political moves are made in a monarchy; the courtier rises by gambling; he guesses that the king (who cannot speak openly) desires that a certain thing be done, so the courtier does it, as a speculation; if the king is pleased, the courtier rises; if the king disowns the action, the courtier must remain silent. In the case of Gloucester's death, it turns out, Richard did rather more than express a vague wish. Perhaps, then, Shakespeare could trust his audience to keep the puzzle about Mowbray simmering at the back of the mind long enough for it to be resolved by Gaunt's explanation in the following scene.

We may remember *1 Henry VI*, in which we saw the medieval simplicity of embattled armies on either side of the stage played against an extraordinary intuition of latency and mystery at the level of causes. So here in Act I, Scene iii, Bullingbrook and Mowbray, horns locked, are medieval, about to fight to the death by the laws of chivalry. That makes the brightly painted surface of the play. What is latent, behind the surface, is the King's involvement. By the time we reach the actual trial by combat, Gaunt has enlightened the audience, but within the scene itself the explanation still cannot be spoken aloud. Silence on this point remains crucial. As soon as the latent dimension is admitted, however, chivalric conflict becomes a complex political problem, with implications. Richard rises to the public occasion. At the last moment he throws his warder down (I.iii.118). This stops the fight, and the King banishes both parties. It is done with flair, and it is easy to think that we are watching a politician of genius. He has defused the situation and got both of the dangerous antagonists out of the way. But flair is one thing, real political prudence another. Richard's performance is good theatre not just for us but for those watching within the play. As the scene unfolds, however, we sense a tremor in the governing hand (Richard's use of the phrase "with some unwillingness" at line 149 gives much away); the King first sentences Bullingbrook to ten years' banishment and then commutes it to six (I.iii.210–11). Mowbray is banished for life (I.iii.150–53). The cleansing symmetry of the King's original action has now gone. The audience wonders why the King is being kinder to Bullingbrook than to Mowbray. To be sure, Bullingbrook is the accuser, Mowbray the accused, and it might seem reasonable to punish the accused more severely. At the same time Mowbray is technically innocent of a crime the King himself had ordered. We wonder if Mowbray has been sent away for life not because of his crime but because of what he might tell people. Also, although the main charges are laid by Bullingbrook against Mowbray, Mowbray accuses Bullingbrook of treachery to the King and prophecies, correctly, that the King will come to see that Bullingbrook is his enemy (I.iii.24, 205).

Here perhaps we move to a latency deeper still. If Bullingbrook knows how Gloucester died, his motives could be deep indeed and might include embarrassing the King. He gives no sign, however, of any such awareness. In terms of plot and known history he is in any case the real threat to Richard, and this makes him like the Duke of York, in relation to the King in *1 Henry VI*. Shakespeare's play about Henry VI is early, but Henry VI himself belongs of course to a later phase of English history. The analogy nevertheless holds: two unstable kings, each threatened. In *1 Henry VI* the House of Lancaster is threatened by the House of York on the ground of the frailty of the Lancastrian claim to the throne. In *Richard II* we are taken back to the time when that dubious Lancastrian grip on the throne was first obtained. Bullingbrook's father is John of Gaunt, Duke of Lancaster. As the drama proceeds Bullingbrook will demolish Richard. Yet he bears with him no discernable consciousness of any such overarching design. He moves one step at a time, each taken, apparently, for a small-scale reason, until he finds himself on a great, unstoppable slide into usurpation. Tania Demetriou said the origin of the Wars of the

Roses was silence and that the conflict grew to a sudden violence through a series of trivial physical actions. Of course Bullingbrook could be a Machiavel, playing his cards close to his chest, knowing very well what he is about, but Shakespeare never presents him to us as a Machiavel. All the *consciousness* of revolution is on Richard's side. Bullingbrook seems merely to move, mutely, into spaces vacated for him, with bitterly ironic courtesy, by Richard. The aetiological silence of the rose-picking scene in *1 Henry VI* is in this play confined to Bullingbrook. He is a walking (fighting, killing) absence of motive—or seems so. Of course he is not literally silent. The part is one of the longer ones in Shakespeare. Bullingbrook has much to say, of a stolid, un-illuminating kind. Richard's part is longer, indeed, but number of words is not the point. Richard, in any case, says much more than Bullingbrook in the same number of lines. Those who believe that plain English is loaded with meaning while poetry is short on meaning may be surprised by this, for Bullingbrook's style is plain where Richard's is poetic. A moment's reflection should show, however, that the richly figurative character of poetic utterance allows simultaneous meaning—and that means more meaning in the same space. The obstinate non-appearance of any explanation, from Bullingbrook himself, of why he overturned the kingdom becomes palpable as the play develops.

Richard, meanwhile, is commonly seen as hopelessly detached from reality. As "the player king" he gives the court good theatre when what is required is good government. Yet it is Richard who sees the real meaning of Bullingbrook's return from banishment. "I just want my rights," says Bullingbrook, in effect (III.iii.112–16). "It means rebellion," says Richard. Richard is right, so does that make him the realist? No, because he remains detached from the truth he perceives. He knows everything about his situation except, somehow, the fact that it is actually happening. He responds to the crisis by suggesting a session of story-telling:

For God's sake let us sit upon the ground
And tell sad stories of the death of kings:
How some have been depos'd, some slain in war,
Some haunted by the ghosts they have deposed,
Some poisoned by their wives, some sleeping kill'd,
All murthered—for within the hollow crown

That rounds the mortal temples of a king
Keeps Death his court, and there the antic sits,
Scoffing his state and grinning at his pomp,
Allowing him a breath, a little scene,
To monarchize, be fear'd, and kill with looks,
Infusing him with self and vain conceit
As if this flesh which walls about our life
Were brass impregnable; and humour'd thus,
Comes at the last and with a little pin
Bores thorough his castle wall, and farewell king!   (III.ii.155–70)

The speech is simultaneously a truancy from crisis, a flight into legend and imagination, and an uncannily accurate perception of what is really coming. Richard, with disquieting, faintly schizophrenic gaiety, expatiates in what is technically known as the *de casibus* tradition, stories of the falls of princes as set out in the immensely popular *Mirror for Magistrates* (editions in 1555, 1559, 1563, 1574, 1575, 1578, 1587, and 1609). Richard turns his own imminent peril into a multiple narrative retrospect. Within the speech he even anticipates the analysis I have just offered and diagnoses his own theatricality, on the words "scene," "monarchize," and "conceit." This degree of awareness might seem to save him from the charge of escapist fantasy, but the relishing love of language betrayed in every line means that the speech comes over, finally, as a shimmering screen of painted images. Anyone who was there, listening to the King talking in this way, would be embarrassed, would smell hysteria, would *not* say, "This man has grip."

The aetiological silence and the roses taken as badges in *1 Henry VI* are rethought and redeployed in *Richard II*. The silence on the origin of the movement that would topple Henry becomes the reticence of Bullingbrook, who will topple Richard. The scarlet and white of the flowers picked in the Temple Garden turn into the garish bravura of Richard's language. In *1 Henry VI* the flowers crystallized the reasons for war. It may be that Richard's fertility in imagery crystallizes his own destruction. If Bullingbrook is from the start a Machiavel, this idea cannot stand. But, as we have seen, Shakespeare consistently refuses to present him in that way. If his motives are genuinely inchoate, the possibility arises that Richard is not just foreseeing his own destruction but may be contributing to it.

There is an old maxim of school-teachers: "Don't say 'Don't.'" Don't say, "Don't draw on the walls," to children who, until that moment, had never thought of doing so. Richard's seemingly extravagant speeches may re-engage the real world by assuming a causal force. His escape from the immediate situation into vivid hypothesis can free the *behaviour* of a less imaginative, more practical listener. This once more is shrewd as historiography. Violent political movements grow not only with the adoption of badges of allegiance but also in response to beckoning images, especially when these are offered by the potential victim. Shakespeare is substituting a multilinear causation for the easier unilinear model. Using the unilinear model we would say, "Ambitious York collected supporters and took action accordingly." By the multilinear model we would say, "York began to move in a certain direction, and his supporters took fire and accelerated the process." In the multilinear version the supposedly passive context is allowed causal input.

Richard is therefore both a fantasist and a realist. Sometimes, indeed, one can begin to feel that he is not one man but two. For example, he is both an unpleasingly "modern" figure, tainted by dodgy financial schemes, and a sacral king, anointed by God, above the laws that bind his subjects, bearing the mystique of a hallowed past. When people remember the play after an interval of time, the sacral figure is usually dominant in their minds (this is partly because of the way the play ends). John of Gaunt's speech about "this other Eden" (II.i.40–66) is remembered as a celebration of Richard's England, as it was before the usurper brought in an age of grey *Realpolitik*. But most of the speech is not about the England of Richard. It is elegiac, saved from vulgar jingoism by its infinite sadness. Gaunt, a dying man, speaks of an England lost, as Eden was lost:

This land of such dear souls, this dear dear land,
Dear for her reputation through the world,
Is now leas'd out—I die pronouncing it—
Like to a tenement or pelting farm.
England, bound in with the triumphant sea,
Whose rocky shore beats back the envious siege
Of wat'ry Neptune, is now bound in with shame,
With inky blots and rotten parchment bonds.   (II.i.57–64)

Who has done this to England? The King. "Landlord of England art thou now, not king" (II.i.113). We are made to feel that the old aristocracy, men whose names are the names of English counties, are rooted in the earth. "Earth," used twice, and "plot" are key words in the speech. But the King is by contrast a modern figure, having to survive by "farming the realm" (I.iv.45), taking out leases, confiscating property. "Farming the realm" means granting certain areas to tax collectors who, on payment of a fee, are free to collect whatever they can get. It is as if the King's possession of all England is merely notional. Because the soil is divided among the barons he is forced to fund his lavish lifestyle by financial ingenuity. We seem to have in Richard a glowing retrospective ideal and a chilling forward-looking possibility. Gaunt is clear that the country he loves, the England that is like a moated manor house, has been destroyed by Richard. There is, however, a latent oddity in all of this.

It is commonly supposed that the further back one goes in time the more unconfined is the power of the ruler. In fact the sixteenth century, the century in which Shakespeare wrote *Richard II,* saw a remarkable shift *towards* monarchical absolutism. In the great medieval treatise of Henry de Bracton the king is under the law because the law makes him king.[2] Where Bracton backs the power of the king, he supports an executive rather than a legislative power (though there are places where Roman law breaks in with confusing effect). Thomas Aquinas is clear that the subject is not obliged to obey a wicked king. Indeed, such kings are tyrants and ought to be deposed (*Summa theologiae,* 2a 2ae, 60.5).[3] This conception of kingship is sustained in the sixteenth century by the profoundly traditional Richard Hooker: "Where the lawe doth give dominion, who doubteth that the King who receiveth it is under the lawe," and "The King is *major singulis universis minor,* greater than any but less than all."[4] The medieval poet William Langland says of the king, "Might of the communes made hym to regne" (*Piers Plowman,* B Text, Prologue, 113). George Buchanan argued similarly in his *De jure regni* of 1571 for a form of monarchy in which kings could be legitimately deposed, but we are now in the sixteenth century; Buchanan's book was condemned by act of Parliament in 1584. Medieval theorists repeatedly asserted the priority of the people to the king. Of course, in practice medieval kings ordered everyone about. This is partly because no one had any idea how to set up a general election. Yet theoretically elective monarchies are common in the period, and there is often a rudimentary election, a throwing up of hats and cheering in the main square. In William Tyndale's *Obedience of a Christian Man* (1528) we suddenly hear a different voice: "The kinge is in this worlde without lawe and maye at his owne lust doo right and wronge and shall geve acomptes but to God only."[5] The idea took hold rapidly. The *Homilie against Disobedience and Wylful Rebellion* (1571?) requires unqualified submission by the subject to the prince, even if that prince be an evil tyrant, like Nero. Any rebel is worse, the Homilist observes, than the worst tyrant.[6]

Of course, as Hooker was Bractonian in the Renaissance, so there were medieval absolutists. Continental theories formed to protect the Holy Roman Empire from papal encroachment contain many pre-echoes of what became "the divine right of kings" in seventeenth-century England. The emperor Frederick II who so dazzled Dante was startlingly absolutist. But the general direction in the sixteenth century is towards rather than away from absolutism. The trend continued after Shakespeare's death until we reach the full divine right of kings promulgated by Charles I and the consequent explosion, the English Civil War.

So Richard's blazing claim to be, as God's anointed, above the petty rules and regulations that restrain his subjects ought to sound as "modern" as his queasy financial dealing.

> Not all the water in the rough rude sea
> Can wash the balm off from an anointed king;
> The breath of worldly men cannot depose
> The deputy elected by the Lord;
> For every man that Bullingbrook hath press'd
> To lift shrewd steel against our golden crown,
> God for his Richard hath in heavenly pay
> A glorious angel.   (III.ii.54–61)

This is the new doctrine, but it does not sound new. The speech is like a stained-glass window. Moreover Gaunt, who represents the old England against tax-raising Richard, backs the new absolutism when he says that he could never lift an angry arm against the Lord's anointed (I.ii.40–44).

There is, however, a tremor in the thought later. Gaunt says, "Thy state of law is bondslave to the law" (II.i.113). He means that Richard, properly above the law, has forfeited that status by his behaviour, has fallen from grace and is now as subject to rules and regulations as his meanest subjects. We are now very close indeed to the medieval doctrine that a tyrant need not be obeyed. But the words of Gaunt still suggest that absolutism is something immemorial, now suddenly threatened, rather than a novel idea. When Richard is speaking, his use of biblical imagery has the effect of a hallowing antiquity.

Is this a conjuring trick? Well, not exactly. To make matters still more complex it turns out that the real Richard II did claim to be above the law, back in the fourteenth century. Historians differ as to how far this was a curious anticipation of later events or how far it was a momentary rhetorical aberration (Richard posing as superman while continuing to operate within the existing legal arrangements, judges, parliaments, royal indentured servants, and so on—he never actually attempted to raise an unparliamentary tax). He is, interestingly, the first English king to require that he be addressed as "Your Majesty." One begins to wonder whether Shakespeare has brought off not so much a conjuring trick as a cunning coup on behalf of "the Tudor Myth" of absolutism. He has taken the disquieting novelty out of Tyndale's doctrine by successfully grounding it in a real medieval absolutist (or one plausibly presentable as such). This complex account assumes that Shakespeare knew that absolutism was a novel doctrine rather than immemorial orthodoxy. Is it not possible, however, that Shakespeare simply believed in the doctrine of sacred supralegal monarchy and was completely unaware that it was not the usual medieval view? This line is a little like the view that the Reformation fails to register in the comedies because Shakespeare was so innocent as to be unaware that it had actually happened.

In fact, neither view is tenable. Even if Shakespeare had somehow remained unaware of the movement in political theory, he certainly read Holinshed with close attention. Holinshed gives a vivid picture not only of the appalling behaviour of the king but also of what counted most heavily against him when his record was scrutinized. Holinshed quotes from the articles of deposition, where much is made of the fact that Richard had said that the laws of the realm were in his head (and sometimes "in his breast"). This is described as a "fantastical opinion."[7] After Shakespeare has put his Holinshed to one side and returned to his manuscript, he makes others apart from Richard support the idea of a sacred, legally untouchable king (Gaunt at I.ii.37–41, York at III.iii.9). This does look, so far, like an attempt to doctor history in the interests of the Tudors. Queen Elizabeth, we may think, could hardly have had a better or more obsequious spin doctor. Oddly enough, we have a glimpse of what the queen thought in the story of the courtier William Lambarde. On an August day in 1601 Lambarde was going through miscellaneous records with the queen when they came to the reign of Richard II. The queen said, enigmatically, "I am Richard II, know ye not that?" Lambarde's mind flew at once to the Essex rebellion against Elizabeth's authority. Elizabeth then spoke of Shakespeare's "tragedie, played forty times in open streets and houses."[8] As we read these words the political import of Shakespeare's play flips inside out. Elizabeth, it seems, was far from seeing the play as astute propaganda on behalf of the Tudors. She sees a play that shows that a monarch can be deposed, predictably used by subversives. At last we notice what Shakespeare's contemporaries would surely have seen at once. This God-defended king who calls on angels to beat back the soldiers of Bullingbrook finds in the event that the angels cannot help him. The deposition scene was cut by the censor from early quarto editions of the play because of its dangerous audacity. In 1601 Robert Devereux, the second Earl of Essex, commissioned a revival of what, almost certainly, was Shakespeare's *Richard II,* to be performed the day before he led an uprising against the queen.[9]

Richard's notion of undefeatable angels is indeed a primitive, magical version of absolutism. He is a little like the Lady's brother in Milton's *A Masque* who held that chastity was an armour of complete steel, so that no chaste girl could ever in fact be raped (line 421). We all know that this is false. Since Richard gave us the long account of princes who were successfully removed, we may surmise that he actually knew the angels weren't a safe bet. If we suppose the power of the king to be divinely given *de jure* rather than *de facto,* we find as we shift to the ideal realm that kingship is after all genuinely indestructible. If the present incumbent is struck down, the power simply slides to the next in line, according to the rules of inheritance.

Shakespeare has made the frailty of anointed kings, on the ground, vivid for all to see. So is Shakespeare after all covertly satirizing the Tudor myth? I think not. Two stories run concurrently in *Richard II*. There is a supernatural story of a divinely ordained line, broken by the deposition of Richard (not righted until after the death of Richard III). This is the Tudor myth of Edward Hall's *Chronicle* and E. M. W. Tillyard's *Shakespeare's History Plays*. That story is clearly there, un-satirized, in the drama. Then there is a naturalist story of a clever but not entirely competent wheeler-dealer, an immoral king in difficulties, who is plainly finding psychological refuge in the sacral role he has inherited. At this level we feel the unreality of the image more than we feel its truth. A play univocally committed to presenting the Tudor myth with maximum power would have shown us a gravely dignified, suffering king (think how royalist writers presented Charles I after his death). But everyone knows that Richard is somehow fooling around; everyone feels that he should take a deep breath and calm down. Richard compares himself with Christ ("Some of you, with Pilate, wash your hands," IV.i.239), but few are less Christ-like than he. Christ loved the world; Richard loves Richard. Have we not heard those words before?[10] We receive the impression of a deep instability, a man with ideals but no convictions, a walking congeries of images, poses, pretences, who, because he is intelligent, ironically perceives what is afoot, but from the side, in narrative profile. This contemplative observer is really at the heart of the action, is its sacrificial victim.

Richard, then, is a complex figure. His self-consciousness leads him into convulsive introspection, and introspection as we saw leads to a splitting of identity. This division creates in its turn a wholly internal field of conflicting forces. We saw how Richard III, left alone, became two, "I and I" (V.iii.183, Quarto). Shakespeare now pushes the idea further, joining it to his first essay on comedic identity in *A Comedy of Errors*. There nature divided herself, producing, in the two sets of twins, objective mirror images. In the happy story of that play the mirroring twins, united at the end, heal the wound of lost identity imagined by Antipholus of Syracuse as water lost in water. If any one had said to Richard before his deposition, "Who are you?" he would have answered, "I am the king." Stripped by Bullingbrook of his social, relational identity he is, like

Richard III, thrown back upon himself and now, like Antipholus, seeks his mirror image. In the middle of the deposition scene he abruptly calls for a glass:

Give me that glass, and therein will I read.
No deeper wrinkles yet? Hath sorrow struck
So many blows upon this face of mine,
And made no deeper wounds? O flatt'ring glass,
Like to my followers in prosperity,
Thou dost beguile me! Was this face the face
That every day under his household roof
Did keep ten thousand men? Was this the face
That like the sun, did make beholders wink?
Is this the face which fac'd so many follies,
That was at last out-fac'd by Bullingbrook?
A brittle glory shineth in this face,
As brittle as the glory is the face,
    [*Dashes the glass against the ground.*]
For there it is, crack'd in a hundred shivers.
Mark, silent king, the moral of this sport,
How soon my sorrow hath destroy'd my face.   (IV.i.276–91)

Richard needs to double himself, as was done so happily at the level of plot in *The Comedy of Errors,* in order to see himself. Or rather, to watch himself. For Richard is enjoying this.

What is happening here is a profound shift in the scope of drama, nothing less than the discovery of human interiority. It happened before, but only once, in the oddly separate history of Greek drama. Euripides' Hippolytus is strangely like Shakespeare's Richard, excitable, narcissistic, doomed. Near the end Euripides gives his protagonist an enigmatic speech (I will translate the Greek as literally as English will bear): "Would it were possible for me, having stood opposite myself, to look at myself, at the evils we are suffering" (1078–79). Hippolytus and Richard both wish to look at themselves and, simultaneously, to watch a great show. In Richard's speech the word "face" recurs with great power. The repeated "Was this . . . ?" must carry a memory of Marlowe's *Doctor Faustus:* "Was this the face that launch'd a thousand ships / And burnt the topless towers of Ilium?" (1604, V.i.91–92), with its burden, the heart-wrenching beauty of Helen, catastrophic destruction, falling towers, Troy in flames. "Face" as Richard uses it is emblematic of the sacral king, but at the same time it suggests "surface," or even "mask." The King, whose fertility in imagery may have accelerated the usurpation, now conducts what Walter Pater rightly saw as an inverted coronation ceremony.[11] Bullingbrook, who in the chronicles overthrew Richard by violence, is here strangely passive, the "silent king." Richard is in charge: "mark me how I will undo myself" (IV.i.203).

When Richard looks in the glass, his first reaction is disappointment: "No deeper wrinkles yet?" In the middle of his splendid tragedy he wishes to check on the appearance of the protagonist and finds, instead of the required countenance ravaged by suffering, a perfectly healthy, youthful face. He smashes the incompetent image in a fit of pique bordering on hysteria. With part of his mind he may even know that the situation could be seen as funny. He turns to Bullingbrook and, with his usual facility in imaginative anticipation (for Bullingbrook has not yet ascended the throne), addresses him as "silent *king.*" "Mark," he says, "how soon my sorrow hath destroy'd my face." Bullingbrook answers sturdily, "The shadow of your sorrow hath destroy'd / The shadow of your face" (IV.i.291–92). It is the answer of a literalist whose patience is wearing thin. Bullingbrook means, "*Of course* sorrow hasn't destroyed your face! What lies broken on the ground is a mere image, and your 'sorrow' too is play-acting." This sounds like good sense. But Richard is not silenced:

> Say that again.
> The shadow of my sorrow! Ha, let's see.
> 'Tis very true, my grief lies all within. (IV.i.293–95)

"Say that again" is aesthetically appreciative. But Richard knocks back the charge that his grief is outward posturing by first accepting it and then denying the implication. He has been posturing, he grants, but meanwhile the true grief is there, tongueless, within him. He has been acting, as if it were a fiction, the person he really is. Bullingbrook, the supposed realist of the pair, is disabled by a kind of tunnel vision. He speaks as if

Richard were exaggerating, as if nothing terrible were happening. But a great objective tragedy is going forward before our eyes. A king is being cast down from his throne. The fancy figurative language of Richard is more *accurate* than the plain language of the usurper.

Shakespeare's mind refuses rest. Having broken through to the notion that introspection in so far as it entails an observer and an observed requires the generation of a second self, he goes on to ask what is involved in this generation. In the background, always, stands Ovid's Narcissus, who saw himself in a pool and fell hopelessly in love with what he saw. Richard III is anti-Ovidian; he, as ugly as Narcissus was beautiful, immediately detests the self he tries to love. Richard II is closer to Ovid's myth. He loves his own face; that is why he uses the word so often. But at this point in the action "face" carries the further meaning "sacral king," and he is thrown by the fact that the "observed self," the face seen in the glass, fails to match the idea of royalty disfigured that has been forming in his imagination. The suggestion is planted that all introspection, because it has to rely on an imagined second self, is systematically imperfect, unreliable. Yet rich interiority of character is dependent on introspection.

To this point in the action the play has been all about the simultaneity of fictive irresponsibility, practical insight, and causal efficacy in Richard. These tensions are given a special force by the prior existence of what E. H. Kantorowicz called "the King's two bodies," the king's physical body as a man and his office as king.[12] After the stripping away of his public identity Richard's verbal behaviour changes. The Richard we see awaiting death in prison is another man in more ways than one. He no longer pirouettes as he did when he had the court for his audience. He always knew that he was playing but somehow could not stop—another case of the spinning wheel that the mind's eye is powerless to arrest. But now the wheel has ceased to turn, apparently of its own accord. He looks steadily at the sad, histrionic sequence through which he has passed:

Thus play I in one person many people,
And none contented. Sometimes am I king;
Then treasons make me wish myself a beggar,
And so I am. Then crushing penury
Persuades me I was better when a king;

Then am I king'd again, and by and by
Think that I am unking'd by Bullingbrook,
And straight am nothing. But what e'er I be,
Nor I, nor any man that but man is,
With nothing shall be pleas'd, till he be eas'd
With being nothing.   (V.v.31–41)

The stories multiply and nest one within another. The reversion to being
king after his time as a beggar precedes the "unkinging" at the hands of
Bullingbrook, as if the deposition were just another pretence. It is here,
however, that the catalogue of fantasies passes into real history—but with
no mark of discontinuity. "*Think* that I am unking'd" catches exactly the
way it all was for Richard at the time; it felt like a dream; actuality still
eluded his grasp, even as he was being, actually, overthrown. But Richard
pauses abruptly after the confident phrase, "straight am nothing." This is
still the easy hyperbole of what I have called the pirouetting style. It is also
in the present tense and announces non-existence. The hyperbole is shrill,
uncomfortable. So far the Richard we have come to know is still there.
When he continues, however, the voice is suddenly quite different,
graver, all trace of lingering hysteria now gone.

Nor I, nor any man that but man is,
With nothing shall be pleas'd till he be eas'd
With being nothing.

The nervous tic of stylistic ingenuity (remember Berowne in *Love's Labour's Lost*) is still there in the chiming of "pleas'd" and "eas'd," but the
thought is suddenly straight and serious. Richard has disengaged himself
from the figurative phantasmagoria in which he has been trapped. He
means, "I, like other human beings, can never rest until I am *really* nothing, that is, dead." Richard has found his "core identity": a sentient,
thinking physical body, and it is entirely different from the "selves" conjured in play-acting or by self-projective introspection.
    It is in this scene that Shakespeare turns his protagonist from player-
king to poet-king:

I have been studying how I may compare
This prison where I live unto the world;
And for because the world is populous,
And here is not a creature but myself,
I cannot do it.   (V.v.1–5)

He is reacting to the falling away of that scaffolding of relation and comparison that enables us in normal circumstances to know who we are, what is what. At the same time he is discovering a central identity.

We have been concerned so far with various models of non-linear causation. First we saw how an irrationally expanding circumambient excitement moved the Wars of the Roses from possibility to actuality. Then, in *Richard II,* garishly coloured imagery of sacral majesty and fallen kings created a field of momentum *around* the taciturn rebel, Bullingbrook (again suggesting that context may be more causally potent than we normally assume). Finally, the question, "Who is Richard?" seems best answered, for long stretches of the play, by "He is the image he creates; he fashions himself in his creative performance." This answer is philosophically congenial to twentieth-century thought and is perhaps still seductive. The Existentialists argued that we play the parts by which we are known in the world and the Structuralists delighted in resolving identity into relation. But Shakespeare will not rest in these thoughts. He will never say, "And that is that."

There is perhaps a fault in *Richard II.* It is hard to reconcile the cold, greedy, *thin* personality that says, before visiting the dying Gaunt, "Pray God we may make haste and come too late!" (I.iv.64) with the figure who dies so bravely at the end. It may be said that this is the live, developing characterization for which Shakespeare is famous; Richard has grown up, matured to the point of full *anagnorisis,* in the sense in which that term applies to Sophocles' Oedipus, self-understanding. Perhaps the trauma of usurpation is itself enough to account for the change. But we do not see enough of the transition. The movement at the end is so profound that it engages the audience entirely. We have no mental leisure to wonder any more how such a thing could happen. Suddenly we love Richard. But I am not sure that we should.

Invisible Acting: *Henry IV,* Parts 1 and 2, *Henry V*

We all think of Richard II as a brilliant actor, and this seems to be in line with the way he speaks of himself. But Shakespeare also shows us Richard through another person's eyes, where, curiously, he appears as a bad actor. York, describing the triumphal entry into London of Bullingbrook, says that Richard in comparison with Henry Bullingbrook seemed like an inept player who somehow manages to lose the audience as soon as he steps on stage:

As in a theatre the eyes of men,
After a well-grac'd actor leaves the stage,
Are idly bent on him that enters next,
Thinking his prattle to be tedious,
Even so, or with much more contempt, men's eyes
Did scowl on gentle Richard.   (V.ii.23–28)

Teachers of literature who have been instructing their pupils that Richard is the dazzler, Bullingbrook the dull dog, tend to avert their eyes from this passage. For York, Bullingbrook with his warm "I thank you, country-men," is the skilled performer, Richard the unskilled. Doubts about the quality of Richard's acting may have been sown earlier. "Over the top," "camping it up," and "ham" are terms of abuse, and they all apply to Richard well before the fifth act.

Setting aside Bullingbrook, is there another player-king in Shakespeare who is truly "well-grac'd"? There is, and his name is Henry V. Henry V appears in the two parts of *Henry IV* as Prince Hal. Hal, no less than Richard, is engaged in systematic pretence, but where Richard's style is high-fantastical, Hal's is naturalistic. Hal plays the good fellow, the boon companion, the pub regular, warm-hearted, spontaneous, never stand-offish. I have said that we should set aside Bullingbrook, but it may be that in making Bullingbrook the good actor in York's speech Shakespeare was preparing the way for the great study of *invisible acting* that was to follow in *1* and *2 Henry IV* and *Henry V.* Bullingbrook's matey, notably un-Ricardian way of addressing his subjects as "countrymen" is not simple reality succeeding false pretence; it is itself a style. Mark Antony, the supreme Shakespearean orator, addresses the Roman citizens as "countrymen" in the speech he delivers over the body of the slain Caesar (*Julius Caesar,* III.ii.13, 73).

Our own age has a taste for formalism and likes to credit earlier artistically successful periods with similar tastes. The Elizabethans, we are told, loved rhetoric, exalted lyricism, schematic images, vivid histrionics. The truth is that rhetoricians long before Shakespeare discovered the efficacy of anti-rhetorical rhetoric. Mark Antony says, "I am no orator, as Brutus is" (III.ii.217). The notion that *ars est celare artem,* "art lies in concealing art," predates Shakespeare by many centuries.[13] The end of *Richard II* caused Shakespeare's mind to swing back from "outside-in" versions of causation to the idea of a surviving core self. This then operates as the central engine of *1* and *2 Henry IV* and *Henry V.* I refer now not to the civil wars of Henry IV's reign but to the inexorable rise from humiliation to glory of Prince Hal. The structure, terminating in *Henry V,* is comedic, not tragic. It has a happy ending. Hal's artful performance does not precipitate events inadvertently in the manner of the over-imaginative Richard, because Hal is completely in charge. The key fact about Hal is that this jovial drinking companion is utterly isolated. But isolation in Hal's case does not lead to introspection and doubling of identity as it did with Richard III and Richard II. It issues at once in action. It is as if (perhaps because of the dubiety of his father's claim to the throne) Hal dare not ask, "Who am I?" What dominates his mind is self-dedication, to maintaining the crown and the kingdom.

In the service of this good end he is a kind of Machiavel.[14] W. H. Auden was the first to notice how in soliloquy he can sound like Iago.[15] Although the dramatic conception of *invisible* rhetorical or histrionic potency begins with Bullingbrook and may seem naturally to imply Machiavellian cunning, I do not believe that Bullingbrook is a Machiavel. We wonder at times if his rise to power was planned in detail from the beginning, but the dominant impression remains one of unarticulated motive (Richard does all the articulation). But the slow rise of Prince Hal clearly is planned from the start. The idea of the invisible actor is now not emergent but fully formed. A mode of Machiavellianism—"white Machiavellianism"—is explicitly entailed. Certainly in his isolation he needs a usable image, but the image he builds is entirely subservient to the plan of gradual but surprising domination. It is utterly practical, and because this player-king produces major effects by design, not accident, he actually is a *central,* unified cause. He, not a fortuitous combination of circumstances, recovers England's greatness. This means that we are now leaving the philosophy I described as congenial to the present age. For Shakespeare the dissolution of central agency into a nexus of relations is an early phase only. In suddenly heading due north, for central substance, he is not in fact contradicting himself. In *1 Henry VI* he never came near to saying anything so metaphysically absolute—so foolish—as "There is no core self." Instead, more modestly, less vulnerably, he says, "Historical causation *can be*" (not "is always") "contextually driven."

We know that Hal is acting because of the important soliloquy placed very near the beginning of the play, in which he takes a long look at the jovial company of the Boar's Head:

> I know you all and will a while uphold
> The unyok'd humor of your idleness,
> Yet herein will I imitate the sun,
> Who doth permit the base contagious clouds
> To smother up his beauty from the world,
> That when he please again to be himself,
> Being wanted, he may be more wonder'd at
> By breaking through the foul and ugly mists
> Of vapors that did seem to strangle him.
>
> . . . .
>
> So when this loose behaviour I throw off
> And pay the debt I never promised,
> By how much better than my word I am,
> By so much shall I falsify men's hopes,
> And like bright metal on a sullen ground,
> My reformation, glitt'ring o'er my fault,
> Shall show more goodly and attract more eyes
> Than that which hath no foil to set it off.
> I'll so offend, to make offense a skill,
> Redeeming time when men think least I will.   (I.ii.195–203, 208–17)

It was once fashionable to argue that this speech tells us nothing about the Prince's character, that it is simply a program note, transposed to the stage, pure information, to allay anxiety in the audience: "The Prince is keeping dubious company but—don't worry—later he will change and amaze everyone." This reading founders on the little words "that" and "to" in lines 200 and 216. These words connote conscious purpose. Even if we stick to the "program note" reading and insist that the speech is pure information, the information includes the fact that the whole sequence is deliberately designed by Hal. The note does not read, "The Prince will change." It reads, "He knows what he's doing; he's using this phase in his career as the base for a surprise initiative, later." It follows that in so far as the Prince leads Falstaff and the rest to believe that he loves them for themselves alone he is deceiving them by a performance.

Everyone is faintly shocked by the coldness of the speech—even, I suspect, those very Elizabethans who, with another part of their minds, were eager to be assured that the Prince was no low-lifer. The sentimentalist is not pleased by the speech. But, we may think for a moment, Machiavelli might not have been too pleased either, from an opposite perspective; the scheme looks crazy if considered as practical politics. Can one really found a successful political career on a carefully contrived early reputation for drinking and keeping wild company followed by sudden seriousness? Surely the plan could easily misfire? It may be that this doubt is conditioned by the democratic conventions of the twenty-first century. If Hal knew that he would have to seek election later he would perhaps be less inclined to burn so many boats ahead of time. But he can be confident, as the heir apparent, that all eyes will be on him and no one else at the moment of transformation. Indeed I was wrong to suggest that Machiavelli would scorn the plan. The idea is Machiavellian—quite literally. The Italian theorist devotes a whole chapter of the *Discorsi* to the proposition "that it is a Very Good Notion at times to pretend to be a Fool," and backs it up with the example of the Roman Junius Brutus.[16] At the same time the scheme Hal sets out smells strongly of the theatre. The muffled figure who suddenly unmasks is immediately familiar to playgoers.

When I say that Hal's friendship with Falstaff and the rest is a pretence, I do not wish to insist that he has no affection at all for the fat knight. Hal's stratagem involves naturalistic acting, and naturalistic actors are often "method actors." That is to say, they work by inducing or finding real emotions in themselves and building on these. I would go so far as to say that Hal is naturally convivial, humorous, and playful. He will, after all, become "the king with the common touch," though that phrase will remind us of the political usefulness of such a character. When Hal thinks that Falstaff is dead on the field of Shrewsbury he says, "I could have better spar'd a better man" (1 Henry IV, V.iv.104). This is to confess ethical division. He loves Falstaff better than he should. But the tone still conveys cold separation more vividly than it conveys love. In the famous rejection of Falstaff—the moment when the sun appears from behind the clouds—Hal, now King Henry, momentarily slips back into the old ragging on the line, "know the grave doth gape / For thee thrice wider than for other men" (2 Henry IV, V.v.53–54). We know that Falstaff spots the crack in the new royal façade (jokes on Falstaff's fatness came thick and fast in the good old times) and that his eye brightens, by the next words of the King: "Reply not to me with a fool-born jest, / Presume not that I am the thing I was" (V.v.55–56). The King slaps down Falstaff, but at the same time he is slapping down something in himself. When at the end of the speech the King rules that Falstaff is not to come within ten miles of his person, we sense that he *fears* the attraction of Falstaff; a truly cold manipulator would not need to make any such provision, would simply forget Falstaff at this point. Despite these moments, the speech of rejection rolls forward unstoppably. It breaks Falstaff's heart and does the trick, politically. We hate Henry as we watch, but then we have to think, if we are English, "He is doing this for us."

Prince Hal knows from the first that he has an enormous responsibility and a very difficult job to do. If he fails, thousands of his subjects, people he will never meet, does not know, will suffer horribly. Civil war, in which father kills son, brother brother, is the worst thing of all. We have already seen how Henry VI, Hal's successor in the tainted Lancastrian line, was unable to prevent these horrors. Although *Richard II, 1* and *2 Henry IV*, and *Henry V* do not really form a tetralogy (a single work of art having four parts) as the Oresteian plays of Aeschylus form a trilogy, they are nevertheless closely linked. It may be that *1* and *2 Henry IV* can properly be termed a "dylogy," if that is the right word. Moreover, Prince Hal at the beginning of *1 Henry IV* is the man we see later, older and somewhat changed, at the end of *Henry V.*

Here we find him proposing marriage to the French Princess. He is still acting, naturalistically, brilliantly. The tone, as we have learned to expect, is jolly. "Here am I, a simple chap," he seems to say, "How about it?" By happy accident the Princess has the same name as the lady in *The Taming of the Shrew*, Katherine, so that Henry can sound, as he modulates from the formal version of her name, like a gentler, sweeter Petruchio: "Do you like me, Kate?" (*Henry V*, V.ii.107). This is followed by a long, immensely persuasive speech by Henry (V.ii.132–68) all about his being no good at smooth talking, more familiar with boxing and horses than with courtly ways but straight as a die—"a plain soldier." Just before the end Henry half-discloses the subtext: "Take a soldier; take a soldier, take a king." Katherine instantly picks up on the word "king" and shatters the atmosphere: "Is it possible dat I sould love de ennemie of France?" (V.ii.169–70). The agreeable oaf addressing her has just altered the disposition of whole kingdoms by slaughtering thousands of her countrymen on the field of Agincourt. These two have never met before. Henry has not fallen in love with Katherine. He is working, as hard as he can, to put together a political alliance. Again, we have to say, his motive is good. It is time to make friends with France. He does an excellent job. If, wildly, we imagine Shakespeare, long before he has put pen to paper, auditioning actors and being confronted by Richard II and Henry V, both hungry for work, one can perhaps begin to see how Henry would get the part (if, that is, the part required conviction—but most parts do). Henry wooing the French Princess is so convincing that we do not notice that he is acting. But he must be.

In the two parts of *Henry IV* the rising star of Prince Hal is played against the setting star of Falstaff. I wrote about Falstaff more than twenty years ago in *A New Mimesis* and think now as I thought then. Falstaff is an astonishing compound of gargantuan appetite (for drink, not food) and sharp intelligence. His love for Hal is deep, his selfishness complete. He can be childlike: "I would 'twere bed-time, Hal, and all well" (*1 Henry IV*, V.i.125). He dies smiling on his finger's end like a baby (*Henry V*, II.iii.15) and tells us how he "was born about three of the clock in the afternoon, with a white head and something a round belly" (*2 Henry IV*, I.ii.187–88), which is pretty much how he looks now. "Something" is a stroke of genius: "Not really *fat* you understand." He is given lyrically beautiful English linking him to saints' days and King Arthur (*2 Henry IV*, II.iv.33, III.ii.280–81). He is the old England.

Shakespeare changed his name to Falstaff from Oldcastle, and the original Oldcastle was a Lollard, a sort of pre-Reformation Protestant. I see no trace of Protestantism in the figure we have in the plays. Tom McAlindon has accurately picked up Puritan expressions used by Falstaff but has in my opinion misunderstood their tone and paid too little heed to context.[17] McAlindon suggests that Falstaff is presented by Shakespeare as a Puritan hypocrite, exposed as a coward when the fighting begins. When Falstaff says, "Would I were a weaver, I could sing psalms" (1 Henry IV, II.iv.133), Shakespeare counts on his audience knowing that many East Anglian weavers were Protestant refugees from Holland, but the humour turns on the unbridgeable distance between Falstaff and any such persons. Falstaff certainly uses the language of Puritan preachers (for example, "Pharaoh's lean kine," 1 Henry IV, II.iv.473), but he does so because he thinks it is funny, much as a consciously low-minded, reactionary humorist might use "politically correct" language today. And it is a coarse criticism that is content to say, without qualification, that Falstaff is exposed as a hypocritical coward. Of course he is "found out" when he boasts about fighting off enormous odds in the Gadshill episode, but the "finding out" does not matter. When the Prince explains that he was there and that he and Poins were the only adversaries Falstaff had to face, Falstaff happily wriggles free at once with the brilliant "Was it for me to kill the heir-apparent?" (1 Henry IV, II.iv.268–69). Some even think that the entire "finding out" was planned by Falstaff. This claim is based on the fact that in 2 Henry IV Hal says to Falstaff, "You knew me, as you did when you ran away by Gadshill (II.iv.306–7). But the Prince is probably speaking sarcastically, remembering Falstaff's bare-faced "By the Lord, I knew ye as well as he that made ye" at 1 Henry IV, II.iv.267–68. What is clear is that Falstaff thrives on such moments. True hypocrites never enjoy being unmasked. As Maurice Morgann saw 250 years ago,[18] the stage direction at the crisis of the Gadshill episode is all-important. It reads, "As they are sharing, the Prince and Poins set upon them; they all run away, and Falstaff, after a blow or two, runs away too, leaving the booty behind them." Falstaff is differentiated from Bardolph and Peto by the words, "after a blow or two." It is enough to show that he is not the simple comedy coward too many take him for. The others instantly panic; Falstaff, redeemed as always by intelligence, takes a second to make sure that he can't win and *then* runs. To be sure he is no warrior. We may laugh at him because he is physically unfit, but he is himself quite aware that he is too fat to fight. Our primitive derision is defused and changed by the anticipatory intelligence of the "butt."

In fact Falstaff is the first person we meet in Shakespeare to have a "philosophy" in the technical sense of the word. He explains it in his speech on honour:

Can honor set to a leg? No. Or an arm? No. Or take away the grief of a wound? No. Honor hath no skill in surgery then? No. What is honor? A word. What is in that word honor? What is that honor? Air. A trim reckoning! Who hath it? He that died a' Wednesday. Doth he feel it? No. 'Tis insensible then? Yea, to the dead. But will't not live with the living? No. Why? Detraction will not suffer it. Therefore I'll none of it, honor is a mere scutcheon. So ends my catechism.   (1 Henry IV, V.i.131–41)

Medieval philosophy saw a debate between two parties, the Realists and the Nominalists. "Realist" has a technical sense that can surprise modern readers. The Realists believed that universal terms such as "beauty" refer to something that exists in its own right. They are a little like Platonists. The Nominalists on the contrary held that only particulars exist; there may be beautiful things, but there is no such thing as beauty, existing separately from those things. This, note, is the philosophy I thought I could detect behind current Historicist criticism.[19] Nominalism can be traced back to the ninth century A.D., to Eric of Auxerre. Falstaff shows himself to be a card-carrying Nominalist when he uses the word "air" ("What is that honor? Air"). The idea that universals were mere words and those words, in their turn, mere breath, *flatus vocis,*[20] became a commonplace of Nominalism. The word "air," with the same hidden Nominalist force, gets into Duke Theseus's speech about the lunatic, the lover, and the poet in *A Midsummer Night's Dream* (V.i.7–22). Imagination, he says, "gives to *aery* nothing / A local habitation and a name," and adds that the poet cannot think of joy, say, without turning it into a concrete "bringer of that joy." Theseus, the materialist, does not rejoice at this materializing tendency in poetry, because of its lawless misapplication of terms. Clearly, he says, abstractions like "joy" are airy nothings, *flatus vocis,* and only confusion can result if we pretend that they are things.

It is a perfectly proper exercise of hindsight to see in Nominalism the seed-bed of modern scientific materialism. There is a line that runs from William of Ockham through the materialist philosophy of Thomas Hobbes to the scientific revolution. Moreover, scepticism about universals has a political dimension. The communist inhabitants of Thomas More's Utopia are unreflective Nominalists who can make no sense of "humanity" but agree at once that there are human beings.[21] For many years this gambit was the rhetorical property of the radical left. Then Margaret Thatcher dished the Labour Party (making *them* appear old-fashioned) by stealing the gambit; she declared that there was "no society," only people (but she recanted later). In general the Nominalist line is felt as a threat to the high-minded ethical—sometimes as revolutionary. Falstaff, though he may be termed a communist in so far as he has absolutely no sense of the sanctity of private property, is no revolutionary. The real revolutionary of the play is Prince Hal, and his revolution is as invisible as his acting.

The Prince's real revolution is not his switch from wild young man to ruler but his turning inside out of English history. The transformation of Hal is indeed made very visible in the play, but at the same time Shakespeare teaches us, gently, that there may never have been any change at all in Hal himself. Hal was never a wild young man. That was all part of the act! Inheriting a throne tainted by his father's act of usurpation, he redirects the aggression of his countrymen from baronial in-fighting to a consolidated assault on a foreign power, France, thereby achieving glory. This is radical. Henry IV thought he would perish in Jerusalem but died instead in the Jerusalem chamber, on his native soil, never winning through to the great imagined crusade. His son never got to Jerusalem either, but he contrives the true simulacrum of a crusade in the defeat of France.

It is sometimes said that political leaders require a "demonised Other" to retain control of their citizens. If the people are to be ruled they must first be scared. This is very nearly the situation at the beginning of *Henry V*. The King desperately needs a war with France if he is to control such as Scroop and Grey. So far, so cynical. Richard II lost control of Mowbray and Bullingbrook; Henry VI will lose control of Yorkist and Lancastrian nobles. If civil war really is the worst thing of all, and if picking a fight with France is the only way to avoid civil war, we may have moved from cynical power politics to an obscure, unlovable *duty*. Even so, however, Henry will not move until it is clear that his claim on France is legally well founded.

The long scene near the beginning of *Henry V* (I. ii) in which the Archbishop of Canterbury sets out the case in tedious detail is often misunderstood. Directors, embarrassed by the grinding technicalities, often tell the actor to play it for laughs—"If you're going to bore them, play it *as* a comic bore—then it will look as if you did it all on purpose." The trouble with this line is that it is the result of tunnel vision. It is always important to attend to everyone present in a Shakespearean scene, not just to the person who happens to be speaking. It is very probable that most of those on stage are bored by the Archbishop's speech, but there is one exception. Henry is on the edge of his seat as he listens. This is enough to impart a strand of latent excitement to the scene by way of group dynamics. The good director will not need to invent a comic apology for the Archbishop if he makes sure that the audience is simultaneously aware, throughout, of Henry's tense figure. The tension is itself morally complex. At one level he is straining at the leash to go to war (for an ethical reason, to bind up the wounds of England); at another he is genuinely constrained by the sense that he must show a true *casus belli*. When Henry, close to desperation, says, "May I with right and conscience make this claim?" (I.ii.96), many today hear only the contained aggression, but "right" and "conscience" are serious words. The King cannot move if he does not receive an affirmative answer.

The ethical drama is intense. The scene in which Henry listens to the legal justification of his act of war is preceded by a scene in which the churchmen—the party that will lay on the required justification—are shown talking in private. It is made clear that they have an interest in coming up with what, they know, the King wants. They are threatened by a bill that would deprive them of the income from temporal lands donated by devout benefactors; if they give the desired legal advice, the effect of the bill may be softened. Shakespeare has planted a presumption of doubt, ahead of the big speech of justification—the speech Henry is relieved to accept. The legal justification they provide could still be good; we just don't know. Similarly, we do not know whether the King has actually promised money if they say what he needs or whether they are simply counting on a reward, given afterwards, more innocently, by a grateful sovereign. The first alternative—that Henry has bought the justification he needs, will, I suppose, be absolutely unacceptable to most twenty-first-century persons. Yet even this might itself be ethically justified, for Shakespeare, by the good gained, the averting of (a far worse) civil war. But the way Act I, Scene ii, is written suggests that the King is not so far the "white Machiavel" that he would go to war without real legal grounds. As the elaborate justification is expounded there is no sign that the King is anxious to rush the business through. Rather he is simply anxious that it be clear that there *is* a legal case. The King has indeed made the claim before consulting the Archbishop, but, manifestly, he makes it clear that the ruling is just that, a pronouncement by which he will be bound. Far more disquieting is the behaviour that follows. Once the war machine is in motion it is obvious that Henry will do nothing to arrest it. The incident of the Dolphin's (Dauphin's) insult, the present of tennis balls (I.ii.258), is joyfully seized, as if it were a *casus belli* in itself. In Act II, Scene iv, we see the King of France shaken by the approach of the English and apparently ready to negotiate. After Henry's demands have been communicated to him, he asks for time (II.iv.140). We are told by the Chorus that opens Act III that the King of France has offered Henry his daughter's hand in marriage and certain territories (but apparently less than Henry demanded). Henry's army rolls forward, and the French King is forced, it might be said, into a posture of defiance. The scene of justification is indeed the place in the play where the modern audience is alienated from Henry. Certainly, Shakespeare has laced this scene with anxiety and uncertainty. The dramatist, I suspect, loves and pities Henry here.

Falstaff's sceptical Nominalism is the real *philosophical* opposition to Henry's strangely ethical *Realpolitik,* his white Machiavellianism. The conflict is much subtler than the usual collision between high-flown martial rhetoric and cynical self-interest. The Prince is saying, "I must involve thousands in bloodshed to prevent worse happening." Falstaff is saying, "I don't believe any of that; war is war; men die and all the grand language is sheer illusion."

Just as the Prince's eagerness for war with France is subject to facile condemnation from readers and auditors, so Falstaff's behaviour in the matter of recruiting is unintelligently condemned. Falstaff turns down two reasonably robust men, Mouldy and Bullcalf, because he gets three pounds apiece by doing so. He then heartlessly signs up Wart, Feeble, and Shadow, pathetic scarecrows. What possible justification can there conceivably be for this? Falstaff has given the justification in the words, "Food for powder; they'll fill a pit as well as better. Tush, man, mortal men, mortal men" (*1 Henry IV,* IV.ii.66–67). This is callous, but at the same time it is intellectually challenging. Would it really have been so much better to send strong young men to their deaths instead of these? In the bleak democracy of death why not take the odd kick-back and spend the proceeds on a cheering drink? The words "mortal men, mortal men" are suddenly resonant. The standard syllogism of the Schools, "All men are mortal; Socrates is a man; therefore Socrates is mortal," collapses into an intuition of the blankly undifferentiated, undifferentiating character of that death that awaits us all, a radical truth that may make nonsense of the Prince's conscientious policy. As Maurice Morgann said, "Falstaff was a kind of military freethinker, and has accordingly incurred the obloquy of his condition."[22]

Falstaff is sceptical about the martial mystique of honour. The Prince, perhaps surprisingly, is not clearly against him. Falstaff's clear anti-type is the wild northerner, Hotspur, who despises poetry, loves fighting, and is caught up into a kind of ecstasy by the word "honor":

> methinks it were an easy leap,
> To pluck bright honor from the pale-fac'd moon,
> Or dive into the bottom of the deep,
> Where fadom-line could never touch the ground,
> And pluck up drowned honour by the locks.　　(*1 Henry IV,* I.iii.201–5)

The dizzy verticality of this, dropping from the moon, as it swims high above us in the night sky, down to the ocean floor, cuts across the complex horizontals of the play's political action. Hotspur, who will never grow old, is unimpeded by thoughts of means and ends, by worries about precedent and consequence. When Henry speaks of honour, we are in a different, more difficult world: "If it be a sin to covet honor, / I am the most offending soul alive" (*Henry V,* IV.iii.28–29). The context is one of mounting excitement before a battle. Henry is saying that he does not share Westmorland's wish that they had more men—the fewer the men, the greater the glory. This is stirring, but we seem to hear also a bat-squeak of doubt. Something in us wants to say, "Is he crazy?" That the speaker and the dramatist are conscious of this element is shown by the convoluted character of the sentence. The question, "Is it a sin?" is allowed to arise in the mind before it is firmly crushed. And we can scent in the self-deprecating confession, "I am the most offending soul alive" (= "I must plead guilty on that one!"), an attempt to manipulate the listener in a manner that would never occur to Hotspur. Henry is counting on the response, "Nonsense! Good for you!" but the "plain man" voice that we have learned to distrust here masks a far from plain engagement with the ethics of war. In detecting this troubling subtext I do not mean to erase the dominant, martial force of the speech.

We few, we happy few, we band of brothers;

. . . .

And gentlemen in England, now a-bed,
Will think themselves accurs'd they were not here.   (IV.iii.60, 64–65)

Words like these, from one facing likely death, still work with an amazing power that has survived all the anti-war poetry of the twentieth century. The thrill is real, and huge. It is also (more quietly) moving, because this is pure courage. But the speaker, unlike Hotspur, inhabits a clouded world. It is nonsense to say that Henry represents the Aristotelean mean between the extreme views of honour put forward by Falstaff and Hotspur. His position is much less clear than that. Two scenes earlier it has been made abundantly plain, both to Henry and to us, that it is just not true that every English soldier is happy to be there. Not all are buoyed by the honour of the enterprise. This is what emerged when the King, emotional eavesdropper that he is, was rash enough to go in disguise among the common soldiers.

The revealing accent of conciliation, the anxiety to be liked that can be heard as an implicit plea in "I am the most offending soul alive," is fully articulated in the nocturnal debate with the soldiers. Stephen Greenblatt argued that authority figures in Shakespeare operate by instilling anxiety in their subjects.[23] In fact, it is the kings who are anxious. They are the ones who cannot sleep at night. *Henry IV* opens with the King's insomnia. This is handed down, a sick inheritance, to the supremely successful Henry V. Henry moves unknown among his men and hungrily engages them in conversation. He falls in with John Bates, Alexander Court, and Michael Williams. This is the first time we have seen him talking on apparently equal terms with working-class persons. Students writing essays on the history plays often refer to the drinkers at the Boar's Head as "low company," and the expression is not wrong—but they are not as low as all that. Falstaff is a knight. Bardolph and the rest are hard to place socially, but they are not of the working class. They are alcoholic, decayed military men, a little like Captain Grimes in Evelyn Waugh's *Decline and Fall*. One can begin to feel, in the Boar's Head scenes, that the social divisions are indeed unbridgeable and that it is simply inconceivable that the Prince could ever talk to an ostler or a tapster otherwise than as to a servant. But now disguise makes a path for truth.

The first thing Henry says in an eagerly pre-emptive response to the sentry's challenge, is that he is their *friend* (IV.i.92). He then gambles (as it turns out, rashly) on their goodwill by suggesting that they are all in for a crushing defeat. He adds, with serpentine indirection, that it might be better not to communicate such fears to the King, who is after all only human and could in his turn dishearten the army. This is dangerous stuff. Obviously Henry has fears, wishes to have them exorcised, cannot obtain exorcism without explaining them, cannot explain them without a risk of—precisely—disheartening the army. In Shakespearean drama figures of authority sometimes pretend that terrible things are happening in order to bring out the glowing loyalty of the temporarily deceived subject. All ends happily with an "I did this but to try thee." Thus in *Macbeth* Malcolm pretends to be vicious in order to bring out the essential goodness of his (briefly horrified) servant, Macduff (IV.iii.1–137). Henry's talk of likely defeat looks like an "I did this but to try thee" that goes horribly wrong. When the disguised sovereign says, as he says here, "The King is but a man, as I am" (IV.i.101–2), there is a joke for the audience to pick up ("But this *is* the King; in saying 'a man, as I am' he isn't really asserting equality at all!") and, at the same time, an eager confession of real frail humanity ("I am just like you, really"). Bates says that although the King may put on a show of courage, he is sure that he would rather be up to his neck in the cold London river than where he is at present. The image of immersion in cold water, independent of the logic of the sentence, reinforces the idea of fear. The King answers with evident sincerity that he is sure the King would not wish to be anywhere but where he is. We believe him, but the exalted "happy band of brothers" tone of the St. Crispin's Day speech is implicitly subjected to an intense strain—before it has been delivered! Bates, who is not in any way presented as other than a good man, refuses to rise to the rhetorical bait: "Then I would he were here alone; so should he be sure to be ransom'd, and a many poor men's lives saved" (IV.i.121–23). Henry, clearly shaken, says he is sure Bates cannot mean that. In an eerie moment of evasive self-projection he suggests that Bates must be talking in this way in order to "feel other men's minds," which is of course exactly what he, the King, is doing. He then stakes all, with the words, "Methinks I could not die any where so contented as in the King's company, his cause being just and his quarrel honorable" (IV.i.126–28). Honour again! Michael Williams's reply is utterly bleak: "That's more than we know." It is a rich man's war and a poor man's fight. Falstaff on the theme of honour exhibited what could be described as reductive philosophic wit. Williams and Bates have none of that. But their position is similarly sceptical. Bates's talk of the King being ransomed is wide of the mark in this case, but the assumption was reasonable. Bates and Williams agree, however, that, if the cause is not good, at least the King will bear the responsibility. It is here that Williams conjures a nightmare image, like something out of Grimmelshausen: a monstrous composite of maimed body parts, growing together and rising up to accuse the King at the latter day, "some swearing, some crying for a surgeon" (V.i.138). It is a hideously distorted pre-echo of the famous title page of Hobbes's *Leviathan*—no co-operative commonwealth, this. The reference to the surgeon, implicitly horrific in an age before anaesthetics, takes us back to Falstaff's dry observation that honour has no skill in surgery (*1 Henry IV,* V.i.133).

Henry replies casuistically: If a father sends his son on a voyage connected with the family business and the ship happens to sink, should we blame the father? The argument is not strong. The shipwreck was not foreseeable, and this absolves the father in the King's analogy. But when a ruler declares war on a large scale, death and maiming are not just foreseeable, they are virtual certainties. The soldiers are so far persuaded as to admit that they too carry a burden of possible sin in this war—not quite the happy bonding Henry had been working for. Of course the soldiers are not entirely fair to Henry, simply because they are imperfectly informed. Unable to bear the misconstruction of his motives, Henry says he is sure that the King would not be ransomed, adding that, if he were to be, then he'd never trust the King again. He is prevented by his disguise from swearing on the Bible that he will do no such thing, but nevertheless he is now engaged, as by a promise. Williams, entirely understandably, dismisses the proposition as claptrap: How could a common soldier ever challenge, on such a point? The ordinary soldiers will all be dead anyway. Henry is now very near the edge. He cannot argue openly. He declares that he has a quarrel with Williams and will wear a certain favour so that Williams can recognize him and challenge him later. Williams genially agrees to box his ears when the time comes. Bates has the last word. He tells them not to quarrel because they need now to be united against the common enemy. Bates, and only Bates, talks like a king.

Afterwards the real king, left alone, expostulates:

Upon the King! let us our lives, our souls,
Our debts, our careful wives,
Our children, and our sins lay on the King!   (IV.i.230–32)

He did not win the argument, and now he sounds almost pettish. He knows that really they were not wrong. All does indeed rest on his shoulders: "We must bear all."

Once more I would guess that the dominant feeling in the dramatist is pity for the King at this point. Henry, the best actor of them all, was always the man with the common touch, the man who, while remaining at the deepest level utterly alone, could always create a warm bond with others. I have suggested that the "outside-in" causality of the earlier *Henry VI* plays is now replaced by a centrist causality, located in a single figure who can, alone, modify history. To be sure, while the *Henry VI* plays are earlier in composition, Shakespeare and his audience would have been conscious throughout of the fact that, historically, Henry V is the remoter, Henry VI the more recent figure. Perhaps the claims of "non-centrist" causality become stronger as the historical material is less remote from current political experience. But the figure of Henry V is not simple. It is itself doubled to meet the needs of the time. The rhetorically accelerating momentum of a group dynamic is now supplied by the outward, expertly put together aspect of Henry himself, the public societal self. He creates an apparent field of warmly co-operating persons, yet all this is exerted, with cold control, from a single originative subject. But now it is not working. Falstaffian scepticism rises up in other places to subvert the grand Henrician program. Falstaff, who loves Henry so much that his heart is broken by the final rejection, remains the fundamental, philosophical antagonist.

There is a wonderful postscript to the debate by night. Later in the play Williams and the King meet again, and Williams realizes that it was the King whose ears he had promised to box. It must be understood that according to the common usage of the time this alone is enough to doom him. Williams comports himself with steady courage. He never intended any offence, he says, to the King's majesty. The King replies witlessly, saying, in effect, "But you offended *me.*" Williams answers, with obvious festering resentment, "Your Majesty came not like yourself. You appear'd to me but as a common man; . . . I beseech you take it for your own fault and not mine" (IV.viii.50–54). The audience holds its breath. But the King, instead of striking him, smiles broadly and gives him a glove full of money.

Anne Barton in an admirable essay sets this moment beside comparable episodes in Robert Greene's (?) *George a Greene, the Pinner of Wakefield,* George Peele's *Edward I,* and Thomas Heywood's *The First Part of King Edward IV.*[24] The general pattern, fed by Robin Hood legends, is that the King, incognito, falls in with social inferiors and is grossly insulted but reveals all and is jovially united at last with the accidentally delinquent party. What is distinctive about *Henry V,* as Barton saw, is that the jovial conclusion fails to materialize. Williams at the precise point at which his heart should be bursting with gratitude and loyalty, says, amazingly, "I will none of your money" (IV.viii.67).

All this works together to compose a sceptical counterpoint to the heroic theme of the play. But the dominant martial theme is still there, still the principal thing. Agincourt is certainly felt as a glorious triumph, against the odds. The King has succeeded and is a good king. Yet Shakespeare has allowed these subtle fault-lines to develop in the majestic structure. Indeed he insists on them. The exchange with Williams shows how even Henrician acting can go wrong, as Richard II's very different style of acting went wrong, so many years before.

I have called Henry "cold" and have stressed his status as a central agent, but there are strange oscillations and weakenings within that central agency. We have seen how real affection for Falstaff could break through at moments in the prolonged white-Machiavellian performance. Henry's need to be reassured on the night before the battle is nakedly, emotionally human. It is right that he be shown as vulnerable at this point. Machiavelli himself enjoyed debating the old question, whether it is better to be loved or to be feared (deciding, perhaps predictably, that fear is the safer bet).[25] Henry evidently wants to be loved, and to most of us this will seem more a redeeming feature than a weakness. One is tempted to say, paraphrasing Aristotle on the unsocial man, that the person who does not want to be loved is either a god or a beast.[26]

The *salus populi suprema lex*[27] argument that justified (?) the war on France could, if stretched to the limit, lead us into darker regions still. The behaviour of Prince John at Gaultree is such a region. Prince John promises solemnly that he will redress all the grievances of the rebels (*2 Henry IV,* IV.ii.59–60). The insurgents scatter:

Like youthful steers unyok'd, they take their courses
East, west, north, south, or, like a school broke up,
Each hurries towards his home and sporting-place.   (IV.ii.103–5)

The familiar imagery expresses pure happiness. Prince John moves at once, coldly, to sentence the now defenceless rebels to death. Once more the talk is of honour. A rebel asks, "Is this proceeding just and honorable?" Westmerland answers for the Prince, "Is your assembly so?" (IV.ii.110–11). The reply seems to concede, formally, that both sides have acted dishonourably. Hotspur's shining ideal is no longer available, to anyone now on the stage. Prince John meanwhile insists that he has not broken faith at all. He promised to redress the grievances and will do just that; he never promised to spare the lives of the insurgents themselves. The moral is clear: when you negotiate with Prince John, have your lawyer go through the small print (and when you sup with him, use a long spoon). Would the Elizabethans have been shocked by this? Portia in *The Merchant of Venice* shows a cast of mind not unlike Prince John's: "The contract allows you a pound of flesh but allows no blood." Portia's legal quibble draws warm assent, perhaps actual applause from the audience, but the matter is complicated by the fact that Shylock is here caught, deliciously, by his own legalism. A. R. Humphreys observed that the story of Cleomenes (who first agreed to a seven-day truce and then attacked swiftly by night, alleging that the agreement had mentioned days but not nights) was seen in the sixteenth century as a tale of dishonourable behaviour.[28] Samuel Johnson and A. C. Bradley both found the Gaultree episode horrifying.[29] But Utilitarian ethics, the principle of the greatest happiness of the greatest number, can perhaps save Prince John as a moral agent. The rebellion was potentially disastrous, in terms of the likely suffering it would cause, far worse, Jeremy Bentham would point out, than a broken promise or a misleading statement. If Shakespeare had wished to ram home the logic of white Machiavellianism in the person of Hal/Henry he would have placed him, not Prince John, behind this unlovable act. But the plot allows a displacement: let the younger brother do this one. Of course, "Delegate odious offices" is itself a Machiavellian injunction. But now Shakespeare is doing the delegating.

The great worry about formalism has vanished, notice, with the death of Richard II. That special horror of consciousness with its fatal capacity to arrest attention at the level of the word, of style, so that a glass wall is erected between the subject and reality, has now gone. Although Henry is an actor, because he plays not "the anointed King" but "the plain man" we do not *see* the acting, and in a way he doesn't see it either. The words uttered in *1* and *2 Henry IV* and *Henry V* are in consequence curiously free from that dramaturgical neurosis, formal self-consciousness. In the earlier work isolation caused the persons of the plays to introspect and to generate the reduplicative images of the self needed by introspection. Yet Henry, though he is both a player-king and more horribly alone than anyone else in Shakespeare except, perhaps, Hamlet,[30] has no leisure for radical introspection. He is after all a player-king only in that he is both a player and a king; he is not playing *at* being a king. His chosen role of affable humanity immediately involves him not only in relationships but in action. When he is in soliloquy we learn his frailty, his anxiety, his hesitation, but he never gazes at himself, in separation from action. It is all oddly practical.

A whole book could be written on the way the word "dream" is used by Shakespeare. Perhaps the strangest instance of the word is in the rejection of Falstaff. The new-made king says,

I have long dreamt of such a kind of man,
So surfeit-swell'd, so old, and so profane;
But being awak'd, I do despise my dream.   (2 *Henry IV,* V.v.49–51)

We shall come later to the place where Cleopatra, looking back, describes her love-vision of Antony as a dream inwardly stronger than common experience. The dream of the moonstruck lovers in a wood near Athens lies behind. Henry V is using—or thinks he is using—the word "dream" as a term of contempt. Regally (a little like Duke Theseus) he consigns Falstaff to a realm of unreality. Yet we can see Falstaff, whose heart is breaking as the King speaks. As in the earlier comedy the word "dream" has resonances unintended by the dismissive speaker. Savagely, the King insists that this "dream" was a nightmare (dreams are naturally nightmares for Hamlet—"In that sleep of death what dreams may come?" III.i.65): a vision of hideous greed, of physical and moral decay. But the audience knows that Falstaff is a figure of enchantment. He too is one who belongs to moonlit nights rather than to sour, political days: "Let us be Diana's foresters, gentlemen of the shade, minions of the moon" (1 *Henry IV,* I.ii.25–26). There is also about him the glow—one can almost say the glory—that will later invest Cleopatra's Antony. "His delights / Were dolphin-like" (*Antony and Cleopatra,* V.ii.88–89) describes Falstaff as well as it describes the rather better-looking Roman lover. The King is not wrong when he says that Falstaff is an aging, profane alcoholic, but it is one half of a reality the other half of which is stored with immense emotional power. Where the King is straightforwardly—almost absurdly —wrong is when he says that Falstaff was never real at all. It may be said that Henry is merely employing a figure of speech and is therefore not "wrong" in any meaningful sense of the word. But the King is at this moment erasing Falstaff, from his love, from the practical universe he has suddenly entered. Street beggars say the thing they cannot bear is to be treated by passers-by as if they did not exist, to be "looked through." The imposing sovereign who grandly consigns his old drinking companion to the category of illusion is, we cannot help noticing, at another level, "in denial."

There was a time in history when chivalry was unknown, when men were perhaps harder and more brutally practical than at any time before or since. Within a year or two of completing the two parts of *Henry IV*, perhaps while he was still working on *Henry V*, Shakespeare turned to the Roman world, and wrote *Julius Caesar*.

4 Stoics and Sceptics

Rhetoric and the Philosophy of Repressed Passion: *Julius Caesar*

Julius Caesar is about political ideology. The anachronism in the word "ideology" is almost painful. It is after all an Enlightenment or post-Enlightenment word. Its life began in Paris in the 1790s. It was, for a very brief space, offered as a suitable name for a new science—"science des idées" (philosophical psychology or phenomenology, in our terms). But then it at once began to be used as a term of abuse, a way of referring to hopelessly unrealistic speculative dreams—the opposite of "science." Napoleon Bonaparte applied it to "every species of theory which . . . could prevail with none save boys and hot-brained enthusiasts."[1] Karl Marx, similarly, used the German *Ideologie* as a pejorative term. Today we speak freely of left- or right-wing ideologies without any sense that we have lodged an insult by the mere use of the term. There is plenty of political theory before the Enlightenment, but it presents itself as analysis, not as a complex social ethic.[2] The peculiar note of entirely godless moral uplift is absent. But in the republicanism of Brutus in *Julius Caesar* that note can be heard with peculiar distinctness. No one ever speaks of Richard II as having an *ideology* of absolute sovereignty, but with the appearance of Brutus the modern word is suddenly clamorously appropriate. The cultural separateness of the Roman world, its independence of Christianity, makes it a perfect laboratory for free-ranging political hypothesis. It may not be as far away in space as Thomas More's island of Utopia (the first such laboratory), but it is actually further off in time.

Shakespeare, who probably didn't know what a pyramid looked like and believed the Romans wore spectacles (*Coriolanus*, II.i.206), is clearly interested in the cultural otherness of the Roman world. He read in Plutarch that the Romans were fascinated by "maleness" and strength.[3] No doubt his reading was conditioned all the while by English contemporary politics. Heather James begins her book *Shakespeare's Troy* by explaining that she will investigate "Shakespeare's use of the political and literary traditions derived from imperial Rome to legitimate the place of the theatre in early Stuart London" and goes on to do just that.[4] But the play, it is important to remember, is about Rome and not about the English theatre. Brutus in Shakespeare's play is that mildly paradoxical thing, an aristocratic republican. The dramatic presentation of Brutus and his circle may be "fed from below" by the playwright's awareness of a certain group (with the socially exalted Sir Philip Sidney at its centre) that was working to safeguard "contractual monarchy" from that absolutism we saw displayed in *Richard II*. We may call this a "reference" to Elizabethan or Stuart politics, but to anyone who has just read or seen *Julius Caesar*, "reference" will seem too strong a word. The play is so obviously engaged with Roman matter, and equally obviously, the Romans are not like us. If there is "sub-reference" to Sidney, that sub-reference exists in tense negotiation with an alien polity.

To begin with, republicanism is not a practical option in the politics of late-sixteenth-century England. In the Rome of the play it is, conversely, hallowed by antiquity. It is still the norm though it is now threatened. Shakespeare's Brutus, intensely theoretical, committed to oppose any hint of monarchy in Rome, is not historically true of course, but he is closer to Roman historical reality than to any available English equivalent. Some historians have described the assassins of Caesar as young men "high" on Greek political theory, on stories of tyrants justly slain, who mistakenly thought there would be popular acclaim for their action. If that is your view of the real episode in Roman history you must then acknowledge that, essentially, Shakespeare has got it right; at a certain level the drama is *historically* intelligent.

It is commonly assumed that the further one goes back in time the more severely monarchical will be the prevailing system, as if there were some natural Law of Increasing Democracy. We have already seen how in the sixteenth century monarchies increasingly freed themselves of ultimate dependence on the consenting will of the people in the great drift towards absolutism (an absolutism that was perhaps anticipated, momentarily and freakishly, by the real Richard II). This movement reached its climax after Shakespeare's death in the divine right of kings asserted by Charles I. The string gradually tightened until it snapped; Charles died on the scaffold. In my lifetime I have watched the governments of Margaret Thatcher and Tony Blair edge, inch by inch, away from parliamentary democracy towards a less fettered exercise of power. Sometimes the people themselves seem simply to lose interest; the day may yet come when hardly anyone will want to vote any more. One of Karl Popper's "paradoxes of democracy" was conveyed by the question, "What is one to do when the *demos,* the people, freely decides to resign its power to a despot?"[5] When I first encountered this question I saw it as the bizarre thought-experiment of a closeted theoretician, despite Popper's insistence that such things had really happened. Then, on a day when I was wandering round the Reichstag in Berlin it dawned on me that there was a day in twentieth-century European history when a society did exactly this. Truly frightening powers were given to Adolf Hitler *by due democratic process.* Democracy can do many things. It can even commit suicide.

Julius Caesar is set at a turning point in Roman history. We watch the process, as the Republican period gives way to the Imperial. Rome was never a democracy as Athens was, but the people had certain voting rights. We see these rights forming in a later play, *Coriolanus* (as usual Shakespeare is writing his history plays in reverse order, late first, early later). Brutus is very conscious of his lineage. Long, long ago there had been kings in Rome and a Brutus had ejected them.

He believes that his friend Caesar, with his growing assumption of power, is endangering what that early Brutus achieved, is threatening the Rome Brutus loves. Therefore he must kill his friend. What is hard for him will be less hard for the people. They are not close personally to Caesar as Brutus is. Therefore the argument for preserving the Republic will have uncontested sway in their minds. "When I tell them what I have done," Brutus says to himself, "they will be grateful."

That is how Brutus supposed it would be. But it is not what happens. Everyone knows how the high-minded Brutus insisted that Mark Antony (who had none of these reservations about Caesar's growing power) should be free to speak at the funeral, how Brutus when the time came made a strong speech justifying the assassination, and how that strong speech was in its turn smashed to smithereens by the overwhelming Caesarean rhetoric of Antony. The interesting thing is what happens before Antony begins to speak.

Brutus brings his oration to a climax with the words, "Who is here so base that would be a bond-man? If any, speak, for him have I offended. Who is here so rude that would not be a Roman? If any, speak, for him have I offended. Who is here so vile that will not love his country? If any, speak, for him have I offended. I pause for a reply" (III.ii.29–34). The people cry out, "None, Brutus, none!" Brutus rounds off his speech amid a storm of applause, and we are momentarily tricked into thinking that his political judgement has been vindicated. But the "third Plebeian," just as enthusiastic as the others, shouts, "Let him be Caesar!" The people are not cheering for Republicanism. Witlessly, they are cheering for Brutus, the new star. His careful explanation of the way in which our love of individual persons must on occasion yield to safeguard central institutions has fallen on deaf ears. The third Plebeian is saying, in effect, to the conscience-racked slayer of Caesar, "*You* be our Caesar!" This is a populace that actually wants to be ruled by an emperor, and soon will be. The wind is blowing strongly in the wrong direction. Those four words placed by Shakespeare in the mouth of the third Plebeian constitute the most telling political moment in the history of drama. What makes it great as a moment in drama is the combination of economy with enormous implication. The third Plebeian is not clever. He is babbling mindlessly. But his words are loaded with meaning, with the burden of a dark futurity.

Brutus's interaction with the mob is a turning inside out of Henry V's second encounter with Michael Williams. Henry has what Brutus has not, "the common touch." But his "plain man" rhetorical strategy of conciliation goes wrong. When instead of punishing Williams for challenging a king he gives him a glove full of money, we expect a warm glow to suffuse all present, especially Williams himself. Instead, as we saw, Henry cannot get the warm response he craves, and this is partly because Williams is too intelligent. The serving soldier is distressed by the stratagem, by the theatrical manipulation of his loyalty. Conversely, Brutus, despite his social remoteness from the people, instantly obtains all the easy warmth he wants, but where Williams was too intelligent, this audience is too stupid. Brutus's rhetoric works completely, but his argument fails to lodge in the popular mind.

When we passed from *Richard II* to *1* and *2* Henry *IV* we left behind the drama of exacerbated consciousness, with its play on mirrors, its multiplied identities, its neurotic attraction to formal cadences. Richard II called for a glass in which he might view his ravaged countenance. The only time a glass is mentioned in *Henry V* is when the King observes that he never looks in one for love of what he sees there (V.ii.147–48). If soldierly fellows like Henry are not given to mirror-gazing, then surely the martial Romans will be even less interested in their own features. But in *Julius Caesar* the image of the mirror is brought back into the drama. Brutus is a mirror-gazer.

Cassius is plotting to remove Caesar from the scene. He knows they need Brutus to lend respectability to the enterprise. How is he to persuade the great man to join them? A man less subtle than Cassius would have gone privately to Brutus and would simply have talked politics: he would have pointed to the dangerously proliferating powers of Caesar, the implicit threat to Republican institutions. He might have ended with a graceful allusion to that Brutus who threw the Tarquins out of Rome— that is to say, on a personal note. Cassius chooses to work with a mirror. Instead of striking a personal note, he begins at the level of lightly personal general conversation: "Tell me, good Brutus, can you see your face?" Brutus treats this as a question in optics and answers ponderously, "No, Cassius; for the eye sees not itself / But by reflection, by some other things" (I.ii.52–53). Cassius moves closer to the ear of Brutus and sharpens the personal reference of his question. Brutus is clearly right, he says; a reflector of some kind is needed, and what a pity it is that Brutus has no such reflector to tell him how he looks. Brutus smells danger, but Cassius warms to his theme, offering himself as a mirror:

> I, your glass,
> Will modestly discover to yourself
> That of yourself which you yet know not of. (I.ii.68–70)

Cassius's objective is political. He hopes to shame Brutus into joining the conspiracy by telling him what people are saying about him, and this shaming crystallizes in the image, in the way Brutus *appears*. The elementary mechanism is powerful. A certain faculty secretary once came up to me in a darkened corridor and said, "Professor Nuttall, you would be very upset if you knew what people are saying about you." My stomach churned. She then produced a dog-eared piece of paper, a "List of Faculty Members not on e-mail." The list was short, but I was on it. Beside my name someone had written, "Silly old sod." The relief was enormous. "Is *that* all?" I asked. "Well," she answered, "I had to get your attention somehow." Her opening line had certainly done just that. Cassius, however, is not simply reporting to Brutus the remarks made by others. He ties that anxiety to what Brutus sees when he looks in a glass. He is exploiting a streak of narcissism in Brutus that he knows is there.

It is said that men and women use mirrors differently. A woman will use it critically, turning her face this way and that to expose any defects so that she can then take remedial action. A man will use the glass narcissistically, instinctively setting his head at such an angle as will produce the most pleasing image, will murmur, "You handsome beast, you," and depart without taking any action. This obviously doesn't work for shaving, but there may be a grain of truth in the general contrast. Male, Roman Brutus, we may confidently surmise, enjoys gazing at his noble countenance.

Richard II at the crisis of his reign called for a real glass. There is no such actual mirror in *Julius Caesar*. Instead Cassius is offering himself as a figurative mirror. Richard does not see what he wishes to see when the glass is brought to him. Interestingly he is not so narcissistic as simply to desire a fine handsome face in the mirror. He is so far invested in the formal, poetic tragedy that is, for him, superimposed on the actual tragedy of his ejection from the throne that he now *wants* the poetically appropriate thing, a tragic, ravaged visage, and, as we saw, is disappointed by the youthful, presumably pleasant-looking face that confronts him. Cassius is intimating to Brutus that he too will be disappointed. Brutus, rather more simply than Richard, is locked into a flattering image. In Brutus's case it is the image of the noble Roman, a straightforwardly admirable figure. Cassius seeks to shock him into action by showing him an ignoble Brutus, shirking his duty. In that purely mental tragedy that, for Richard, unfolds alongside the real tragedy, the doomed King is an especially terrible figure because he is sacred, anointed, God's regent in England. Wilfully private and sonorously public imagery join in his half-accurate perception of what is going on. For Brutus the self-image and the public image are one, from beginning to end. But in tying his appeal to what this proud, self-loving, highly moral man sees when he looks in a glass, Cassius knows that he is planting a hook and will soon wind in the fish.

It appears that these soldierly Romans can revel unexpectedly in a special kind of interiority, a mode of introspection that is distinct from what we have seen elsewhere. We have reached Stoicism. Plutarch's Brutus was a Platonist,[6] but Shakespeare's is clearly a Stoic. The Stoics believed that the passions should be subjected to rational control. Sometimes the ideal Stoic is seen as simply passionless, as wholly rational. At other times the admired figure is the man (almost always a man, hardly ever a woman) who successfully subdues enormous passions within himself. Where the first idea is essentially static, the second is dynamic and so lends itself to dramatic treatment. Reason's right to rule in the human breast is clear *de jure. De facto,* however, reason may not always be able to impose its lawful authority; the passions can on occasion prove too strong. This is as much as to say, "The rational soul *ought* to rule—is an obviously regulative faculty—but it cannot always do so." When the Stoics try to imagine the relation between reason and passion their language is often military. The idea of a *psychomachia* or "battle in the soul" is largely a Stoic invention (*psychomachia* in older Greek just meant "fighting to the last gasp"). For the Stoics, to follow nature and to follow reason are one and the same. "Nature" is here "the way things actually are," "the way the world is organized," and reason, meanwhile, is not confined to ratiocination—that is, working logically from premises to a conclusion—but includes a cognitive element, the just appraisal of the proper weight and character of things. The pastoral/romantic tradition, by making nature "green" (that is, like a forest and unlike a computer), will produce a philosophy in which following nature and following reason are profoundly opposed. David Hume will argue that the morally cognitive faculty, the just appraisal of things, belongs to feeling, not reason: " 'Tis not contrary to reason to prefer the destruction of the whole world to the scratching of my finger."[7] In another place Hume set down the grandly anti-Stoic sentence, "Reason is, and ought only to be, the slave of passion."[8] But within Stoicism itself the link between reason and nature gradually weakens. Stoic "comforters" told exiled persons that the rational man was a citizen of the world and therefore could not be exiled.[9] Love of country was by implication an aberration, a local convention. The bereaved were told that the death of a child was no cause for grief because we all die anyway. The steady maintenance of such doctrines becomes increasingly a subjective exertion against the manifest character of reality as experienced. When the Stoic philosopher in Johnson's *Rasselas* loses his daughter, the weeping man is reminded by one present (a little tactlessly) of his philosophy. "What comfort," the father answers, "can truth and reason afford me? Of what effect are they now, but to tell me, that my daughter will not be restored?" The philosophy of just appraisal is turning as we watch into a philosophy of heroically asserted indifference, a systematic refusal of the world. Shakespeare, the ignoramus who thought the Romans had chiming clocks (*Julius Caesar*, II.i.192), exhibits a complete grasp of this philosophical and cultural material.

He finds in it a fascinating variant on that queer reduplication of the self he had explored in the English history plays. There is one place in the writings of the Stoic Epictetus where he suddenly says that he doesn't want us all to be like statues.[10] The sentence comes as a surprise because elsewhere the pressure to be as statue-like as possible has been unrelenting. Seneca writes, "As the hardness of certain stones is impervious to steel . . . so the spirit of the wise man is impregnable."[11] If one thinks of oneself as a statue—a marble, Roman statue—perhaps unconsciously one arrogates to oneself a certain grandeur. The kaleidoscopic strutting of Richard II gives place in this Roman play to a motionless posture of contempt for the irrational mess of the world. Cassius reminds us of the statue of Brutus's ancestral namesake at Act I, Scene iii, line 146, and later the "second Plebeian" cries out that the living Brutus should have his own statue, to match those of his ancestors (III.ii.50). In a brilliant preliminary destabilizing of Stoicism Caesar is described as a "Colossus" (I.ii.136) and, simultaneously, as having "the falling sickness" (I.ii.254). When rational pride is linked to image in this way a new species of narcissism is set free. There is nothing erotic about it. In Brutus it is intimately involved with morality. By isolating the element of narcissism Cassius finds the chink in the armour of Brutus. But the moral breastplate is still there. Cassius himself marvels that the noble Brutus should be less than rigid, should be malleable, manipulable (I.ii.308–10).

Two scenes later we see Brutus alone with his conscience and his self-image. We have here not the black horror of Richard III left alone at the end with a self that is devilish but instead something colder, more philosophical, almost pedantic. Brutus reviews the situation in which he finds himself as a result of responding to the expert persuasion of Cassius:

It must be by his death; and for my part,
I know no personal cause to spurn at him,
But for the general. He would be crown'd:
How that might change his nature, there's the question.
It is the bright day that brings forth the adder,
And that craves wary walking. Crown him that,
And then I grant we put a sting in him
That at his will he may do danger with.
Th' abuse of greatness is when it disjoins
Remorse from power; and to speak truth of Caesar,
I have not known when his affections sway'd
More than his reason. But 'tis a common proof
That lowliness is young ambition's ladder,
Whereto the climber-upward turns his face;
But when he once attains the upmost round,
He then unto the ladder turns his back,
Looks in the clouds, scorning the base degrees
By which he did ascend. So Caesar may;
Then lest he may, prevent. And since the quarrel
Will bear no color for the thing he is,
Fashion it thus: that what he is, augmented,
Would run to these and these extremities;
And therefore think him as a serpent's egg,
Which, hatch'd, would as his kind grow mischievous,
And kill him in the shell.   (II.i.10–34)

Is Brutus weakly rationalizing in this speech? In *A New Mimesis* I argued that he was not. When people rationalize actions fuelled by pre-rational forces they prefer not to acknowledge, they don't produce flimsy skeins of half-probability, as Brutus does here. They shout, claim certainty, stress the coercive force of their own utterance. When Hamlet has the perfect opportunity to kill Claudius (usually surrounded by guards but here alone, on his knees, praying), he finds that he cannot do it. Admittedly some argue that the reason he gives for not striking, as he had promised his dead father he would, is to be taken straight. Most feel, however, that the situation is psychologically complex, that Hamlet is obscurely impeded and *covers* his culpable inaction with a sudden parade of reasoning (*making* reasonable that which is not naturally so). Hamlet says he will not kill Claudius because he is at prayer and may be in a state of grace; Claudius himself had killed Hamlet's father with his sins heavy upon him; it would be but feeble vengeance to send the regicide straight to heaven. This has the proper marks of rationalization because of a fiercely asserted logical completeness and simplicity, already in implicit contrast with the known complexity and hesitancy of Hamlet's nature. Moreover its ferocity, the declared wish to send Claudius to everlasting pain in hell, exactly meets the psychological need. Failure to strike, of itself, looks like a softening, but "I will wait until I am sure that he will burn for ever" sounds hard. The ferocity is compensatory. Brutus is not like this at all.

If Brutus is rationalizing in this soliloquy, what is the action or attitude he is trying to cover with this screen of reasoning? Is it an impulse to kill Caesar or a reluctance to kill? The rationalizer normally argues strenuously and one-sidedly to defend the line he will actually take. Brutus argues *for* killing Caesar but does so with an ostentatious emphasis on the weaknesses in his own case. He is therefore the exact opposite of Hamlet. Instead of finding himself unable to strike and having to cover his inaction with a plausible excuse, Brutus finds himself powerfully drawn towards the action of killing a friend for political reasons. The ordinary rationalizer would at this point begin to shout; he would make a heavily public case: Caesarean power is killing the Roman Republic; therefore, if the Republic is to live again, Caesar must die. But this is not what Brutus does. Instead, as I argued in *A New Mimesis,* he looks for weaknesses in his own position. With donnish scrupulousness he reminds himself that the case against Caesar is hypothetical. Caesar, he says, has done nothing discreditable with his enormous power. It is just that power on this scale could lead to horrific consequences. The apparent categorical simplicity of statements like "Republicanism is good" dissolves, under Brutus's probing, into a cloud of probabilities. An absolute monarch may rule wisely, but when monarchy becomes absolute there is no way to restrain the monarch who rules unwisely or cruelly. The people and the state may make bad decisions, but these can readily be reversed. The consequences of adhering to a republican system are likely to better than the consequences of permitting absolute monarchy. Brutus is saying to himself in effect, "I must not kid myself; I am doing this on the basis of a guess. The guess is supported by a generally accepted maxim, that power can corrupt, and by nothing else." This then, is not Brutus evasively rationalizing a bloody purpose, it is Brutus at his most intellectually honourable. That was my argument.

The awkward thing is that few feel its force. William Poole took issue with my reading in an admirable article.[12] First he pointed out that a man honestly wishing to test the strength of an argument would hardly begin by assuming its truth, yet Brutus begins, "It must be by his death." One could answer that this opening sentence is there to show the degree to which the conspiracy has already hardened, closing in as it were upon Brutus. We could paraphrase: "So it has to be assassination—God!—but let's think, while we can, about this!" The reply could be sound as far as it goes, but the ghost raised by Poole is not exorcised. A sense that Brutus is "in" any way, is inwardly committed to bloodshed, is meanwhile inserted in our minds by these words. That is why the reader of the play can be found anxiously turning back the pages to see whether Brutus has already given his word that he will join the conspiracy. Poole then detects a subtle but important discrepancy of tone between the public comfort of the maxim, " 'Tis a common proof" and Brutus's private voice. The word "I" recurs with palpable effect. The word "I" can express intellectual modesty as easily as egoistic assertion, but the oscillation between the two voices certainly assists the feeling that the speaker is rationalizing. Poole then finds "I grant" odd ("then I grant we put a sting in him"). This, however, I can deal with easily within the terms of my original reading. My "donnish" Brutus was concerned above all not to corroborate his chosen line but to expose its areas of frailty. This entirely honourable impulse to falsify one's own pet notions has become the habit of his mind. Such a habit can result in convolutions of syntax bewildering to persons of a more practical bent. Brutus has begun to put, against himself, the case for sparing Caesar. Within that counter-case he begins to look, *again,* for weaknesses and objections. The fact that what he here offers as a momentary concession will form the principal ground of his case *for* killing Caesar may seem odd, but it is psychologically plausible in a man like Brutus. Our modern English paraphrase will now be a little longer: "It looks as if this means assassination. I mustn't kid myself on the arguments here. So far Caesar has done nothing wrong. But in certain circumstances he could change. Hmmn. OK, I grant that there could be a danger there. So . . . ."

But then Poole moves to his clincher, the inescapably queasy effect of the words "colour" and "fashion":

> since the quarrel
> Will bear no color for the thing he is,
> Fashion it thus,　　　　　　　　　　　　　　　　　(II.i.28–30)

In *A New Mimesis* I paraphrased "Fashion it thus" as the academic's "Put it this way," but admitted even then that my paraphrase softened the uneasy impact of "fashion." I allowed the hint of an uncomfortable division between Brutus as he is morally involved in practical action and Brutus as taking refuge in abstract theory, seeing the world in profile, as if he were contemplating an abstract philosophical problem. Poole says more roundly that the weakness of the personal voice in contrast with the robust public maxim suggests a latent agenda. In so far as I allowed a certain doubleness in the speech, agreed that it was not at all points the morally luminous affair I was in general arguing for, it might seem that I really conceded, ahead of the game, Poole's fundamental point against me. But we still differ. Poole is, I think, arguing for rationalization. He deals with my insistence that rationalization likes to sound confident by locating the confidence (or pseudo-confidence) in those parts of the speech that employ common maxims—the "public voice." These do sound robust in exactly the right way. The hesitant personal parts of the speech then, for Poole, betray the presence of another layer in Brutus. I meanwhile continue to insist, much more strongly than Poole would, on the morally conscientious character of those hesitations, the parts of the speech Poole sees as "impoverished."

So is Brutus rationalizing or not? I suppose it all depends on what is meant by "rationalizing." If the word means "presenting an artificially constructed array of reasons to cover the real reason for a certain action, about to be carried out," Brutus is not rationalizing. If the word means "assuming by an act of will a certain rational manner, to persuade oneself that one is behaving well and that all this will look all right when viewed in retrospect," then Brutus is rationalizing. Certainly the sense of doubleness, of the fact that an attitude has been assumed, does permeate the speech, and I am sure that it is this that prompts so many readers and watchers of the play to use the term. But two further things must be said. It is the first meaning that is the central ordinary Freudian meaning of the term, and in any case, allowing the appropriateness of the word in its second sense does not oblige us to say that the moral reasons conjured by this unhappy divided man are utterly hollow. They could be good reasons, thought up by a naturally virtuous mind, still.

"Fashion" and "color" are disturbing because they imply a wholly hypothetical state of affairs as their context. "Color" hovers between the senses "specious or plausible reason" and "allegeable ground or reason" (senses 12.a and 12.b in *The Oxford English Dictionary*). Both these senses were current in Shakespeare's time. The suggestion that Brutus feels weirdly free to dress the case in any way that helps is disturbing. "Color" in particular suggests through one of its senses that Brutus is thinking, sub-ethically, of how he can make all this sound when he has to explain to an admiring audience later (this is the Brutus who can be caught by the thought of a mirror). But although both these terms *describe* rationalization or something similar, they cannot for that very reason be *specimens* of rationalization in action. A person who says, "I could rationalize this," is not yet rationalizing—indeed is being oddly honest. Hamlet, who is the star case of rationalization, obviously studiously avoids giving the game away in this fashion. It is another instance of the law that says, "Real rationalizers avoid any impression of uncertainty." But this time Brutus (that honourable man) virtually tells us that he is going to rationalize, so, if Brutus is a truth-teller, what follows will indeed be rationalization. I answer, if so, it is very effectively checked in advance by the lead-in. But in any case, "I am going to rationalize," is less good as a paraphrase than, say, "Let's see how we can make sense of this."

The root of our unease is a sense that Brutus is contriving to forget or erase actuality. Richard II as we saw was both politically astute and eerily cut off; he knew everything about his situation except the fact that it was actually happening. Shakespeare is here rethinking that strange capacity to transpose the world into a presentational profile and placing it in a Stoic context. Stoicism pretended to be a philosophy that deals with distress by rational engagement but soon proved to be a philosophy of disengagement, a system of unconfessed denial. In Brutus's soliloquy we sense that the careful assertion of moral reasoning, in itself noble, has somehow come adrift. There is even a streak of self-satisfaction, an obscure interior equivalent to the public pride of the statuesque Stoic. *Love's Labour's Lost* and *Richard II* are both shot through with the worry of formalism, with a horror at the substitution of an idea of reality for reality itself. In *Richard II* the mode of the supervening formula is that of a story, "The Death of Kings." In *Julius Caesar* it is theoretical reasoning. Shakespeare is here criticizing Stoicism. He is suggesting that it is a philosophy pathologically subject to degeneration into detachment. This detachment is not the detachment of the Olympian observer, permitting a comprehensive prospect. It is the detachment of the frightened fugitive, a way of hiding from an over-rich and hurtful universe. And he is right. Stoicism is at bottom a pusillanimous philosophy. It "talks tough" exactly as Hamlet "talks tough."

If anyone else had seen so deeply into the unacknowledged evasions at the heart of Stoicism that writer would have had to give us a contemptible Brutus, one whose silly pretensions have now been seen through. But Shakespeare can see all this and still think Brutus an honourable man. I for my part continue to believe that the hesitations expressed in the soliloquy are fundamentally honourable. There is no irony in "This was the noblest Roman of them all" at the end of the play. Brutus, perhaps alone of the conspirators, acted from unselfish motives in what he conceived to be the public interest. Always he tried to be good. The same final respect for this complex, flawed, evasive man can be seen in the great quarrel scene in Act IV.

There, if the Folio text is not corrupt, we have the curious "double report" of Portia's death. Brutus and Cassius fall out over the conduct of the war. Then Brutus suddenly explains that he has just learned that his wife has died. Cassius is deeply contrite and wishes to sympathize. But you can't hug a Stoic. Then a messenger arrives and tells Brutus—what?—that his wife has just died. Brutus behaves as if he were hearing the news for the first time and puts up a tremendous show of serene acceptance. The messenger is duly impressed: "Even so great men great losses should endure" (IV.iii.193). We who know that Brutus was informed in advance of the bad news may be tempted to say, "You fraud!" But Cassius, who knows all, says, "I have as much of this in art as you, / But yet my nature could not bear it so" (IV.iii.194–95). I think this means, "I am as good as you are at artificial performance, but I haven't got your sheer guts." He notes the artifice and, vividly aware as he is of the courage Brutus is showing in the midst of terrible grief, has no difficulty in forgiving it. Cassius loves Brutus even more than Brutus loves Brutus. But Brutus evidently loved Portia. His love for his wife and his grief at her death, "affections" Brutus is proud to be able to repress, actually redeem him as a human being. Cassius understands this, and so does the audience if the performance has been good. As Brutus is redeemed, Stoicism is damned. The socially climbing Shakespeare who emerges from Katherine Duncan-Jones's biography, *Ungentle Shakespeare,* seems as a personality ethically thin, far from admirable. But the Shakespeare who can uncover so much frailty and continue to perceive goodness, the Shakespeare behind the plays, is a figure of immense, intelligent charity.

Julius Caesar is also a play about rhetoric, the art of persuasion. Teachers of literature often maintain that Shakespeare and Shakespeare's audience were in general happy with rhetoric, as we are not. Brian Vickers in his monumental study, *In Defence of Rhetoric,* is too learned to be unaware that from the earliest times philosophers have been hostile to rhetoric, but he thinks the poets, including Shakespeare, simply loved rhetoric, immersing themselves in its tropes with unaffected delight.[13] Certainly the hostility of the philosophers is perennial. Rhetoric is attacked because of its dubious relation to truth-telling. Plato, himself a consummate rhetorician, attacks rhetoric in the *Phaedrus,* 266D, and the *Theaetetus,* 172–73. In the *Phaedrus* the rhetorician-sophist Gorgias is pilloried: such persons by argument "make the little appear great and the great little." There is something alarming about the real-life Gorgias. Plato's fears of an epistemological meltdown may not have been baseless. Gorgias held that truth and knowledge were illusions and that the power of the word was supreme.[14] Helen of Troy was seen as the cause of countless deaths in war. Gorgias accordingly wrote his rhetorical "Praise of Helen." At the end he says it was all a joke, but he also says, chillingly, "So I, by words, have made a bad woman good." The implication can make one shiver. Words can do *anything.*

Vickers cites Aristotle as a philosopher friendly to rhetoric, yet the note of philosophic contempt can be heard when Aristotle says that it is important to get an emotional hold over the judges in a court-room—"especially the weak-minded ones" (*Rhetoric,* 1415b). The story of philosophic hostility that begins long before Shakespeare was born continues after his death. Locke attacks rhetoric and so does Kant.[15] The end of rhetoric is persuasion, and not infrequently a lie or a distortion will persuade more effectively than the truth ever could. I am told that a study was made of the effect of television party-political presentations at election time; it showed that if the presenter offered reasons for voting for the party presented, enthusiasm for that party actually fell; but if the candidate was shown walking in a field, holding hands with his wife while a spaniel trotted about and Elgar music could be heard in the background (Edward Elgar for Britain, Aaron Copland for the United States?), enthusiasm rose.

Julius Caesar contains the greatest oration in the English language, delivered by Mark Antony over the still-bleeding body of Caesar. Shakespeare is writing at the height of his powers. All this may seem to support the "teachers' line" that at this period poets, playwrights, and audiences simply loved rhetoric and had no problem with it. But Shakespeare is not happy with his own facility any more than he was happy with the different facility of courtly language in *Love's Labour's Lost.* He stands with the worried philosophers, shares all their doubts. Antony whips the crowd up to a frenzy, induces in them a passion that he shares, good method-actor that he is ("His eyes are red as fire with weeping," III.ii.115). When he has finished he says coldly to himself, "Now let it work. Mischief, thou art afoot" (III.ii.260). The mob runs riot in the streets, and when they meet a poet called Cinna, they tear him to pieces because he has the same name as one of the assassins. This is what really powerful rhetoric can do.

No one but Shakespeare, knowing that Antony's speech must blow away any earlier words from Brutus, would have dared give Brutus the strong speech he actually gets from Shakespeare. Brutus, as Antony half-ironically observes, is himself an orator. Quintilian in his *Institutio oratoria* (XII.x.17) distinguishes two styles, "Attic" and "Asiatic." The Attic style is refined, polished, and free from superfluity; the Asiatic is swelling and exultant. Quintilian prefers Attic to Asiatic, and that is what Shakespeare gives to Brutus. He challenges the intelligence of his auditors with ethical choices: "If then that friend demand why Brutus rose against Caesar, this is my answer: Not that I lov'd Caesar less, but that I lov'd Rome more" (III.ii.20–22). The speech in its flinty way is thoroughly rhetorical. For example anaphora, the repetition of an opening phrase, is heavily employed ("Who is here? . . . "). Yet even before Antony speaks we may sense, in this most carefully ethical of orations, the unintended dominance of the wrong emotion. That Plebeian who cried out at the conclusion of the speech, "Let him be Caesar!" (III.ii.51), has understood nothing, but the rhetoric has done its job; the man has been persuaded. Mindlessly, he is now on Brutus's side. But then comes Antony's huge, "Asiatic" speech. Shakespeare himself never uses the term "Asiatic," but it is likely that he knew the distinction between the two kinds of oratory (it can be found in other authors besides Quintilian). Antony is the figure who will appear later in *Antony and Cleopatra,* a play that explores the tension between classical restraint and opulent Asiatic emotion.

I have said that rhetoric was always subject to philosophical attack from outside. At the same time it is naturally liable to a self-consuming, internal solvent. If we become aware that we are being persuaded, we are at once armour-plated against persuasion. This generates "anti-rhetorical rhetoric": "I am no great persuader, I'm a plain man" (Antony's "I am no orator, as Brutus is," III.ii.217). Indeed a streak of negation runs through developed rhetoric. The figure known as *occultatio* is a good example. By this figure information is slipped into the hearer's mind, as it were, by the back door: "I'll skip the fact that he has been embezzling funds for the last five years and I won't dwell on the fact that he has been taking bribes." Instead of bludgeoning the auditor into assent through sonorous repetition, the vital material is cocooned in disclaimers. The effect of course is to activate fierce curiosity at once, precisely because the listener is led to believe that he or she is no longer being persuaded, that the rhetoric is over. Anaphora belongs to the primary level of oratory, *occultatio* to the secondary. It is as if rhetoric can succeed only by denying its own nature. *Occultatio* is everywhere in Antony's speech. It reaches a climax when, with careful timing, he suddenly explains that he does not propose to read Caesar's will—that will in which the people are made beneficiaries of his generosity (III.ii.130–36, 140–45, 238, 247–50).

Shakespeare had written just one oration on this scale earlier—the speech given by Henry V before the critical battle. There morality and emotion are almost fused. Almost but not quite. As we saw, the nocturnal debate with the common soldiers drove a wedge between the stirring excitement of a genuinely honourable war and bleak reality. It is as if Shakespeare went on thinking about that division and decided to make it wider, in the Roman play. We are confronted once more by a separation of language from reality but in a new mode. For, at the level of description, Antony's words are weak. "You all did see," he cries in triumphant scorn,

> that on the Lupercal
> I thrice presented him a kingly crown,
> Which he did thrice refuse. Was this ambition? (III.ii.95–97)

The crowd roars its agreement, and what is more sinister still, the theatre audience is swept along by the same stimuli. Yet we have been told earlier, by Casca, what actually happened on the Lupercal. Caesar did indeed refuse the crown three times, but he did so, seemingly, *with increasing reluctance* and fainted at the last refusal (I.ii.236–50). Shakespeare makes it clear that at the deepest level Caesar and Rome with him are drifting towards monarchy. Mark Antony's scorn for the suggestion is a mistake, or else culpable pretence. But if the speech is short on truth, it is long on practical agency. W. H. Auden wrote, "Poetry makes nothing happen."[16] But rhetoric makes things happen, on a frightening scale.

It is as if the implicit critique of Stoicism we saw in Shakespeare's presentation of Brutus, a man who feels he must repress even the love he feels for his dead wife, is now strangely mirrored in an implicit critique of Antony and his sinister ability not to repress but to foment extravagant emotion. We begin to see that the Roman world as a whole is a place of malfunctioning emotion. In this society love is an ill-nourished, un-developed thing. Either it is crushed by Stoic repression or it is rhetori-cally manipulated and converted into aggression.

The seeming serenity of Roman Stoicism is seen by Shakespeare as the source both of a peculiarly Roman narcissism on one hand and of Roman bloodlust on the other: every man a hero in his own proud psychomachia. In the comedies we saw male same-sex bonding happily invaded by the love of women. In the ultra-male world of Rome's military society this assumes a more extreme form. Women play no direct part in the real business of the drama. There is a mild pre-echo of this in the English martial milieu of *1 Henry IV,* where we see Hotspur's wife excluded from her husband's bed and from the deliberations of the rebellious lords (*1 Henry IV,* II.iii.37f.). In *Julius Caesar* this is re-run, in a darker, fiercer mode. Portia, Brutus's wife, is excluded from the plot and left alone in her bed. In the film *The Godfather: Part II* there is a moment of great visual power when a door closes, shutting off the brighter room beyond in which beautiful women sit with children; the Mafiosi have to discuss business. In her distress Portia first wounds herself in the thigh and then dies by swallowing fire. Brutus's reaction to her desperate act of self-harm is glowing admiration: "O ye gods, / Render me worthy of this noble wife!" (II.i.302–3). No clearer evidence of the sickness of this society could be given.

It remains a curious fact that in later ethical philosophy we shall see reason displaced as the proper director of moral action and feeling substituted—and this switch is first made in the handbooks of rhetoric. Hume said that he could detect no *rational* error in the man who preferred the destruction of the world to the scratching of his finger, but only an error of feeling,[17] and many historians of ideas locate the change at this point. But Sir Philip Sidney argued in his *Defence of Poetry* for passionate language as a better motor of moral action than the "wordish description" of the philosophers.[18] Sidney was swiftly followed by Thomas Wright, Benet of Canfield, Jean-François Senault, Edward Reynolds, and Walter Charlton, all authors of treatises on the passions in which the moral status of feeling is enhanced.[19] Brutus speaks coldly but is quite clearly a loving husband. Antony speaks warmly and we never know whom or what he really loves. The Antony of the later play obviously loves Cleopatra, but although it is historically the same person Shakespeare has re-conceived the character for the later play. In *Julius Caesar* Antony is an ever-increasing, wholly inexplicable political power. From the moment when he walks in among the assassins on the Capitol, we know his strength and at the same time we learn Brutus's weakness. The knives of the killers are still wet with blood. Antony knows that they must be wondering whether they need to kill him too. Coolly he singles out with his eye the weak man and addresses Brutus.

"You shall give me reasons / Why" (III.i.221–22). It is a gamble but he knows his man. The donnish Brutus could never refuse a request for a full, rational explanation. It would be inconsistent with his profound self-respect to do anything but what he does. As Brutus offers the Caesarean Antony full freedom of speech, including the right to speak at Caesar's funeral, Cassius's head, we may surmise, is in his hands.

Perhaps they should have killed Antony there and then. That is a moral "should," not just an expedient recommendation. Had they done so, thousands of lives would perhaps have been saved: no Battle of Philippi, no Civil War. But the words "Let him be Caesar!" rise before our minds. Perhaps killing Antony would not have been enough, after all, to save the Republic. Rome is lurching towards monarchy.

Cicero, that clever statesman of the Republic, ought to have had words of wisdom for the first crisis of the play, when Caesar fainted at the offer of the crown. "Did Cicero say any thing?" Cassius asks, and Casca answers, "Ay, he spoke Greek" (I.ii.278–79). Cassius presses him: "To what effect?" but Casca answers, "Nay, and I tell you that, I'll ne'er look you i' th' face again. But those that understood him smil'd at one another, and shook their heads; but, for mine own part, it was Greek to me" (I.ii.278–84). The passage seems to be unimportant, negligible nonsense, and in general the commentators have been content to take it so, troubling themselves no further. Yet it is not difficult to find out what Cicero said. In Suetonius's *Life of Julius Caesar* (xxx), in the context of a possible bid for the monarchy on Caesar's part, Cicero delphically quotes a couple of lines from the *Phoenissae* of Euripides (524–25). Suetonius gives them in Greek and then translates: "If law is to be violated, it is best to do it for the sake of dominion—and in all other things to preserve piety."[20] Cicero is saying that a revolution carried out in the spirit of mastery is better than one carried out in a spirit of mere anarchy—and adds that meanwhile the gentler habits of traditional religious sentiment should be retained. I am sure that Shakespeare knew the words that eluded Casca. Yet the dramatist does nothing to help us as we sit listening in the theatre—that audience he has so scornfully subjected to the mind-destroying rhetoric of Antony. It is another piece of buried learning, like the allusion to Ovid on genealogy in *The Taming of the Shrew* (III.i.27–28).

But there is a better example. At the point of the assassination Shakespeare famously leaves his native English for Latin. Caesar, looking at his killer, says, *Et tu, Brute?* "You too, Brutus?" (III.i.77). The sudden gravity of the ancient language suggests that this is some sort of marker. This is a moment of special significance. But Shakespeare does not explain. Again, the answer is not in Shakespeare's principal source, Plutarch, but in Suetonius. For Suetonius also switches at this point, from his native language, Latin, into Greek. The alien letters jump out from the page: *Kai su, teknon?* "You too, child?" Geoffrey Bullough in *Narrative and Dramatic Sources of Shakespeare* says that there is nothing in the text of Shakespeare's play to prove that he read Suetonius, and indeed Philemon Holland's translation of Suetonius, which Bullough prints, did not appear until 1606, some seven years after *Julius Caesar*. But Shakespeare could easily have read Suetonius in Latin. "Prove" is a fierce word. The fact that *Et tu, Brute?* is not in Plutarch but is in Suetonius falls short, we may concede, of absolute proof, but meanwhile it places Shakespeare's knowledge of Suetonius beyond reasonable doubt.

When Suetonius has Caesar use Greek the effect is not so much of gravity as of intimacy. It is a little like the use of French by Russian aristocrats in Leo Tolstoy's *War and Peace.* But the all-important word is *teknon,* "child." The story in the background (and this is fully set out by Plutarch) is that Brutus was the natural son of Caesar. That Shakespeare knew this story is clear from the phrase "Brutus' bastard hand" in *2 Henry VI* (IV.i.136). Something very odd is going on. Shakespeare signals, with the Latin phrase, to those few in the audience who know Suetonius but gives nothing away. It is as if he moved to incorporate the frightening theme of patricide but then chose to crush it before it could appear fully. If we entertain the thought that a father is here speaking to his son, we shall find that it adds to the power of the tragedy and works consistently with the rest. One wonders if that almost pathological habit of concealment in Shakespeare that fascinates Richard Wilson is somehow behind the suppression. Perhaps Shakespeare crushed the story not because it seemed inappropriate or embarrassing but because it was too strong. It is displaced, sideways. Shakespeare needed to write a whole new play to accommodate the thought. It is called *Hamlet.*

The Introversion of Stoicism: *Hamlet*

Hamlet followed closely upon *Julius Caesar.* The mutual involvement of the two plays is obvious. When Brutus says,

Between the acting of a dreadful thing
And the first motion, all the interim is
Like a phantasma, or a hideous dream. (II.i.63–65)

Brutus is thinking about Caesar, but Shakespeare is thinking of the play to come. *Hamlet* is seen in the distance and is described before it is written. Then, conversely, *Hamlet* keeps glancing back at *Julius Caesar.* Polonius says he once played the part of Caesar and was "kill'd i' th' Capitol" (*Hamlet,* III.ii.102). He adds, "Brutus kill'd me" (*et tu, Brute, Kai su, teknon*). Horatio remembers how before Caesar fell "the sheeted dead / Did squeak and gibber in the Roman streets" (I.i.115–16). Now, as we look through northern eyes, the classical scene becomes a Gothic nightmare, a *Walpurgisnacht.*

Stoicism, also, spills over from *Julius Caesar* into *Hamlet* and becomes a subjective nightmare. Polonius's set speech of advice to his son is in part Stoic:

to thine own self be true,
And it must follow, as the night the day,
Thou canst not then be false to any man. (I.iii.78–80)

This is the doctrine of the Stoic Cato: "He that striveth with himself shall full evil agree with other men . . . is not meet for the company of other men."[21] But the shadow of an encroaching subjectivism is already discernible. I remember saying to my teacher when I was about fourteen, "But sir, if your nature was mendacious, and you were true to that, wouldn't that mean that you would tell lies all the time?" and was appropriately slapped down for wasting class time.

Polonius is covertly substituting a prescribed, ideal self for the self as it would appear in a straight description. Laertes is invited to conjure from nowhere a splendid version of himself, a Laertes who could not possibly betray a friend; if he can be true to *that,* his virtue is indeed assured. This slippage from "Be true to reality" to "Be true to your version of reality" happens behind an unchanged linguistic surface. Formally the word "self" still looks like a straightforward descriptive or referential term. But the change will bear strange fruit. Proto-Romantic Rousseau in the French eighteenth century asks, "What greater good can a truly good being expect than to live in accord with his nature?"[22] Two pages later he explains that he derives these principles not from a "Higher Philosophy" but from the depths of his heart: "What I feel to be right is right." The reader thinks, "Can Stoicism, the anti-passion philosophy, be turning into, of all things, Romanticism?" That is exactly what is happening. As Stoicism is subjectivized, as the impersonal, rational cosmos fades, a curious internal excitement develops. Shakespeare's *Hamlet,* in which the slow process of subjectivization is meticulously observed, became a key text for the Romantics. The *Weltschmerz* and *Ichschmerz* ("world-pain" and "I-pain") of Goethe's *Werther* is immediately reminiscent of *Hamlet.* George Chapman's *Bussy D'Ambois* was written some three years after *Hamlet.* The play opens with the withdrawal of a neo-Stoic Providence from the fabric of the universe: "Fortune, not reason rules the state of things." When Bussy says, "Who to himself is law, no law doth need" (II.i.208), we no longer infer that this is simply a man who does not need to be told that he should stop at a red traffic light. Bussy is a wild man.

At III.ii.65f. Hamlet gazes at his friend Horatio ("more an antique Roman than a Dane," V.ii.341) with a kind of envy, as one who "in suff'ring all . . . suffers nothing," "is not passion's slave." Hamlet, lost in a new subjective darkness, sees in Horatio an innocent Stoic. But when Hamlet appropriates Stoic language to himself, all this is gone: "There is nothing either good or bad, but thinking makes it so" (II.ii.249–50). Harold Jenkins in his note on this line in the Arden edition of 1982 is clear that the sentiment expressed is a Stoic commonplace and that there is no suggestion at all of ethical relativism. Certainly the observation is common, and equally certainly, it is Stoic in origin. But Jenkins's confidence is misplaced. We have seen how the exertion of reason by Roman Stoics can increasingly become a way of denying rather than truly representing reality. Brutus's pretence that he is unmoved by the death of his wife is heroic because of its manifest un-realism and is humanly forgivable for the same reason. Normally, indeed, the commonplace observation Hamlet makes here is relatively undisturbing. In Hamlet's mouth, however, it is suddenly vertiginous.

The old Stoic was insulated from the conventions of any particular society but remained "a citizen of the world," whatever that means. Hamlet's isolation is more profound. He has been ordered by a dead man to become a bearer of death and, in consequence, to die himself. Henry V was isolated from happy courtship and from convivial friendship by his political dedication. Hamlet is cut off in a more elemental fashion from sexuality and procreation. That is why he must turn on Ophelia and repel her from his tainted, shadowy presence. Clearly the words as Hamlet utters them are pivotal between a Stoicism that retains some grip on ethical objectivism and a modern radical uncertainty. "Kidding on the level," he insists, to Rosencrantz and Guildenstern, that Denmark is a prison. Jenkins thinks he means that that he finds the place depressing even if they don't, because he is depressed; it is not an ethical judgement. But Hamlet has been told by his dead father that Denmark is controlled by the murderer of that father. The notion of being trapped by circumstance in the ogre's castle is not far away. To exclude the ethical from consideration is absurd. Hamlet means that *he* can see that Denmark is a wicked kingdom in which he is confined. Denmark is bad. But then whimsically he allows that this could be a subjective view—others might assess the situation differently. Obviously ethical subjectivism is much more disquieting than subjectivism in the field of happiness. Epistemological relativism, doubt not about whether anything is objectively good but about whether anything can be known to be there at all, is more radical still.

Yet Hamlet is ready to push his scepticism to the point of epistemological doubt: "O God, I could be bounded in a nutshell, and count myself a king of infinite space—were it not that I have bad dreams" (II.ii.254–56). Hamlet is thinking about the fallacies of experience. Empiricism, the philosophy that says that all knowledge is founded on sensory experience, was to become the dominant mode in the course of the seventeenth century, after Shakespeare's death. The question, "How do I know that I'm not dreaming?" is a chestnut of empiricism (it is indeed the point at which empiricism can mutate into its apparent opposite, scepticism). Just as Stoicism, for all its insistence on reason, held the seeds of a strange subjectivism, so empiricism, though it begins by sounding thoroughly down to earth, had in it that which could foster immaterialist idealism. As long as "experience" means "the things we experience," this sunlit wall, that tower in the distance, all is well. But the empiricists became committed to a causal or representative account of perception. That sunlit wall is replicated in an image on the retina. The mind, it seems, has immediate access to "ideas" only, that is to images that represent (with what degree of fidelity we can never check) external things. So now "experience" refers to the private television screen, behind the eye. A shiver of solipsism, a fear that there may be nothing at all out there, can be felt behind the robust philosophy of John Locke: "Since the *Mind,* in all its Thoughts and Reasonings, hath no other immediate Object but it own *Ideas,* which it alone does or can contemplate, it is evident, that our Knowledge is only conversant about them."[23] It recurs in Hume: "Let us chace our imagination to the heavens, or to the utmost limits of the universe; we never really advance a step beyond ourselves, nor can conceive any kind of existence, but those perceptions, which have appeared in that narrow compass."[24] We wish to check that the unending show of images is true; we think we can pop outside to see. But the mind cannot leave its cell inside the head. Checking—"having a look"—can be done only via the optical apparatus we had hoped to corroborate externally. It is interesting that Hume feels the difficulty in spatial terms. The most distant heavenly bodies we can see are available to the mind only as insubstantial images too close for comfort. Hamlet says he can think that he is master of infinite space, but all this might be happening within the confines of a tiny shell. Elsewhere in the same scene his mind passes from the "firmament . . . fretted with golden fire" to a "foul and pestilent congregation of vapors" (II.ii.301–3).

There is no sign that Shakespeare has worked out, ahead of history, a full causal or representative theory of perception. But he has clearly seen that the world as it appears to a suffering subject can shift and change alarmingly. The difficulty of separating dream from reality haunts him. With breath-taking cleverness Hamlet wittily transposes his "dream" to another place in the system. Instead of saying, "It is my dream that the world is foul" or "I feel that I am a wretched prisoner in darkness," he says that he could believe himself free, *but for* his bad dreams. What are the bad dreams? The sceptical intuition itself, that nothing is real? Or, what the audience by now believes for a fact, that Denmark is a place of wickedness? By the second interpretation the bad dream is the site not of an illusion but of shocking veracity. The general effect, however, is of profound, intractable disorientation.

In *Hamlet* the concern with acting and identity that ran through the early plays reaches a climax. It is a curious experience to turn from twentieth-century critics as they laboriously excogitate, one at a time, such notions as "self-reference" and "self-fashioning" to Shakespeare himself. For Shakespeare these notions are merely preliminary approximations, the springboard for a far more complex and acute interrogation of the subject.

Hamlet envies the simple Stoic, Horatio, but there is no doubt in our minds but that Hamlet is the greater man of the two. This is odd because he is so very close to being an anti-hero, or even a clown. His very name as it is given in Saxo Grammaticus probably means "fool" or "weakling," but I do not think Shakespeare knew this.[25] Faced with a challenge to his honour, the murder of his father, he dithers. He hangs about in his mother's room. He jokes nervously when action is needed. He is incapable, seemingly, of a normal sexual relationship with a loving woman. It is remarkable technically that this figure should become a colossus of world literature. The very hesitations of a Hamlet loom larger in our minds than the massacres of a Tamburlaine. Richard II was one kind of player-king, Henry V perhaps another. Hamlet is not so much a player-prince as a player-avenger. Like Richard he is "playing himself," but where Richard was sustained in his role by the shining public image of the sacred king, Hamlet has been led by a ghost out of the green area of common existence into a parched desert.

We know that there was an earlier play with the Hamlet story, perhaps by Thomas Kyd. This play is lost, but we have Kyd's *Spanish Tragedy,* an inverted *Hamlet,* about a father avenging his son. It is likely that the earlier *Hamlet* was melodramatic and bloody. The pre-existence of this older version makes it possible for Shakespeare to engage in a virtuoso range of stylistic registers, some half-parodic. When Hamlet tells the players who visit Elsinore to avoid extravagant gestures and to speak "trippingly" (III.ii.2), we may detect a sophisticated distaste for the kind of acting Kyd's plays actually demand. Hamlet recommends an altogether cooler manner. William Empson in a brilliant essay conjectured that when Shakespeare was invited to do a re-write of the old play he discovered a "hole" in the drama: the hero kept failing to act. This made for suspense, but meanwhile no reason for the delay was offered within the play. Shakespeare knew that he had to deal with a mildly difficult audience—one genuinely enthusiastic about the old play but no longer easily terrified—perhaps too ready to smile where they would once have gasped. Suddenly Shakespeare knew what he had to do. Instead of supplying a plausible explanation of the delay within the plot, he would make the hole in Kyd's play huge, would turn the original dramaturgical incompetence into a psychological mystery. He would have his hero marvel, aloud, at his own inaction. He now has a way to deal with the too comfortably omniscient audience. They can be given what they have paid to hear, plenty of echoes of the old revenge play, but these Kydian elements will now figure as a one-man play within the play, as a performance put on by Hamlet, as "antic disposition" or pretended madness. Now, whenever he wishes Shakespeare can wipe the complacent smile from the spectator's face with the implied challenge: "Can you understand this man? You can't, can you?" The resultant play with its strange stylistic duplicity had an enormous effect on the revenge tragedies written by later dramatists. There is a sense in which they are all "pastiche revenge tragedies" rather than "straight." That is because, after *Hamlet* had made the formal character of the genre so explicit as to be almost comic, any dramatist who hoped to appear "street-wise" was obliged to show a similar consciousness of "manner." What the later dramatists could not do was to write two plays at once, a mock-revenge and a real, terrifying, murder-answering murder. Only Shakespeare could do this.

Empson's ear was good, and his analysis of the complex stylistic orchestration of *Hamlet* masterly. But his essay had two great faults. First, he decided that once one has seen that Shakespeare's method is to daze the audience there is no point in speculating about the reasons for the hero's delay. The play is set up as a conundrum without a solution. That means that we can all relax. In fact, as we shall see, Shakespeare lays down lines of clues and suggestions, leading away from the eye into a gradually increasing obscurity. Audiences have always responded to these clues, and there is a sense in which the critic who has decided that they should be ignored is no longer receiving Shakespeare's play. Second, Empson failed to see how the histrionic behaviour of the Prince reacts upon his own sense of self. That Hamlet should employ actorly tricks to impose upon others (as when he fixes Ophelia with his eye and walks backwards from the room) is one thing, but what are we to make of the speech beginning, "Now could I drink hot blood" (III.ii.390)? This is in the manner of Kyd. It demands a melodramatic delivery. But Hamlet is not here working on another person. He is alone. Since we know that these tragic mannerisms are a means of manipulation, we are propelled into the thought: Hamlet must be using the black-revenge style *to practise upon himself.* The role-playing that was a means of evading action for Richard II is in Hamlet a desperate attempt to galvanize muscles that are inert. As early as the Temple Garden scene in *1 Henry VI* we saw "outside-in" motivation, the mere behaviour of a faction, the adoption of badges, metamorphosing into violent war. There we were looking at group behaviour. But there are modes of outside-in motivation that work at the level of the individual. Richard II's strutting is a way of comforting himself. Hamlet's is an essayed self-therapy.

Once more we begin with isolation. The visiting ghost has separated Hamlet from the sustaining link with continuing life. As a result, his motivation decays. The young, ordinarily likable Hamlet we glimpse in the letter to Ophelia ("O dear Ophelia, I am ill at these numbers," II.ii.120) has given way to one from whom all ordinary, natural relationships have been withdrawn. Normal identity, which is bound in with such relationships, has gone with them. The left-over darkened self is haunted by a single thought: "I am to kill my uncle." Hamlet watches an actor reciting a speech about Hecuba. He is amazed and also, in a way, envious when he sees a tear in the actor's eye: "What's Hecuba to him, or he to Hecuba?" (II.ii.559). *From the outside in* role-playing has created a real emotion. Hamlet therefore keeps up the Kyd style, now, when he is alone, to activate the required bloodlust.

The usual picture is that a human being has a certain nature to begin with and from this nature the expected actions will flow. Anne will give more than the others because Anne is a generous person. But the sequence can be reversed. Remember here the James–Lange theory; "We fear, because we run."[26] A certain Roman Catholic chaplain to a university used to say to students who had lost their faith, "Behave as if you had it still. Hang around in churches. Do a lot of kneeling. It will seep back in from the outside." Baron von Hügel, a little chillingly, said that he embraced his child "*in order to* love it."[27] The basic notion of a walking negation that seeks a more substantial identity through role-playing is obviously close to Jean-Paul Sartre's Existentialism, as set out in *L'Étre et le néant*. This is a chronologically scandalous thing to say, but I claim similarity only, not influence. Shakespeare has probably read Seneca and has certainly not read Sartre. But Hamlet is more like Sartre's man than he is like Seneca's.

One chronological scandal to which we have almost become accustomed by repetition is the Freudian interpretation of Hamlet's delay, as set out by Ernest Jones in his *Hamlet and Oedipus* (1949). The suggestion is that Hamlet sexually desires his mother at an unconscious level. When his father returns from the grave to tell him that he was murdered by Claudius and urges Hamlet to avenge the crime, Hamlet finds himself inexplicably unable to move. The reason is that Claudius, in removing the sexual partner of Hamlet's mother, did what Hamlet himself wanted done; he removed the rival. In striking Claudius, Hamlet would be striking himself, or a projection of himself. This bizarre theory, the fruit of a later age, turns out to have extraordinary purchase on the text. In particular, the play of stylistic registers supports it. A good Freudian would predict that such an Oedipally impeded hero would use the language of the super-ego (conscientious, high-minded) when speaking of his father, because the super-ego presides over the business of repression, tells us what we ought to say as distinct from what we wish. But in moments of passion he will use earthy, sexual language, as when he begins to see Claudius not as the man who removed old Hamlet but as the new lover of Gertrude. And that is exactly what we get. In the intimate context of the closet scene (the closet is the room where the Queen readies herself for bed) Hamlet praises his dead father in educated, classical language (Hyperion, Mars, Jove, Mercury), but when he switches to Gertrude's re-marriage, we have at once the authentic accent of the Freudian id: "the rank sweat of an enseamed bed / . . . honeying and making love / Over the nasty sty" (III.iv.92–94). The phrase "Hyperion to a satyr" (I.ii.140) mythically encapsulates the Freudian opposition of the super-ego and the id. "Hyperion," another name for Apollo, means "travelling on high"; satyrs are libidinal creatures, hiding in undergrowth. Freud himself was willing to use classical mythology to articulate his theories. Hamlet does seem oddly arrested when praising his father, yet he can strike when Claudius has become the new rival. When Hamlet stabbed the arras in the closet scene he believed that Claudius, not Polonius, was on the other side. All this is exactly what the Freudian would predict—on the English stage in 1600–1601.

Best of all, for the Freudians, is one freak of imagery. Old Hamlet was murdered by having a poison, a "leprous distillment," poured into his ear (I.v.63–70). In Act III Hamlet says to Gertrude, "Here is your husband, like a mildewed ear" (III.iv.64). It is an odd simile. The mildewed ear in the main story of the play is old Hamlet's. In this queer synecdoche Hamlet is now at one level confounding Claudius with the dead king. Perhaps the slippage from one person to another is triggered by the words "your husband" at the beginning of the line. The Freudian reading makes all this intelligible. Hamlet's mind can slip sideways, with the image of the corrupted bodily organ, from the dead king to his brother because that brother has now become what old Hamlet used to be, the person having sexual relations with Gertrude.

The chronological scandal remains. Is there any way of mitigating it? In fact there are several. First, Freud was deeply influenced by his reading of Shakespeare. Then, Shakespeare is famous for his love of murky, undisclosed factors—"Something nasty lurking under the fine silk." Given this, it is perhaps not so very surprising that he should plant a hint of incestuous feeling in the Prince to mirror the public incest of Claudius ("Our sometime sister, now our queen," I.ii.8).[28] It must be added that Shakespeare never committed himself to the lunatic idea that all male infants desire to have sex with their mothers and to murder their fathers. Hamlet is a one-off, a manifestly peculiar case.

Samuel Taylor Coleridge saw Hamlet as a man paralysed by excess of thought.[29] It has long been almost embarrassingly evident that when Coleridge described Hamlet he was describing himself—as clear a case of unconscious projection as one could wish for. Coleridge, notoriously, could never carry through his great designs, perhaps indeed because his brain worked overtime. The case of Coleridge is therefore taken to corroborate a view of the play very close to Empson's: *Hamlet* is the equivalent in literary art of a Rorschach blot—that is, it is expressly framed for maximum ambiguity so that when onlookers think they are interpreting, they are really only revealing their own nature. Presumably, once we know this we austerely cease to offer explanations of the play. Shakespeare, who has a strange ability to anticipate anything we might later think of, produces a spectacular, really uncanny anticipation of the Rorschach blot theory:

HAMLET Do you see yonder cloud that's almost in shape of a camel?
POLONIUS By th' mass and 'tis, like a camel indeed.
HAMLET Methinks it is like a weasel.
POLONIUS It is back'd like a weasel.
HAMLET Or like a whale.
POLONIUS Very like a whale. (III.ii.376–82)

Hamlet cruelly draws Polonius into warm, positive agreement and then hits him with the emergent truth that a cloud can be made to resemble pretty well anything we like. Polonius is left stammering agreement with the last interpretation given, and we sense that he would now agree with anything. So Polonius is made a fool of, as the play *Hamlet* makes a fool of any critic who offers a single positive interpretation. But, as always with Shakespeare, there is another level. Polonius may not be the complete fool after all. He thinks Hamlet is both dangerous and mad and therefore to be "humoured."

So is Coleridge's account of the play a futile, wholly subjective affair? Not at all. Coleridge accurately seizes something that is there in the text: "sicklied o'er with the pale cast of thought" (III.i.84), "thinking too precisely on th' event" (IV.iv.41). The most telling moment for Coleridge is a curiously disconcerting simile; Hamlet says that he will sweep to his revenge "with wings as swift / As meditation, or the thoughts of love" (I.v.29–30). "As swift as thought" is a common simile, for thought can in a second fly to the ends of the earth. But thought in the Prince of Denmark is an impediment, not a release. So Shakespeare interposes the retarding, polysyllabic word "meditation," and suddenly the phrase takes on the character of an inadvertent oxymoron. Coleridge was right. This book is about Shakespeare as thinker. Hamlet is Shakespeare's prime example of a thinker, and thought is making Hamlet ill. It is a mistake to suppose that Hamlet's problem is weakness of will. If will is involved with wishing, then we must grant that Hamlet's will to do what must be done is huge. His malady is disjunction of the will. The very act of mental willing has assumed a strangely separate existence and has become disengaged both from the normal corroborative emotions and from action. Voluntary action is often explained as action following a movement of the mental will, but there is no such discernible succession in ordinary voluntary behaviour. G. E. M. Anscombe once observed that, just as one can stare at a matchbox in an intense and distracted way and "will" it to move, so one can "will" one's arm to move. Both matchbox and arm remain inert.[30] Real voluntary action—just moving one's arm to pick up a pen—is a simple thing. Reflexive consciousness in Hamlet has destroyed this ordinary simplicity. In classical philosophy, long before, the felicitous *adjective* "voluntary" is transformed, by an excess of abstraction, into a queerly separate *noun,* "will." In *Love's Labour's Lost* conscious elegance of language is seen as a pathological condition. Berowne confesses at the close, "I am sick" (V.ii.417). Perhaps in both places Shakespeare is strangely ashamed of things in himself we see as strengths. For the Shakespeare who wrote *Love's Labour's Lost* was a master of elegant language, as the Shakespeare who wrote *Hamlet* could obviously out-think all his rivals.

Empson's wish to halt all speculative criticism with the simple assertion that *Hamlet* is designed as an insoluble conundrum implicitly freezes and sanitizes a work that buzzes with possible explanations: the Existentialist Hamlet, the Freudian Hamlet, the man paralysed by excess of thought, and so on. These are not the only lines available. It is surprising that so little has been made of a possible religious reason for Hamlet's delay. Christianity forbids revenge, but Hamlet is under an obligation to avenge the murder of his father. This gives the ethical conflict on which tragedy thrives. G. W. F. Hegel observed that tragedy is not about the conflict of right and wrong but about the conflict of right and right.[31] In Greek tragedy the primitive ethic of pollution, linked to certain taboos, is in tension with a more developed moral understanding. Oedipus marries his mother and is therefore stained forever. But he did not know she was his mother. And so his fate is terrible, pitiable. There is nothing in English tragedy to correspond to the taboo as it figures in Greek tragedy. Taboo is a primitive prohibition. What we do have in English tragedy is a *primitive obligation,* at odds with a more developed ethic. Revenge, at the deepest, oldest level, is something one must do. It is a matter of honour. If you do not kill the murderer of your father, you are less than a man. But the Bible says that revenge is wrong. It has been said that in all the philosophizing and questioning in *Hamlet* no one ever seems to notice that revenge is forbidden. In fact, Hamlet obviously knows that revenge is a sin. When he is listing his own faults he says, "I am very proud, *revengeful,* ambitious" (III.i.123–24). It may be that the ethical problem of revenge is not mentioned elsewhere in the play because it is too obvious to need stating.

The Bible gives two reasons for not taking revenge; first, because revenge should be transcended by love (Matt. 5:38), and second, because it is God's job ("Vengeance is mine, saith the Lord," Rom. 12:19). In the early sixteenth century it was commonly felt that God did in fact look after the necessary acts of retaliation and that when he did so he used human beings for the purpose. Yet revenge remains forbidden to human beings. Only the grimmest theologians were happy to say that God might use John to carry out an act of revenge and that John sinned even as he carried out God's will. A devout young sixteenth-century Christian whose father had been murdered would think, "This must be left to God." In other words he would "go limp," exactly as Hamlet does. Although in the early part of the play we may begin to think of Hamlet as a brilliant Machiavel who will trap Claudius and finish him off, perhaps with some novel poison, notoriously Hamlet's glittering cleverness expends itself in vacancy, and the final killing of Claudius is something that emerges by accident from a tangle of confused circumstance. It is true that at the very last moment, when Hamlet forces the poison down the King's throat (V.ii.326), he is an agent, and we shiver. But all the rest is more reaction than action. The chaos at the human level leaves God free to ensure the proper end. It is only because of this confusion that we are able to think of Hamlet as not necessarily bound for hell. The Machiavel avengers of later Jacobean tragedy all have a whiff of brimstone about them. The play certainly makes the order of divine, over-arching causation evident to us: "There's a divinity that shapes our ends" (V.ii.10), "There is special providence in the fall of a sparrow . . . the readiness is all"

(V.ii.219–22). Passivity in revenge is the only path left to one both honourable and Christian. As Charlemont says at the end of Cyril Tourneur's *Atheist's Tragedy* (1611), "Patience is the honest man's revenge."

None of these explanations of Hamlet's delay is powerful enough to displace the others. All are relevant to the play. Plato set himself to refute those who confuse "the many beautiful things" with "beauty itself," the prior essence with its local accidents.[32] Hamlet, lost in the vacancy at the heart of revenge, reaches out to "the things of revenge," the gory apparatus of the old play, black clothes, skulls, blood, and poison. But Shakespeare pushes the Platonic thought further. The audience is slowly taught that it has long been confusing "the things of death" with death itself. The negation of death is so complete as to be logically unique. The poets think they are writing about death but take pusillanimous refuge in "the things" —worms, epitaphs, and winding sheets—that are so much more tractable by the mind. When Hamlet first soliloquizes on death, he sees it as a "positive negation," an "undiscover'd country" (III.i.78). It is remarkable in the face of this obvious agnosticism in the most famous of Elizabethan plays that teachers continue to assert that agnosticism was unknown in Shakespeare's day, that all believed firmly in a Christian eschatology. The much more dangerous Hamlet who returns to Denmark after his voyage no longer sees death in terms of an obscure landscape. Instead he is briskly *chosiste*. Death is subjected to an abrupt materialist redaction: "Imperious Caesar, dead and turn'd to clay, / Might stop a hole to keep the wind away" (V.i.213–14). This is the last we hear of the Roman play from which *Hamlet* sprang. Great Caesar is now a lump of mud. Yet the effect of this hearty language is to make the sheer otherness, the ineffability of death more importunately present to our minds than it was in the earlier, metaphysically ruminative soliloquies. There was always an edge of hysteria to Hamlet's humour and it is there still.

When Ludwig Wittgenstein said that death is not an event in life, he went on to speak of that which lies outside the border of one's visual field.[33] But "border," it turns out, is a misleading word. If one is asked, "What shape is your visual field?" one has to work surprisingly hard to come up with an answer. It might be thought that nothing could be clearer, more empirically elementary, than the shape of the view we have of the visible world before our eyes. People say, "A horizontal oval . . . I think." They hesitate because they cannot check the border. As Wittgenstein says, our life is actually *endlos,* "endless" in the sense that our visual field is *grenzenlos,* "without limit." There is, for example, no clear blackness along the edge where the visual information gives out. There is "what we see" and "what we don't see." It is impossible to align the two.

Of course by Wittgenstein's criterion Shakespeare is guilty along with all the other poets of filling his death play with dying (dying, unlike death, is another "event in life"). But he is less guilty than most of evading the central mystery of un-being. By stressing the inadequacy of the theatrical apparatus bequeathed by Kyd (though it may successfully activate vengeful passion, it is itself unreal) and by making us feel the off-target coarseness of Hamlet's conversation with the grave-digger, Shakespeare propels us into a more fundamental bewilderment.

It is hard to think of anything in *Hamlet* of which one can be finally sure. Shakespeare knew from the first second of the play—from the first two syllables—that his task was to enlarge uncertainty. "Who's there?" are the opening words. One sentry, on the icy battlements of the castle, throws a challenge into the darkness. His words are humorously thrown back at him. The noise he heard was made, it seems, by the other sentry arriving for his spell of duty. So is there nothing to fear? Someone or something else is actually there, waiting: the spirit who may be Hamlet's dead father. He, or it, by a command to kill, destroys Hamlet, Ophelia, Gertrude, as well as Claudius, who looks genuinely guilty. According to Protestant theory of the period the ghost cannot be a revenant, a dead person returned. When the Protestants abolished Purgatory they had nothing left beyond the grave but heaven, from which no soul would wish to return, and hell, from which no one could escape. Most people after watching *Hamlet* are pretty sure that the ghost was Hamlet's father, but one can never be completely certain. In the Folio stage directions he is always called "Ghost," never "old Hamlet." Even if he tells the truth about Claudius he could still be a devil. When the play is over, we can still ask, "Who *was* there?"

Troilus and Cressida: Hamlet's Play

Hamlet is a sick, clever man. *Troilus and Cressida* is a sick, clever play. So, clearly, Hamlet is the author of *Troilus and Cressida*—or, at least, *Troilus and Cressida* is the play Hamlet could have written. The sickness of the play troubled nineteenth-century critics more than it troubles critics today, perhaps because the present century is itself sick. The Victorians were right to be upset. *Troilus and Cressida* is drawn from "the matter of Troy" and is the story of the faithlessness of a frightened woman in time of war. Chaucer's long poem *Troilus and Criseyde* is deeply humane. We feel above all the sadness of that far-off breaking of faith. Chaucer's Pandarus, the middle-aged, fussy figure who brings the two young people together, is absurd, a little prurient, and, at the same time, curiously benign (he runs for a cushion so that Troilus, the suitor, can kneel in comfort, at iii.964). The final effect of Shakespeare's play is nothing as warm as pity; rather, it leaves a sour taste in the mouth. His Pandarus is a figure of horror, riddled with venereal disease. Act II, Scene i, opens with a dialogue between the "deform'd and scurrilous" Thersites and the "blockish" Ajax:

THERSITES Agamemnon, how if he had biles [= "boils"]—full, all over, generally?
AJAX Thersites!
THERSITES And those biles did run—say so—did not the general run then? Were not that a botchy core?
AJAX Dog!
THERSITES Then would come some matter from him; I see none now.

(II.i.2–9)

Technically this has the structure of a fool's routine, a joke. Thersites puns on the word "matter." One meaning is "good sense." So Thersites is saying that Agamemnon is incapable of speaking to the point. The other meaning is "pus," the suppuration from a boil. The imagery is so disgusting that the laugh is killed by it. Note that Thersites gets no applause, within the play, from the uncomprehending Ajax. Thersites' wit is no longer sociable as wit should be but is yoked to a private relishing of nastiness for its own sake, a sort of mental coprophagy. The drama itself, meanwhile, is, like the Prince of Denmark himself, systematically unclassifiable. The editors of the First Folio were obviously uncertain where to place it. Modern editors have in general settled on the designation "comedy" (or "satirical comedy"), but this play is not in the least like the satirical comedy of, say, Marston. True, the hero and heroine are left (remorselessly) alive at the end, and so one primary requirement of tragedy is not met. Nor do we have the grandeur proper to tragedy. At the same time, however, we have none of the happiness proper to comedy. It is not so much that the play is too sad (after all it grew out of *Hamlet, not Romeo and Juliet*), but it is just too nasty. The way in which Thersites' joke is eclipsed by nausea illustrates with precision the generic vanishing-act performed by the play as a whole. Hamlet, whose very age is curiously problematic (I.i.170, V.i.147–62), is himself a perpetual student; the atmosphere of the University of Wittenberg clings to him like a miasma. In *Hamlet* we have the notion of corruption hidden by cosmetic paint (III.i.50), in *Troilus and Cressida* the "putrified" knight in splendid armour (V.viii.1–2). *Troilus and Cressida* was probably written for a student audience, for one of the Inns of Court. In Shakespeare's time undergraduates at Oxford and Cambridge were younger than their successors today, but those at the Inns of Court were a little older and therefore more like modern bright students than anyone the universities could have produced. This is where the really clever young men were to be found, the intellectual cream. John Donne, that great playgoer, was at Lincoln's Inn.[34]

So in this play Shakespeare is more intellectual, more technically philosophical in the full meaning of the word, than in any other. At the same time he presents such exaggerated mental activity as a pathology, a kind of illness. In *Hamlet* only the Prince is made ill by thought. In *Troilus and Cressida* the whole world is sick with intelligence. Polonius is there in *Hamlet* to attempt a diagnosis of a manifestly disturbed condition. He suggests "love melancholy" (II.ii.92–106, 164–65, 187), which is about as close as Elizabethan terminology can get to Freud's "libidinal disorder." In *Troilus and Cressida* we find no one anxiously trying to alleviate the condition because all are infected. Where there is no health there can be, in a way, no consciousness of sickness. All this accords perfectly with the conceit: "Hamlet wrote *Troilus and Cressida*." But Shakespeare, the real author, knows they are sick.

First we need to characterize the style of the play. This is subtle, beyond the competence of most modern audiences or readers. Shakespeare, that supposed cultural innocent long deemed wholly unaware of historical difference, here essays a dazzling synthesis: a consciously medievalized, mannered picture of classical antiquity. We have mock-chivalry, for example, in Hector's repeated challenge to the Greeks (I.iii.260–83) and in the doddering Nestor's love vaunt (I.iii.291–301). This is joined to Homeric burlesque: the array of heroes suddenly seen as a collection of subnormal grotesques. Long before, Rabelais had called Achilles "a scald-pated maker of hay-bundles" and Agamemnon "a lick-box."[35] Some will say that what I take for stylistic sophistication is a simple product of the sources; we get "medievalized antiquity" because Shakespeare happens to have found his way to this particular classical story through the medieval poet Chaucer. But the play of (medieval) honour against (Greek) cynicism is too expertly handled for this simple explanation to hold.

It remains a Greek, not a Roman, play. We shall, however, look in vain for the conscientious examination of an historically embedded culture that we have in *Julius Caesar*. "Roman" for us means war, Stoicism, Epicureanism, Empire succeeding Republic, and all of these are in *Julius Caesar*. "Greek" for us means early democracy, Attic drama, Plato and Aristotle, Periclean Athens, sculpture, and architecture, and none of these are in *Troilus and Cressida*. Admittedly, Aristotle is mentioned in passing, but the passage is chiefly notorious as a spectacular anachronism. Hector magisterially observes that Aristotle thought young men unfit to hear moral philosophy (II.ii.166–67), but Hector, alas, died hundreds of years before the birth of Aristotle. "Greek" to Shakespeare means "fluid, tricky, clever, a-moral, abstract, cynical." In a curious way the Greek theme licenses the a-historical freedom of the play, its shape-shifting rootlessness. This picture of the Greeks is heavily influenced by Virgil. While Homer, the earlier Greek epic poet, shows the antagonists in the war, Greeks and Trojans, on strangely equal terms, Virgil in his later Latin epic has clear "good guys" and "bad guys." The Roman race, in Virgil, is derived from the defeated Trojans; the Trojans are good and the Greeks, who won through the deception of the Wooden Horse, are despicably clever.

While concrete history is now set aside, Shakespeare's sensitivity to Greek literary *structures* is astonishing. So far, Rome is matter but Greece is *form*. When the Prologue speaks of "beginning in the middle" (28) the reference is to the Greek idea that the best narratives begin *in medias res,* "in the midst of things," as Homer had in both his epic poems.[36] Shakespeare then out-Greeks the Greeks by not only beginning but also ending his play in the middle—I refer to the notoriously withheld tragic ending.

The erudition is worn with an un-Jonsonian lightness. Act I, Scene ii, the scene in which Cressida first sees Troilus, is rightly derived by the commentators from Chaucer. Criseyde sees Troilus pass by, badly wounded, at ii.1247–56.

What is not noticed is the way Shakespeare re-casts the episode in a distinctively Greek form. Shakespeare unlike Chaucer gives us a comparative display of figures. Aeneas passes, then brave Hector with his fine "countenance," then Paris, and later Troilus. The Greeks had a technical term for this: *teichoskopia*, "the Viewing from the Wall."[37] Again the fundamental version is in Homer. In Book iii of the *Iliad* Helen watches from the wall as the Greek heroes pass to and fro before her eyes. Agamemnon goes by, taller than the rest, then Odysseus, then the gigantic Ajax (iii.161–229). When Virgil rewrote Homeric epic for the Romans he transposed into his poem a great many Homeric motifs, but this one he did not adopt. One suspects that the gossipy, excited character of the Homeric passage, with its Greek interest in male beauty (the heroes are like models on a catwalk), would have seemed undignified to Virgil.

It is one thing to burlesque ancient epic, as was done on festive occasions at both the universities and the Inns of Court in Shakespeare's time. It is another to find and register shockingly "low" elements in Homer himself, as distinct from the more gentlemanly Virgil. Chapman's translation of Homer, some of which had appeared by the time Shakespeare wrote *Troilus and Cressida,* made people realize how raw, how brutal, how uncivilized the first epic was. In the *Iliad* Ajax is likened to a donkey that has broken into a cornfield: small boys beat it with sticks but cannot shift it (ix.558–65). The humanist Marco Girolamo Vida was appalled: "But the animal is so *base!*"[38] In Book xxiv Achilles, with the air of one offering a guest a cup of coffee, casually rises and slaughters a sheep (xxiv.621–22). Shakespeare's swift *teichoskopia* shows that he understands that real Greek material can affront the standards of a later classicism, uneasily conscious of its proper dignity.

I have said that "Greek" for Shakespeare connotes morally dubious abstraction; at the same time, however, because of the prospect opened by Chapman and by Arthur Hall's *Ten Bookes of Homers Iliades* (1581), it simultaneously connotes gross physicality. Act I, Scene iii, is studded with phrases that are relishingly physical: "nerves and bone of Greece" (where "nerve" means "muscle," 55), "his mastic jaws" (73), "ribs of steel" (177), "large Achilles, on his press'd bed lolling / From his deep chest" (162–63), "blockish Ajax" (374), "sinew" (136 and 143). This language begins to compose a Mannerist picture—exaggerated musculature, turbulent graphic panache, a classicism on the brink of grotesquerie—akin to that displayed by Giulio Romano in the Sala de' Giganti at Mantua. Shakespeare is no Warwickshire innocent, insulated by a parochial culture, ineptly essaying a classical theme beyond his understanding. He instantly masters the classical manner and then, brilliantly, subjects it to a series of transformations. It is the modern reader who is commonly unable to match the sophistication of the Elizabethan dramatist.

Shakespeare ensures that we feel the alien quality of the Greek world by giving the opening Prologue a language on stilts, full of strange words: "orgillous," "immures," "corresponsive," and Chapmanesque compounds. This, Shakespeare's "Trojan style," was used in *Hamlet* (at II.ii.446–91) to register the ecphrastic[39] space between the player's narrative of Priam's death and the main, Danish action. Here in *Troilus and Cressida* the two poles of "Greekness," abstraction and grossness, are eerily fused.

Troilus and Cressida has no natural beginning, no natural grand conclusion in death. The world it depicts is fractured, chaotic, indefinite. The passage of days here confers no shapeliness on the succession of events. "Time hath, my lord, a wallet at his back, / Wherein he puts alms for oblivion" (III.iii.145–46). Troilus, saying good-bye to Cressida, has a similarly bleak view of time:

Injurious time now with a robber's haste
Crams his rich thiev'ry up, he knows not how.
As many farewells as be stars in heaven,
With distinct breath and consign'd kisses to them,
He fumbles up into a lose adieu;
And scants us with a single famish'd kiss,
Distasted with the salt of broken tears.   (IV.iv.42–48)

I said earlier that *Troilus and Cressida* replaces the humane pity and fear of tragedy with a sour taste left in the mouth. So here even a kiss from the lips of the beloved Cressida leaves a salt, unpleasant taste behind. Time mishandles the rich materials that fall into his fumbling grasp. The strongest word in the speech is "broken" at the end.

Although the play inhabits a super-educated medium of burlesque classicism,[40] a sense must survive that the story of Troy is the grandest of all stories. If it were not for some such expectation, behind the play, Shakespeare's unremitting reduction of honour, love, and courage to chaos would become itself formally tedious, dramatically null. Certainly the persons of the play have none of the rich humanity of those in the other plays. Here, for once, L. C. Knights's idea that dramatic character begins and ends with what we see, holds.[41] No one watching the play is moved to wonder about latent motives as we all do, to the point of extreme discomfort, when watching *Hamlet*. The mystery of self-hood and relational identity, tenderly explored in the context of dramatic action in earlier plays, is now thoroughly abstracted and becomes, explicitly, a matter of academic philosophy:

ACHILLES What are you reading?
ULYSSES   A strange fellow here
    Writes me that man, how dearly ever parted,
    How much in having, or without or in,
    Cannot make boast to have that which he hath,
    Nor feels not what he owes, but by reflection;
    As when his virtues, aiming upon others,
    Heat them, and they retort that heat again
    To the first giver.
ACHILLES   This is not strange, Ulysses.
    The beauty that is borne here in the face
    The bearer knows not, but commends itself
    To others' eyes; nor doth the eye itself,
    That most pure spirit of sense, behold itself,
    Not going from itself; but eye to eye opposed,
    Salutes each other with each other's form;
    For speculation turns not to itself,
    Till it hath travell'd and is mirror'd there
    Where it may see itself. This is not strange at all.
ULYSSES I do not strain at the position—

It is familiar—but at the author's drift,
Who in his circumstance expressly proves
That no man is the lord of any thing,
Though in and of him there be much consisting,
Till he communicate his parts to others;
Nor doth he of himself know them for aught,
Till he behold them formed in th' applause
Where th' are extended; who like an arch reverb'rate
The voice again, or like a gate of steel,
Fronting the sun, receives and renders back, his figure and his heat.

(III.iii.95–122)

Ulysses is trying to move Achilles to action. This passage is therefore a rewriting of the moment in *Julius Caesar* when Cassius draws Brutus into the conspiracy by offering himself as a metaphorical glass. The idea of a mirror is running still in the words of Ulysses. But we know by now that Shakespeare is the poet who continually recycles but never repeats himself. So there are crucial differences from the earlier version. Where Brutus was set up as a high-minded theorist, we now have something both narrower and more intense than theorizing. This is technical, academic discourse. The opening question, "What are you reading?" sets the tone. It can be heard every day in university common rooms. When Ulysses says, "I do not strain at the position—/ It is familiar," we have, again, the idiom of academic chit-chat, exactly caught. Stoics like Brutus delight in well-worn truths; academics are notoriously touchy if anyone suggests that what they are saying is common knowledge, a cultural "given." When Achilles says he sees nothing startling in the proposition, Ulysses is eager at once to distance himself from the naive reader who mistakes a commonplace for a novelty. In modern English he would say, "I'm not bothered about the basic line—this is something every schoolchild knows." He then suggests that the author's "drift" takes one into less familiar territory.

Curiously, modern commentaries on the play do not really listen to Ulysses. The commentators, like Achilles in the present dialogue, are happy when they can place an observation. So they point out that much of this material is proverbial, and how Erasmus in his *Adagia* wrote of the negligibility of things unheard. It is one thing to say that the eye cannot see itself but by reflection or that Narcissus can never gaze directly at his own beauty, and another to say that there is no such thing as a truly intrinsic quality, that the question, "But what is it like, *in itself?*" is a doomed, unanswerable question. When Ulysses says, "No man is the lord of any thing . . . / Till he communicate his parts to others," he suggests that the very fabric of language forces us to construe individual persons relationally and that *there is no other way.* The word "lord" was probably prompted by the philosophic term "property." A property is an attribute that *belongs* specifically to some person or thing ("owes" at line 99 means "owns").

This generates a paradox: "That which is yours is not private to you but is logically shared." Corin says in *As You Like It* that "the property of rain is to wet" (III.ii.26); the inmost character of rain shows only as it acts on other things. We may normally assume that a relation is something that holds between two things that exist prior to the relation. If that is right, we ought to be able to say something about the things in themselves, before we proceed to the relation. But if we say (as we did earlier), "Anne is a generous person," we are saying there and then that Anne gives more than other people do. The generosity is not a pre-existing, separate thing that causes the giving. If we say, "John is a recluse," we are saying that John noticeably absents himself from the company of *others.* The supposed prior substance, where we thought true identity inhered, dissolves before our eyes. We are close to the Structuralist intuition that context is not posterior to identity but on the contrary confers identity. Of course Ulysses has a practical end in mind: to get Achilles moving. His argument therefore runs, "If you do no brave action you cannot think, 'But I am Achilles' because 'Achilles,' now, is nothing." The general *drift* (Ulysses' word) is meanwhile to turn substance into relation, and this can be felt as obscurely chilling.

The philosophizing is so fundamental that to a surprising degree it breaks free from the contextual matrix of the early seventeenth century and becomes "just philosophy," as close to twentieth-century Structuralism as it is to the proverbs cited in the commentaries. Nevertheless to those hungry for Renaissance analogues I offer Sir Thomas Elyot's *Boke Named the Governour* (1531). Elyot argues there that identity is not opposed to relation but is rather the product of relation.[42] Shakespeare, however, far more than Elyot, is dialogically in touch with thinkers of a later century who worried that "qualities," which they first conceived as attached to a pre-existent object as qualities as a colour is painted on a ball, had somehow engulfed the original object, so that it became "a mere congeries of qualities."[43] Roundness, redness, solidity, weight, all these are abstractions, yet when they are removed from the object, what is left?

Of course when solidity is instantiated in a given case there is no need to worry about the object dissolving into air. But the ghost of just this anxiety can be felt, a sudden sense of slippage into the insubstantial, behind Ulysses' words. This vertigo is expertly managed by the dramatist as part of his concerted picture of Greek sterility.

In mythic history the Trojan line led to Britain, as the poet of *Gawain and the Green Knight* explains in the opening lines of that poem. One might therefore expect that academic philosophy, with its taint of incipient nihilism, would be confined to the Greek party. But the Trojans, too, philosophize. They talk about the rights and wrongs, the sense and nonsense of fighting to the death in order to hang on to one abducted woman:

HECTOR Brother, she is not worth what she doth cost
   The keeping.
TROILUS   What's aught but as 'tis valued?
HECTOR But value dwells not in particular will,
   It holds his estimate and dignity
   As well wherein 'tis precious of itself
   As in the prizer. 'Tis mad idolatry
   To make the service greater than the god,
   And the will dotes that is attributive
   To what infectiously itself affects,
   Without some image of th' affected merit.   (II.ii.51–60)

The opening, note, is profoundly different from the conversation between Ulysses and Achilles: not the studied neutrality of "What are you reading?" but the down-to-earth assertion, "She is not worth what she doth cost / The keeping." So we begin, indeed, with an affirmation of ethical substance. But Troilus's answer is utterly relativistic. What, he asks, is this "value" of which you speak? Value, he implies, is not something we read off from the objective world, it is something we assign. The Trojans have *given* Helen a high value; the rest follows. We are again plunged in real philosophy. The fact that Trojans talk in this way would appear to blur the picture we are given elsewhere of subtle,[44] tricky Greeks in contrast to virtuous Trojans. Kenneth Palmer in the older Arden edition of the play gave the basic answer: it is only the Trojans who consider ethical ends; the Greeks are cynically concerned with means only.[45] It is only the Trojans who get as far as to *ask* whether the war is morally worth fighting. Within that Trojan discussion, however, Troilus's position is dismayingly close to pure subjectivism. My fantasy that Hamlet is the author of *Troilus and Cressida* was never so plausible as in Troilus's "What is aught but as 'tis valued?" After all Hamlet himself propelled a certain proverbial commonplace into dizzy subjectivism when he observed, "There is nothing either good or bad, but thinking makes it so" (II.ii.249–50).

Shakespeare ensures nevertheless that we can see clear blue water between Troilus and the tricky Greeks by joining the philosophy of freely assigned value to medieval chivalry. The play as a whole, as we have seen, is a dance of classical and medieval motifs. For Troilus, Helen is like a flag. It does not matter that a flag is only a bit of cloth fixed to a stick; once you have made it your flag, honour requires absolute devotion, even unto death. This is the philosophy that Hector rebuts with magisterial ethical objectivism. The modern reader or spectator may be thrown, because of a presumption that ethical objectivism is the old-fashioned thing, belonging naturally with the Middle Ages. But one can tell already in the *Henry VI* plays that Shakespeare saw the honour ethic in rather different terms. Hotspur, who dies young and represents the warlike adolescence of England itself in historical time, is violently, joyfully committed to a conception of honour notably ungrounded in ethical responsibility. Prince Hal in contrast is harrowed by ethical questions: Is the war justified? An ethic that so easily resolves itself into mere caprice can, then, as easily be the product of an undeveloped culture as of a wearily sophisticated late culture. At least, I suspect that Shakespeare saw it so.

It is possible that many modern responses to this scene are unconsciously conditioned by an uncritical presumption: that ethical objectivism is naive, that myriad-minded Shakespeare cannot seriously be backing such a view. Graham Bradshaw in his brilliant book *Shakespeare's Scepticism* (1987) felt obliged to take Troilus's view as fundamental and argued strenuously for a *secondary* ethical objectivism, resting on the fact that man really is a value-assigning animal. But there is nothing jejune about Hector's statement of ethical objectivism, as Shakespeare gives it. I will here risk my arm. When Hector says that value dwells not in particular will, he is simply right. Philosophically. If value were freely assignable it would collapse at once into purely subjective preference and lose its power. As things stand we *argue* about the rights and wrongs of the war in Iraq. If value is entirely free-floating, these arguments are instantly vacuous. When Jane says, "I feel fine this morning," and Joe says, "I feel terrible," they do not go on to argue. The situation is reminiscent (or "pre-echoic") of a moment in early-twentieth-century philosophy, when G. E. Moore decided to take on those relativists who said that "This is good" meant no more and no less than "I like this": "Whoever will attentively consider with himself what is actually before his mind when he asks the question, 'Is pleasure (or whatever it may be) after all good?' can easily satisfy himself that he is not merely wondering whether pleasure is pleasant."[46] Hector's observation, " 'Tis mad idolatry / To make the service greater than the god," is especially telling, clever and profound at the same time. It outclasses anything the wilful young Troilus can offer.

Which makes it the more distressing when Hector suddenly caves in—

> yet ne'er the less,
> My spritely brethren, I propend to you
> In resolution to keep Helen still,
> For 'tis a cause that hath no mean dependance
> Upon our joint and several dignities. (II.ii.189–93)

Critics defend this volte-face by invoking the cynicism of the play, taken as a whole. This is a world in which no one is good; the Trojans may look better than the Greeks, but all are hollow men. They point to Act V, Scene vi, where we have the damp squib of Hector's long-awaited head-to-head encounter with Achilles on the battle-field. They agree, apparently from sheer fatigue, not to fight that day. Immediately afterwards Hector turns aside to slay a foolish knight for his splendid armour. As he puts off his own armour, Achilles and his Myrmidons suddenly surround Hector and kill him, unchivalrously.

I am not sure that this sequence is enough to account for Hector's collapse in the debate with Troilus. When he asks Achilles if he will pause in the fight so feebly begun, we sense not deep ethical cynicism (that would alone explain the capitulation to Troilus) but a strange, engulfing lassitude, a slipping away. Hector's "Ne'er the less my spritely brethren" is unprepared for, unintegrated, unexplained. It may be that there is no reason for it at all but only an external explanation. It is not inconceivable that Shakespeare wrote the first, eloquent part of Hector's speech, adjourned to the pub for a heavy lunch, and returned thinking, "I have to turn the action round here—Hector must after all give way because, damn it, the Trojans never did agree to restore Helen to the Greeks . . . hmmmnn. . . . The word I need is 'nevertheless'—that'll do it." The real trouble is that the sentence introduced by that happy "ne'er the less" is catastrophically weak compared with what went before—especially with what was *just* before. Hector had reached an ethical climax on

> Thus to persist
> In doing wrong extenuates not wrong,
> But makes it much more heavy.   (II.ii.186–88)

To switch from this without warning to a view flat contrary, based on nothing but "our several dignities," will not do. Well might Troilus cry out in happy surprise, "Why, there you touch'd the life of our design!" (II.ii.194).

This rough handiwork at the end of Hector's speech is something Shakespeare normally avoids. Why did it happen here? It does indeed flow from the general conception, but not as a matter, simply, of showing that all are contemptible. It is not artistically managed in that way. Rather it is an unforeseen consequence of Shakespeare's experiment in withdrawing rich humanity from the persons of the play. *Troilus and Cressida* alone of Shakespeare's plays contains no "characters of love," as John Bayley defined the term in his book of that name in 1960. When the poet does not love his characters, his attention will wander. Had he been holding, before his inner eye, a fully conceived Hector, really wrestling, as

Henry V wrestled, with the ethics of war, he could never have left that mismanaged non-transition on the page. But the attenuation of humanity is meanwhile essential to the bleak artistic logic of the drama. The special human crisis that produced in *Richard III* and *Richard II* a retortion of the suffering subject back upon himself and a psychomachia as rich as the public action of the play is in *Troilus and Cressida* projected upon a screen. The divided soul of the protagonist is re-construed as divided ontology. When Troilus learns that Cressida is false, he says,

If beauty have a soul, this is not she;
If souls guide vows, if vows be sanctimonies,
If sanctimony be the gods' delight,
If there be rule in unity itself,
This was not she. O madness of discourse,
That cause sets up with and against itself!

. . . .

This is, and is not, Cressid.   (V.ii.138–46)

The agony of learning that the Cressida he loved is unfaithful to him is dealt with, mathematically, by dividing Cressida in two. The loved Cressida is different in essence from the faithless Cressida. And yet they are one. We see here a flinching from human complexity, a flight to theoretic diagram that is emblematic of the entire play. At his crisis Richard III said, "Richard loves Richard, that is I and I" (V.iii.183, the First Quarto reading). He looked inward. Troilus says, "This is, and is not, Cressid." He looks outward but not at reality. He looks at a screen he has erected.

If we go back to the exchange before Troilus's big speech on broken faith, we find Troilus saying to Ulysses, "Rather think this not Cressid" (V.ii.133). The idiom is academic. We should remember the theoretically minded Brutus, meditating and flinching from his political situation, hypothesizing with the donnish phrase, "Fashion it thus." There was in the word "fashion" a hint of artificial manipulation that persists here in *Troilus and Cressida*. Troilus wildly suggests that all women are tainted by Cressida's treachery. Ulysses answers this exactly as a tutor might speak to a student who has committed a gross error in reasoning: "What hath she done, Prince, that can soil our mothers?" Troilus's mind in response reels from the irrational extension of falsity to the entire female sex to the discovery of absolute contradiction *within* the figure of Cressida. What has she done? Nothing, unless *this* is she. In other words, why worry about generalizing from the individual? The individual no longer exists.

If we think of Othello and how he spoke, in anguish, to the Desdemona he had loved and now believed to be false, we shall feel at once the diminished humanity of the sequence in *Troilus and Cressida*. That straying into a faintly parodic, grey philosophical manner would be unthinkable in *Othello*.

But after all even in this play the characters are not completely hollow. We never glimpse "an interior Troilus," but we are given enough sense of his pain to know that the very abstraction I have been noting is something he, a human being, has been driven to, by a distress that is pre-technical, simple, and moving. If we think of the great aubade in *Romeo and Juliet,* where the lovers must part at daybreak, we shall find the parting of the lovers in *Troilus and Cressida* lifeless. Yet here in the Greek play there is a residual humanity that is almost the more moving because of its very weakness. Cressida says how sad a figure she will make among the merry Greeks and asks, "When shall we see again?" (IV.iv.57). Troilus replies, "Hear me, love. Be thou but true of heart—." Cressida interrupts him; how can he ask such a thing? Troilus stumblingly explains that he intended no serious questioning of her faith, that the phrase was a conventional prefix to what was to follow. He then gives her the complete, supposedly innocuous sentence: "Be thou true, / And I will see thee" (IV.iv.66–67). Cressida talks of the dangers to which Troilus will be exposed and adds, implying as she does so that Troilus after all required an answer, "But I'll be true" (IV.iv.69). They exchange tokens, a sleeve and a glove, and Troilus says (!), "But yet be true." Now Cressida reacts strongly: "O heavens, 'be true' again!" (IV.iv.74).

Obviously Troilus's initial claim that his first "Be true" was merely conventional can be sustained no longer. He comes clean and explains that he can't help knowing that she will be among attractive men, away from him, and that he is afraid. Cressida on her side tries to keep up the notion that Troilus's doubts are shocking and insulting to her, but does not carry her point. Half-playfully, half-evasively, she turns the tables and asks Troilus if *he* will be true to *her*. His answer is utterly simple; he can do nothing else; it is the way he is made. There is nothing now for Cressida to say. Though Troilus is true, this cannot stand as a great love story. But there is a special, entirely human sadness in the very falling short. The sub-tragic, ignoble fear of Troilus is one of the things that saves *Troilus and Cressida* from being itself a work of cold, abstract art.

5 Strong Women, Weaker Men

Much Ado about Nothing: The Impediment of Wit

In moving, as was natural, from *Julius Caesar* to *Hamlet* and then to *Troilus and Cressida* we stepped over the happy love comedies, *Much Ado about Nothing, As You Like It,* and *Twelfth Night. Julius Caesar* is probably 1598, *Hamlet* 1600–1601, *Troilus and Cressida* 1601–2; *Much Ado about Nothing* is 1598–99, *As You Like It,* 1599, and *Twelfth Night,* 1601–2. *The Merchant of Venice* (1597) we shall keep on one side, as a way in, later, to the most difficult of the problem plays, *Measure for Measure.*

In turning back to *Much Ado* we must reawaken memories of *Two Gentlemen of Verona, Love's Labour's Lost,* and *Romeo and Juliet.* The slowly burning fuse of Shakespeare's intent preoccupation with identity, lit in *The Comedy of Errors,* smouldering in *Richard III,* blazing in *Richard II,* and finally exploding in *Hamlet,* is not to be seen in this play. The characters are solid, but not problematically deep. The strange impulse, already strong in *Two Gentlemen of Verona,* to make male friendship simultaneously moving and (because one of the friends is despicable) uncomfortable is there, as is a sense that such friendship must give way to all-transcending heterosexual love (remember now the friendship of Romeo and Mercutio, across which the love of Juliet falls like a spear of light). Remember also the happy, ill-conceived, all-male academy disrupted by the arrival of the ladies in *Love's Labour's Lost.* That fear of verbal dexterity as an impediment to truth (the wheel that won't stop spinning) that makes *Love's Labour's Lost* an oddly frightening play at bottom reappears in *Much Ado about Nothing* in the wit-combats of Beatrice and Benedick. These look at first like displays of festive freedom but at last compose a glittering cage in which it impossible for either party to say, simply, "I love you."

The play begins with the men coming home in high spirits from a successful military action. The ladies are waiting for them. Sarah Duchess of Marlborough is said to have written in her diary, "His Grace returned from the wars today and pleasured me twice in his top boots"—but that was a married couple.[1] What we see at the beginning of Shakespeare's play is a confluence of marriageable persons. The weddings will come at the end, because this is a comedy. The audience will understand that the men will have "bonded" before the action of the play starts. Claudio and Benedick are firm friends, comrades in arms. But then Claudio's eye falls on Hero, the daughter of Leonato, and he is in love. At once he babbles about her beauty to his friend who (not being in love with Hero) just can't see the colossal attraction. The humour is subtle. It is in a way naive of Claudio to assume that Benedick, who has until this moment seen the world as he sees it, will agree on the beauty of Hero. Claudio does not begin to understand that, if Benedick did see Hero as a love-object, this, far from cementing their friendship, would actually threaten its existence. That is allowed to happen, with painful consequences, in *Two Gentlemen of Verona*. Here all remains good-humoured. Benedick benevolently regards his friend's new passion as a local loss of sanity. *Of course* he cannot see Hero as Claudio sees her. What is implied by the exchange is nothing less than the absolute incommensurability of same-sex friendship and heterosexual love.

The bastard, Don John, for no reason at all, tricks Claudio into believing that Hero is false to him. Claudio's reaction does not render him sympathetic in our eyes. First, he believes Don John at once (Iago has to do a slow, expert job on Othello). Second, in a violent revulsion of feeling he decides to humiliate her publicly. In church, in front of her father and her friends—at the moment when she thinks she is going to be joined to him—he rejects her, in coolly vicious language. As her father moves forward to "give her away," Claudio says, "There, Leonato, take her back again. / Give not this rotten orange to your friend" (IV.i.31–32). Claudio's language is odious.

Nevertheless Claudio has taken his stand in good faith, and in crises comrades stick together. He will assume that he can count on the support of Benedick, but Benedick has been invaded too. He loves Hero's great friend Beatrice. Benedick is becoming aware that it is not only men who form strong same-sex friendships. Beatrice loves Hero (not sexually) and knows her perhaps better than Benedick knows Claudio. She sees at once something that the eye of passionate love (at least as far as Claudio is concerned) cannot see, that the story about Hero is a foul lie. Beatrice is right.

Next we must understand how anxious the audience has become about Beatrice and Benedick. Because they are mysteriously trapped in a running wit-combat, it has become impossible for either party to confess the love that is actually there. Some years ago the program note for a Stratford production of *Much Ado about Nothing* expressed great scorn of the sentimentalists who thought that Beatrice and Benedick were drawn to each other from the beginning. But the sentimentalists are correct. The first words we hear from Beatrice are her inquiry whether Benedick has returned from the war (I.i.31). She refers to him satirically as "Signior Mountanto," but she wants to know. She says savagely, "I wonder that you will still be talking, Signior Benedick, nobody marks you" (I.i.116). The very excess of rudeness betrays her. Obviously there is one person on stage who does "mark" (that is, "notice") Benedick, namely Beatrice herself. Beatrice and Benedick are electrically aware of each other from the start. Both are good. Therefore we desire their happiness. In the event, their friends, benign panders, free them from their formal prison and bring them together. Beatrice is tricked into overhearing a pre-planned conversation in which Hero and a gentlewoman chat unguardedly, as if they were alone, about Benedick's passion for Beatrice and Beatrice's cruel scorn. Benedick has already been caught by like means. Beatrice, left alone, says, "Benedick, love on, I will requite thee, / Taming my wild heart to thy loving hand" (III.i.111–12). Elsewhere in Shakespeare deliberately arranged overheard conversations are designed to deceive. These are done to un-deceive. The players in the charade tell the simple truth. It is "everyday life," as played out by Beatrice and Benedick, that has become a lie, in need of correction.

The audience is delighted that everything is coming right, but we do not see Beatrice and Benedick together until the moment in the church we had reached, when Claudio humiliates Hero. After the shock has had its full effect and all seem to be leaving, Beatrice remains, and Benedick stays with Beatrice instead of going out with the others. Anne Barton in her introduction to this play in the *Riverside Shakespeare* rightly seizes on the significance of this purely spatial state of affairs. It means that Benedick is now aligned, not with Claudio, but with his lady.

They speak quietly together with none of the old bantering. If one listens one can tell that, although both say they believe in Hero's innocence, there is in Beatrice an edge of outrage that Benedick, in his separateness from Hero, cannot feel (just as before, in the lighter mode of the exchange with Claudio, he could not see her overwhelming beauty). Suddenly the difference between them becomes explicit:

BENEDICK Come. Bid me do any thing for thee.
BEATRICE Kill Claudio. (IV.i.288–89)

Benedick's response is immediate, strong, and instinctive: "Ha, not for the wide world." Of course he cannot kill his best friend. Beatrice answers, "You kill me to deny it. Farewell."

The audience is appalled, not, as Benedick is appalled, at Beatrice's request, but at the fact that the union of these two good people, achieved with such difficulty, is unravelling before our eyes. As Beatrice turns to leave, Benedick reaches out to her: "Tarry, sweet Beatrice." The dialogue that follows is fascinating. One would expect Benedick, in such extreme circumstances, to say to Beatrice, "Can you *prove* that Claudio is as bad as you say?" In the event he says the more dangerous, the more loving thing: "Think you in your soul the Count Claudio hath wrong'd Hero?" In other words, "Do *you* believe this?" Beatrice answers in the affirmative and Benedick says, without further fencing, "Enough, I am engag'd" (IV.i.331). The clipped language is aggressively male—almost "man to man." But Benedick is talking to the woman he loves. The effect, finally, is very touching. All his habitual moral responses have been transferred from the male world in which they were formed. Beatrice is now as important as—more important than—the war from which he has recently emerged. Of course the idea of soldiers of love is old. Ovid wrote, *Militiae species amor est*, "Love is a kind of military service" (*Ars amatoria*, ii.233), and *Militat omnis amans*, "Every lover is a soldier" (*Amores*, I.ix.1), but those were jokes. In the courtly love literature of the Middle Ages the language of knightly service was re-applied in the sphere of courtship. But Benedick's "I am engag'd" is neither Ovidian nor courtly. It is absolute commitment—faith—expressed in the language of a world he has left forever.

The tension between same-sex solidarity and heterosexual love, first explored in *Two Gentlemen of Verona,* here reaches a climax. Perhaps something snaps. It is never as strong again in the later comedies. Not everything in *Much Ado about Nothing* has this strength. Don John, the bastard, who, motivelessly, seeks to destroy Hero, is weak if set beside the inexplicable killer Tybalt in *Romeo and Juliet* or the ineffably evil Iago in *Othello,* later. Shakespeare is just not interested in Don John and is content to let the cosmic dissonance of his illegitimacy cover the case. The bastard Edmund in *King Lear* is similarly at odds with natural goodness but receives a quite different quality of attention from the dramatist.

The worry we ascribed to the young Shakespeare, that stylish language can act as a screen, cutting us off from reality, persists in *Much Ado about Nothing* in the curious difficulties into which Beatrice and Benedick fall simply because they are both very witty. If we set this beside the situation in *Love's Labour's Lost* where the cadenced elegance of sentences begins to work against the truth or credibility of what those sentences seek to assert, we shall see that *Love's Labour's Lost* is primarily philosophical, where *Much Ado about Nothing* is, more narrowly, socio-psychological. The earlier play gives voice to a fundamental fear about reality slipping from us (usually it is only a philosopher who can contrive to lose so large a thing as the real universe). In *Much Ado about Nothing* Shakespeare forgets this fear and looks very hard at social practice. The play is intelligent mimesis. In the eighteenth century people liked to say that Shakespeare was good because he held the mirror up to nature. They said it so often that it came to seem either boring or mistaken. But that is exactly what Shakespeare does here. This is shrewd social observation. It is as if baiting and merriment serve a useful purpose in the preliminary phase of courtship but can become counter-productive if they harden into a fixed habit. I remember teenage girls in my native Hereford in the late 1940s clustering in a corner of the town park, flinging verbal abuse with much laughter at the boys casually circling them. The dating columns of popular newspapers in Britain today insist so frequently on "a good sense of humour" that "g.s.o.h." has become the accepted, immediately intelligible abbreviation. But it has to be possible for the parties to move out of this bantering, this careful sparring at arm's length, if the union it all serves is ever to be attained. It is hard to make complicated jokes and to kiss at the same time. All this Shakespeare observed, I would say, empirically. What he no longer does is investigate the categories of perception or question the status of data. *Much Ado about Nothing* is a tender play and a very shrewd one—and it is innocent of epistemological implications.

There is a Great Detective in this play as there is in Sophocles' *Oedipus Rex*. Dogberry, the local copper, finds and arrests the guilty party. He does so, however, more by luck than judgement. It is a major lexical injustice that we speak of Dogberry's glorious linguistic slips and adventures as "malapropisms." The word derives from Mrs. Malaprop in Richard Sheridan's *The Rivals* (1775). But Shakespeare got there more than a century earlier. There is something emblematic in making the impresario of the dénouement a simpleton. Bottom in *A Midsummer Night's Dream* had his own moment of strange profundity: "It shall be call'd 'Bottom's Dream,' because it hath no bottom" (IV.i.215–16). But no such intuition of mystery is given to Dogberry. In *Much Ado about Nothing* Shakespeare himself has chosen not to think hard.

As You Like It: Rosalind Triumphans

This could not last. *Much Ado about Nothing* was followed by *As You Like It,* and *As You Like It* contains dialogue like this:

TOUCHSTONE Truly, I would the gods had made thee poetical.
AUDREY I do not know what "poetical" is. Is it honest in deed and
    word? Is it a true thing?
TOUCHSTONE No, truly; for the truest poetry is the most feigning, and
    lovers are given to poetry; and what they swear in poetry may be said
    as lovers they do feign.
AUDREY Do you wish then that the gods had made me poetical?
TOUCHSTONE I do, truly; for thou swear'st to me thou art honest. Now
    if thou wert a poet, I might have some hope thou didst feign.

(III.iii.15–27)

We are in the Forest of Arden, to which Duke Senior and his company have fled. Touchstone, the Duke's fool, is talking to a simple country wench. The actor who first played Touchstone was probably Robert Armin. Armin, something of an intellectual, was influenced by Erasmus and wrote a book, *Fool upon Fool* (1600). He drew a distinction that has force still between the "natural" and the "artificial" fool. The "natural fool" is funny before he speaks. He is likely to be fat, pink, and slow of mind. The "fool artificial" is a "gag man"; he is witty and others become the object of *his* mirth. Armin was himself an artificial fool, and Dogberry clearly is a natural fool. When Falstaff remarks that he is not only witty in himself but is the cause that there is wit in other men (*2 Henry IV*, I.i.9–10), he anticipates Armin's distinction and confounds it by occupying both parts simultaneously. Falstaff is funny before he speaks and is also highly intelligent. The entry of the artificial fool in *As You Like It*—Touchstone replacing Dogberry—results at once in a marked increase of intellectual activity.

When Touchstone says he wishes the gods had made Audrey poetical, the audience is at first not much clearer than Audrey herself. Is he wishing that Audrey (herself a female natural fool who may be chewing a straw as we watch) were more like the pretty girls in the poetry books? We are not sure. Audrey tells him she has never heard the word before, and Touchstone "explains" in a manner designed to make the head spin: the truest poetry is the most feigning, the most replete with un-truth. He is exploiting double senses in *true* and *honest*. *True* can mean "truth-telling" or it can mean "genuine" or "authentic." "Your true tennis-player practises for two hours a day" doesn't mean that truth-telling tennis-players behave in this way. *Honest* meanwhile can mean "virtuous," "honourable," or (again) "truth-telling." The coexistence of the two meanings is enough to generate temporary bewilderment: "Genuine poetry is not concerned with factual accuracy" does not sound like a paradox; "True poetry is all untruth" feels like contradiction. But why did Audrey ask, "Is it honest?" Audrey is a simple soul, but she is perhaps a little sharper than most modern audiences, who just can't follow the dialogue. She is using *honest* in the sense of "virtuous"; she suspects that Touchstone's intentions may not be honourable, and she is absolutely right. Touchstone chooses to reply as if she had used *honest* in the other sense, "truth-telling." "Not at all," he answers, "Lies all the time!" Indeed, enraptured by his own wit, he perhaps gives too much away to Audrey when he adds that lovers swear undying devotion but this is all feigned. Audrey, who is basically a good girl (no irony here), is puzzled that anyone would want another person to be a liar. Touchstone genially explains again; if Audrey were a poet and as careless of truth as other poets are, her protestations of chastity would be feigned and he might have some chance of working his evil will on her.

This, it might be said, is more dazzling than profound. But it is embedded in a pastoral, and pastoral has built into it a certain philosophical potency. Touchstone is fooling around with dangerous materials. Pastoral, the poetry of shepherds, was bequeathed to the Renaissance by classical antiquity, as was Stoicism. But whereas Stoicism is a philosophy that aims at static unity, a closed and invulnerable integrity, pastoral is systematically ambiguous from the start. For the Stoic, as we saw, following reason and following nature are the same. For the pastoral poet they are opposites. "Nature" in pastoral literature is made antithetical to "art" and so becomes, distinctively, *green*. Nature is good, art bad. A wood is natural but a city is not. Yet there is one enormous snag. The celebrants of the pastoral ideal are poets, and poetry is itself art, not nature. It may be thought that the genre "pastoral" derives from the artless songs of real, simple shepherds so that there was a time when this problem did not exist. In fact, however, quite apart from the fact that there is in any case a latent oxymoron in the "*songs*" of "*artless*" shepherds, pastoral seems to have started not in the country but in the first cities to feel uncomfortably big, disquietingly civic—first Alexandria, then Rome. "Pathos of distance" is essential to the genre. Nature turns green when people begin to say, "It was all fields here when I was a child." The country assumes its poignancy when it is no longer immediately available. Technology and cleverness are now construed as an epistemological Fall of Man (Eden, the lost garden, was a green place; the civic New Jerusalem is for—ugh!—forward-looking politicians). The fact that the pastoral poet is forever divided from his ideal by his poethood could have led to comedy, but in fact it led to a poetry of yearning, of confessed impossibility, in the hands of the best practitioners. The poets, in a kind of secret agony, are driven to a strange self-projection; they invent versions of themselves that can be happily part of that golden world on the other side of the glass wall conscious art has formed. Virgil's Tityrus, who lolls in the shade of a beech in the first Eclogue, is Virgil himself, but a Virgil who is no longer learned, literate, Roman but is instead an untutored shepherd, like the other inhabitants of the landscape. Nevertheless Virgil, because he is a great poet, knows that the wound of art cannot be healed so easily. His Tityrus is teaching the woods, as he plays on his oaten flute, to re-echo the name of fair Amaryllis (*Formosam resonare doces Amaryllida silvas*). The strange generic pain of pastoral is latent in this line. With great delicacy the words confess that there may after all be no such thing as wholly innocent poetry. When Tityrus begins to play he is a tutor in duplicity (*resonare,* "re-echo"); he *teaches* the woods, inarticulate till now, eloquence, gives them the art of language, makes them conscious.

All this lies behind the dialogue of Touchstone and Audrey. Touchstone is urban, courtly, clever, and corrupt; although Audrey is a comic figure, she upholds the core pastoral values; she is artless and virtuous. It is deeply appropriate that she should need to ask what "poetical" means; she, as nature, must be artless, and poetry is an art. Artful Touchstone is hardly satanic, but he is certainly subtle (the word applied to the serpent in Genesis). He introduces sexuality into Eden/Arden and seeks to induce a Fall. One might have predicted that when an artificial fool takes on a natural fool there can be no contest: the artificial fool will run rings round the natural. But this is a pastoral comedy, and so, wonderfully, the natural fool wins. Audrey repels the serpent Touchstone (who has to wait like everyone else for the wedding at the end); her simple virtue is unshaken.

There are further implications. These are articulated in the speech Duke Senior gives on arriving in the green world:

Now, my co-mates and brothers in exile,
Hath not old custom made this life more sweet
Than that of painted pomp? Are not these woods
More free from peril than the envious court?
Here feel we not the penalty of Adam,
The seasons' difference, as the icy fang
And churlish chiding of the winter's wind,
Which when it bites and blows upon my body
Even till I shrink with cold, I smile and say,

"This is no flattery: these are counsellors
That feelingly persuade me what I am."
Sweet are the uses of adversity,
Which like the toad, ugly and venomous,
Wears yet a precious jewel in his head;
And this our life, exempt from public haunt,
Finds tongues in trees, books in the running brooks,
Sermons in stones, and good in every thing.   (II.i.1–17)

This is an "aria," like Mercutio's Queen Mab speech, inviting—and get-ting—inclusion in yesterday's anthologies of "beauties from Shakespeare." Note that the Duke himself is no shepherd. He has been projected into Arcadia not by a process of imaginative transformation (as with Virgil's Tityrus and Marvell's "Mower") but by political violence. One great difference between Virgilian and Shakespearean pastoral is that Virgil gives us a rural world that may indeed be lost but is, on the page, continuous; in Shakespeare pastoral is always an interlude, framed by civic or courtly action. Typically a power-figure is driven to take refuge in a wild place, praises its simplicity, but returns eagerly to court at the first opportunity.

Duke Senior's praise of the country life is so radical that we are involved once more in epistemology and ontology, with the questions, "What do we know?" and "What is real?" There is nothing especially philosophical in his observation that rural life is free from the flattery that poisons life at court. It becomes philosophical when it is joined, as here, to a special claim for reality status. A. O. Lovejoy and G. Boas in their classic study *Primitivism and Related Ideas in Antiquity* (1935) drew a distinction between "hard" and "soft" primitivism. Soft primitivism depicts the pastoral life as idyllically free from toil, the shepherd lolling in the shade. Hard primitiv-ism springs not from the *Eclogues* of Virgil but from his *Georgics,* poems concerned not with shepherds but with a later phase of rural economy, ploughing, sowing, the cultivation of crops. This shows country life as hard.[2] Wrestling with a plough stuck in the black earth forms the charac-ter. It produced, Virgil says (*Georgics,* i.63), the *durum genus,* the "hardy race" of Romans that would conquer the world.

Shakespeare allows Duke Senior to pass from soft to hard primitivism in the course of his speech. The first clue is his reference to a less than idyllic cold wind. We see no more of this testing weather in the play that follows. *As You Like It* as a whole remains firmly in the line of the *Eclogues;* it is not Georgic. But the Duke is no ordinary hard primitivist. He is not content to say that toil makes you tough; he says that rural hardship acquaints you with reality. We have returned to the anxiety about formalism that haunted *Love's Labour's Lost* but now it is recast according to the conventions of pastoral. The Duke suggests that the court is a mere tissue of forms, that eloquence is mendacity and style a mere truancy from the real. The cold wind cannot lie, but it can apprise him of his bodily humanity, the fundamental truth of his condition.

The idea of Eden is present in the speech, in the phrase "the penalty of Adam." What follows is a well-known textual puzzle. The Duke appears to say, first, that they do *not,* in this happy place, feel the penalty of Adam (as if the Fall were miraculously reversed), then to specify the penalty not as work, as at Genesis 3:23, but as seasonal change with its concomitant discomforts, and then to dwell cheerfully on the fact that they *do* feel the winter wind and how good it is for them. The best answer to the puzzle is to say that the sentence sets off as a question: "Feel we not" now means, not "We do not feel," but "Don't we feel?" and the final question mark gets lost because the sentence proves in the event to be so very long. The meaning meanwhile is radical indeed. The only "telling" we can trust is prelinguistic. There is no duplicity, no re-presentation in this truthful wind. Here the senses of "true" that Touchstone punned on, "truth-telling" and "real," are in play, but now with serious force. This is "the philosophy of pastoral" at its most fundamental. We have reached the point at which all that is not natural, in the new sense of that word, is tainted.

But we must now remember the central psychosis of pastoral: it is in art that the artless is celebrated. And the Duke is himself spectacularly artful in the way he puts his case. The language is mannered and cadenced (terms we used earlier in connection with the prison of words confining the bright young courtiers in *Love's Labour's Lost*). Shakespeare is clearly aware of the paradox, since with delicious irony he makes the imagery work against the Duke's ostensible "message." Even as he condemns language, the Duke is turning everything into language. He finds *sermons* in stones, *tongues* in trees, *books* in the running brooks. "Il n'y a pas de hors-texte" indeed.[3] When he has finished the smooth courtier, Amiens murmurs,

> Happy is your Grace,
> That can translate the stubbornness of fortune
> Into so quiet and so sweet a style.   (II.i.19–20)

The lexical tremor in this use of *translate* betrays much. It is usual to speak of translating from French, say, into English, from one language into another. But Amiens applauds a translation of unpleasant fact (he takes it for granted that their situation is, objectively, pretty bad) into, of all things, *style*. Amiens, who is no doubt expert in the courtly flattery condemned by pastoral, sees the Duke's little performance as a splendid instance of what might be called philosophical flattery: the Duke has flattered the ugly old dame Nature by pretending not just that she is beautiful but that she is somehow the only real thing there is. What the Duke has just attacked as a vice is made the ground of Amiens's compliment. The Duke, however, is not indignant. He genially accepts the kind words. "Happy," as Amiens employs the word, means not "contented" or "in a good situation" but "felicitous," "stylistically apposite," as in "a happy phrase."

I said earlier that the "artful-artless" paradox could have generated comedy but instead produced a subtly poignant effect. Here, however, we really are on the brink of comedy. Duke Senior is within a hair's breadth of being funnier than Touchstone and—irony of ironies—he would then be natural fool to Touchstone's artificial fool, since we would be laughing *at* the Duke whereas we laugh *with* Touchstone. The despised Audrey speaks better for truth and simplicity than Duke Senior ever could. The play goes surprisingly far in the direction of debunking pastoral, that most haunting of genres. Certainly the plot line does not show courtly persons educated by shepherds as pastoral requires. Instead we have a wild place made courtly, simplicity usurped by mannered sophistication. The word "usurped" may remind us that the Duke himself has been usurped by his wicked brother, as a matter of brute political fact, and that he in his turn will usurp the deer, to whom the forest really belongs. His act of *stylistic* usurpation in this speech becomes, in the circumstances, a peculiarly brilliant grace-note.

But while the courtly persons of the play never learn simplicity, the real rustics are there, a standing answer to all this cleverness, as the Brueghelesque songs of Winter and Spring answered all the verbal display at the end of *Love's Labour's Lost*. Silvius admittedly is a cardboard cut-out, a love-lorn literary shepherd. But Audrey, Corin, and William are genuine rustics, of the earth earthy. Corin reminds us of the "hard" hands of the shepherd, "uncleanly . . . [from] handling our ewes . . . their fells you know are greasy" (III.ii.59, 50, 53–54). When Touchstone speaks of the "cow's dugs" and the "pretty chopp'd hands" of Jane Smile, who milked them (II.iv.49–50), he is satirizing country life, but the raw imagery has a force that defeats his wit. It is a counter-attack from nature, reversing the defeat of nature by style we saw in Duke Senior's speech.

Some say the golden world of pastoral was always, intentionally and manifestly, hollow, a conflation of artificial tropes. It will be evident that I regard this view as a mistake. If it were true, all the intricate imaginative negotiation would be over before it had begun. It is essential to the dialectical tension of the genre that the simple world be loved before it is eclipsed by conscious art. The landscape glows in the *Eclogues* of Virgil. Without this warmth there would be no poignancy in the strange exclusion of the artist from the world he describes. For his pastoral to remain vividly alive, Shakespeare had to counter the solvent effect of things like Amiens's compliment to the Duke with harshly realistic rusticity. That is why he admits to this dancerlike comedy rebarbative social and economic detail, like the continuing bond of villeinage among Elizabethan herdsmen (II.iv.78–79). When Rosalind, newly arrived in the forest, speaks easily of buying a cottage (II.iv.92), one thinks at once of rich buyers "pricing out" local farm labourers when they pay over the odds for cottages in Wales, say, today. This thought occurs because Shakespeare has allowed a note of economic realism to enter the play. It might be supposed that such things are anti-pastoral. On the contrary, they enable *As You Like It* to become a real, strong pastoral.

Although Corin never effectively teaches the courtly party anything at all, he is given a space in which he too can philosophize. He says, "I know . . . that the property of rain is to wet and fire to burn; that good pasture makes fat sheep; and that a great cause of the night is the lack of the sun" (III.ii.23–28). Such wisdom is very close, as Corin knows, to tautology ("Water wets because of its wetness"). We may compare it with a famous sequence near the end of Molière's *Le Malade imaginaire* (1673).

In the French play a candidate is being examined in philosophy by members of faculty. I will give it first in Molière's mixture of French and dog-Latin, and then translate:

BACHELERIUS Mihi a docto doctore
  Domandatur causam et rationem quare
    Opium facit dormire:
      A quoi respondeo,
    Quia est in eo
    Virtus dormitiva
    Cujus est natura
    Sensus assoupire.
CHORUS Bene, bene, bene, bene.[4]
CANDIDATE I am asked by the learned doctor
  The cause and reason why
  Opium makes you sleep:
  To which I answer:
  Because there is in it
  A *dormitive virtue*
  Of which it is the nature
  To lull our senses.
CHORUS OF EXAMINERS Excellent, excellent, excellent, excellent!

The student has explained that opium makes you sleep because it has the power of making you sleep. As Molière handles the scene the tautology is exposed and is straightforwardly satirized. "*Virtus dormitiva* explanation" has passed into common usage among philosophers as a term of good-humoured abuse. The way Shakespeare treats similar thoughts when they are offered by Corin is quite different. There is a strange strength in the gentle reminder, countryman to townsman, that the rain can wet you and that black night will come when the sun, the only source of light hereabouts, has gone. The notion towards which Duke Senior strained, that the wind can apprise you of your own bodily reality, is implicit in Corin's words, but he never slides into the slick metaphors, "tongues in trees" and the like, that did for Duke Senior. Instead, with a smile, he rests in the oddly instructive tautology. In Molière's lines we are made to feel that

tautology is vacuous, in Corin's, that it is strangely *full*. We may suppose
that the notion of meaning is dependent on there being a space between
word and thing. But pastoral teaches—or strains towards the notion that—
nature alone is truly wise. All that water can say is "I am wet." We sense
that the necessary space between word and thing is vanishing. In his poem
"The Garden," Andrew Marvell rejoiced in this pastoral collapse into a
kind of tautology: "a green thought in a green shade."

Where the educated Duke Senior was unaware of the contradiction
into which he had blundered, Corin knows that his words will sound like
folly to many. The icicles in the song of Winter at the end of *Love's
Labour's Lost* become the drenching rain of Corin's brief meditation and
will afterwards become the rain that "raineth every day" in the vacuous/
haunting song of Feste at the end of *Twelfth Night*.

As You Like It is, then, true pastoral. Indeed it is the greatest pastoral in
the English language. Although Duke Senior is implicitly satirized as a
man incapable of grasping the nature he thinks he admires, Nature herself
is made strong enough in the drama to act as a healing antidote to the self-
dissolving intricacies of courtly consciousness. It is not simply that the
rural world is made to seem real. It is also made irreducibly mysterious. In
some strange way the forest is outside time ("There's no clock in the
forest," III.ii.300–301). This is foreshadowed indirectly in an eerie slippage into "double time" before we ever reach Arden. The most famous
double-time sequence is that attributed by critics to *Othello*. The suggestion, in the case of the later tragedy, is that the plot as it stands is impossible. Only a few hours elapse, as we watch, after the wedding of Othello
and Desdemona, yet within that time, it is supposed to be plausible that
Desdemona could have carried on a love affair of several weeks' duration
with Cassio. In fact there is no need to postulate a double-time scheme for
Othello.[5] I know that when I first saw the play I assumed that Othello was
made to believe that Desdemona *had been* unfaithful during the period of
courtship preceding the wedding. No problem.

But in *As You Like It* there is genuine temporal doubling. As we learn
about the friendship of Rosalind and Celia in the first act it is made clear,
first, that it was only the other day that Rosalind's father fled the court
("He is already in the Forest of Arden," I.i.114), and, second, that since he
left the two girls have grown up together (I.iii.71–76). Of course it could

be careless writing. Or it could be a way of disorienting us before we are taken to the wild place, a subtle anticipation of the later suggestion that time may be different, *there*. It is an old chestnut of classes on *As You Like It* to ask the students why Rosalind doesn't change her clothes when she finds Orlando in the forest. The presumption is that we can see at once why Rosalind needs to assume male attire during her journey, in order to fend off rough, importunate persons. But when she is happily reunited with the man she wants, she might be expected to put on a nice dress and begin emitting feminine signals. Usually the students say that her doublet and hose give Rosalind a freedom to be herself that would be abruptly terminated by suffocating convention as soon as she put on a dress, or that by remaining in disguise Rosalind can eavesdrop on the way her lover talks about her when has no idea that she is present—an amazingly happy exercise since, unlike eavesdroppers elsewhere in Shakespeare, she hears nothing but love and praise of herself. But I cannot forget the day when a student gave an answer of a completely different kind: "Rosalind does not change her clothes because time stops when she enters Arden; this is reflected in the structure of the play; the *action* is crowded into the courtly preliminaries and the dénouement; the extended centre is a pastoral meditation, and is timeless."

In *Two Gentlemen of Verona* Shakespeare tried out the idea of the lady who puts on male attire to go after the man she loves. It is an idea that gradually intensifies in the comedies that followed, reaching a disquieting climax in *All's Well That Ends Well*. In this play the notion, germinal in *Two Gentlemen of Verona*, half-suppressed in *As You Like It*, that the pursuing lady redeems the inadequate male lover at the close is very strong. Helena, who hunts Bertram down, is positively alarming to male spectators. One feels hot breath on the back of the neck. In *As You Like It* Rosalind clearly outclasses Orlando in intelligence and practical energy, but while Theseus in *A Midsummer Night's Dream*, similarly outclassed by Hippolyta, leaves a sour taste behind, Orlando is a perfectly agreeable young man. Rosalind understands him very well and is content with what she sees. She was wretched and restless, we know, until she found a way to join the young wrestler she had watched.

Now, however, she has found him. He meanwhile has not found her. He still thinks his lady is far away. But Orlando is bearing up very comfortably! Rosalind is slightly piqued by this (but also finds it funny). She explains that the marks of a lover are: "A lean cheek, which you have not; a blue eye and sunken, which you have not; a beard neglected, which you have not . . . your hose should be ungarter'd, your bonnet unbanded, your sleeve unbutton'd, your shoe untied, and every thing about you demonstrating a careless desolation. But you are no such man; you are rather point-device in your accoustrements, as loving yourself, than seeming the lover of any other" (III.ii.372–84). Rosalind's picture of the unrequited lover is humorously over the top, but for all that she touches a vulnerable point in Orlando, this well-dressed, healthy, unsubduably cheerful young man. What she hits is his (to her entirely forgivable) shallowness. Notice that in her flight of fancy she has exactly described Hamlet—him of the down-gyved stocking, pale as his shirt (II.i.77–78)—and the one thing we all know about Hamlet is that he is *deep*.

Rosalind is a little like Juliet, but a Juliet for whom everything goes right. She is wildly in love, giddier in her desires, as she says herself, than a monkey (IV.i.153). At the same time, like Juliet she is a clear-eyed realist: "Men have died from time to time, and worms have eaten them, but not for love" (IV.i.106–8).[6] We hear the same realism in her friendly tip to the proud Phebe, "Sell when you can, you are not for all markets" (III.v.60). Amid the glassy refracted "natures" of this pastoral comedy she is magnificently natural, the only member of the upper-class party that can, perhaps, look old Corin in the eye.

Given this earthiness, it is the more remarkable that she is almost divinized at the end of the play. Rosalind is one of Shakespeare's impresario-figures (others are the Duke in *Measure for Measure,* Prospero in *The Tempest*). She majestically orders from above the resolution of the comedy in which, against all expectation, Mr. Right marries Ms. Right in every case. In so controlling the plot of the drama she is analogous to the dramatist, above the action, transcendent. At the very last moment, however, Rosalind is displaced, by an actual divinity. Hymen, the god of marriage, appears to join the parties together. It is strange but true that *The Winter's Tale,* a play that everyone feels is in some way enchanted, contains (apart from the Oracle) no supernatural event or appearance, whereas *As You Like It,* the play of joyous common sense, has a god descend (in a curiously unobtrusive manner) at the close. It is as if Shakespeare felt at the last moment, that, because of the humanized Platonism, the intuition of transcendence that informs all the marriage endings in Shakespeare, Rosalind was becoming too explicitly divine, and to save the ordinary woman, Marriage itself in visible shape was wheeled in to take over. Rosalind, still, rules the play.

We began in the Temple Garden in *1 Henry VI,* where political causality was seen as a shimmering thing, operating not so much in a linear manner as laterally, enforced and nourished by its physical context. There is a remote amatory echo of this in *As You Like It:* "The sight of lovers feedeth those in love" (III.iv.57). The line suggests a faint perversity: falling in love ought to be the most personal of experiences, yet "peer pressure" plays its part. This movement of the spirit that seems so individual, so intimate to the originating self, may happen in part because other people are doing it. There is even a hint of a simpler impropriety, of lovers turned on not privately by each other but by simple pre-personal erotic imagery. In general, however, *As You Like It* is a very "straight" play—for some, disappointingly so. Rosalind is disguised as Ganymede, and Orlando is invited to woo her in her disguised state. The stage seems to be set for homo-erotic comedy. "Ganymede," the name of Jupiter's boy-love in mythology, signals this in advance: "Jove, slyly stealing from his sister's bed, / To dally with Idalian Ganymed" (*Hero and Leander,* i.147–48). This is Christopher Marlowe, the now dead rival poet, notorious for his homosexuality. And Marlowe haunts this play, as the "dead shepherd" (III.v.81), his death in a quarrel over a bill in a tavern perhaps alluded to in "a great reckoning in a little room" (III.iii.15). In fact, however, the humour of the Orlando/Ganymede scenes turns again and again on Orlando's insuperable heterosexuality—good news for Rosalind, if not for Ganymede. As long as Orlando thinks he is dealing with a young male his kisses are passionless. He arrives late and would clearly prefer a female. There is one hilarious moment when he begins to respond to *Ganymede* and Rosalind jumps back in alarm. It happens when she first sets out the program of "pretend-wooing," as a purgative exercise, leading finally to monastic withdrawal from the world. "Come every day to my cote," she concludes, "and woo me." Orlando is spell-bound: "Now, by the faith of my love, I will" (III.ii.427–28). The form of his oath is deeply ironic, but the irony is inadvertent, on Orlando's part. Rosalind hastily puts him right: "You must call me Rosalind" (III.iii.434). For the rest of the play heterosexual love is in the ascendant.

It is in accord with that movement we have seen repeatedly in the comedies from same-sex friendship to love and marriage with a member of the opposite sex. This comedic privileging of heterosexuality was easily accepted for centuries by the current culture as obviously right-thinking. We seem now to have reached a point where it requires a defence. It is odd, still, when one considers the bisexual nature evident in Shakespeare's sonnets, his charitable sympathy with those homosexual figures such as Antonio in *The Merchant of Venice* who are necessarily marginalized when the weddings happen at the end. The real answer is that Shakespeare chose to make comedy revolve around procreation. There was then no question of homosexual marriage, and such unions are infertile. The plays certainly celebrate marriage, but Shakespeare is never the uncomprehending, intolerant bigot, trapped by tunnel vision.

Twelfth Night: The Unsociable Man

VIOLA What country, friends, is this?
CAPTAIN This is Illyria, Madam.
VIOLA And what should I do in Illyria?
  My brother, he is in Elysium.   (I.ii.1–4)

Viola, having survived shipwreck, thinking her brother drowned, here enters the world of *Twelfth Night*. Because she believes that her twin, Sebastian, is in Elysium, she feels that she, because they are identical, should be there also. She thinks that she should be—perhaps is—dead. Shakespeare the poet knows the power of assonance: "Elysium" and "Illyria" are similar sounds, similar words. "Lyrical," meanwhile, may be lurking in the background (one is tempted to suggest that "Illyria" could feel like a compound of "lyrical" and "idyllic," but "idyllic" seems to be post-Shakespearean). If she has indeed died, this place in which she finds herself could be a paradise, an Elysium in truth. We have a momentary sense that Viola may have entered Arcadia through the gate of death. "What should I [a dead woman] do in Illyria?" is a half-echo of *Et in Arcadia ego*, "Even in Arcadia, I [death] exist." In Poussin's painting of this name shepherds marvel at the inscription as at something hitherto unknown in their world of perpetual spring. Erwin Panofsky traced the phrase back before Poussin to Guercino, but not alas to a date early enough for Shakespeare.[7] The most learned man I know said, "Oh, it's a lot earlier than Guercino," but couldn't come up with a reference. So my "half-echo" may be merely fortuitous. The underlying idea, the incongruity of death in Arcadia, is certainly something Shakespeare understood. In the timeless Forest of Arden the bloody napkin (when Oliver is gored by the lion, IV.iii.114–56) is like a wound in the very genre of the comedy. We can't have bloodshed *here!*[8]

Shakespeare reorders the conventional elements of pastoral: Golden Age, Happy Place, Alternative World, Eden. Certain major images are common to the classical and Hebraic traditions. Naturally the Renaissance falls upon the coincidences with delight. The shepherd is important in the New Testament especially, and the idea of a lost garden is there in the Old Testament. True, the Christian idea of the shepherd is different from the classical; the Christian shepherd is above all responsible; this gives us *pastor* in the sense "minister of religion." The classical shepherd of soft primitivism is blissfully at ease. Elsewhere, however, we find not contrast but a strong assonance. Pastoral as linked to the Golden Age, to childhood, and to innocence has warm affinities with the Christian story of the lost garden. W. H. Auden thought the human race was divided into "Arcadians," who instinctively locate happiness in the past, and "Utopians," who locate it in the future. The happy place for the Arcadian is green, rural; for the Utopian it is urban, the New Jerusalem. Retrospective Arcadians are aesthetes, prospective Utopians are politically energized, working towards that civic bliss that is yet to be realized.[9]

Yet there is one way in which Arcadia may suddenly seem to lie not in the past but ahead of us. This happens if we turn Eden into heaven. The semantic development of the word *paradise* encapsulates the shift. Its first meaning from Greek and Old Persian is "enclosed park, or garden." Adam and Eve before the Fall were in Paradise. But then it comes to mean the happy place some reach after death. Dante's *Paradiso* is not about Eden but about the life to come. Yet in a way Auden's rule still holds. For Paradise in the new sense is not so much in the future as outside time. It remains a–historical and apolitical. There is no clock in heaven.

Shakespeare has used the pivotal character of the word to bathe his comedy in the light of transcendence. This new way of relating death and Arcadia will assume great power in the late Romances, which are all about persons thought dead in sea-storms but re-united at the end, children lost and found. The pattern was first tried, indeed, at the beginning of Shakespeare's career. *Twelfth Night* stands between *The Comedy of Errors* and the last plays, *Pericles, Cymbeline, The Winter's Tale,* and *The Tempest.*

Of course *Twelfth Night* taken as a whole is not a pastoral. The hint of a secular Paradise is fleeting. The audience knows with complete security that Viola has not died and that Illyria is simply a rather jolly country where people drink late and enjoy music. There is music in the half-anagrammatic names, not only Illyria and Elysium but Viola, Olivia—Malvolio.[10] The last name jars. To begin with, it means "ill will." Then, Malvolio is the unassimilable, unattractive, unlovable, windowless monad of the play, at odds with the festive society. He is described as a "puritan" (II.iii.139), and this is a word on which we should pause. Today the word is heavy with the baggage of later English and American history, puritan opposition to Laudian Anglicanism and the rest. When Shakespeare wrote *Twelfth Night* such clear factional grouping was not yet in place. *Puritan* means something like "precisionist"; a kind of moral pedantry is implied, with a correlative disapproval of the surrounding cheerful slackness. John Whitgift wrote in 1572 that puritans "think themselves to be *mundiores caeteris,* more pure than others as the *Cathari* dyd, and separate themselves from all other Churches and congregations as spotted and defyled."[11] One is reminded of the Pharisee in the Bible who thanked God that he was not as other men (Luke 18:11). The separateness of which Whitgift speaks certainly applies to Malvolio. He is one of the most interesting of an interesting group, the set of those not assigned a partner at the end of the comedy. Malvolio is unintelligent, deficient in natural affection, contemptuous of others, censorious, and complacent. He does not like others to have a good time. Lord Macaulay once observed that the puritans opposed bear-baiting not because it caused pain to the bear but because it gave pleasure to the spectators.[12] Malvolio has no business to be wandering about in a happy comedy. But he is here, a gauche, walking affront to the festive spirit, and the comedic society deals with him in the only way it can, by making him a butt.

I have said that Malvolio should not be there, but there is perhaps a sense in which he is actually needed. Nietzsche wrote, "Not so very long ago a royal wedding or great public celebration would have been incomplete without executions, tortures and *autos da fé,* a noble household without some person whose office it was to serve as a butt for everyone's malice and cruel teasing. . . . There is no feast without cruelty, as man's entire history attests. Punishment, too, has its festive features."[13] Nietzsche's blood-chilling observations can have a certain shrewdness. One begins to wonder whether, when spirits are high, there has to be someone to suffer the impact of the aggressive element in all this joy. Malvolio is "ill will," in contrast with the others, but Nietzsche implies that this description can be turned inside out: the butt is there to receive the malice of the happy persons. Who better for such a role than one who despises merriment?

We saw earlier how Ernst Cassirer praised Shakespeare for his discovery of a new form of laughter, laughing with rather than laughing at.[14] The older comedy of cruel derision has given place to a comedy in which players and audience alike are wreathed in smiles at the end of the play.[15] But now the redeemed inhabitants of this new comedy of love themselves belong, as they shift status from players in *Twelfth Night* to spectators of the drama *they* have set up, to the old party, the party of cruel mirth. In Auden's terms the play called *Twelfth Night* is a Christian comedy of charity;[16] the play within it, called *Malvolio Gulled,* is Roman-Jonsonian.

We have already seen the "mechanicals" mocked by the grand people in *A Midsummer Night's Dream* and Holofernes similarly ridiculed in *Love's Labour's Lost.* But Bottom and his friends are clearly part of the "dance" of the comedy, and the same is true of the dotty schoolmaster and *his* friends. Malvolio is anti-comic and isolated in a far more radical manner. Jonathan Bate noticed a link between Malvolio and the Ovidian myth of Actaeon that is certainly working in the play.[17] Actaeon was the hated onlooker who watched Diana and her nymphs as they bathed and was in consequence first transformed into a deer and then torn to pieces by his own hounds. The last words of Malvolio are "I'll be reveng'd on the whole pack of you" (V.i.378). One can still hear, Bate suggests, the baying of the hounds in that one word, "pack." This is not "over-reading" but literary criticism at its most acute. Bate looks back to Roman antiquity; others look forward. The line is indeed prophetic. The puritan will have his revenge indeed on these merry players. The puritan Long Parliament closed all the theatres in England in 1642.

Even in the earlier plays there was a point when the mockery became uncomfortable and Shakespeare made his counter-move. Holofernes was given his "island" of dignified remonstrance: "This is not generous" (V.ii.628); Bottom was given the haunting words, " 'Bottom's Dream,' because it hath no bottom" (IV.i.215–16). But these earlier figures are both stagers of plays; they are not made the matter of a miniature derisive comedy set up by others. In *Much Ado about Nothing* Beatrice and Benedick are each tricked, as Malvolio is tricked, into believing that they are loved, but the deception in *Much Ado* is at bottom hardly a deception at all. A tale is spun to Beatrice that Benedick loves her—and he does. The same thing is done for Benedick, symmetrically. The entire enterprise of the tricksters is benign; this is indeed a happy comedy laughing both at and with its characters. But in *Twelfth Night* our discomfort at what is done is suddenly much greater. Maria, Olivia's gentlewoman, and Sir Toby Belch concoct a letter, written in a passable imitation of Olivia's hand, designed to make her steward Malvolio believe that he is the object of the great lady's affection. The letter itself is all about the social gulf that lies between them; it urges him not to be frightened by this. The jokers assume that Malvolio will be caught by the chance of social climbing. In fact he is caught by something more elementary, by the thought that he is loved. There is a subtle pathos in the fact that this inadequate human being, so deficient in warmth towards others, should still be vulnerable at this point. Suddenly we see, Malvolio is human.

The elaborate charade of a supposed courtship conducted through the symbolism of clothing may seem far removed from social practice, but the autobiography of Thomas Whythorne (1528–1596) supplies a real-life equivalent. The impecunious Whythorne (who published the first book of English madrigals) worked as a tutor in music in various households. He was in service to a flirtatious widow who, from her socially exalted position, taunted him with his faint-heartedness in matters of love. Whythorne, thus prompted, appeared before her dressed in russet (the colour of hope), and she at once slapped him down, with a mocking rhyme: "The suds of soap / Shall wash your hope."[18] Of course the yellow stockings, the cross-gartering, and the fixed glassy smile are hilarious. As they lead, however, to sensory deprivation in the cell and the charge of madness laid on Malvolio, everyone wants to cry, "Enough! This has gone too far." Malvolio's name may connote malice, but he has nothing devilish about him as Tybalt does in *Romeo and Juliet* or Don John, the destroyer of young love in *Much Ado about Nothing*. His pride and intolerance are moral faults, but his principal crime is to be unattractive.

Meanwhile there is the main plot, the story of Viola, Orsino, Olivia, and Sebastian. Orsino loves Olivia but is getting nowhere. Viola, having survived shipwreck, disguises herself as a young man in order to be taken on as servant to Orsino. Orsino deputes the disguised Viola to press his suit once more with Olivia. Olivia remains proof against Orsino's pleas but falls for the messenger, thinking she is a young man. All is resolved at the end when Olivia is happy to marry Sebastian (who looks exactly like his sister with the added advantage of being genuinely male) and Orsino finds that he can love Viola (who has long loved him). Orsino's story is the one that falls short of full bliss. He never got his Olivia after all. But we feel this less than we might have because from the first Orsino is a dreamy, etiolated figure, an Aubrey Beardsley decadent, as much in love with love as with Olivia.

When Viola, herself the mirror image of her twin, performs the *proxy* wooing of Olivia on behalf of Orsino, we might be lulled into expecting the drama to become flimsy, insubstantial: a person who is herself an image can offer no more than a decaying after-image of the Duke's original passion. But Viola voices overwhelming, vivid love:

Make me a willow cabin at your gate,
And call upon my soul within the house;
Write loyal cantons of contemned love,
And sing them loud even in the dead of night;
Halloo[19] your name to the reverberate hills,
And make the babbling gossip of the air
Cry out "Olivia!"   (I.v.268–74)

Where Rosalind as Ganymede invited Orlando to practise his technique on her, Viola as Cesario redirects the passion she actually feels for Orsino at Olivia, and does so as a selfless act of service to that same Orsino. The possibility of a homo-erotic love finding expression in this confusion of gender roles is actually even smaller than it was in *As You Like It*. Orsino is not going to respond to the boy Cesario, nor will Olivia respond to the young woman, Viola. Yet a current of perversity (if that word can, somehow, be purged of pejorative force) runs through the play.

Shakespeare must have known that the idea of identical twins of opposite sexes is a biological nonsense. The gross thought, "But, dammit, Sebastian must have a penis and Viola has none, so how can they be called identical?" is inescapable. In the bisexual world of Shakespeare's sonnets we meet with the fantasy of a figure who looks female in every way except for his sex organs. The poet acknowledges his disappointment that nature will never provide this:

And for a woman wert thou first created,
Till Nature as she wrought thee fell a-doting,
And by addition me of thee defeated,
By adding one thing to my purpose nothing.
  But since she prick'd thee out for women's pleasure,
  Mine be thy love, and thy love's use their treasure.   (Sonnet 20)

In *Twelfth Night* Shakespeare has brilliantly entwined the sea-sundered twins of *The Comedy of Errors* with the cross-dressing of *As You Like It*. By the power of the comic plot Viola elicits love in a manner that seems independent of her actual sex. This is because of her beauty, a beauty possessed in equal measure by her brother. This intersexual beauty has a Platonic flavour: it suggests a transcendent sphere played against the farcical mistakings of the fallible persons of the play. The figure in mythology for "beauty linked to mirror-image" is Narcissus.

In Ovid Narcissus has no double apart from the unreal image he sees in the pool. But there was another version of the story. Pausanias in his *Description of Greece* (IX.xxxi.6–9) pours scorn on the idea that a grown man could be fooled by a mere reflection and prefers to follow the version in which Narcissus had a twin sister with whom he fell incestuously in love. In this version, when he gazed into the pool he knew, sadly, that he was looking at his own face but could at the same time entertain the fantasy that he was gazing at his delicious sister. As this Narcissus sees the girl in the reflected boy, so Olivia divines the boy Sebastian in his reflection, Cesario-Viola, standing before her. It may be said that Shakespeare would have taken his mythology from Ovid, not Pausanias, but Elizabeth Story Donno has pointed out that Pausanias was available in both Latin and Italian in the sixteenth century.[20] It is just possible that Shakespeare read it or was told about it by a friend—or even thought it up by himself.

Malvolio remains the obstinately unassimilable man we have described. Hamlet, removed from social existence by a command from a dead man, becomes himself a walking darkness. Malvolio is in a comedy and is, unlike Hamlet, a rather silly man. But he too is a walking, asocial darkness, and a space without light is created for him in the middle of this radiant play. The lock-up in which he is confined is a "dark house" (III.iv.135, V.i.342). The cell is emblematic of his nature. The Clown visits Malvolio in his confinement and carries the idea of darkness into his mind by insisting that all is imagined by him, that the room is brilliantly lit (IV.ii.36). We are within earshot, so to speak, of those notorious experiments conducted in the twentieth century, in which a group of persons would agree in advance to tell the subject of the experiment that, for example, *they* could all see that the shorter of two lines on a piece of paper was really the longer, to see when the subject would cave in to peer pressure. Malvolio knows as firmly as he can know anything that he is without light, and the Clown assures him that the sun is shining through the window. If the Clown is right, the darkness apprehended by Malvolio is madness indeed. There is a peculiar antic cruelty in the brief philosophic catechism conducted by the Clown, ostensibly as a sanity test: "What is the opinion of Pythagoras concerning wild-fowl?" (IV.ii.50). Poor Malvolio does his best, giving the rather interesting answer that Pythagorean "transmigration of souls" from people to birds implicitly debases the notion of a soul. The Clown tells him that he has, alas, failed the test; "Remain in darkness still" has perhaps a double meaning: "Stay here in the cell" (betraying the fact that the lock-up really is without light?) and "Remain in your insuperable ignorance."

Scholars and commentators may strain to explain how very unpleasant Malvolio is so that we can feel less bad about the way he is treated. Nietzsche would say that it is only modern milksops who get upset about this. But it is clear that Shakespeare is conscious of the streak of cruelty in the play as just that—cruelty. The note is indeed audible earlier in the mockery of "Pyramus and Thisby" in *A Midsummer Night's Dream* and of "The Masque of the Nine Worthies" in *Love's Labour's Lost,* but here it is obviously allowed to grow stronger. In *As You like It* Rosalind says, "Love is merely a madness, and I tell you, deserves as well a dark house and a whip as mad men do; and the reason why they are not so punish'd and cur'd is, that the lunacy is so ordinary that the whippers are in love too" (III.ii.400–404). She echoes the sentiments of Theseus in *A Midsummer Night's Dream* ("The lunatic, the lover, and the poet") but has some difficulty in keeping a straight face as she does so. Theseus, ponderously, intended every word; Rosalind is fooling. Yet the grim picture of the confined madman makes itself felt. In *Twelfth Night* the terms of the analogy are shifted. It is not the happy lovers who are mad but the loveless—or the unsuccessful lover. *They* confine *him*. But Rosalind has anticipated this. In her fantasy those who scourge the poor mad lover turn out to be themselves in love. The phrase "dark house" occurs in one other place in Shakespeare, in *All's Well That Ends Well,* where the alignment of terms, including the phrase, "dark house," shifts again, this time convulsively.

The End of Comedy: *All's Well That Ends Well*

"Wars is no strife / To the dark house and the detested wife" (II.iii.291–92). Bertram is speaking. By "dark house" he means "married life." Rosalind pretended that she thought lovers deserved confinement of this kind; in *Twelfth Night* those who marry (for Maria marries Sir Toby) impose it on one who never will. Now the phrase is applied, with a degree of social realism, to marriage without love. Bertram is not thinking of a Bedlam. He is thinking of an ordinary Elizabethan or Jacobean house, ill-lit, smelly, loud with the ranting of oppressed women. It is vivid expression of a distinctively male horror of marriage.

Bertram has been trapped by comedy plotting, by the logic of fairy-tale, and is not unnaturally resentful. Helena, the daughter of a physician and therefore several steps below Bertram, Count of Rossillion, emerges from obscurity to cure the King by means of a remedy she learned from her father. The King's disorder is less than glamorous. He has a *fistula* (I.i.34)—that is, either piles or, more loosely, an abscess. Before the cure is applied, Helena makes a bargain with the King: if she is successful, she is to be married to the man of her choice, whoever that may be, so long as he is not of the royal house. The King agrees, his fistula is cured, and Helena claims the Count of Rossillion. The King sees no problem: "Why then, young Bertram, take her, she's thy wife" (II.iii.105). Bertram is aghast: "In such a business, give me leave to use / The help of my own eyes." Already Shakespeare is deliberately bringing out the "lack of fit" between fairy-tale and real life. Later in *King Lear* he will do it again, in a more frightening manner, as an old king, confronted by two bad daughters and one good one, thinks he can proceed by the logic of fairy-tale and reward the good daughter—and is suddenly engulfed by psychological and political realism. Here Bertram is saying in modern terms, "Marriage is a serious business, in which the parties concerned must surely—in the real world—be allowed some say!" The King is baffled, thinks that Bertram must be upset about Helena's low social status, and happily explains that this is something that he, as king, can "build up" (II.iii.118). Bertram is brought to heel; he says that he had thought Helena base but thinks so no longer. The wedding is performed on the spot. Bertram emerges from the ceremony to tell Parolles, "I will not bed her" (II.iii.270). His overwhelming wish is to run, if need be into the cannon's mouth, from marriage with Helena. It is here that he speaks of "the dark house and the detested wife."

I have said that the fairy-tale opening breaks upon human reality, and this might seem to imply the flimsiness of fairy-tale. In practice, however, in the theatre, these ancient patterns have their own enormous power. We know from our prior knowledge of stories, not of life, that Helena is the heroine, that Bertram is uncomprehending in his pride and must be reclaimed for the happy ending. Helena catches him at last exactly as she caught the goodwill and compliance of the King, by a bargain. This time, however, the bargain is not one proposed by Helena. Bertram, having fled to the wars, left a letter in which he said he would never accept Helena as his wife until she got the ring from his finger and a child fathered by him. For Bertram this was merely a cruelly picturesque way of saying, "Never." For Helena, the clever physician's daughter, it is of course a deal—and a challenge. She gets the ring and the child by a "bed-trick," that is, by taking the place of another woman under cover of darkness. Bertram thinks he is having his way with one Diana, a lady he encountered while campaigning, but is in fact impregnating his lawful wife.

Of all the women in the comedies who set out on the road to hunt down the desired man, Helena is the most formidably determined. Neither Julia in *Two Gentlemen of Verona* nor Rosalind in *As You Like It* has the gall to run down a man who has made his dislike crystal-clear, but that is what Helena does. The modern reader thinks, "Has she no pride?" Indeed in a way she has none. When Helena sets out in pursuit of Bertram, she is "habited like a pilgrim," in the garb of humility. But her action is authorized by the fact of marriage. The marriage is itself like a chunk of fairy-tale plotting transposed to the plane of efficacious reality. The wedding was at once humanly hollow (with one psychologically unconsenting party) and Platonically sovereign. It justifies any low trick performed in its service.

But it does not follow that all is harmonious. Helena's humility is fused with steely, domineering courage. No man stands a chance against this alpha female. If it is all right to be shocked by Petruchio in *The Taming of the Shrew,* perhaps it is all right to be shocked by Helena also. Someone should write a play—*The Taming of the Snob*—about the marriage, in a parallel universe, of Helena and Petruchio. I think Helena would win. I have already suggested that male spectators find Helena positively frightening. If the authority of the wedding is deeply grounded in popular culture, so too is the myth that weddings are occasions on which women trap men, not vice versa. The traditional humour of the stag-night party, an all-male get-together held on the eve of the wedding, attests to this: "Another good man gone" and the like. I was told in my youth that it was bad form to say, "Congratulations!" to a newly engaged woman precisely because the expression was too tactlessly close to the truth (hers the triumph, his the loss). The tone of stag-night merriment, meanwhile, was one of rueful condolence and acceptance of the inevitable. Perhaps this is true no longer, in 2007.

All's Well That Ends Well is a strange fusion of cynicism and idealism. That Shakespeare's intelligence is working in a sceptical or even destructive manner can be seen from the speech on virginity he gives to Parolles. Parolles to be sure is a contemptible character, but it is characteristic of Shakespeare to give some of his most challenging intuitions to such despised persons. "Virginity is peevish," he says, "proud, idle, made of self-love, which is the most inhibited sin in the canon" (I.i.143–44). With remarkable directness Parolles confronts an ethical difficulty that has been lurking in Christianity for centuries. The chaste lady who, in order to secure her place in heaven, scorns sex and marriage, is held up as supremely virtuous. At the same time selfishness is a sin. The cult of virginity is hopelessly entangled with a peculiarly ungenerous form of self-interest. In the words of the old hymn,

Whatever, Lord, we give to thee
Repaid a thousandfold will be.
Then gladly, Lord, we give to thee.

We may insist that Parolles has simplified the situation, that the virtuous virgin behaves as she does not out of love of self but out of love of God. Yet Parolles's dart draws blood. It is partly a matter of lost innocence. If one has a system of immense rewards in heaven for good behaviour in this world, then that good behaviour, once the agent has become aware of the reward, will cease to be innocently disinterested. The form of Parolles's speech on virginity mirrors that of Falstaff's speech on honour (1 Henry IV, V.i.129–41). Falstaff's "deconstruction" of honour is countered in the same play by the presence of the painfully conscientious Price Hal. But All's Well That Ends Well is a marriage comedy. This means that the deep logic of the play backs Parolles. The comedy celebrates marriage, and marriage is not for virgins.

Parolles, the liar and coward, is the site of active intellection in this play. When he is on stage Shakespeare is thinking aloud and thinking hard. In general, fools in Shakespeare are players within the plays who are never seen "out of the part." They have few soliloquies. We do not see them, for example, trying to think of good gags to use in tomorrow's performance. There is a half-exception to this rule in King Lear, where we are allowed to glimpse the Fool as an ordinary human being—when we are told how, since Cordelia's departure to France, the Fool has not been looking well (I.iv.74). Both Falstaff and Parolles are given soliloquies. This immediately marks them off from the professional clown. In Act 4, meanwhile, Parolles is granted that curious thing, an overheard soliloquy (IV.i.24). He racks his brains, aloud, for a way to escape humiliation, and the two brothers, the Lords Dumaine, hear every word he utters. They are astounded because they find that Parolles, the congenital fraud, is actually capable of speaking truthfully about his actions—if only to himself. The second lord asks, "Is it possible he should know that he is, and be that he is?" (IV.i.44–45). He means, partly, "How can he be aware of his own behaviour and not change it?" But there is a deeper puzzle: "How can a man be systematically mendacious in all his social relations and yet be, in isolation, a person with a full grasp of what is actually the case?" Henri Bergson thought comedy was essentially bound up with "thinghood" and automatism, and therefore with unconsciousness.[21] Parolles's slippage from hilarious unbroken mendacity into self-awareness marks a shift out of the comic into the serious. Naturally it brings Dumaine up short in his tracks. *This* Parolles is no longer funny, can no longer be used as a butt in an unproblematic fashion. The second lord's question also reactivates the preoccupation, so strong in *Richard II,* with the difference between public, relational identity and "core identity." Which comes first? Parolles offers an answer to the question a couple of scenes later. Richard II wondered for a moment whether to be "unking'd" meant annihilation, but Parolles is clear that utter disgrace (the equivalent in his case of deposition) means nothing of the sort. "If my heart were great," he says, " 'Twould burst at this," and adds, "Simply the thing / I am shall make me live" (IV.iii.330–31, 333–34). There is a Parolles behind the grotesque composite of false boasts (his name means "words"). This Parolles is a physical body that eats and drinks—and will continue to do so. In *As You Like It* Corin, the true voice of nature in the play, countered the shimmering verbal dexterities of the courtly party with a near-tautology: "The property of rain is to wet" (III.ii.26). Parolles is given the subjective equivalent appropriate to a poltroon—again, a near-tautology: "I shall continue to be because I am a continuous being." Considered as articulate propositions, tautologies are nonsense. But a tautology can be used to hint a pre-articulate truth. The "Parolles strand" in *All's Well That Ends Well* is skilfully drawn out. It is Shakespeare's last skirmish on the problem of *paroles,* words.

But at the end of the play we have pre-articulate thought of a different kind. It manifests itself first as a curious discomfort. I tried to make sense of it in an essay dealing primarily with *The Winter's Tale.*[22] At the close of the comedy Bertram is abruptly reunited with Helena, the lady he has scorned and, until this moment, has believed dead. Shakespeare's comedies, we all know, end with weddings. *All's Well That Ends Well began* with a wedding—but it came to pieces. Now it is made solid. "One that's dead is quick" (V.iii.303). We expect to be told how Bertram came to repent of his rejection of Helena, became aware slowly of how much he loved her, as preparation for this moment. There is no question but that Shakespeare could easily have done this had he wished to. In Sidney's *Arcadia* (1593, i.17), when Parthenia, having recovered her lost beauty, comes as a disguised suitor to Argalus, Argalus persists in fidelity to the supposedly dead Parthenia but at last perceives with joy that she is standing before him. This is the humanly satisfying version of the story-pattern. Shakespeare himself used it later in *The Winter's Tale*. But here he works against the natural logic of the comedy. The odious, shallow Bertram is entirely willing to marry (as he sees it) another lady altogether until only minutes before he is joined to Helena. He says, indeed, that he will love her, but observe how he says it: "If she, my liege, can make me know this clearly, / I'll love her dearly, ever, ever dearly" (V.iii.315–16). He says it to the King, not to Helena. The future tense, "I'll love her," is substituted for an expected present tense, "I love her." The undertaking is technically conditional (there is an "if"-clause). Yet we sense an incipient warmth in the repeated "ever." Most important, the tone is not so much that of profound love discovered in the end as that of dazed incomprehension. Bertram had set the action in motion with a lofty, mocking "if"-clause—if Helena could get the ring and a child from him, he'd take her. Now we have another condition laid down, as if it were some sort of tic that Bertram cannot help, but the position is now reversed. Bertram can no longer pretend to himself that he is in imperious control. He has been grossly abused, overtaken, and outplayed by a comedy plot. No wonder he is saying, "Will someone please explain?" Shakespeare has gone out of his way to emphasize the bare theatricality, the artificiality, of the dénouement: the comic plot reaching its proper resolution not in alliance with deep human motivation but independently.

Has Shakespeare, then, turned formalist? Has he joined those for whom final wisdom consists in a confession that all is merely text or verbal invention? Not so. The effect of the heightening of the theatrical stratagem at this point is not to satirize or "deconstruct" marriage itself but to make one feel the reality of marriage at a level deeper than that of conscious relationships. There is perhaps one sense in which Shakespeare might after all be called a formalist here—a Platonic sense. But there is a huge difference between a Platonic Form and the forms proposed in modern critical theory. The substitution in our time of culturally variable, fluid form for essence is seen—and sold—as a draining away of substance; the Platonic Form on the contrary is super-objective, epistemologically "hard," *more* real than concrete objects.

At this moment in the text the modern reader is aghast. In the theatre, mysteriously, the old magic works. Everyone suddenly smiles. Shakespeare knew that they would. They smile because these imperfect persons are getting married. It is as simple as that. I have called this "comedic alienation." The term is Brechtian. Bertolt Brecht wanted the "human detail" of his plays to recede in importance; what mattered was the Marxian pre-personal laws of historical and economic causation. So he deliberately imparted to the individual persons of his plays an air of cardboard artificiality.[23] The underlying laws for Brecht are rather like Platonic Forms but are now charged with causal efficacy. They are profoundly objective, not cultural fictions but that which underlies all subsequent fictions, all subsequent knowledge. We expect of a happy ending that the parties should love one another, and we think that in order to love one another they should at least know each other. Shakespeare says, "But as often as not they don't, really; yet marriage is marriage; that is how the world goes on." In the background is a sense that early modern people thought of love not as something that happens to a person but rather as something that a person might *do.* By the older logic it makes sense to undertake to love someone, to promise love, as people still do in the marriage service. Bertram undertakes—once his head has cleared—to love Helena. The original audience might have thought, "He can damned well do so." But I believe the discomfort we feel today was always there in the play, deliberately planted by the dramatist.

In like manner Shakespeare refuses to back the second half of the happy ending formula, "and they lived happily ever after." Touchstone and Audrey, as we saw, are actually promised a life of quarrelling at the end of *As You Like It* (V.iv.191). The refusal to hand out post-marital happiness to all comers can look cynical. But meanwhile the conception of marriage is, in the philosophical sense of the word, idealist.

Søren Kierkegaard thought that the difference between ancient and modern tragedy lay in the fatal hypertrophy of subjective consciousness in modern times. The Greek chorus, an embarrassment to the modern sensibility, "expresses the more which will not be absorbed in action and situation."[24] The post-classical tragic hero is responsible for his downfall with a sense of individual agency we never see in Greek tragedy; modern tragedy leaves behind a clarified despair, ancient an open sorrow: "Our age has lost the substantial categories of family, state and race."[25] It is odd how much of this applies to Shakespeare's systematic reduction of the subjective in *All's Well That Ends Well*. That he should do it in a comedy and not in a tragedy is somehow predictable. Tragedy for Shakespeare has indeed become the territory of the isolated individual, as Kierkegaard says. But comedy is the genre of a larger social continuity.

An incipient Platonism is at work within the dramaturgical art. I suggested that the substitution of Hymen, the god of marriage, for the all-controlling Rosalind at the end of *As You Like It* was caused by a quiet shock, experienced by the working dramatist, at the growth under his hand of a kind of transcendence, the transcendence of marriage itself, prior to the accident-prone flux of human, conscious life. It may seem that I am accusing Shakespeare of reifying a simple legal contract, but the glowing value associated with the marriage event suggests a greater ontological strength. Nevertheless, when I speak of an incipient Platonism I have to add at once that, although a kind of transcendence is discernible, the hard Platonic *chorismos*, the severe separation of the Form from the turbulent half-reality of the sensuously available world, is not there, in Shakespeare's mind. All remains this-worldly, fully human.

6 The Moralist

Mercy Conquers Justice: *The Merchant of Venice*

Troilus and Cressida is about the sadness of broken faith in a world of hollow men. At the same time it is a philosophical play and it deals with the foundation of ethical judgements. *The Merchant of Venice* and *Measure for Measure* are about the application of ethical principles. Each play interrogates the standard notion, "Mercy is higher than justice."

Because *The Merchant of Venice* is set in Venice it is also all about money. The splendour of Venice, with its palaces of porphyry and marble, was based on commerce. Aristotle condemned usury (in Greek, *tokos,* "begetting") as an unnatural form of generation, but in Venice money seemed to beget money in a way that was bewildering to land-based northerners. Hence "merchant" in the title. If Shakespeare had been writing in the 1960s, say, he would have called this play *The Capitalist*. Antonio, the merchant of the title, is a homosexual, virtuous Christian. At the beginning of the play he is strangely sad. We may think of Helena's sadness at the beginning of *All's Well That Ends Well*. There our first thought is that she is weeping for her father who has died. But we are wrong: "I have forgot him. My imagination / Carries no favour in't but Bertram's" (I.i.82–83). Helena is weeping for that "bright particular star," the young Count of Rossillion. Prospective, potentially fruitful romantic love displaces inert, retrospective grief. There is a similar *volta* or turning point in *As You Like It:* Rosalind is sad—for her banished father? No, for Orlando, the handsome young wrestler. Antonio's mysterious depression at the beginning of the comedy looks as if it might be part of a regular pattern.

His friend Solanio, who must be a theatre-goer to catch on so swiftly, says at once, "Why then, you are in love." Antonio answers, "Fie, fie!" (I.i.46). The words express reproof, not denial. Antonio does not say that Solanio is wrong but suggests that he should keep quiet. Join this to the end of the play, where Antonio is not assigned a lady in the final pairing-off, and we have enough already to infer homosexuality.

There is one slight snag. I illustrated the supposed repeatable comedy pattern by referring to *All's Well That Ends Well* and *As You Like It*. But both these plays were written after *The Merchant of Venice*. It is therefore unlikely that anyone in the original audience could have matched the swift intuition of Solanio. Solanio, the poet's creature, has meanwhile access to his maker's mind. He gets it absolutely right. This, the first example we have of the comedy *volta*, is itself a harshly modified case. There can be no marrying for the truly faithful homosexual. We have seen in *Romeo and Juliet* and *Two Gentlemen of Verona* the tension between same-sex solidarity and heterosexual love happily resolved. But in *The Merchant of Venice* same-sex solidarity becomes profound homosexual love, felt by one party only. Antonio loves Bassanio, but Bassanio is unaware of the fact. He loves Portia, a seriously rich lady who lives on a hill, above the clatter and money-changing of Venice ("above" here connotes more than merely physical separateness). Bassanio is one of the half-contemptible young men who recur in Shakespearean comedy (Claudio, Bertram . . .). He is very nearly a fortune-hunter (he speaks ecstatically of Portia's wealth), but he loves sincerely with the little love of which he is capable. He asks his friend Antonio to advance him money to cover the expenses of the courtship. Antonio can deny him nothing, but this is peculiarly painful. He is being asked to pay for a process that will seal his exclusion from Bassanio's love. We saw how in *Twelfth Night* Viola was asked by the man she loves to plead his cause with another and how she did so, selflessly. But we knew it would all come right in the end. Viola is dressed like a young man but is really a woman, and so the time will come when Orsino will see sense. Antonio both looks like and is a man and therefore has no chance with the heterosexual Bassanio. We know that the comedy ending will not save him. This does not mean that all dramatic tension falls away. The inaccessibility of Bassanio still hurts. Nor does it diminish the generosity of Antonio to Bassanio. Antonio is a successful merchant, but his wealth is not like Portia's, so great as to be insulated from fluctuations in the marketplace. At the time of Bassanio's request Antonio is waiting for his ships to come in. But his credit is good; he can raise the money he needs to help his friend by going to the moneylenders. So he goes to see Shylock.

Shylock the Jew proposes a "merry" bond (I.iii.145). Should Antonio fail in repayment, Shylock has the right to carve a pound of flesh from a point of his choosing on the person of the debtor. So far it all seems fun. But some in the audience are already wanting to cry out, "Don't sign!" Antonio has engaged to have his heart torn from his breast for love of his friend—if necessary. And of course it becomes necessary. The ships fail to arrive; Shylock claims his bond. Portia, disguised, sits in judgement on the case. She appeals to the Jew to show mercy. He refuses, taking his stand on the law. Portia says that the Jew is right, and the audience draws in its breath. At the last moment, however, Portia draws Shylock's attention to the fact that the bond allows him a pound of flesh but no blood. The tables are now turned, since no one can carve out a pound of flesh without shedding blood. Antonio is saved by Bassanio's lady, not through mercy softening the heart of Shylock, but by a legal quibble.

The sequence of the play makes it clear that Shakespeare respects the love of Antonio for Bassanio. There is no question of turning him into a satirically conceived grotesque. He is an outsider, but he is a good outsider. His love of another man is not set in contrast with his Christian virtue but is instead the strongest example of Christian goodness in the play. At a certain point in the trial scene the shallow Bassanio cries out that he would sacrifice his wife and his own life to save Antonio. The words mirror what Antonio has actually done: he has sacrificed his own love and is now sacrificing his life for Bassanio. But we do not believe Bassanio. If he meant what he said he could have stabbed Shylock there and then in the court-room. Antonio's words are quieter:

Commend me to your honorable wife,
Tell her the process of Antonio's end,
Say how I lov'd you, speak me fair in death;
And when the tale is told, bid her be judge
Whether Bassanio had not once a love.

(IV.i.273–77)

The speech is unreservedly generous. Antonio makes no claim on Bassanio, who belongs, he knows, to Portia. The tone is controlled and courteous, without any of Bassanio's shrillness. "Speak me fair in death" is touched with humour—"You're supposed to be nice about people after they've died, you know!"—but there is within it a more serious plea for both charity and recognition. "Commend me to your honorable wife" is masterly; it is the equivalent of our "Give my regards to your wife," but the words are charged with extra force by the fact that Portia is Antonio's insuperable antagonist, the rival he could never have defeated. Therefore behind the entirely real magnanimity we hear a primitive cry: "Who loved you more—she or I?" "Bid her be judge" then has a resonance of which Antonio is quite unaware, for Portia is there, in disguise, and will act as judge.

That entirely human, wholly forgivable "What about *my* love?" behind the generosity breaks open when the trial is over, in the ring-begging scene. Portia, as herself, had given Bassanio a ring and made him swear that he would never give it to another. After Portia, as the learned Doctor Bellario, has beaten Shylock on his own ground, the law, and the rescued parties are crowding round the rescuer, overcome by relief and gratitude, Portia/Bellario protests that she wants no payment—and adds lightly that if they really want to give her something, the ring on Bassanio's finger will do very well. Bassanio, deeply embarrassed, first mutters that the ring is virtually worthless and then explains that he has promised his wife that he would never give it away. This is the moment at which Antonio cracks:

My Lord Bassanio, let him have the ring.
Let his deservings and my love withal
Be valued 'gainst your wive's commandment.   (IV.i.449–51)

Antonio's thought is, "Don't I mean anything to him?" He suddenly, quite explicitly, stakes his love, unauthorized by social institutions, against the marital love of the woman, and amazingly, he wins. Bassanio in his turn cracks and runs after Bellario to hand over the ring. Antonio has won, however, only through the moral thinness of Bassanio. Portia, more godlike even than Rosalind in *As You Like It,* controlled the entire sequence. It was Portia, not the non-existent Bellario, who set the test for Bassanio and doubtless knew from the first how he would fail. Perhaps she did it because she was irritated, as I am always irritated, by Bassanio's earlier cry that he would give his wife to save Antonio (at the time Bellario/Portia commented drily, "Your wife would give you little thanks for that," IV.i.288). If she is only half as fair-minded to Antonio as he is to her, she must be aware of the moral strength of the appeal Antonio will make to Bassanio, though, interestingly, Shakespeare sends her off-stage so that she does not hear Antonio's actual words when the time comes. But the Shakespearean fusion, in a single female nature, of clear-eyed perception of a man's weaknesses with unswerving love of that same man remains disquieting. We ask, "How can Hero love Claudio of all men? How can Helena love Bertram? How can Portia, who could have had anyone (including that very nice Prince of Morocco), love Bassanio?" Shakespeare does it so often, he must be doing it on purpose. I fancy that if we put our question to him he would answer, "Whatever made you think love had anything to do with desert?"

The implicit opposition of love and desert is set squarely before us in the trial scene. Love goes with mercy, pity, and forgiveness, desert with justice, reciprocity, retaliation. An eye is a fair price for an eye. Shylock asks under what compulsion he must show mercy. Portia answers,

The quality of mercy is not strain'd,
It droppeth as the gentle rain from heaven
Upon the place beneath. It is twice blest:
It blesseth him that gives and him that takes.
'Tis mightiest in the mightiest, it becomes
The throned monarch better than his crown.
His sceptre shows the force of temporal power,
The attribute to awe and majesty,
Wherein doth sit the dread and fear of kings;
But mercy is above this sceptred sway,
It is enthroned in the heart of kings,
It is an attribute to God himself;
And earthly power doth then show likest God's
When mercy seasons justice.   (IV.i.184–97)

The word "strain'd" means, initially, "forced." Portia is telling Shylock that he is making a fundamental mistake in looking for any element of compulsion in mercy; the whole point of mercy, she says, is that it removes you from the sphere of compulsion to the moral freedom of love. Marvellously, the word "strain'd," as it is uttered, melts into another meaning, "filtered as through a grid." As Shylock's world-view is made to dissolve, so the imagery becomes that of rain falling with indiscriminate, life-giving kindliness on all alike. The absolute transcendence of love over power and judgement has never been put with greater force. Instead of the suggestion (which we have met already in *Hamlet* and will meet again later) that retaliatory *justice* is peculiarly God's work, we have the proposition that, while force may be appropriate to merely earthly kings, God himself is, above all, love.

Portia's argument fails in the court-room. Shylock is not persuaded. The comedy plot, with that logic of alienation we have seen in *All's Well That Ends Well,* works itself out at the sublunary level of fallen humanity— not to satirize the ethic of mercy but to make its heavenly beauty the more poignant.

If we compare Shakespeare's Shylock with Marlowe's earlier figure, Barabas, in *The Jew of Malta,* it may seem that Marlowe is the original, subversive sceptic, Shakespeare the inert, prejudiced traditionalist. After all, Marlowe starts the hare of cultural relativism with the line, "For Christians do the like" (V.ii.117). While Shakespeare places the Jews squarely with the Old Law of an eye for an eye and a tooth for a tooth in contradistinction to Christian love, Marlowe wittily draws on observable behaviour and makes his contrast turn on the fact that the Christians are bellicose and the Jews financial operators. The finest moment in *The Jew of Malta* comes when Barabas has Rhodes at his mercy. The Christian governor assumes that they are going to be killed; Barabas smiles genially and explains that he'd be silly if he killed them all; Rhodes is a place where he can make money (V.ii.64–73). Shakespeare, however, is just as sceptical, but in a subtler manner.

The action of *The Merchant of Venice* ironizes Christian charity. We learn with a shock that the good Antonio has spat on the hated Shylock (I.iii.126–31); the glitteringly rich Portia is relieved to be rid of the Prince of Morocco, a thoroughly decent man who reacts far better than Bassanio to the challenge of the casket, on grounds of race: "Draw the curtains, go. / Let all of his complexion choose me so" (II.vii.78–79). I am sure that Shakespeare knew that this remark would be received by the 1590s audience with uncritical warmth, and I am equally sure that he saw its profound unfairness. The Christians who are notionally the party of forgiveness bay for Shylock's blood as soon as they have him on the run. It is true that he is not finally executed—and this is important—but he is deprived of his livelihood by the court (IV.i.375–77). Only Antonio's last-minute intervention prevents Shylock from being cast out to starve.

Antonio, with real charity, gives up his claim on half of Shylock's goods. But there are strings attached. Shylock must turn Christian. Is this also charity? Many in—most of—the original audience would have thought it was. Yet Shylock is being forced to deny his inmost essence, his Jewishness, and to abandon an ethical principle on which he has just staked his life. There is a dark symmetry to all this. Shylock wanted to tear out the heart of a Christian, and now, at another level, the Christian court wants to tear out the heart of Shylock, his Jewish faith. When Shakespeare turned Marlowe's "O girl, o gold!" (*Jew of Malta*, II.i.54) into "My daughter, and my ducats!" (II.viii.17), he made a cardboard figure into a living man in a way we find uncomfortable. Cynics want to say, "Look, he cares only for his money!" Sentimentalists say, "Look, he loves his daughter!" In fact Shylock loves both. Incidentally, his love for his wife is made fully clear in the play, as is his fundamental humanity in the speech that moves from "Hath not a Jew eyes?" to the unanswerable, "If you tickle us, do we not laugh?" (III.i.59–65). In the theatre, however, the physical horror of Shylock's knife so close to Antonio's skin—legally authorised!—is overwhelming. It would be understandable for someone who had just watched this scene to ask, "Can this devil-man really be acting on an *ethical* principle?" But Shylock may be doing exactly that.

When Christian Gratiano shouts that he'd like to string Shylock up (IV.i.379) we can deal easily with the discrepancy between Christian theory and Christian practice; Gratiano is a fallen man, an imperfect Christian, and that is that. But when we become aware of the systematic symbiosis of Jews and Christians in the mercantile triumph of Venice, we are less sure of our ground. Writers of the time were aware, as Shakespeare is clearly aware, that Venice depended on the Giudecca, its Jewish community, to carry out the more visible processes of usury, lending with interest, without which the whole complex venture could not exist.[1] The sixteenth-century Venetian diarist Marino Sanuto wrote, "Jews are even more necessary to a city than bakers are, and especially to this one."[2] What Shylock is seeking from the Christians is a just acknowledgement of the truth: that they depend upon people like him, depend upon their willingness to do things the Christians want done but cannot be seen to do. In effect he is saying to them, "You know me. I'm the man of hard bargains and fiercely extracted payments. This is what I am *for*. I now turn the skills that are so useful to you when employed upon the money-men of Rhodes, say, against you. In mere consistency you must back, in this court, the principle you have implicitly backed elsewhere. Your very charity is 'luxury goods,' dependent on monetary wealth that is in its turn dependent on people like me." This is an ethical argument. If justice is Jewish and mercy Christian, it should not surprise us that Shylock's argument should be all about fairness. After all it is a mistake to suppose that mercy alone can submit an ethical case. Justice has its own case to make. This will return, with increased power, in *Measure for Measure*. No wonder Shylock suddenly feels sick when Antonio offers to waive his right to Shylock's goods. He glimpses perhaps a kind of Christian charity that escapes his argument. *The Merchant of Venice* is Shakespeare's most Marxist play—economics determines consciousness[3]—and, at the same time, it is his most Christian. Portia's moving argument for the utter transcendence of justice by mercy is not dislodged or even threatened by Shylock's counter-ethic. He remains a figure of darkness, she of light. But it is not over yet. *Measure for Measure* is still to come.

Redemption by the Devil: *Measure for Measure*

Shakespeare's Venice is constituted not organically by earth and water but by gold. It is a Christian state that prefers not to acknowledge its dependence on unloving, hard men. The Duke in *Measure for Measure* discovers at the beginning of the play that he needs a hard man to put right the human damage done by mercy. He finds that it is *morally* needful—not just expedient—to apply legal penalties to offenders. Portia gave transcendent mercy a basis in theology. *Measure for Measure* pursues those theological implications. These turn out to be so extraordinary, so heretical, that they must be approached with circumspection, in a roundabout way. I need, also, to speak more personally than is customary in a critical study.

Some years ago I became interested in a certain violent heresy: that of "Ophite Gnosticism." "Ophite" is from *ophis,* the Greek for "serpent"; these are "the Gnostics of the Serpent." The Ophite Gnostics read Genesis in, to put it mildly, a different manner. They thought that God the Father was the evil party and the serpent good. This was made easier for them by the fact that Gnostics already thought, unlike Christians, that the God who made this dreadful world was wicked. They readily identified the evil creator, Ialdabaoth, with the Jewish Jehovah.[4] Also, as Gnostics, they thought knowledge was a good thing (*gnosis* and *knowledge* are etymologically cognate). As soon as the Ophites read that God told Adam and Eve that they were not to eat from the Tree of Knowledge, they said, in effect, "You see? Anyone who forbids knowledge is an oppressor. Jehovah is a jealous tyrant." Meanwhile the serpent, against the orders of the tyrant, leads Adam and Eve to knowledge. The reader may already be wishing to protest that this was, after all, a knowledge that brought death into the world and all our woe, so that the serpent was hardly doing Adam and Eve a good turn. It is hard for us, belonging as we do to a Christian or post-Christian culture, to see how Genesis might read to an outsider. We have built into us before we begin to read the presumption that the serpent is Satan, the enemy of humankind. But the text of Genesis never says that. The serpent is just a snake. God tells Adam and Eve that if they eat from the tree they will die, and most of us feel that he did not lie, because after this primal sin Adam, Eve, and all humankind become subject to death. But an outsider could easily draw a different conclusion. When Eve says that God told them that if they disobeyed him they would die, the serpent answers, in William Tyndale's admirable translation of Genesis 3:4, "Tush, ye shall not die."[5] A literal way—one might say a natural way—to understand God's threat or warning would be to suppose that Adam and Eve would fall down dead immediately upon biting into the apple. This certainly seems to be the way the serpent, who was actually there, takes it. But this obviously does not happen. After telling them that they won't fall down dead, the serpent adds that the real consequence of their rebellious action will be that their eyes will be opened and they will become as gods, knowing good and evil (Gen. 3:5). Here the serpent is certainly not lying. After the eating of the apple, we read, "And the eyes of them both were opened" (3:7), and later we find *God* saying, "Behold, the man is become as one of us, to know good and evil" (3:22). We can see how a Gnostic reader could think that it is obvious that God is a jealous, punitive figure and the snake his noble antagonist, the champion of humanity. And now the Ophites say the really subversive thing: "The serpent is Christ."[6] From this derives what I have called, in a book of that name, "the alternative Trinity." In orthodox Christianity the Trinity is a happy family; the Father and the Son get on well, see things from the same ethical point of view. For the Ophites the Trinity is a dysfunctional family; the Son is the antagonist of the Father.

I first got into this material as result of giving tutorials on William Blake. I used to ask my pupils to tell me whether Blake was a Christian. The replies were various, but nevertheless I found after a while that I could predict the result. Those who concentrated on the figure of Christ as he appeared in Blake's writings came back and said, "He is a great Christian poet." Those who concentrated on the Father said, "He is an anti-Christian subversive." The reason for this is simple. Blake's Trinity is plainly Gnostic. His father god, Urizen (clearly identified with Jehovah),[7] is an oppressor; his Christ is a liberator. In his notebook for 1810 Blake wrote, ungrammatically but still intelligibly, "Thinking as I do that the Creator of this World is a very Cruel being and being a Worshipper of Christ I cannot help saying the Son O how unlike the Father."[8] I was at first puzzled; the immense interval between Blake and the Gnostics of the second century A.D. seemed to preclude influence. As I looked into the matter, however, I became more and more confident that there was no interval, that I was dealing with a *haeresis perennis,* or perpetual heresy that never disappeared in the intervening period, though it lived underground for long periods. I do not wish to insist on a continuous stream of Ophite discourse but rather on the continuing *availability of the thought.*

In *The Alternative Trinity* I argued that traces of Ophite Gnosticism can be found in Marlowe's *Doctor Faustus* and even, as a faint antiphonal subtext, in Milton's supposedly monist, authoritarian *Paradise Lost.* Antinomian Protestants of the seventeenth century liked to denounce the Ten Commandments given by the Father to Moses and to say, "In Christ all things are lawful unto me" (1 Cor. 6:12). Blake liked to demonstrate that Christ broke every one of the Ten Commandments.[9]

Now this is pretty wild stuff. That it should be found in Blake, who was a sort of professional oppositionalist, is predictable. That we should meet it in Marlowe, who had a reputation for diabolical heresy, is on the cards. That it should be intermittently discernible in Milton, given the constant presence in his writings of an anti-Milton, a second self with whom he is locked in tense argument, is perhaps just credible (I believe it). But surely we shall not find this kind of weirdness, this harshly eccentric way of viewing the world, in Shakespeare? Shakespeare, after all, is nothing if not central. He is seen, with reason, as embodying the natural humanity of the nation, as radiantly sane.

But it is also true that Shakespeare, as we say loosely, "did everything." Teachers of literature learn over the years to hesitate when embarking bravely upon sentences of the form: "This will not be found before 1750," because again and again it turns out that Shakespeare has actually done it, whatever it is—sometimes briefly, but he has done it. If we set aside technological advances like mobile telephones, it is remarkably hard to think of anything Shakespeare has not thought of first, somewhere. Marxian, Freudian, feminist, Structuralist, Existentialist, materialist ideas are all there. Did he never consider Gnostic theology?

I think he did, and the work in which he did so is *Measure for Measure*. The play is a comedy with an unusually neat and intricate plot. The Duke of Vienna has become aware that his indulgent rule has led to hideous disorder and sexual disease in the city. He accordingly appoints the severe Angelo to enforce the laws that have long lain idle. The Duke then tells everyone that he is going away but actually remains on the scene, disguised as a friar. Angelo, applying the law, sentences one Claudio to death for contracting a clandestine marriage. Claudio's sister, Isabella, who is about to become a nun, pleads with Angelo for her brother's life. Angelo tells her he will spare her brother if she will submit to his base lust. Isabella, horrified, tells her brother of the vile proposal and is horrified again when he entreats her to comply. The disguised Duke, having previously told Claudio to prepare for death, then steps forward to solve the problem. Angelo was formerly "espoused *de futuro*" (rather like our notion of engagement) to a certain Mariana. Before the action of the play begins Angelo had pulled out of this "betrothal." Any *de futuro* espousal is automatically converted to full matrimony if the parties consummate the relationship. The Duke arranges that Mariana be substituted for Isabella in

Angelo's bed under cover of darkness so that at the very moment when Angelo thinks he is working his will on Isabella he is in fact cementing the marriage with Mariana. Angelo, ratting on his promise to Isabella, proceeds meanwhile with the execution of Claudio, but here he is again tricked by the Duke, who arranges that the head of Ragozine, a pirate who died on the same night, be substituted for Claudio's. The play ends with forgiveness for all, including Angelo. In the warm glow the Duke offers his hand in marriage to the novice, Isabella. Substitution mirrors substitution with a satisfying elegance. The play is like a minuet.

But, if it is a minuet, it is danced to crashing discords. Shakespeare appears to be writing deliberately to achieve maximum discomfort at the ethical or ideological level. The "good" characters in the play are disquietingly inconsistent. When the Duke appoints Angelo he has two motives, which sit uneasily together. He wants to find out if Angelo is a hypocrite, and he wishes to put in place a strong magistrate who will deal with the social evil. More important, he obviously accepts from the beginning that there is an *ethical* case for severity, but at the end of the play he undoes any good that might have been achieved by forgiving everyone in sight (he will need another Angelo in fourteen years). Why does he not apply the rules himself? He can hardly start punishing them now, he explains, when by his leniency he practically told them to abandon restraint (I.iii.35–37). Although sixteenth-century political theorists held that there could be a thoroughly moral reason for delegating odious offices (essentially, to save the *office,* rather than the person of the prince from potentially damaging obloquy),[10] the thought that the Duke is pusillanimously getting someone else to do the dirty work is hard to avoid. Isabella is clear that Claudio deserves punishment (she argues, precisely, for *forgiveness* of a real sin, not that her brother is guiltless). Yet she welcomes the morally parallel stratagem of the bed-trick (the private marriage of Claudio and Juliet and the marriage by consummation into which Angelo is tricked are both equally clandestine and therefore strictly illegal—no priest officiated on either occasion). Isabella has resolved upon celibacy but makes no audible protest at the end when the Duke does not so much propose as assume that the two of them will be married. The one person who is utterly consistent at the level of moral principle from beginning to end is Angelo.

When Isabella went to Angelo to plead for her brother she thought she had a "knock-down" argument. She could afford, she thought, to explain how she agreed with Angelo (and she did agree) that Claudio deserved punishment, because she had in reserve an argument that would blow all such reasons away; Angelo is right at the level of justice, but justice itself is transcended, eclipsed, by mercy. This is the argument put by Portia in *The Merchant of Venice* with an eloquence that makes it triumph over the social and economic ironies simultaneously advanced in that play. Isabella says, as she thinks, unanswerably, "Yet show some pity" (II.ii.99). But Angelo has an answer. He says, "I show it most of all when I show justice; / For then I pity those I do not know." To Isabella's claim that mercy gloriously soars above mere justice he replies, in effect, "No; the one is entangled in the other." He means that if you are responsible for the inhabitants of a city, know that unrestrained crime will hurt large numbers of people, and then you do *not* restrain it, that is itself a kind of cruelty, is unmerciful to the unnamed, faceless innocent. Isabella challenges Angelo with the scriptural argument, "He that is without sin among you, let him cast the first stone" (John 8:7)—in effect, that only the sinless can properly judge and punish. But again Angelo has an answer: obviously one cannot let the rapists and murderers do as they like simply because there are no sinless policemen or magistrates; what one can do is make sure that the agents of the law are themselves subject to that law, so that if a magistrate is caught out, he too is punished. He applies this expressly to himself, saying that if ever *he* offends, he must be punished by the same rule (II.i.29). At the end of the play his last words are an insistence that he, Angelo, must be punished (V.i.474–77). There is a sense in which the Duke's ultimate forgiveness insults him, as Antonio's final generosity to Shylock—on condition that he become a Christian—insults Shylock.

Substitution, that slick mechanism of comedy plotting, is the key to the play, because, at another level—the ethical—substitution becomes the locus of an intense discordancy. The Duke makes Angelo a substitute for himself, bestows upon him the office of governor: "Be thou at full ourself" (I.i.43). In the Italian source, Giraldi Cinthio's *Hecatommithi* (1565), Maximian (who corresponds to the Duke) sends his officer away to Innsbruck, where the events of the story take their course. Shakespeare's Duke, as we saw, tells everyone that he is going away but in fact never leaves. He remains in the city, a shadowy figure—"the old fantastical Duke of dark corners" (IV.iii.157)—standing behind Angelo, watching him at work. The effect of the change is greatly to intensify our sense that Angelo, himself far from shadowy but, rather, brilliantly illuminated, represents the Duke, is his substitute. When Claudio is forfeit to the law Angelo invites Isabella, in effect, to take Claudio's place, to suffer instead; her virtue is to be a price paid for Claudio's life. Mariana is substituted for Isabella in Angelo's bed. Then Ragozine's head is substituted for Claudio's. It is the idea of substitution that finally carries us into the realm of theology. Central to Christianity is the doctrine of the atonement. This is, precisely, an act of substitution. When Christ died on the cross, he gave himself as a substitute for humankind; he bore the pains that our sins deserve. According to one version of the doctrine, in doing this Christ paid off the Devil, who had a right to us because of our wickedness.[11] Later a feeling grew that it was beneath the dignity and power of God to do any sort of deal with the Devil, and Anselm said that Christ suffered on the cross to satisfy *God's* own requirement of justice while simultaneously affording mercy to humankind.[12]

Usually Shakespeare steers clear of theology, but in *The Merchant of Venice* a breach is made and theology streams in. In *Measure for Measure* the stream becomes a flood. Isabella, with a wonderful hesitancy as at a truth too shaming, too glorious to be put into words, reminds Angelo of Christ's merciful atonement:

Why, all the souls that were were forfeit once,
And He that might the vantage best have took
Found out the remedy.   (II.ii.73–75)

It will be said that there is nothing Gnostic about this; Isabella is offering Angelo a beautiful, healing, reconciling thought. I answer, yes, but Isabella is not the only person in the play. We have already seen how she does not have uncontested ethical sway over the drama in which she figures. When Portia makes her splendid speech about the quality of mercy in *The Merchant of Venice,* it appears to carry all before it, to be indeed absolutely higher than the retributive justice of the Old Law of an eye for an eye and a tooth for a tooth. The doctrine she voices is certainly to be found in the

Gospels: "Love ye your enemies; be ye therefore merciful as your Father is merciful" (Luke 6:35). Here the reason for avoiding retaliatory justice is that justice is simply transcended by mercy, as Portia explained. But the passage in Luke continues, "Judge not, *that ye be not judged.*" Suddenly we are given another reason; justice belongs to the Father, not to you; if you usurp his place, *substitute* yourself for him—he may not be so merciful after all; he may judge *you*. We now have, already, an implicit collision. According to the first proposition humankind has, so to speak, emerged from the benighted ethic of retaliation into the upper air of unconditional mercy, but then the second proposition suggests that God the Father remains locked, meanwhile, in the Old Law of "Thou shalt not." There is now an implicit tension between the judging Father and Christ's doctrine of loving forgiveness (Christ rejects the *lex talionis* at Matt. 5:38). The title of this play, note, is not *Love Triumphant* but *Measure for Measure*. It points to the second, darker proposition, "With what measure ye mete, it shall be measured to you" (Mark 4:24). We are in the world of "Vengeance is mine, I will repay, saith the Lord" (Rom. 12:19).

Many years ago Roy W. Battenhouse wrote an article called "*Measure for Measure* and the Doctrine of the Atonement."[13] Battenhouse sought, with some difficulty, to identify the Duke's role in the play with God's role in his universe. If we forget Christ and think only of the Father, this can begin to work (the phrase, "like pow'r divine," is applied to the Duke at V.i.369). But the doctrine of the atonement forces us to think of Christ also. Is there a Christ figure in the play? There is, but it is not the sort of person we might expect to see in such a part. We have to ask who takes upon his shoulders the burden of sin so that we can be happy. The answer is Angelo. Yet Angelo, we all know, is diabolically wicked. I said earlier that it is hard to think of anything Shakespeare has not thought of first. It is so here. We have reached a point where we are suddenly halted, mentally paralysed by a figure simultaneously redemptive and Satanic. But Shakespeare knows what he has done. In Act V, Isabella says, looking at Angelo, "You bid me seek redemption of the devil" (V.i.29).

Of course in orthodox Christianity Christ remains sinless and Angelo, very evidently, does not. Christ bore the *consequences* of *our* sins. It may be supposed that people of the early modern period, if they were sure of anything, were sure of this. It turns out, however, that Protestant theologians of the sixteenth century had doubts on precisely this point. To begin with, the language of scripture is distinctly odd: "He took our infirmities" (Matt. 8:17), "For he hath made him to *be* sin for us, which knew no sin" (2 Cor. 5:21, Geneva Bible, the edition of 1602). Calvin was not content to say that Christ simply took our punishment; our guilt also was passed to him (*Institutes,* II.xvi.6). In his 1535 lectures on Galatians Luther is scornful of the idea (which he thinks popish) that Christ took only the consequences of our sins, insisting that the words of scripture clearly mean that Christ actually sinned; to flinch from this truth, to "unclothe" Christ of our sins, "This is to abolish Christ."[14] Christ's cry of dereliction on the cross, "My God, my God, why hast thou forsaken me?" (Matt. 27:46, Geneva Bible; cf. Mark 15:34) has always embarrassed orthodox Trinitarians; if Christ is God, how could he think that God had abandoned him? It also seems to work against the doctrine of the sinlessness of Christ. It looks very like despair—perhaps the worst sin of all. Luther believed that Christ despaired.[15] The humiliation of Christ is absolute. We are being propelled not by cranks and eccentrics but by revered doctors of the Protestant Church into a twilit region; we may begin to think of the wretched "sin-eater" of the medieval village, the desperately poor individual who in return for a tiny sum of money would eat a loaf of bread beside the body of a newly deceased person; the eating of the bread signified that the eater took upon himself the sins of the departed—in effect, pawned his soul. Or else we may think of the scapegoat (Lev. 16:10), which lies, the author of the Epistle to the Hebrews, early biblical exegetes, and late-born anthropologists all tell us, behind the figure of the suffering Christ.[16]

The Ophite blurring of the line that separates the Devil, the enemy of the Father, from Christ, the redeemer of humankind, is present in *Measure for Measure.* There is a story by Jorge Luis Borges called "The Three Versions of Judas" about a theologian who held that, in order to identify the true Christ, we must ask, first, "Who is necessary to the economy of salvation, who must be there, bearing the burden, that the load may fall from the shoulders of the rest of us?" and, second, "Who has been hated and reviled ever since?" The theologian tries one answer after another. These are the three "versions" referred to in the title of the story. In the third he concludes that Christendom got it wrong, that Judas was the true

Christ. The realisation drives him mad. Angelo is simultaneously the redeemer of Vienna and the polluted one. Borges' theologian has wandered into Gnostic territory.[17] The Gnostic Gospel of Judas (or, possibly, "of Jude") does not indeed say that Judas was Christ, but it does say that Judas was the best beloved disciple and that in "betraying" Jesus, he was fulfilling the secret will of Jesus himself.[18] These various blurrings and inversions echo one another. The Ophite merging of the serpent of Genesis with Christ remains the most radical of all.

I have said that the Ophite version can be glimpsed in Marlowe's *Doctor Faustus*. Marlowe, demonstrably, was aware of Gnostic writings linked to the figure of Simon Magus, "the first of the Gnostics," who haunts the play. Shakespeare obviously knew Marlowe's writings and probably knew Marlowe personally. But in Shakespeare's hands these subversive ideas take on an energy, a capacity for fresh moves, that I cannot find in Marlowe, Milton, or even Blake. Shakespeare's main innovation is to make the sacrificed Christ figure himself a champion of retribution. Angelo is a legal precisionist, a believer in punishment; *this* is his sin.

It will be said that Angelo's greatest sin is his blackmailing of Isabella for sexual purposes. How does this (surely unequivocal) evil figure in the heretical paradox of the play? As far as I can see, it does not figure there at all, in any direct fashion. Of course the whole episode is necessary to the comedy plot and in due course helps to generate the dance of substitutions already noticed. But the Duke never authorized Angelo's vile behaviour. Angelo, however, is absolutely clear that this sin was indeed a sin. There is a certain ethical heroism in his readiness to apply the principle of punishment in his own case. In this steely consistency he differs notably from the good Duke. At a deeper level, perhaps, it is necessary that the sacrificial bearer of sins should be completely humiliated, that the ice-cold Angelo should experience the blackest sexual desire, just as Luther felt that the sacrifice of Christ was less than complete if Christ did not actually sin. The completed sequence operates to enhance our sense of the possible moral dignity of punitive government and this, in its turn, makes it just a little easier to expose the assumed supremacy of mercy to criticism. But the heretical paradox becomes importunately evident when we turn to Angelo's other sin, the sin of unforgiving judgement. In the eyes of the happy persons of the comedy, punitive judgement is itself wicked when set beside the transcending ethic of mercy. The sin that is carried by Angelo—and "carried by" now means "committed by"—is the sin of judging. Of course by Angelo's ethic all this is turned around. From his point of view (though he never argues egoistically in this way) the hated officer bears the *consequences* of *their* sins (as in orthodoxy)—since for *him* irresponsible leniency would be the sin! So he shoulders the burden of being (in the eyes of the world) the bad guy. Shakespeare knows that most people in the audience will detest Angelo and will warm to Isabella's words on pity (whether she wins the argument or not). But meanwhile it is equally clear, as the good Duke conceded at the beginning, that somebody has to be the bad guy, if the rest are to find space to be happy again. Pope Innocent's "concession" to Leon Norsa of Mantua in 1489 made it clear that confining obvious usury to Jews was a proper way to save the souls of Christians.[19] In *The Merchant of Venice* being the (necessary) bad guy meant practising usury; in *Measure for Measure* it now means being the policeman. Angelo is certainly the metamorphosis of Shylock. He does the Duke's dirty work as Shylock does the dirty work of Venice. Both are legalists. Shylock believes as Angelo believes, in measure for measure. Both are fired by intellectual energy. When Portia rules initially in Shylock's favour, Shylock is immediately delighted not just by the fact that he is one step nearer carving out the heart of a Christian but by the legal correctness of Portia's words (IV.i.223–24); we sense, together with Shylock's hatred, a *disinterested* intellectual enthusiasm. Both are scapegoats. But in the later play questions that are merely hinted in *The Merchant of Venice* become clamorous.

As Christianity hardens into orthodoxy the absolute assumption of the superiority of mercy perhaps becomes automatic. It is all too easy. In a way Ophite Gnosticism provides an exaggerated version of this way of thinking. In Gnosticism the Father is bad, and in William Blake it is plain that the Father is bad because he is "judgemental"; the practice of justice is itself a kind of tyranny. Christ, the friend to humanity, is the opposite of all this. The Ophites said that the serpent was Christ but largely confined their attention to the narrative of Genesis. But who is Christ? Christ is the redeemer. By introducing the device of substitution and ringing the changes on its possible implications, Shakespeare sets fire to the whole scheme. The atonement rather than the Garden of Eden is now at the centre. Yet the atonement itself, especially as interpreted by thoroughly orthodox Anselm, can reawaken the Gnostic idea of a harsh Father and a loving Son. Anselm, as I said, held that Christ suffered on the cross not to satisfy Satan but to satisfy *God's* requirement of justice even while being merciful to humanity. If we hold strongly to Trinitarian orthodoxy there is no great ethical discomfort here: the Father and Jesus are both equally God, so God gives himself to himself, in agony, to meet the requirement of pure justice. But it is very easy to get the feeling (partly because of the sheer oddity, which Wittgenstein would seize on, of being constrained to a strange transfer of payment to meet, technically, a rule one has made oneself) that we are dealing here with separate persons, that the Father requires justice ("Vengeance is mine") and is willing to let the Son do the suffering. Anselm himself hesitates between the two versions.[20] The second, note, is not a million miles away from the Ophite scheme, in which the Father is a tyrant and the Son our friend, but all is now played out in the field of substitutionary theology.

Now observe what Shakespeare has done. He has identified the humiliated redeemer with the authoritarian judge, but because of the now settled ascendancy of the ethic of mercy, this judge is no longer an unfettered tyrant, having uncontested power. He is on the run, defeated before he starts, at the hands of the Happy Ones. They are the blessed, standing in the light; Angelo, stained by his rigorism, stands in shadow. "Vengeance is mine," says the Lord, secure in his omnipotence. "Justice is mine," says Angelo—and must then continue lamely (like a suffering servant), "It's all right—you people don't have to do a thing—you can keep your hands clean."

When the Christians were an underground sect, meeting in catacombs in Rome, they could afford to be absolutely merciful because the non-Christian Roman cops would deal with anything really nasty. Then the Emperor Constantine was converted to Christianity and suddenly the cops were Christians, and so were the magistrates. As Angelo quietly observed to Isabella, if you are *in charge,* and know that leniency will cause many people (whom you may never meet) to be hurt, leniency becomes, by context, cruelty. What could the Christians do now? Famously, they came up with the theory of vicarious judgement, whereby the magistrate decides not as himself but as the vicar or representative of God (who, very fortunately, is still allowed to be "judgemental"). As we saw, various structures of substitution are brilliantly explored in *Measure for Measure*. Because the Duke appoints Angelo expressly to enforce the law strictly, Angelo is now his vicar or substitute and the Duke bears responsibility for the resultant severity, just as God bore the responsibility in the post-Constantinian courts. Shakespeare's Duke, however, by withdrawing to the shadows almost succeeds in making his instigating role invisible, or at least obscure. Although he wants measure to have measure he manipulates the lighting. Lucio's careless remark about the Duke resonates beyond its immediate context: he "would have dark deeds darkly answer'd" (III.ii.177). But the great substitution, implicitly central to the play, is the atonement. Shakespeare gives us a redemption in which the demonized Angelo is the Christ figure. This is audacious enough. He then moves again and makes this hated Christ a God-the-Father figure, a bearer of justice. This, it seems to me, is breathtaking. Meanwhile, as William Poole has observed, the actual atonement required by justice never takes place. It is aborted by the happy operation of the comedy plot.[21] Because of the reversal of roles within the Anselmian trinity we can sense that the merciful *Father* has chosen to pardon the judicial *Son,* to let him off the hook of justice, and the Son, Angelo is shocked. In the Bible, Poole adds, Christ asks that the cup be taken from him; Angelo asks to drink from it, and his request is benevolently/insultingly denied.

I do not claim that *Measure for Measure* is a clear Gnostic critique of orthodox Christianity. We are dealing here with hints and suggestions only. But it is clear to me that "steady, central Shakespeare" could visit the wilder shores of thought. He did so on many occasions. *Measure for Measure* is his most daring essay on the relation between ethics and theology. The preliminary structure is Ophite Gnostic in its readiness to merge the Devil with Christ, but I do not claim that Shakespeare is drawing on any specific Ophite source. There is no great problem, as I have already suggested, in supposing that he could have known something of the Gnostics. Marlowe, it seems, knew the (pseudo-)Clementine *Recognitions,* which contains some vertiginous Gnostic material, and could easily have rambled on about this in some pub (we have a fair idea, from "the Baines note," how unguarded Marlowe could be in casual conversation).[22] Donne, who was born eight years after Shakespeare, knows about the

Gnostics.[23] This was dangerous stuff but less completely hidden than many scholars suppose. Yet my guess is that Shakespeare got there simply by thinking very hard about the moral resonances of substitution. There is an electric intelligence in the placing of the word "grace" in Angelo's final plea for punishment: "Immediate sentence then, and sequent death, / Is all the grace I beg" (V.i.373–74). Of course the first meaning of *grace* here is the human, social meaning, "the favour of a superior." But in a play so theologically fraught the theological meaning cannot be wholly absent: "the un-earned, inexplicable generosity of God." Normally this takes the form of the remission of punishment, the lifting of damnation. But for Angelo mercy is the suffocating thing and, conversely, the principled application of punishment he knows he deserves would be a favour. I have referred to Portia's speech in *The Merchant of Venice* as a simple example of an unproblematic ethic of mercy. But in fact a fierce scepticism is already discoverable in the subtext of this, the earlier play. That said, fragments of remembered chat with Christopher Marlowe may well have speeded up Shakespeare's thought processes. I said that after Shylock sought to cut out the heart of Antonio, Christian Venice in response moved to cut out the heart of Shylock in a figurative manner, in that they required him to renounce his religious faith, his very Jewishness. But I had to acknowledge at the same time that they spared his life, that Antonio, especially, was merciful. Mercy itself is still uncompromised. At the end of *Measure for Measure* it is the mercy itself that tears the ethical heart out of Angelo. Suddenly, the knot is drawn tight. Angelo begs to be punished because punishment alone can save the intellectual and moral honour of his entire existence. Having accepted punishment he will have been true, after all his sins, to what is for him the most important thing of all. The smiling Duke denies him this final dignity and emasculates him with forgiveness.

As a result, now, in 2007, he still challenges our deepest assumptions. We are the natural heirs of the Duke and his friends. Throughout the play Angelo's name is dinned in our ears, meaning what?—"angel"? "messenger"? "Lucifer"? Or just a coin, stamped with another's face?[24] The Duke meanwhile is never addressed by name in the play, but we know what that name is: Vincentio, "the winner." Today we have come to use "heresy" and "subversive" as terms of praise and welcome, or think we welcome, the rebel. But a rebel who is immediately welcome cannot, it seems to me, be much of a rebel at all. Who in such a society is *really offensive?* Not the law-breaker. In the writings of Foucault the word "policing" carries an automatic charge of condemnation. All is well in a way as long as the heretic is preaching indulgence. But when this very doctrine becomes orthodoxy, a new kind of heretic, depised as the early apostles of mercy were despised, appears: the believer in punitive justice. One can imagine Shakespeare quietly smiling as we condemn—how "judgemental" that word is!—the new heretic. Where subversion is universally applauded the true subversive may be the authoritarian. I said earlier that if mercy is absolutely higher than justice, a justice-dispensing Father God is himself relegated to the shadows, denied the enlightenment vouchsafed to humankind (but this same God is invoked with some relief by a society pressed by the practical difficulties of dealing with crime, to do the dirty work). It is as if Shakespeare, who is famous for being able to sympathize with anyone, had a grain of sympathy for the now degraded omnipotent Father! Angelo is both Christ figure and Father figure, and Shakespeare undoubtedly feels with Angelo. This is deeply uncomfortable for us (for me, too). But all this—the warmth and the discomfort—he certainly foresaw.

7 How Character May Be Formed

An Expert Makes a Man: *Othello*

In *1 Henry VI,* one of the first plays Shakespeare wrote, the idea of lateral causation was broached. Individuals find themselves acting strenuously not because of a pre-existent inner drive but because those round them are behaving in a certain way. If others run fast, we too, by some primary mechanism, want to run with them. The idea grew and changed under Shakespeare's hand. We have seen how, in *Julius Caesar* and *Troilus and Cressida,* Cassius and Ulysses avail themselves of the power of lateral causation to stir certain persons to action. Hamlet then uses outward behaviour (his own outward behaviour) to practise upon *himself,* to induce motivation and perhaps consequent action from the outside in. In *Othello* we return to the model employed in *Julius Caesar* and *Troilus and Cressida*—one human being manipulates another.

At the end of the play Othello attempts to sum up:

Soft you; a word or two before you go.
I have done the state some service, and they know't—
No more of that. I pray you, in your letters,
When you shall these unlucky deeds relate,
Speak of me as I am; nothing extenuate,
Nor set down aught in malice. Then must you speak
Of one that lov'd not wisely but too well;
Of one not easily jealous, but being wrought
Perplexed in the extreme; of one whose hand

(Like the base Indian) threw a pearl away
Richer than all his tribe; of one whose subdu'd eyes,
Albeit unused to the melting mood,
Drops tears as fast as the Arabian trees
Their medicinable gum. Set you down this;
And say besides, that in Aleppo once,
Where a malignant and turban'd Turk
Beat a Venetian and traduc'd the state,
I took by th' throat the circumcised dog,
And smote him—thus.

(V.ii.338–56)

On the word "thus" Othello stabs himself and dies. The act is a repetition, for he is both the foreigner in the story, slain in loyalty to Venice, and the slayer, himself inescapably alien from the state to which he is true. By this point in the play he has strangled his wife in an agony of jealous rage. Indeed Othello is the literary paradigm of the jealous man. But in this important final speech he says that he is not easily jealous. Does he not know what he has just done? Is he completely deluded about his own nature? Not necessarily. What strangled Desdemona was conceivably not the natural Othello but a substituted artificial man. Shakespeare has prepared his ground. Earlier in the play Desdemona tells her confidante, Emilia, that she is very upset because she has lost the handkerchief Othello gave her and adds that, but for his nature, he might in the circumstance have been suspicious. Emilia asks, "Is he not jealous?" and Desdemona answers, "Who, he? I think the sun where he was born / Drew all such humors from him" (III.iv.29–31). Of course Desdemona could be wrong too. In a way her judgement is immediately disconfirmed because Othello enters and, finding her hand damp (a sign of sexual vitality), begins to speak wildly of the need for chastity and discipline. Obviously the man who speaks such words is jealous and suspicious. But, once more, the artificial man is speaking. The clue is in the word "wrought" in Othello's final speech—"but being wrought / Perplexed in the extreme." "Wrought" is often misused as if it were the past tense of the verb "wreak." In fact it is the old past tense of "work" and is so used here. Othello is saying that he has been worked upon, wrought as a clay figure is wrought by the finger and thumb of the artist. He does not name Iago in the speech, but the sentence points at him and at no one else. The supposition is that whoever "wrought" Othello was an expert, an artist at the top of his profession. The original sunny, unsuspicious nature of Othello is perhaps essential if Iago is to perform a *spectacular* feat of manipulation. There would be little credit in making Leontes, the king in *The Winter's Tale,* jealous, simply because Leontes is jealous already, spontaneously.

If the cardinal problem of *Hamlet* is the hero's delay, the cardinal problem of *Othello* is the hero's gullibility. We shall be less puzzled, perhaps, if we look more closely at Iago's methods. Certainly, while Othello may really have been an unsuspicious man, he has that in him which Iago can use, to form the monster of suspicion we see before the end of the play.

Many years ago I wrote that *Othello* was a play about a hero who went into a house.[1] Othello has lived the life of a soldier under the open sky. Throughout the play imagery of wind and weather is played against imagery of confinement:

But that I love the gentle Desdemona,
I would not my *unhoused* free condition
Put into circumscription and confine
For the sea's worth. (I.ii.25–28)

In Act II, Scene i, Othello comes down from high, stormy seas first into the encircling bay and then into the arms of Desdemona. After Iago has planted doubts in his mind he has a soliloquy that begins as a farewell to marital content but turns as he speaks into a farewell to "the big wars," the male world he has lost (III.iii.349). Thomas Rymer's notorious attack on *Othello* in his *Short View of Tragedy* (1693) is all about the ignobility of the action. The tragic hero is undone by, forsooth, a handkerchief! Rymer was sharp enough to notice how this martial hero was overwhelmed by small domestic details. But that which earns Rymer's principled contempt, the low domesticity, is entirely deliberate. It is indeed the point of the play. This man who should have died on the field of battle is destroyed by small-scale household stuff. Remember Bertram's words, "Wars is no strife / To the dark house and the detested wife" (*All's Well That Ends Well,* II.iii.291–92). But Othello could never detest Desdemona, even when he thought her false. When Hamlet says he cannot kill Claudius at his prayers because that might send him to heaven, Othello expressly asks Desdemona to pray before death: "I would not kill thy soul" (V.ii.32). A black man can rise to eminence in the Venetian army; racial feeling becomes evident when a black man marries a white woman, crosses the threshold from public to private, familial life. Othello the soldier has no difficulty in dealing with a lynch mob (I.ii.59), but the newly married Othello falls apart when Desdemona asks to be allowed to go with him to the wars, so that the marriage can be consummated (I.iii.260–65).

This is the raw material of Iago's plastic art; not constitutional jealousy, but sudden insecurity. This is what he can use to *make* jealousy. Iago foments racial feeling about the marriage among the Venetians. Othello knows they are thinking of him as a lascivious Blackamoor, and this alone is enough to bring him to his knees. He does not really know Desdemona and marvels that she, so beautiful, could love one like him. So he turns, as Iago knew he would, to the familiar: to the genial male friend, the experienced soldier, "honest Iago." There is something frightening about the strength of the love of a woman when it comes to one till then cocooned in comforting male solidarity. It is as if we had a Romeo who instinctively felt he could not be loved by Juliet, turned back to his old friend Mercutio —and found that Mercutio hated him. The shock is profound. Othello is visibly the outsider, black amid the glittering Venetians. But good old Iago is the real outsider of the play; his evil is not human, it is Satanic.

That is how Iago enters the soul of Othello and remakes it. In the dialogue that opens Act IV, Scene i, Iago is so close to the Moor's ear, has insinuated himself so deeply into Othello's very thoughts, that one can hardly tell which speaker says which words:

IAGO Will you think so?
OTHELLO   Think so, Iago?
IAGO   What,
  To kiss in private?
OTHELLO   An unauthoriz'd kiss!
IAGO Or to be naked with her friend in bed.

Those critics who scent latent homosexuality in Iago could be right. The lovely Titania entwined herself about innocent Bottom. Now the morally hideous Iago entwines his own mind with Othello's and moves in very closely, in physical space, as he does so. The language, "naked . . . friend," assists the thought.

Here in the tragedy that engages even more than *Romeo and Juliet* did with an upper-middle-class setting appropriate to comedy we have a final perversion of the resistance put up by same-sex solidarity to heterosexual love. Mercutio derides romantic love and is good. Antonio is defeated by Portia and is, again, good. Iago is opposite to love itself and is entirely evil. And because this is a tragedy not a comedy, marriage is not triumphant at the end. Instead marriage is defeated by pure hatred.

We have returned to the theme of "outside-in" motivation begun in *1 Henry VI*. Iago is one of the "prompters," like Cassius, like Ulysses, but he is more creative than either of them. Where they release pre-existing energies, Iago makes a murderer. Now the "prompter" and the "impresario figure" (Rosalind, Vincentio, Prospero) join. From the first the impresario figure is eerily analogous to the dramatist, the manipulator of human beings. Where Rosalind is to her people, as Jane Austen is to hers (and Shakespeare to his in most of his comedies), a matchmaker, Iago is the match-breaker.

Iago demonstrates how one can put together a figure whose actions flow from a passion of jealousy, felt internally by the subject, yet not original to that subject. Othello's murderous passion is formed in the relational space between persons, by the public medium of words audible to us, the watchers of the play. But what motivates the motivator? Together with the lavish account of the manner in which Othello came to kill his wife, Shakespeare offers a deliberate reticence. Iago has no motive in the sense of "public reason" for doing what he does. Admittedly the play begins with Iago confessing to a perfectly ordinary motive of resentment. Cassio has been promoted over his head. But this does not begin to explain what he does to Othello. More pertinent is this speech:

For that I do suspect the lusty Moor
Hath leap'd into my seat; the thought whereof
Doth (like a poisonous mineral) gnaw my inwards;
And nothing can or shall content my soul
Till I am even'd with him, wife for wife.   (II.i.295–99)

Iago entertains the thought that Othello has had sexual relations with his, Iago's wife, Emilia. This, it might seem, is a perfect, "straight" motive for what Iago does later. But in fact it is not straight at all. All this matter about Othello and Emilia is in the realm of hypothesis, not categorical fact. Shakespeare carefully prepares his ground with the earlier speech in Act I:

> I hate the Moor,
> And it is thought abroad that 'twixt my sheets
> H'as done my office. I know not if 't be true,
> But I, for mere suspicion in that kind,
> Will do as if for surety.   (I.iii.386–90)

Here Iago tells us that he has decided consciously to treat a story that could be false as if it were true. He is clear that he does not know whether Othello and Emilia have done anything wrong. It is here that we glimpse the original nothingness that is Iago, a pure existential darkness that knows its own emptiness and fills the void with a histrionic performance: "I can play the wronged husband—that will serve." "Gnaw my vitals" in the later speech, however, sounds passionately sincere. It is as real as the jealousy of Othello later. Iago has successfully induced a violent emotion in himself, but it is wholly factitious, and he knows what he has done. This means that the origins of his action remain completely obscure. Coleridge's famous phrase, "the motive-hunting of motiveless malignity," is brilliantly exact.[2] There is an earlier "walking darkness" in Shakespeare: Hamlet. Hamlet became an outsider when a dead man came to him with a command. Thereafter his motivation decayed until he sought to induce emotion from the outside by playing "the Avenger," even in soliloquy. Iago, the dramatist of his own psyche no less than that of Othello, *decides* to be motivated in certain ways and then rants accordingly. This means that all the careful construction of character conducted in this play is performed by one who in a certain sense has no character at all. Iago is as invisible as the author of the play. I remember a certain poet and novelist saying, with a slight shiver, "You do realize that all writers of fiction identify at once with Iago."

The sense of eeriness in the villain of the play is assisted by the clear suggestion, running from the start, that Othello is in any case not the sort of person who would have carried on a clandestine affair with Iago's wife. Ask anyone who has just watched the play, "Do you think Othello had an affair with Emilia?" and you will receive the answer, "Of course not! Look at the way Othello first approaches Iago to ask his help—you can tell from the way he speaks that he is not concealing any sort of guilty secret." Any ordinarily shrewd person can see this at once, and Iago, who is more than shrewd, must know it too. He knows for example that the stereotype of the lascivious black man that he uses to whip up feeling in Venice is grotesquely inapplicable to Othello himself. In one of the most uncomfortable moments of the play (uncomfortable, because we sense a grain of truth in what is said), Iago observes that Othello is in fact a little old for the lively Desdemona (II.i.229). This does not sound like a man who seduces other men's wives.

In claiming that Iago is motiveless I was careful to say that "motive" here connotes "intelligible public reason." This leaves open the possible presence of internal, private motivation: love of power, say, or the hatred of goodness in another. Both of these are applicable to Iago. But to say that Iago is motivated by hatred is to do little more than describe and summarize his behaviour—the *explicandum*. It is as much an inference from the behaviour as it is a pre-existing instigator. It accounts for nothing.

Has Shakespeare failed, then, at the centre of his dramatic enterprise? Is it not the mark of a good dramatist to offer characters that are both complex and intelligible? Not necessarily. There is a place in the surviving collection of crabbed lecture notes known as the *Poetics* of Aristotle where the philosopher remarks that moral character is shown when a person makes an "unobvious decision" (1450b8). The commentators make heavy weather of this passage, but if one thinks about drama one can see what Aristotle probably meant (and would have explained in the classroom). If I am about to cross a road but decide not to, because I see a bus coming, I have made an obvious decision and an observer will have learned absolutely nothing about my moral character. If a man smelling faintly of whisky knocks at my door and asks politely for the price of a cup of tea, it is not obvious what I should do. If I kick the man down the steps, an observer will have learned a lot about me, at once. If it were unequivocally clear that Othello had slept with Emilia, Iago's behaviour would be, forthwith, more understandable and less wicked. To those who like formulae we can offer the following law: "Ethical character is in inverse proportion to external motivation." There is no evidence that Shakespeare read the *Poetics*. He understands the principle because he is a working dramatist. Also he relishes the contrast between the explained behaviour of Othello and the unexplained behaviour of Iago, the prime motor.

The Trigger: *Macbeth*

The most economical feat of dramaturgy ever, the place where most is done in least time, is not, as might be thought, "Let him be Caesar" in *Julius Caesar* (III.ii.51). It is in *Macbeth* and it lasts less than a second. It is the famous "start" when Macbeth is told by the Weird Sisters that he will be king thereafter. Shakespeare makes sure that we don't miss this minute bodily reaction by making Macbeth's companion say, "Why do you start, and seem to fear / Things that do sound so fair?" (I.iii.51–52). What does the start mean? Some say that it simply signifies surprise. Others more shrewdly say, "No, it means recognition." If he had merely been surprised, Macbeth would have said, in Jacobean English, "Why on earth do you say *that?*" The companion, Banquo, is himself puzzled, as he would never have been by simple amazement, and detects a note of fear. Macbeth's start means, "How do they know that I have already thought about this happening?"

Once more we have "outside-in" causation, but now it assumes yet another form. There is no expert manipulator here, no Iago to coax the malleable psyche to the desired outcome. This time the crucial element, ambition, clearly pre-exists the moment of external activation. The effect of the prophecy of the Weird Sisters is simply to translate thought into action. They are a trigger. A gun is fired that might have remained safely in the cupboard.

The nearest analogy I know to this moment in *Macbeth* is in a work having no connection with Shakespeare. In Fyodor Dostoevsky's *Crime and Punishment* the hero or anti-hero, Raskolnikov, has been brooding on the more frightening implications of Utilitarian ethics. Russian Utilitarianism is a more violent affair than its English counterpart: if the greatest happiness of the greatest number is the sole criterion of ethical behaviour, the Ten Commandments no longer hold. It is right to kill if this killing is the only way to prevent two other people from being killed. Even, say, torturing a child to death could be right, if one knew that it was the only way to prevent the torturing to death of two other children. Truly independent spirits can rise above biblical morality and, when necessary, spill blood. Raskolnikov, with these thoughts surging in his brain, happens to overhear a conversation between a student and a young officer. They are talking about one Alyona Ivanovna, an aged, grasping pawnbroker. "On the one side," the student says, "we have a stupid, senseless, worthless, spiteful, ailing, horrid old woman, not simply useless but doing actual mischief," and on the other side we have "fresh young lives thrown away for want of help . . . . a hundred thousand good deeds could be done on that old woman's money which will be buried in a monastery."[3] It follows, ethically, by the principle of the greatest happiness of the greatest number, that the old woman must be killed and her wealth re-employed. Raskolnikov, hearing this, starts: "the very same ideas had been running in his mind." This is the point in the novel at which hypothesis becomes action. That is what a psychological trigger does. Brilliantly, Dostoevsky makes the officer say to the student, "Would you kill the old woman *yourself?*" The student answers, "Of course not," and adds, "I was only arguing the justice of it."[4] But although the student falls back into the softer medium of hypothesis the hard action is passed to Raskolnikov, who, because of words accidentally overheard, will now do what he had previously only thought of doing.

We certainly cannot infer that Macbeth would have killed Duncan in any case, even if he had never met the Weird Sisters. Where Iago is a baffling individual psychology operating purposefully to a deliberate end, the Weird Sisters are *ontologically* baffling. *Weird* or *wyrd* in Old English means "fate." The sisters are three in number like the classical Fates. At the same time they are witches, a relatively familiar feature of the rural social scene. In the village on the Welsh border where I lived as a child we had a "cunning woman" who had spells and simples, written out in a Herefordshire County Council school exercise book, for curing various ailments, animal and human. The community never rose against her, but one could imagine it happening (should a cow die, say, after receiving her medicine). The Weird Sisters are not grand, as the Fates are. They belong to a northern, Brueghelesque world of cooking pots and greasy kitchen scraps. But they are not straightforwardly physical: "The earth hath bubbles, as the water has" (I.iii.79), says Banquo as they vanish. The close alliance of almost squalid domestic familiarity with supernatural fear carries us, not into a Sophoclean landscape of Apollonian determinism, but back, into early childhood. The very working out of the prophecies in *Macbeth* is terrifyingly infantile: "I bear a charmed life," cries Macbeth, "which must not yield / To one of woman born." Macduff answers,

> Despair thy charm,
> And let the angel whom thou still hast serv'd
> Tell thee, Macduff was from his mother's womb
> Untimely ripp'd. (V.viii.13–16)

"The angel" here is a bad angel. The structure of the exchange can be found to this day among children, in school-yards and back streets: "You can't so! Nobody born from a woman can kill me, so I can't be killed!" "Yes I can. *I* wasn't *born* from a woman, I was *torn* from a corpse. That had you!" Of course the content of the exchange is sheer terror, on a grand scale. But the quasi-magical force accorded to the literal meaning of terms, so that one party is undone by a single unguarded word, is primitive, twilit stuff.

It has often been noticed that the protagonists of the early tragedies are highly intelligent but those of the later tragedies less so.[5] Hamlet, Brutus, Richard II (*Richard II* is generically perhaps the purest tragedy Shakespeare ever wrote) are all clever men. Othello and Lear are not. It is mildly odd that *Macbeth* post-dates both *Othello* and *King Lear* because *Macbeth* dramatizes the transition from "tragedy of thought" to "tragedy of passion"; if in *Hamlet* action is muffled by consciousness, in *Macbeth* consciousness is progressively muffled by action. Macbeth begins as a man of acute, intelligent awareness and then grows or shrinks into a roaring monster. I say "grows or shrinks" because the imagery of the play points in both directions:

He cannot buckle his distemper'd cause
Within the belt of rule.

. . . .

        Now does he feel his title
Hang loose upon him, like a giant's robe
Upon a dwarfish thief.   (V.ii.15–16, 20–22)

This movement away from crackling intelligence, men who wear their brains on their sleeves, to figures of elemental simplicity may seem to mean that, for one writing about Shakespeare as a thinker, there will be a sharp drop in material as we reach these later plays. You cannot write dialogue for Hamlet without philosophizing. Lear and Othello (rather like Audrey with the word "poetical") do not know what philosophy is. But the fact that the protagonists suddenly abstain from articulate intellection does not mean that the playwright, likewise, must have ceased to think. In *Othello* the protagonist is a simple man, but the environment, Venice, is super-sophisticated. Iago, the "antagonist" of the play, is nothing if not clever, and he does meditate on his own bizarre psychology. In *Macbeth* the *process* of simplification is itself complex. Here we find Shakespeare anticipating later notions of the unconscious and repression, just as he did in *Hamlet*. Lady Macbeth seems more resolute than her husband, but it is she on whom the dream life takes a Freudian revenge. She walks in her sleep, dreams that her hand is marked by a spot she cannot wash away. This is quite obviously, without any straining of language, a case of repressed guilt. As he makes Polonius comment in the terminology of Elizabethan humour psychology in *Hamlet* (II.ii), so here he has a doctor of physic on hand in the sleepwalking scene. We are now to think in terms of pathology.

The reduction of a world buzzing with fascinating multiple meaning to a level simplicity can itself be philosophized:

To-morrow, and to-morrow, and to-morrow,
Creeps in this petty pace from day to day,
To the last syllable of recorded time;
And all our yesterdays have lighted fools
The way to dusty death. Out, out, brief candle!

Life's but a walking shadow, a poor player,
That struts and frets his hour upon the stage,
And then is heard no more. It is a tale
Told by an idiot, full of sound and fury,
Signifying nothing.

(V.v.19–28)

This is almost an inverse mystical experience. While the great mystics speak of a world suddenly enhanced, blazing with fresh significance, Macbeth describes the draining away of all meaning from the universe. In E. M. Forster's *Passage to India* the mystical lesson of the Marabar caves was similarly crushing. The echo the visitors hear—"Boum"—means "Pathos, piety, courage—they exist but are identical, and so is filth. Everything exists, nothing has value."[6] What is technically interesting about Macbeth's speech on hearing of his wife's death is that an intuition of universal meaninglessness should be at the same time an explosion of lyric power.

The gradual diminution of intelligence in the protagonist need not imply a failure in the tragedy, taken as a whole. The ferocity of the ending has overwhelming dramatic strength, though there is a problem, linked to the reduction of intelligence, in the tragic status of Macbeth himself. "This dead butcher" (V.ix.35) cannot, some feel, command the pity and fear common to both Greek and early modern tragedy. A nasty piece of work who gets what he deserves is not tragic, and Macbeth at the end of the play is close to this. More important, however, for the purpose of this book, the slow diminution of intelligence is itself of philosophical interest. It all started with the babble of the Weird Sisters. One could imagine a version of the play in which there were no witches but Lady Macbeth, as "prompter," worked on her husband until she made him murder Duncan. But Shakespeare, pursuing yet another form of lateral motivation, makes the movement start from a humanly unrelated external stimulus. The Weird Sisters are not, like Cassius and Ulysses, political experts pursuing a certain design. They are primitive organisms (or even mechanisms), grinning and chattering, witlessly rhyming out their habitual predictions. Of course at the same time they are right, and this proves their supernatural status. But the situation is very different from that in, say, *Oedipus Rex*. There the Oracle predicts that the newborn Oedipus will murder his father and marry his mother. His parents in fear leave him to die. He survives and grows up believing that Polybus and Merope of Corinth are his parents. He hears about the Oracle and at once strains every nerve to prevent it from coming to pass. He leaves Corinth, and every step brings him closer to his real father, whom he kills in a fight at the place where three roads meet. Thereafter he marries Jocasta, not knowing that she is his mother. In this story the supernatural status of the predictor, the Oracle, is high, because everything in the subjective motivation of the protagonist is in direct opposition to the prediction, but the prediction holds firm. Where the protagonist strives against Apollo and fails, Apollo is *causally* crucial in the story. But in *Macbeth* the Weird Sisters trigger a pre-existing tendency in Macbeth's mind. They are telling a man to do something he had already considered doing, something he partly wants to do in any case. In this second story the supernatural status of the predictor is much lower. The play I imagined in which a privately ambitious, honourable soldier is persuaded by his wife to murder a king would be, if it were written, recognizably a version of *Macbeth*. But *Oedipus* without the god who governs and causes all would be inconceivable. There would be no story.

The "trigger" in *Macbeth* belongs to the darkened, primitive world I have set in opposition to the dwindling light of reason in the protagonist. Although Hamlet is impeded throughout by his unresting intellect, his actions were set in motion by a dead man, after which he was himself gradually engulfed by negation and death. This sequence has something in common with the way emissaries of blood and darkness set Macbeth in motion, after which he gradually becomes himself a bloody, primitive organism. It is now as if Shakespeare has become interested in how small a thing, how simple a thing, could impinge from outside and radically transform the sequence of events. When biologists speak of giving a stimulus to a developing organism, outsiders often assume some complex process must be involved and do not realize that a prod with a small metal object will do the trick. What the Weird Sisters do to Macbeth is oddly like what a practised hypnotist can do to a subject, using post-hypnotic suggestion. The post-hypnotic "trigger" can be trivial in itself. But its power is astonishing.

It will be said that I am overplaying the meanness of the Weird Sisters.

They are after all very frightening in a good production. But the imagery of the kitchen (they squat round a great cooking pot) would have stamped them as low, for early modern audiences. Visitors to old English houses are often puzzled to find that the kitchen is a long way from the hall in which people dined. "Weren't they worried that the food would get cold?" is a question frequently asked. The answer is, "They were still more anxious not to be troubled by the smell of the cooking." Think of the kitchen wench in *The Comedy of Errors* (III.ii.95f.) and "greasy Joan" in the song of Winter at the end of *Love's Labour's Lost*. The Witches' familiars are a grey cat and a toad (I.i.8–9). The "second witch" likes to kill pigs (I.iii.2). They drop into their stew the "Finger of birth-strangled babe / Ditch-deliver'd by a drab" (IV.i.30–31). This is the starved underbelly of society, like the other England of beggars driven off by dogs that Lear discovers when he is cast out from his palace. They are as far as one can be from the brightly illuminated academic mind. Ulysses' speech on identity in *Troilus and Cressida* (III.iii.103–22) actively invites an academic response, intellectual analysis. The voice at the ear of Macbeth is immemorial, pre-academic, pre-intellectual. *Macbeth* is after all the play of darkness, fog, and blood.

Another Expert Man-Maker: *Coriolanus*

Othello seems to belong to 1604, *Macbeth* to 1606. *Coriolanus* followed in 1606. We are now jumping over *King Lear* and *Antony and Cleopatra* in order to find our next "prompter." This time it is a lady, and she does an even more fundamental job than Iago—but she had more time in which to do her work. The lady is the Roman matron Volumnia, and the person she remakes is her own son. Having first produced him biologically, she embarks upon a process that we would call conditioning. The play does not show the childhood of Coriolanus, but the playwright wants us to know what this woman has done to him. It is made clear in a single brilliant scene, Act I, Scene iii.

The atmosphere of this scene is from the beginning "womanly." Volumnia and her daughter-in-law, Virgilia, are at first the only persons present (later they are joined by Valeria, a gentlewoman). There are no men. The stage direction reads, "They set them down on two low stools and sew."

The sole textual authority for this play is the Folio of 1623. Its stage directions are famously more richly descriptive than those in other plays. They are likely to be authorial.[7] We seem to be looking at a genre painting, a "Dutch interior," half a century before Vermeer. Sewing is a stereotypically feminine activity. Those men in the audience who are curious about the way women talk when there are no men present become especially alert. Of course Shakespeare was a man, and had to guess. He has the women talk about family, about Coriolanus, who is Volumnia's son and Virgilia's husband. When Valeria arrives, she asks after Virgilia's son, little Marcius. Virgilia says he is well. Volumnia cuts in warmly with "He had rather see the swords and hear a drum than look upon his schoolmaster" (I.iii.55–56). It is clear that she speaks with benevolent approval. Valeria then recounts how she saw the little fellow chase a pretty butterfly, catch it, tear it, and, in his rage, chew it to pieces (I.iii.60–65). This ghastly behaviour obtains immediate loving admiration from the ladies, most markedly from an entranced Volumnia: " 'Tis a noble child." Virgilia, perhaps wishing to lighten the atmosphere, says "a crack" (in modern English, "a lively lad"). The playwright has only to show that we are watching a replication of what must have happened when Coriolanus was a small child for the idea of conditioning to enter. This he does with Valeria's "A' my word, the father's son" at line 57 and Volumnia's "One on's father's moods" immediately after the narrative of the torn butterfly. Aggression, then as now, was rewarded with love. This is how you make a Roman military killer. The women do it—or, rather, one woman has done it.

I have said that the initial setting is stereotypically female; the end of the scene, where the gossips depart to visit a pregnant lady who lives nearby, is, again, conventionally "what women do." We need to stay with the stereotype a little longer. What, for example, is the stereotypical mother supposed to be like? I would guess that the answer is "tender, nurturing, life-giving, protective." Now listen to the way Volumnia imagines her son, at the time when she is speaking:

His bloody brow
With his mail'd hand then wiping, forth he goes,
Like to a harvest man that's task'd to mow
Or all or lose his hire.   (I.iii.34–37)

This is too much for her daughter-in-law. Virgilia cries out, "O Jupiter, no blood!" Volumnia brushes this pusillanimity aside; it is interfering with her vision:

Away, you fool! it more becomes a man
Than gilt his trophy. The breasts of Hecuba,
When she did suckle Hector, look'd not lovelier
Than Hector's forehead when it spat forth blood
At Grecian sword, contemning. (I.iii.39–43)

There is a professional gentleman in Dickens who momentarily frightens the reader by saying that he is firmly of his wife's opinion that "Other things are all very well in their way, but give me blood!" The wife eagerly chimes in. "We meet it in a chin and we say, 'There it is! That's blood!' "[8] These blameless persons are in fact talking about pedigree. But Volumnia really does like blood. The mature ladies who used to hand out white feathers (symbols of cowardice) to young men not in uniform in the First World War were as nothing to this Roman lady.

This nurturing mother desires above all to see her child shedding the blood of others, but also as bleeding himself. She has carefully fashioned him to this end. The remarkable thing about Volumnia's reply to Virgilia is the way it entwines the maternal with the erotic. When she speaks of the beauty of Hecuba's breasts the first impression made by the words is sexual—male sexuality, at that. But these are the breasts of a suckling mother, and so we are returned to Volumnia herself, the mother in play. What is even more beautiful than these perfect, milky breasts, however, is the blood that sprang afterwards from the forehead of the son. Note that I have had to put in the word "afterwards" to make sense of the speech. Volumnia telescopes the sucking child and the bleeding warrior. For her they are one.[9]

There is a yet more violent juxtaposition of suckling and blood-letting earlier, in *Macbeth*. Lady Macbeth says,

I have given suck, and know
How tender 'tis to love the babe that milks me;
I would, while it was smiling in my face,

Have pluck'd my nipple from his boneless gums,
And dash'd the brains out. (I.vii.54–58)

Lady Macbeth is here trying to turn her husband into a killer. She sees this task as directly antithetical to her own female-ness: "Unsex me here" (I.v.41). Lady Macbeth's words are horrifying, but Volumnia is finally the more disturbing of the two. Lady Macbeth knows that her own thoughts are dreadful and is, so far, still a moral being. Volumnia perceives no conflict between the maternal and the murderous. Elsewhere Shakespeare reverts repeatedly to the idea of sucking not milk but blood. "Drones suck not eagles' blood," says Suffolk, scornfully, at *2 Henry VI,* IV.i.109. In *Henry V,* Pistol, in a kind of drunken hysteria, eager to show his willingness to fight, shouts, "To suck, to suck, the very blood to suck!" (II.iii.56), and later maintains his virile status even an in act of leniency when he says, "As I suck blood, I will some mercy show" (IV.iv.64). Most powerful of all is Caesar's dream, in which he saw his own statue spouting blood and the people of Rome bathing their hands in it. Decius interprets the dream: the vision "Signifies that from you great Rome shall suck / Reviving blood" (*Julius Caesar,* II.ii.87–88). We half expect to be told that the Roman mother gives blood, not milk to her baby, by the breast. That after all is a fair figurative description of what Volumnia has done. The thing she actually says, that the child's bleeding forehead is fairer than the mother's breasts, may seem a less violent thought than that of sucking blood. Once more, however, Volumnia's words are more shocking than the other passages precisely because she is not thinking figuratively. The "bloody child" of the "second apparition" at *Macbeth,* IV.i.73, becomes a literal bleeding child, Hecuba's Hector, Volumnia's Coriolanus. Volumnia is thinking of real blood in a real battle and gives her pleasure in the thought an erotic charge completely absent from the other examples.

Shakespeare clearly saw Rome as a place where blood-letting is fetishized and, at the same time, deemed heroic. Brutus, when his desperate wife resorted to self-harm, was enchanted: "O ye gods! / Render me worthy of this noble wife!" (*Julius Caesar,* II.i.302–3). After the assassination of Caesar the high-minded Brutus wished not to wash away the blood but to steep his arms in it so that they could afterwards stalk through the streets "waving our red weapons o'er our heads" (III.i.109). "Blood" and "wound" are heavily recurrent words in *Titus Andronicus* and *Julius Caesar,* but "wound" especially dominates *Coriolanus.* Readers of the source, Plutarch, may find this odd, since there is far less emphasis on wounds in the real ancient author than there is in the Renaissance play, though Plutarch does refer to the ancient practice of exhibiting wounds to solicit political support (*Coriolanus,* xiv.1).[10] As for the protracted play-business in which Coriolanus is pressed to show his wounds to the electorate and refuses (not because he thinks them unimportant but rather because he thinks them too sacred for political use)—this is thoroughly grounded in Roman practice. Scholars working on Shakespeare's classical sources tend to confine themselves to the obviously relevant places in Plutarch and the rest. But Shakespeare himself evidently read more widely. It is in Plutarch's Life of Aemilius Paulus that we find the closest analogue to Coriolanus as he appears in Shakespeare's play. Aemilius Paulus treats the crowd with Coriolanian scorn and uncovers his breast to reveal an unbelievable number of wounds.[11] Shakespeare may well have found his way to the place in Seneca where the philosopher says that virtue is like the good soldier, who will submit to wounds and will *count his scars.*[12] Nevertheless, even in this environment Volumnia is uniquely bloodthirsty.

The scene in which we are told about little Marcius and the butterfly shows, then, how Coriolanus was conditioned in his childhood to become the controlled killer we see triumphing in the first part of the play. Near the end, where Volumnia tries to persuade her son to spare Rome, her arguments make no impression on him, but as soon as she simply reminds him that his mother is speaking, he is hers to command (V.iii.161–88). The telescoping of the infant with the warrior that we saw in Volumnia's speech on the breasts of Hecuba is replicated at leisure by Shakespeare in the drama taken as a whole. Coriolanus is an awe-inspiring soldier, and he is also, at a certain level, Volumnia's baby still. Coriolanus is not, like Brutus, a reflective Stoic. That is to say, he is not conscious of himself and his high principles. Therefore when Volumnia seeks to manipulate him, she need not bring a mirror to the task as Cassius did (figuratively) when he sought to manipulate Brutus:

> I, your glass,
> Will modestly discover to yourself
> That of yourself which yet you know not of.   (*Julius Caesar,* I.ii.68–70)

Nevertheless Coriolanus does unthinkingly exemplify certain Stoic ideals: integrity, self-sufficiency, self-rule, contempt for popular caprice. Or he can seem to. The proud phrase "author of himself" is employed by Coriolanus to express his own rational independence of local loyalties and of biological kindred. The phrase in isolation blazes with Stoic confidence, but the circumambient grammar of the sentence in which it occurs has a different effect: Coriolanus says he *will* stand (future tense, not present) "*As if* a man were author of himself, / And knew no other kin" (V.iii.36–37). "As if" implies reference to a state of affairs that does not exist, implicitly confesses the artificiality of the Stoic stance. Then the word "kin" reminds us of Volumnia. His assumption of a power to make himself, as a moral being, is comprehensively undermined by the fact that all this courage, all this aggression, was formed and moulded by the mother. His sturdy independence is itself an artefact. Stoicism is all about self-control. But when self-control is created artificially by an external agent is it any longer *self*-control?

In *A New Mimesis* I suggested that Coriolanus' "I banish you!" (III.iii.123), hurled back at the citizens as they eject him from the city, is simultaneously an echo of Senecan advice to the stateless ("Reflect that you are a citizen of the world and cannot be banished from *that*") and the angry cry of a stamping four-year-old.[13] When Coriolanus's seeming mastery of himself finally cracks, it is the word "boy" that undoes him (V.vi.103). Aufidius, the half-barbaric Volscian warrior, tells him that he has nothing to do with Mars, the god of war, but is "a boy of tears" (V.vi.100). The words detonate in what is left of Coriolanus's mind. It is another proto-Freudian moment. Aufidius's words have their extraordinary effect because they are, at a certain level, true.

Coriolanus belongs with the figures of lesser intelligence that we found in the middle and later tragedies. But, again, this does not mean that the dramatist himself has stopped thinking. I raised, in connection with *The Merchant of Venice,* the notion that economics or "social being" may determine consciousness. *Coriolanus* certainly engages, achronically, with Marxian thought, and it is no accident that Bertolt Brecht felt the need to rewrite this play. When the people are starving and ready to revolt, the smooth-talking Menenius silences them with the celebrated "fable of the belly" (I.i.96–160). He explains how there was once a time when the limbs rebelled, claiming that they did all the work and gave the product to the belly, after which the belly unjustly kept everything to itself; but the belly answered the foolish limbs by explaining that it was the storehouse and that all the good things the limbs received came in due course from the belly. The story seems expressly designed to form the target of a Marxian attack. The fundamental question for the Marxist is, "Who creates the wealth?" The usual answer is "the Proletariat." Here in the play Menenius begins by conceding that the limbs win the bread for the body at the beginning of the process. This can seem to have made nonsense in advance of his later assertion (I.i.152–53) that all the benefits the people receive come to them from the Senators (who correspond to the belly in the fable). His words are doubly offensive when we realize that in any case the Senators are not in fact redistributing the wealth to the starving people. That was what the civil unrest was all about in the first place. Obviously Menenius is fobbing them off with an empty tale.

It may be said that to read the scene with this degree of scepticism is not just "achronic," it is anachronistic and plain wrong; the audience of Shakespeare's time would have been guided by an instinctive respect for social superiors to accept that Menenius had both refuted and made a fool of the rebellious Plebeian and that the whole notion of "fobbing off" is an exclusively twenty-first-century response. But Shakespeare uses exactly the same phrase at the beginning of the episode: "You must not think to fob off our disgrace with a tale" (I.i.93–94). There is nothing arcane or "unavailable-in-1606" about the idea that the Senators were behaving unjustly. Plutarch himself says that sedition arose because "the Senate did favour the riche against the people."[14]

So far, so Marxist. But what the playwright does next throws the Marxist into confusion. Shakespeare makes a fundamental move on the question, "Who creates the wealth?" Menenius, as we saw, casually conceded at the beginning that the people were the true creators of Rome's wealth. This notion, however, is gradually destroyed as the play unfolds. *Coriolanus,* though set at an early period in Roman history, shows us not a primitive agrarian economy but an economy distorted by military success. The wealth is made not by honest ploughmen and reapers but by military campaigns that result in the exaction of tribute from the subjected peoples. Gaius Marcius Coriolanus is clearly upper-class, but he is no parasite on the labour of those socially below him. As a spectacular killer he is himself a primary wealth-creator. The people of Rome, meanwhile, increasingly take on the aspect of an idle mob, as if they were parasitical on the courage of such as Coriolanus. We are told that in battle they proved to be of no use (III.i.122–50). It may be said that we should not believe this, because it is said by Coriolanus, who is abominably proud. But no one contradicts Coriolanus, who, though he may indeed be proud, is nowhere given to lying. The "bite" of this Shakespearean character comes from a disturbing coincidence of pride with truth in much of what he says. Plutarch says, apropos of the insurgency, that many of the people exhibited terrible wounds to show what they had done for Rome, but Shakespeare suppresses this.[15] His populace is hungry but without honourable scars.

If the people are in truth parasitic, does this make Menenius's fable, after all, cogent? Is the complacent conservative who rejoices in his victory over the poor citizen proved essentially right by what follows? The answer, surely, is no. To read in this way is to flatten the play with its lurching momentum into a flat monotone. Shakespeare *first* creates a sceptical space around the seemingly duplicitous Menenius and *then* has fun working against the grain of the scepticism he has created. That is Shakespeare's way.

Volumnia stands behind all. If we think of her as a woman interested only in the exercise of power, she is a sad failure. She has failed to understand how Rome is ceasing to be a place of simple bellicose values and is becoming a complex society, with an interest in the the new "co-operative values."[16] Having constructed a warrior, she finds that she needs a politician. Coriolanus, we can see at once, was not built for electioneering. But the speech on the breasts of Hecuba with which we began suggests a darker, more primary drive in Volumnia, a lusting for death. And in this she succeeds, for *Coriolanus* is a tragedy, and the tragedy is largely of her making, just as the tragedy of *Othello* was largely of Iago's making. Iago is the "male best friend" who desires your destruction. Volumnia is the mother who at a certain level is working to a like end. Of course she does not contrive the catastrophe of the play, but we have learned by now to ask Marxian questions about deep causes—not, this time, "Who creates the wealth?" but "Who creates death?" The answer is, the mother.

In the later twentieth century "construction" became a word of power.

People, we were told, are not causative essences using their bodies, they are constructed by relation, society, context—or even "text." Shakespeare in a way feeds the appetite for discernibly "constructed" human beings as he feeds every appetite. But he never falls into that easy universalization of the idea that rendered so much of late-twentieth-century "construction-ism" so vulnerable, philosophically. He never says, "*All* is externally con-stituted; there is *no* 'core self.'" Where all is construction, construction ceases to be felt as threatening or as some kind of distortion. The tension falls away. In Shakespeare that tension is always there. The co-presence of a possible un-manipulated self is persistently maintained. The truth is that when Shakespeare wrote the notion of publicly constituted identity was readily available. The new, exciting thing was the inner, truly originative self. The seventeenth century after all was to be the century of Descartes, who in his *Discourse of Method* (1637) made "I think therefore I am" the foundation of his philosophy and bequeathed to academic metaphysics an almost intolerably sharp distinction between the ego and the body, a distinction from which it has been struggling to escape ever since—partly by accepting the notion of "socially constructed selves"! Coriolanus nev-ertheless might seem to be so extreme a case of construction as to be total; to twist George Herbert's words, he must confess that nothing is his own.[17] Richard II was always in some degree in charge of the parts he played; even Othello was visibly a good artless man until Iago remade him, and the good Othello is still there at the end of the play. Volumnia, however, had Coriolanus under her hand (or at her breast) from birth. There is no pre-existing Coriolanus, before the manipulation starts. But we are wrong.

The most exciting moment in the play comes when, against all our expectations, Coriolanus is able to speak from his core identity. It is indeed a little like the moment in *Richard II* when the King noticed that he did not in fact become "nothing" when deposed, that although he had lost his legal status, he was still there (V.v.40–41). In *Coriolanus* the crisis comes when Volumnia has broken her son, before the walls of Rome. The strongly formed soldier resists her reasoned plea for mercy but cannot hold out when hit by the word of simple, terrifying, conditioning power, "mother." It is here that we have the remarkable stage direction (surely Shakespeare's), "Holds her by the hand, silent." Coriolanus says, "O mother, mother, / What have you done?" (V.iii.182–83). He then tells her that she has won and may have brought him to his death. The voice is not that of the constructed automaton, the thing "made by some other deity than Nature" (IV.vi.90–91). The person speaking is the person *to whom* all these things have been done. Coriolanus is granted the instant of final *anagnorisis*—recognition of the truth—that Shakespeare refuses to give to King Lear. He is no thinker, but suddenly, he knows. The bravest, strongest, fiercest male protagonist in Shakespeare is in the end a figure of pathos because he is psychically stunted, undernourished, deprived by the mother who bore him of all those things that would have allowed him to grow normally as a human agent. But he is still *there*.

8 Shrinking and Growing

Harrowing Hell: *King Lear*

When students are asked when Shakespeare thought King Lear reigned in England they usually say, "Early Middle Ages?" This is not a good shot. Holinshed's Chronicle, Shakespeare's principal source, places Lear's accession to the throne in *anno mundi* 3105.[1] *Anno mundi* ("in the year of the world") is a system of dating that counts years from the original creation. Unfortunately Holinshed is confused about the relation of *anno mundi* dating to the B.C./A.D. system. In Book ii, chapter 6, Holinshed says that after Lear's death, Cordelia became queen in *anno mundi* 3155 and adds that this was fifty-four years before the founding of Rome. Since we have an accepted date for the foundation of Rome (754 B.C.), this means that Cordelia became Queen in 808 B.C. and that the creation took place in 3963 B.C. At the beginning of the following chapter Holinshed, with a great show of precision, says that the reign of Rivallus, the son of Cunedag, began in *anno mundi* 3203 and explains that this was fifteen years before the foundation of Rome. The date of creation, we notice with dismay, has slipped back by some nine years to 3972 B.C. There are other wobbles elsewhere. The nearest synchronism of these dates—and they are not so far apart as to be utterly unmanageable—*places Lear's reign in the later ninth and early eighth centuries B.C.* The earlier account in Geoffrey of Monmouth provides no dates but says that Lear ruled for sixty years after Bladud the aeronaut, a contemporary of Elijah.[2] This gives the rough dating, 820–760 B.C. These numbers chime eerily with the dates of the reign of George III, 1760–1820, who was thought to be mad and identified closely with Lear. So Lear is a figure of primeval antiquity, long before the Middle Ages, long before the birth of Christ, long before Julius Caesar or Coriolanus, long before Aristotle or Sophocles.

Shakespeare, one may safely bet, would not have engaged in arithmetical calculation when he read Holinshed, but he certainly took in the fact that Lear belongs to very early history. He is aware that this is a pre-Christian world. That is why Lear swears "by Apollo" (I.i.159)—a pagan oath. *King Lear* is one of the chronicle plays, and the 1608 Quarto describes it as a "true chronicle history," but the editors of the 1623 Folio placed it not with the histories but with the tragedies. We all now think of it as a different kind of play from *Richard III* or *Henry V.* Are we wrong? The Folio editors may simply have made a mistake, or else they made a critical decision and the designation of this play as tragedy is no mistake. Of course the categories are not mutually exclusive. As we have seen, *Richard II* can be called a tragedy with perfect propriety. But they are distinct. Tragedy is all to do with pity and fear (Aristotle's terms, but they apply after his time). History is all about the evolution of England. One aspect or the other may carry greater weight in a given case. It may well have been evident to the editors when they came to *King Lear* that they were dealing with work of a different order. They were looking at the greatest tragedy ever written.

Pedantic precision over dates is not Shakespeare's line. But there is in *King Lear* a strange preoccupation with mathematics. It is a play about the breaking down of a king who descends into madness, learns charity, but then loses the daughter he loved most. These emotional heights and depths are married in the bloodless sphere of mathematics. Has Shakespeare made a mistake, in choosing to interweave, in this most humane, most passionate of plays, a strand of pure numerical abstraction? Surely, it might be said, this can only weaken the tragedy. But *King Lear* is also about the fear of madness. The very incongruity of the mathematics can work as a bat squeak of hysteria within the complex chords of the major action. We sense the mind breaking free from its moorings. The extremes represented verbally by "all" and "nothing" can both be converted into the sign "o." David Willbern has noticed, behind the word "nothing" that reverberates through the play, a pun on "hole" and "whole" (the round world)—both represented by the figure "o."[3] As early as *Henry V* one can find Shakespeare thinking half-humorously about the odd union of nullity and multiplying power in the zero, in that Arabic notation that had by Shakespeare's time virtually ousted the old Roman numerals. In the Prologue he describes the Globe Theatre ("Globe" = "the round world") scornfully as "this wooden O" and then interjects a curious apology: "O, pardon! since a crooked figure may / Attest in little place a million" (lines 15–16). In *King Lear* the interest in the exponent power of zero falls into the background, and Shakespeare's imagination is instead engaged by the notion of a nothingness that is universal and therefore equal to all. In Act I, Scene iv, the Fool says to Lear, "Thou art an O without a figure . . . Thou art nothing" (I.iv.192–94). Earlier in the same scene the Fool, living dangerously, calls the King fool and adds,

Nuncle, give me an egg, and I'll give thee two crowns.
LEAR What two crowns shall they be?
FOOL Why, after I have cut the egg i' th' middle and eat up the meat, the
   two crowns of the egg. When thou clovest thy crown i' th' middle and
   gav'st away both parts, thou bor'st thine ass on thy back o'er the dirt.
   Thou hadst little wit in thy bald crown when thou gav'st thy golden
   one away.   (I.iv.155–63)

Together with putting over his moral lesson that the King has made a dreadful mistake in resigning his power, the Fool must fool around with circles. A crown is one kind of circle:

Within the hollow crown
That rounds the mortal temples of a king
Keeps Death his court.   (*Richard II*, III.ii.160–62)

The bald head of the old King is suddenly abstract, another kind of circle. The egg is nothing. In scoring tennis we say "Thirty love" for "Thirty nil"; "love" here is a corruption of French *l'oeuf*, "the egg," "zero." The Fool sees that these circles may be filled or empty. Eat the boiled egg and you have two half-shells, empty roundels. These ragged, scraped-out circlets later become the gouged eye-sockets of Gloucester—"bleeding *rings*" (V.iii.190). Shakespeare links Gloucester back to the image of the egg by having the third servant say that he will fetch egg-white to treat

Gloucester's wounded face (III.vii.106) and by having Edgar say that if Gloucester were to throw himself from the (imagined) height of Dover Cliff, he would be smashed "like an egg" (IV.vi.51). Lear's nothingness becomes, entropically, the final nothingness of the universe in the words of the blinded Gloucester when he meets the King (by this stage in the play truly mad): "O ruin'd piece of nature! This great world / Shall so wear out to nought" (IV.vi.134–35).[4]

The mathematical obsession shows elsewhere, sometimes in what could be mistaken for a mere accident of phraseology—"all th' *addition* to a king" (I.i.136)—sometimes in more evidently painful contexts. When Lear speaks of shedding the addition to a king—that is, of resigning all the grand apparatus of practical sovereignty as part of his retirement plan—he gives a mathematical form to a sentiment expressed earlier, with serious tragic import, by Richard II, when he presided over his own dethroning: "Now mark me how I will undo myself" (IV.i.203). Sometimes the line of mathematical reasoning is in contradistinction to the world of human compassion. When the unloving daughters, Goneril and Regan, with cruel relish gradually subtract persons from Lear's retinue, they end with the words, "What need one?" (II.iv.263). Here mathematical calculation is emblematic of inhumanity. Lear's answer is strong: "O, reason not the need! our basest beggars / Are in the poorest thing superfluous" (II.iv.264–65). Even a destitute woman, sleeping rough, will have about her some object "of sentimental value," something not rigidly calculated as necessary to survival.

But Cordelia, the good daughter, is also given to mathematical calculation. At the beginning of the play Lear embarks upon what he has obviously planned as a happy family occasion. He has a map of England already divided in three, a part for each daughter, with the best part reserved for Cordelia, who indeed deserves it. Each daughter is to say how much she loves her father and because Cordelia is the most loving of the three she will easily earn her share. It all goes wrong. Cordelia will not play. She is clear that she cannot possibly offer all her love to her father:

Why have my sisters husbands, if they say
They love you all? Happily, when I shall wed,
That lord whose plight shall take my hand shall carry
Half my love with him, half my care and duty.   (I.i.99–102)

The King is appalled by this and so in a way is the spectator in the theatre. Surely it is only the wicked who quantify love in this way? Cleopatra will say, later, "There's beggary in the love that can be reckon'd" (*Antony and Cleopatra,* I.i.15).

Lear's plan for the day had a fairy-tale simplicity in easy accord with the uncritical simplicity of his own mind. Now fairy-tale founders upon human complexity. It is often said that Cordelia answers as she does because she is a truth-teller. But she is not invited to lie. The question is, "Which of you loves me most?" The true answer to this, from Cordelia, is, "I do—by far the most." Cordelia feels acutely what Lear has not even noticed: that if she speaks warmly of her love where it is known that warm words will obtain a huge reward, her declaration will be infected in advance by a presumption of mercenary intent. Brilliantly, Shakespeare makes Goneril employ the "inexpressibility topos" in her speech to Lear: "Sir, I love you more than words can wield the matter" (I.i.55). Now, even to say, "I cannot express my love" (Cordelia's position) will also be tainted by the rhetoric of self-interest. Indeed she does say, "I cannot heave / My heart into my mouth" (I.i.91–92), but she must say this to herself, not to the King.

It is made clear that the stilted tone of Cordelia's words to her father gives a wholly misleading impression of the love she really feels. Can we say then that she lies when she says that half her love will go to her husband? Is she talking nonsense when she says she loves according to her bond, "no more nor less" (I.i.93)? We think of the phrase, "Not a penny more, not a penny less." There is no easy answer. In Holinshed's Chronicle, Cordelia says, "If you would more understand of the love that I beare you, assertaine your selfe, that so much as you have, so much you are woorth, and so much I love you, and no more."[5] In Shakespeare's play by this point realistic psychology has taken over completely from primitive story. In Holinshed's Chronicle the logic of fairy-tale still holds. The words of Holinshed's Cordelia have magical, prophetic force. Lear is being told by a voice that is in a way superhuman that he must look into his own heart and discover what he lacks. In Shakespeare this secondary level of prophetic import is present too, but in an uneasy relationship with the character of Cordelia, now fully humanized.

Perhaps we are to suppose that the young woman, Cordelia, disabled by embarrassment, nevertheless clings (because of her habitual truthfulness) to a cooler version of the situation, set out now according to the very different test of justice. The difficulty is that if *she* were to say challengingly to Lear, "How much love do *you* deserve?" as her counterpart virtually does in the Chronicle, the implied Olympian censoriousness would be intolerable. So Shakespeare avoids the frontal accusation. Instead he makes her clutch at an impersonal mode, an escape from the hotly personal situation in which her father has placed her, by referring to justice. This can then work in the play *in alliance with* the mathematical language of reduction and annihilation that follows. The Chronicle's Cordelia says that Lear must "assertaine him selfe" and Shakespeare reminds us that the King "hath ever but slenderly known himself" (I.i.293–94).

When Goneril and Regan subtract "all the addition" of Lear's state they are wicked. When Cordelia, almost against her own will, pitches King Lear into an abyss of negation she is part of a mythic logic. Lear must be broken down before he is remade. When Lear invites her to speak on her own behalf she answers famously with a single word, "Nothing" (I.i.87). Lear thinks at first he has misheard, so Cordelia says it again: "Nothing." Now Lear, confronted by what must seem to him a moral impossibility, wildly attempts to re-run time itself (though his words are made less crazy by the fact that the daughters are being asked to lay on a *performance* of filial love). "Let's cancel that," says Lear, "And start again," or, in his own words, "Nothing will come of nothing, speak again" (I.i.90). The disyllable uttered by Cordelia has a resonance beyond its immediate conversational context. A black hole opens in the fabric of the play. Lear falls through the hole into a dark counter-world of continuing subtraction, a reduction now authorized by the moral movement of the drama itself. He passes from the upper-class England of the map—good hunting here, good fishing there ("with . . . forests . . . rich'd, / With plenteous rivers," I.i.64–65)—to an under-nation of wretched poverty and madness, where beggars are driven by dogs from filthy farm-yards and people hammer nails into their arms to extort charity (IV.vi.154–55, II.iii.16). When Richard II undid himself and ceremonially discarded the outer signs of royalty, he was half-able to enjoy the process of his own unmaking. Lear, mad on the heath, tears off his clothes in an agony of spirit, straining to reach the "poor bare fork'd animal" that lies beneath (III.iv.107).

I said that the mythic resonance of Cordelia's "Nothing" held a suggestion that the King must be unmade before he is made anew. The latter
part of the sentence implies that we should expect an upward-turning at
the end of the play. In the scenes on the heath and in the reunion with
Cordelia we seem to find that upward-turning. The man who when sane
was coarsely insensitive to the feelings of others learns, from his descent
into hell, to pity the naked wretches and homeless people and to repent of
his own negligent kingship (III.iv.26–33). Reunited with the daughter he
had wronged he seems inwardly to grope his way, even as they are being
hauled off to prison, to a charity that extends, with full Christian force,
even to his captors. Cordelia's "Nothing" has annihilated the old Lear and
made possible the regenerate man. So far we appear to have moved from a
scheme in which bloodless mathematical subtraction is a simple foil to
human compassion to a more profoundly imagined scheme, in which
subtraction and division work in alliance with good, as the necessary
preliminary to redemption. The story of the foolish king who descended
into hell and learned charity is a Christian *commedia* (comedy in the
medieval sense, "story with a happy ending"). Johnson, Tolstoy, and many
other strong Christians have felt that this is the proper form of the play.[6]
For Christians, meanwhile, the proper form of the universe is itself comedic, not tragic. We are in God's hands and God is good. That is why the
greatest religious poem of the Middle Ages, the poem reflecting the
structure of the universe, is called the *Commedia*. Even the death of Christ
on the cross, terrible as it is, is finally a comedy, not a tragedy. Thus,
Nicholas Grimald's neo-Latin poem on the death and resurrection of
Christ, *Christus Redivivus* (Cologne, 1543), is described on the title page
as a *comoedia tragica*—that is, not "a tragi-comedy" but a "tragic *comedy*."
But Shakespeare, having completed his *commedia*, went on to smash it.
When Lear and Cordelia are taken off to prison we can easily think,
"Everything that can be done to human beings has been done to these
two, and yet they love all humankind; a love that rises in this way above
circumstance and confusion is transcendent, is what Christ taught." But
Shakespeare says, "Wait a moment; look what happens when I kill his
daughter." Lear tells us how he instantly killed "the slave" he found
hanging Cordelia and *the audience is almost moved to applaud*. He is no
longer the exemplar of regenerate love but has reverted to the primitive

figure we saw at the opening—but now with an immense charge of tragic power. Then, in the Folio text, he dies not with that final insight that is supposed to dignify the tragic hero at the close but in the pathetically mistaken belief that Cordelia is still alive.

There has been a general drift in the criticism of this play from "redemptive" to "bleak" readings, from A. C. Bradley and J. F. Danby to Barbara Everett and John Holloway.[7] Sometimes the "bleak" reading reaches a point of intensity at which the word "nihilism" is used.[8] Dr Johnson seriously averred that he could not endure to read the play through and avoided doing so until as an editor he was forced to.[9] *King Lear*, up to Act V, Scene iii, is a profoundly moving Christian drama. To take that away from us, not by any august mechanism of causal necessity, but through the trivial accident of a message sent too late (V.iii.244–62), is indeed hard to endure. Naught for our comfort. Does this mean that the fundamental import of the play is a negation of all value, that there is a final decay of all moral hope to correspond to the physical entropy with which we began?—"This great world / Shall so wear out to nought" (IV.vi.134–35).

I have long argued that the savage ending of *King Lear*—Shakespeare's destruction of his own Christian *commedia*—makes it an anti-Christian play. If there is any divine power it is as Gloucester imagines it: the gods are morally squalid beings who delight to torture us as boys delight in tearing the wings off butterflies (IV.i.36–37). I was shaken in this view by an essay by Stephen Medcalf.[10] Medcalf like many before him sees Cordelia as a type of Christ. The entry of Lear with Cordelia dead or near death in his arms immediately evokes for Medcalf the Pietà of Christian iconography, in which the dead body of Christ is shown in the arms of his mother. The transposition of sexes, a female Christ and a male mother, has always ruled this out for me. But let us now remember the law that says, "Whatever you think of, Shakespeare will have thought of first." This applies to Medcalf's thought. Shakespeare too has seen that Cordelia is a Christ: after all, he gives her the words, "It is thy business that I go about" (IV.iv.24).[11] It is too easy for the sceptic to shoot this down by pointing out that the business to which Cordelia here refers is sordidly political, the recovery of Lear's power, so that the scriptural reference is at best parodic. In fact the echo of Christ's words in Cordelia's speech is never received by an audience as parodic. Instead we seem to hear, for a second, another music, from the upper air. Medcalf corroborates his case with a strong frame of reference to romance materials. He is perfectly aware, as was Bradley, that *King Lear* shows no justice in this fallen world. After all Christianity has always affirmed that we live in just that, a fallen world, and that the kingdom of Christ lies elsewhere. To look for justice *here,* then, is a theological mistake. The *commedia* of natural justice in which the good end happily, the bad unhappily, the play Johnson wanted, would have been at best a coarsely materialized Christianity.

In the course of history Christians have said many things. The undoubtedly Christian armies that fought in England's Civil War took victory in the field to mean that Christ was on their side. The whole notion of providence, that we are held here and now in the hand of a benign power who ensures that all things turn out as they should, is prominent in Christianity, and this is clearly thoroughly exploded in Shakespeare's play.

Since the tide turned against the "redemptive" reading it has become customary to dismiss Bradley's intuition of transcendence in the death of Cordelia as a self-indulgent critical evasion. But Bradley was a great Shakespearean critic, and nothing that he says is foolish. He is aware of the supremacy of evil forces in the world of the play; he observes that not only are the wicked parties strong, the evil they do leads to no good; it founds nothing.[12] He is likewise aware that Lear's last words in the Folio, "Look her lips, / Look there, look there!" (V.iii.311–12), are spoken by a man who is making a mistake in thinking his daughter is alive, and are therefore pathetic rather than nobly tragic, and that they bring "a culmination of pain."[13] He says that *King Lear* does not contain "a revelation of righteous omnipotence or heavenly harmony or even a promise of the reconciliation of mystery and justice."[14] Yet he speaks of Cordelia as one mysteriously exempt from the events of the play, as "a being calm and bright and still," and says that she resembles certain other tragic figures in that she is rather "set free from life than deprived of it."[15] Cordelia, he says, is "a thing enskied and sainted."[16] Interestingly, Bradley has borrowed the phrase "enskied and sainted" from Lucio, the streetwise libertine of *Measure for Measure* (I.iv.34). Such language can sound to modern ears like so much Edwardian sentimental twaddle, but it is possible that a mind still open to a diffuse religious resonance—a mind such as Bradley's or Medcalf's—will perceive things in the play that are actually there.

Cordelia is swiftly characterized in Act I, Scene i, as a socially awkward, deeply moral young woman, but she is also haloed by a certain light that never leaves her. That is why the line in which she says she is going about her father's business remains obstinately beautiful, despite the "low" context of political manoeuvring. When Bradley argues for a transcendental reference on the ground that Lear at the very end experiences joy (while we experience pain), he does not persuade me. The very intensity of Lear's joy increases our sense of his error and so deepens the pathos. But when Bradley writes, "If we condemn the universe for Cordelia's death, we ought also to remember that it gave her birth," he hits something important.[17] Suddenly we realize that *King Lear* is not *ethically* nihilist. An ethically nihilist play would leave one thinking that "good" and "evil" have no meaning. *King Lear* leaves us with a sharpened sense of the difference between good and evil, and, lying behind that, of the difference between goodness and nothingness.

The bitter practical sequence of events in the play does, still, work against the Christian transcendental belief. Christianity is at bottom optimistic, because God is all-good as well as omnipotent. Samuel Johnson was disgusted by the shallow quasi-Leibnizian theological optimism of his time. but in the very review in which he reduced the optimists to a heap of rubble he knew that meanwhile every Christian must finally affirm that the world is a good world.[18] The action of the play supports the pessimist, but the whole point of transcendent value is that it exists elsewhere—not here. This is a kind of goodness that, *ex hypothesi,* is instantiated nowhere in our experience but is rather heard far off, like distant music. My reading earlier in this book of the "alienated" comic ending of *All's Well That Ends Well* actually works against my resolutely anti-transcendentalist reading of *King Lear.* There I argued that the very imperfection of the human participants worked not to satirize or falsify the value of marriage but to throw it into relief, as something independent of the variously shoddy fallen individuals who are drawn, blinking, into the circle of light. To affirm that "good" and "evil" are meaningful terms is to reject full nihilism yet does not carry us as far as transcendentalism. But my word "independent" begins to do just that. There is nothing "tragically cleansing" about the death of Cordelia, and Lear is denied the kind of final insight into truth that gives grandeur and dignity to other tragic heroes. It may be that this very withholding of the usual consolations of genre also operates finally to isolate rather than to abolish the goodness of Cordelia.

The transcendence is still a very "this-worldly" transcendence. The absolute separation of Plato's Forms is a thing alien to Shakespeare's genius. This is true both of beneficent marriage as it sanctifies the union of errant persons in comedy and of the goodness of Cordelia, powerless but mysteriously operative in a darkened world. The final tension in *King Lear* is between Nothing and Good, and Nothing proves, indeed, frighteningly strong. In the "Dover Cliff" episode Nothing fights a rearguard action and almost triumphs over value.

The "Dover Cliff" episode does not take place on Dover Cliff, but one of the persons involved and three quarters of the audience are persuaded, for a good ten minutes, that that is the location. The newly blinded Gloucester is led by his son Edgar to believe that he is standing on the brink of a high cliff. Edgar, who is at this stage in the play disguised as a crazy beggar, knows that his father is close to despair and wishes to die. Edgar becomes yet another of our "prompters," close at the ear of Gloucester as Iago was at Othello's. He implicitly invites Gloucester to hurl himself from the cliff edge. Gloucester pitches forward, towards what he thinks is certain death, and falls abruptly on level ground. This could have been the moment at which the old man realized he had been tricked, the moment of "disconfirmation," but Edgar steps forward at once and speaks in an altered voice, expressing amazement that Gloucester should still be alive after so terrible a fall. From Gloucester's point of view an independent witness has confirmed everything his Bedlamite companion had said to him seconds before. Gloucester believes that after all he did fall from the cliff-top—and has been saved. Edgar explains to the audience that his motive in this strangely cruel piece of trickery was benevolent; he was teaching his father to reject thoughts of suicide and to trust in the benevolence of divine power. Indeed, the stratagem works. Gloucester is grateful to the power that has so miraculously preserved him.

The snag is that there was no miracle. The old man has bumped his nose in a sequence having a certain affinity to other instances of rough late medieval humour (the blind leading the blind and all falling into the ditch, and the like). Everyone who sees the scene is made uncomfortable by a sense that Edgar is partly the loving son, partly devilish. Eerily, when

Edgar speaks to Gloucester after the fall, he says he saw a hideous devil standing beside him at the top of the cliff, just before Gloucester jumped. This makes perfect sense as part of the benevolent therapy: Edgar, by suggesting that a devil prompted the death-leap, drives home the idea that suicide is a sin. But the devil is described as standing exactly where he, Edgar, had been standing, close at the ear of the despairing man. We may say that all is still well. If Edgar played the devil, temporarily, in prompting suicide, it was all in the service of the happy outcome. But the discomfort persists, because Edgar lies. God has not saved Gloucester through a miracle. The brilliance of Edgar's theatrical stratagem is infected with moral dubiety. Power like this is unholy, as is perhaps the power of the dramatist to coax the indefinite otherness of human beings into dapper formal sequence.

The pain of the episode arises from the discrepancy between theatricality and human suffering. It is sometimes maintained that the entire "Dover Cliff" episode is manifestly an implausible fiction, a game. I once explained the sequence to a distinguished experimental psychologist who knew nothing about Shakespeare. "Could a man, in these circumstances, be made to believe that he had really fallen and survived?" I asked. He replied, "He was in shock, had just been violently blinded so that he is now dependent on any voice he hears; he fully expects to die, the shock of the impact on level ground merely dazes him, but then the second, confirming voice, describing his spectacular fall would do the trick. You can make people believe far odder things than that." Like Richard III's seduction of Lady Anne, the episode is both astonishing and credible.

The entire passage is especially disquieting for the author of this book, because it is very nearly a destructive parody of that redemption through comic form I have discerned elsewhere. In *All's Well That Ends Well* the stratagem of the bed-trick results in the real marriage of the principals, a thing good in itself. In *King Lear* Edgar's stratagem brings about the repentance of Gloucester and his subsequent turning towards life. But in *King Lear* there is a spillage from the corrupt trick into the supposedly happy outcome. The devout and virtuous state attained by Gloucester is predicated on the lie. He now believes *because* he thinks, wrongly, that he has been divinely saved. If *All's Well That Ends Well* had told the story of a young man who fell deeply in love with a lady because he believed, quite erroneously, that she had behaved generously to him, the comedy would have been as disquieting as *King Lear* is at this point. In *All's Well That Ends Well* as we have it there is a clean division between, on one hand, the human participants, the formidable Helena and the baffled Bertram, and, on the other, the wedding, merry, immemorially traditional, simultaneously ideal and able to accommodate human frailty. Marriage in the comedy is in one respect thoroughly this-worldly, but at the same time it is actually more fully transcendent, more unproblematically separate than Gloucester's regeneration, compromised at its heart by the fact that it is founded on a lie. If one thinks of Christian Goodness and Nothing as forces contending mythically in the play, Nothingness has here entered the very sanctum of Goodness, like a poisonous gas. The gloriously redemptive plot-trick of the comedies really seems for a moment to become a nihilist victory. No wonder Samuel Beckett responded strongly to this play.[19]

But Christian love is an evident reality in the dreadful pre-Christian world of *King Lear*. Shakespeare probably did think of Christ when he conceived the character of Cordelia, and he took steps to ensure that some in his audience might think along the same lines. Nothing in the play, meanwhile, backs belief in God the Father. Bradley, with that readiness to admit spiritual resonance that our age too curtly dismisses as absurd, rightly identified a quasi-transcendent moral music in the play. This music is set against the almost unrelieved pain of the practical sequence. This gives us a Cordelia above the pain of events, above the pain of her own death, but it does not clearly enforce a doctrine of immortality. At the end of the play we are not sure that Cordelia is in heaven, but unless we are entirely brutalized, we do feel that we have glimpsed, beyond the chaotic horror, something of infinite sweetness that we cannot fully comprehend.

Misanthropus: *Timon of Athens*

King Lear sets the process of reduction to near-nothingness against love and goodness. The word Lear uses, thunderously, to describe what is done to him is "ingratitude" (I.iv.259, I.v.39–40, III.iv.14). One can feel as one listens to Lear that he is failing to see the point: Goneril and Regan are not just ungrateful for all their father has done for them, they are cold, loveless, almost machine-like in their destruction of the old king, and this is where the horror lies. But Shakespeare is linguistically sensitive. He is aware of a paradox in the word "gratitude" that we in the twenty-first century may miss. "Gratitude" is the proper response to "grace" or "graciousness." As long as we think of gratitude in terms of simple repayment its real force will escape us. The nexus of related terms is: grace, gratitude, gratuitous.

In Christian theology the grace of God is an inexplicable generosity; it is essentially unearned, unmerited, a freely given extra. Calvin thought human beings totally depraved and despised the Pelagian idea that good people earned their place in heaven by doing good things. Thus for Calvin all beneficent action from God to humankind has the character of amazing grace. In social, non-theological usage grace is the favour of a superior and is sharply distinguished from wages. When Lear cries out against filial ingratitude he is in part lamenting the decay in Goneril and Regan of any human response at the level of generosity, the absence of *spontaneous* moral life, and this hits the mark. But it is quite obvious that, despite the initial strong distinction between the grace-gratitude nexus and mathematical, monetary justice, Lear does expect a return for the generosity he showed his daughters. He expects, not payment indeed, but spontaneous love in return. There is a lurking paradox here, and Shakespeare explored it in *Timon of Athens*.

If the writer of *King Lear* was strangely drawn to mathematical notation, *Timon of Athens* has the form of a demonstration in Euclid. One almost expects to read at the end the words, "Quod erat demonstrandum." Although there are some rough edges in *Timon of Athens* (the play as we have it may be an unfinished version of a collaboration between Shakespeare and Thomas Middleton) the central structure has an icy clarity—and it is all about ingratitude. Timon gives freely to all comers; he then falls on hard times. The friends he had showered with gifts reject him. He who had loved all mankind becomes in consequence a hater of mankind, a misanthrope. Timon is Lear without any of the old king's grandeur of language and, more important, without any family. He has only friends, or perhaps I should say, "friends."

In the first part of the play it is clear that Timon's gifts are lavished on others with no expectation of a material return. Indeed, one sure way to secure an expensive present from Timon is to give *him* something. He seems to be driven by some inner force to outdo the giver, on a spectacular scale, at once. A notion of reciprocal payment is beginning to emerge here, but it operates in a reverse direction: Timon is not worried about securing a return from others, he is rather harassed by the thought that he *must* give back more than he received. Marcel Mauss observes how in certain societies this very different reciprocity-of-honour could become codified. He writes of the American Indians of the Northwest, "One does not have the right to refuse a gift or a potlatch. To do so would show fear of having to repay."[20] He adds interestingly that in certain circumstances a refusal can be an assertion of strength. Mauss is describing a society composed entirely of Timons. In Shakespeare's play he is alone. The recipients of Timon's gifts feel no obligation whatever to reciprocate his generosity. Their indifference to obligation can make them seem strong and Timon, inversely, weak, in Maussian terms.

We may think for a moment that Timon in the first half of the play is like one of those sad children who take presents to school in the hope of buying friendship. But Timon did not give with the conscious intention of obtaining anything for himself. He really does give freely (freedom is at the heart of the grace-gratitude-gratuitous complex of terms). The thought of a return does not cross his mind until he is financially ruined. Then indeed he assumes that his dear friends will come to his aid as he would certainly have gone to theirs in like circumstances. When Timon poured out his good things upon others they really were gifts, gratuitous extras, outside and above the low world of contracts. But now he thinks that after all a return is in order. Gracious giving is properly answered by gratitude, and gratitude may even be expected on occasion to express itself financially. This does not mean that he has slipped back into the sphere of legally enforceable bonds. Timon is not looking for "the money due to me," he is looking for an *ethical* response. The freedom of his original beneficence depended on his continuing unawareness that an obligation was being created in the recipient. But the grateful recipient is conscious of obligation. How, then, can we say that he makes his grateful return freely? The freedom lies in the fact that the return is not enforced by any legal sanction. The recipient of bounty responds only because he wants to, but, from the ethical point of view, *he ought to want to*. A wholly sincere suspension of all legal obligation can without inconsistency coexist with an implicit belief in ethical obligation. That said, we must add that the original giver must retain a certain innocence. If the giver is too vividly aware that the secondary ethical obligation is always there, he may begin to give with an eye to having help at hand later, as a sort of insurance policy. If this happens, his giving is no longer gracious, disinterested, and the whole scheme is now tainted. But Timon (who is not one of Shakespeare's clever characters) is entirely innocent.

Nineteenth-century critics tended to see Timon as a noble spirit vilely used by others. Earlier critics saw him as less than admirable, a fool or an extravagant show-off.[21] Ethically, his generous actions ask for a generous response. On the practical level his near-hysterical giving virtually invites abuse from the recipient. There is the low idiom: "He asked for it."

We now have an extraordinarily subtle structure in counterpoint to that we saw exposed in *The Merchant of Venice*. In the earlier play Shylock, the man of legal bonds, takes the Christians at their word. In effect he says, "You all know very well that I function usefully in your society as the man who deals not in charity but in strict business terms—and now I want what is owing to me," and the Christians are aghast. In *Timon of Athens* the faithless friends take Timon at his word and say in effect, "You are the man who is above bonds and contracts, the free giver, the man to whom we owe nothing, right?" and *he* is aghast.

In *The Merchant of Venice* it is clear that the opposite of *grace* is *bond*. Portia never uses the word "grace" in her famous appeal to Shylock to be merciful, but for all that she is talking about grace (to this day we can feel that the Christian Venetians are graceful and that Shylock is graceless without understanding the full meaning of the terms we continue to use). In *Twelfth Night* the Fool says, "Words are very rascals since bonds disgrac'd them" (III.i.21). This is far too clever for your average twenty-first-century audience. The Fool means, "You may give me your word and this would have been fine in the good old days when gentlemen were gentlemen and people like Shylock were kept out of sight, but now the growth of legal safeguards has removed the old element of gentlemanly generosity ('dis-grac'd') in promises. Since then words can no longer be trusted." My paraphrase is long because it is adapted to the reduced understanding of modern readers (of whom I am one).

Because Timon is not intelligent he does not philosophize as Ulysses does in *Troilus and Cressida*. But it is no straining of terms to say that Shakespeare philosophizes in *Timon of Athens*. The analysis of the intricate dance of social giving in which obligation is first erased and then re-inscribed, conducted with careful attention to linguistic usage, would have delighted J. L. Austin. It is his sort of thing but, I am tempted to say, cleverer than anything in Austin's writings. The subsequent embedding of this paradox of giving in a bleakly cynical society then throws further light on the way causes operate (sometimes in unexpected ways) between individuals and groups—something that as we have seen fascinated Shakespeare from the beginning. This also is very intelligent but perhaps belongs more with social psychology than with philosophy (if a label must be attached). Certainly, Shakespeare is *thinking* in this play.[22]

The connection with *The Merchant of Venice* is strong, but the link to *King Lear* is stronger still. I am assuming that *King Lear* is earlier than *Timon of Athens,* but the date of *Timon* is hard to fix. It could belong to 1604, the year of *Measure for Measure,* with *King Lear* following in 1605. When Lear says, "Our basest beggars / Are in the poorest thing superfluous" (II.iv.264–65), his thought flows from his grief at what he calls ingratitude in a way that modern audiences, again, usually miss. He has moved into the logic of the "grace" nexus. The essence of grace is that it is superfluous to desert or requirement. When Alexander Pope wrote of the "nameless graces" of poetry, he was setting aside the rational Augustan scheme he had set up in order to acknowledge the possibility of inexplicable splendours the scheme itself could never generate.[23] The whole point of a *gratuity* to a waiter is that it be over and above the sum named on the restaurant bill. If play is allowed to speak to play, when Lear notes that even the poorest will have about them odd, gratuitous objects that are not valued solely for their efficacy in the practical business of survival, he counters one central drive of *The Merchant of Venice,* which is to suggest that grace is a luxury that only the rich can afford, something unavailable to the economic work-horses on whom Venice depends.[24] "No," says Lear, "Such graces are the property of humanity, in whatever condition." Yet when Lear says later,

> Take physic, pomp,
> Expose thyself to feel what wretches feel,
> Then mayst thou shake the *superflux* to them,
> And show the heavens more just
> (III.iv.33–36)

he implicitly assents to the claim of rational justice: that the extra wealth should be distributed not in pure, unsystematic freedom but in accordance with demonstrable need and desert. But of course Lear is here speaking at the level of the ethical, not the contractual. What shows in the word "just" is that the scheme deemed contrary to cold justice, the scheme of grace, can lead us, as we move from contract to ethical desert, back to the claim of justice—now having high moral status! This is exactly the sequence played out in *Timon of Athens.*

In fact it looks as if Shakespeare's mind must have passed from *The Merchant of Venice* to *Measure for Measure* before he wrote *King Lear.* In *Measure for Measure* Angelo offers the unlovable proposition that in practical life the rigorous application of punitive law may in the long run be more merciful (that is, may cause less pain) than the generous forgiveness the Duke has been freely granting to criminals. In *King Lear* the supremacy of unconditional charity is reasserted with even more power than Portia could give it in *The Merchant of Venice.* But to make the good, loving Cordelia the mouthpiece of *quantified* love, as she is when she says she will need so much love for husband, leaving so much for her father (I.i.100–102), is as disconcerting as it was to make the wicked, punitive Angelo the mouthpiece of practical mercy. Lear expects reciprocal gratitude after his gift of the kingdom to his three daughters at the beginning of the play. Goneril and Regan are like Timon's false friends. They profess love but are insensible of any ethical obligation. They simply hang on to whatever they can get. Lear's folly, we could say (as we said of Timon's), "asked for it." This the King could have borne, but when Cordelia begins to "mathematize" and hesitate, he snaps. Cordelia has perceived that the King's free (though hierarchically ordered) generosity has become enmeshed in its predictable practical effect: the creation of a mercenary temper in the recipient. Political economists used to like to point out that charity pauperises the supposed beneficiary. This also is like *Timon of Athens.* Cordelia is bewildered by her sudden apprehension of the dangerous social context, tries to resolve the matter by moving into the cooler medium of rationally demonstrable desert. This makes her language uncomfortably similar to that employed by her sisters in their wholly destructive application of mathematics to human flesh and blood.

"Grace" normally refers to the initial act of generosity, but "Grace before meat" is prayer of thanksgiving, the other side of the equation. This too gets into *Timon of Athens* at III.vi.70–84, where the protagonist utters a parodic Grace. Man to God, giver to Giver, he warns the Supreme Being not to give, because the recipients will only despise the giver. He ends by asking God to destroy his creatures and by explaining that his own guests will be given no food at all: "In nothing bless them, and to nothing are they welcome" (III.vi.83–84).

With these words Timon modulates from a parodic Grace into something even more shocking, a parodic Eucharist. It is entirely natural when staging this scene to place Timon in the centre of the far side of a long table, with his guests on either side. Already the composition of innumerable Last Suppers, from Leonardo da Vinci and earlier to Luis Buñuel's version in the film *Viridiana* (as savage as Shakespeare's), is in place. This is Timon's last supper and he is, as we think, on the point of inviting his guests to "take, eat," but then we hit—or are hit by—the word, "nothing." On this word, according to the Folio stage direction, "The dishes are uncovered and seen to be full of warm water." It is possible that the stage direction is incomplete and that the words "and stones" should be added. As the terrified and embarrassed guests fall over each other in their haste to get their hats and coats and leave, one says, "One day he gives us diamonds, the next day stones" (III.vi.120). If Timon has indeed served them stones in water we have a reversal of Jesus' words, "If a son should ask bread of any of you that is a father, will he give him a stone?" (Luke 11:11). These words follow closely on the passage in which Jesus teaches his disciples the Lord's Prayer: "Give us this day our daily bread."

"Grace before meat" is the giving of thanks for that physical sustenance God has given us in response to our prayer, "Give us this day . . . ." This elemental form can be seen in one of the Graces printed in *The Primer set furth by the Kinges Majestie and his Clergie* of 1545: "Most mightie lord and merciful father we yeld the hartie thankes for our bodely sustenance," but the prayer of simple thanksgiving immediately slides into a petitionary prayer for the grace of God (*grace* in its primary sense). Further conceptual contortions followed in later Graces, until we get, instead of "Thank you for this food," a plea *to be made grateful* ("For what we are about to receive, may the Lord make us truly thankful"). Christian devotion is invaded by the convulsive neurosis proper to competitive courtesies among fallen human beings. In the original Last Supper, meanwhile, a more fundamental transposition of terms takes place, as the bread and wine become the body and blood of Christ, the host of the supper. *Eucharist* belongs to the "grace-gratitude" nexus. In modern Greek *eucharisto* means "thank you." "*Charity*," we now see, belongs to the same family of terms.

The question whether the body and blood of Christ are actually consumed by participants in the Mass or Holy Communion, or whether the whole business is to be understood figuratively, was a matter of hot contention in the sixteenth century. The transition from ordinary bread and wine to Christ's body can seem, especially in an Anglican context, a move to a higher plane. But the notion of eating one's god and drinking his blood carries simultaneously a charge of barbarous magic. I am sure that Shakespeare was sensible of all these things. The heavily recurrent cannibalistic imagery of the play, joined as it is to the parodic Grace and Eucharist, presented as a great set-piece, must have the effect of sensitizing us to the primitive force latent in the doctrine. The most interesting instance is at I.ii.41, "So many dip their meat in one man's blood."[25] This evokes the moment in the Last Supper when Jesus dips the sop and passes it to the traitor, Judas (John 13:26). Nor is this the only one. "The fellow that sits next him, now parts bread with him . . . is the readiest man to kill him" (I.ii.46–49) and "Who can call him / His friend that dips in the same dish?" (III.ii.65–66) keep the thought alive.

Does this mean that Timon is a Christ figure? G. Wilson Knight had no doubt about the matter. After all we have seen Angelo as a redeemer. *Measure for Measure* and *The Merchant of Venice* are not the only plays in which Shakespeare allows his mind to be engrossed by theology. If Timon is a Christ figure he is so, in a curiously trivial manner, in the first half of the play only; thereafter he becomes, as the hater of all mankind, an inverse Christ figure. He is monumentally inconsistent, moving from witless love to insane loathing. But Angelo is frighteningly consistent. If he is a Christ figure he is so from beginning to end. Even in the first part of the play Timon's bounty never seems Christlike. If he is crucified he is crucified as much by his society and his own stupidity as by treachery. Even in his final phase of total misanthropy he lacks moral grandeur. The phrase "inverted Christ" might suggest a frightening devil, but that is not what we are given. Instead, the prolonged ranting begins to sound unreal in our ears. Perhaps, in the words of Albert Camus, he is "the only Christ we deserve."[26]

When Timon tells his guests he is giving them nothing, we may think of Cordelia's more frightening "Nothing," the key word of *King Lear.* Timon really is a kind of nobody. It may be that pure negation, as distinct from the slow approach to negation, is un-dramatizable. The approach to nothingness is exciting, but nothingness itself is boring and featureless. Even Hamlet, unmanned though he was by an enervating darkness within, was able to embark on the strenuous business of filling the inner void with fictive, histrionic "selves": "the joker," "the bloody avenger," and so on. Lear is broken down and dies in error, but he dies on a loving error. "Love survives" is, I suppose, a cliché, but at the end of *King Lear* it is no cliché. But Timon in the wilderness is thoroughly dehumanized. Aristotle said that the unsocial man is either a god or a beast (*Politics,* 1253a). Coriolanus is unsocial and is an artificial god-man operated by his mother. Timon, having turned his back on society, is a beast. He can still talk but he uses language only to curse. This is tedious, but it is necessitated by the strong intellectual form of the drama.

It may be an accident arising from the unfinished character of the text before us, but this boring sub-man in one way embodies a more perfect negation than any other figure in Shakespeare. What I mean is that he simply vanishes. We do not see him die as we see Lear die. As with the visual field as Wittgenstein described it,[27] there is the visible Timon, and then elsewhere, later, there is no Timon. The eye cannot check the line between them any more than it can check the border of the visual field. *Timon of Athens* has an oddly Greek feel to it. We seem to be looking at figures in profile, in a frieze. The pattern of a hero humiliated to whom come, in succession, various figures soliciting his aid can be seen in Sophocles' *Philoctetes* and *Oedipus at Colonus,* in Aeschylus's *Prometheus Bound* (if the play is indeed his), and, after Shakespeare's death, in Milton's ultra-Greek *Samson Agonistes. Timon of Athens* is consciously frigid from the opening *paragone,* or "contest of the arts." Instead of dying Timon dissolves, and then re-forms as a succession of monuments, recording his strange, tick-tock life. Imagery of dissolution runs through the play. Perhaps this is enough to justify the inference that the mysterious ending is deliberate. Even the letters incised in stone on the surviving monument are transferred as we watch to a softer medium, as the passing soldier takes their impression in wax. When the good servant departs, he goes "Into this sea of air" (IV.ii.22). Later Timon says, addressing himself,

Then, Timon, presently prepare thy grave;
Lie where the light foam of the sea may beat
Thy grave-stone daily. (IV.iii.377–79)

Later still he says,

say to Athens,
Timon hath made his everlasting mansion
Upon the beached verge of the salt flood,
Who once a day with his embossed froth
The turbulent surge shall cover. (V.i.214–18)

Timon's identity dislimns. It merges first with stone and then with the eroding sea and air. If he remains he remains only in his epitaph—as words. Notoriously it is difficult to set up a murder trial if there is no body as central exhibit. In like manner it is hard to have a tragedy in which the protagonist, as physical being, slips through our fingers before the end comes. The generic status of *Timon of Athens* is a puzzle. *Is* it a tragedy? It is the strangest of Shakespeare's plays.

An Autumn That Grew by Reaping: *Antony and Cleopatra*

Antony and Cleopatra, like *Romeo and Juliet*, shows by its title that it has two main characters not one, and this is already, implicitly, a move against the singleness of focus natural to European tragedy. It is hard to imagine a Greek tragedy called, say, *Theseus and Phaedra*. In *Romeo and Juliet* the double title signalled a negotiation with comic form. In *Antony and Cleopatra* the doubling is the product of a reduplicated metaphysic: the tragedy of a Roman soldier and the tragedy of love. The story of Antony in the play is the story of a political and military leader who fell in love, gloriously and disastrously, with an Egyptian queen. The story of Cleopatra is the story of an erotic free spirit whose life became entangled, gloriously and disastrously, with imperial Rome.

Julius Caesar, *Coriolanus*, and *Timon of Athens* are all Plutarchian plays.

Plutarch himself was a Greek and therefore sees the Romans from outside, as a harshly masculine culture. This immediately sheds a chill on the resulting Roman plays. *Julius Caesar,* compared with, say, *Macbeth,* feels like a black-and-white film. Coriolanus, we sense, might have been fully human but only if he had been born into another culture. As it is he is a titan, a machine, an emotionally stunted child—a *man* perhaps, but never (except for just one instant) a human being. The sense of coldness may be increased by an underlying awareness that these people lived before the birth of Christ. One wishes to speak of an "impoverished" world but the word suggests that things have got worse when the main idea is that on the contrary they are about to get better—and that is what makes the ancients, relatively, poor. Perhaps the right word is "un-enriched." A. C. Swinburne, indeed, thought that the world turned grey with the coming of Christ.[28] It may well be that Shakespeare, as he read his Plutarch, would have thought that the world was grey *before* Christ came to redeem it. Certainly a sense of undernourished humanity fills *Timon of Athens,* which deals with Greeks, not Romans. But in *Antony and Cleopatra* colour suddenly blazes.

The most likely date for *Antony and Cleopatra* is late 1606. It would be nice for my argument if it were the last of the three Plutarchian plays, coming after both *Coriolanus* and *Timon of Athens.* It may well be so. One could then see the play as a planned break-out from an increasingly claus-trophobic Graeco-Roman world. *Julius Caesar* is earlier by several years. If *Coriolanus* is later than *Antony and Cleopatra* we are looking at a temporary gaol-break.

Antony leaves cold, dry, military-political Rome for the wet, formless, erotic East (and South), for Egypt, much as Gustav von Aschenbach in Thomas Mann's novella centuries later would leave the Germany in which he had lived "like a clenched fist" for warmth, love, and death in Venice, itself intensified in Aschenbach's reverie to a tropical, steaming marshland of islands and alluvial channels.[29] It has often been observed that the idea of loss of form or outline pervades the imagery of *Antony and Cleopatra,* from "Let Rome in Tiber melt" (I.i.33) to the marvellous speech about the way we form pictures and lose them when we look at clouds:

Sometime we see a cloud that's dragonish,
A vapour sometime like a bear or lion,

A tower'd citadel, a pendant rock,
A forked mountain, or blue promontory
With trees upon't that nod unto the world,
And mock our eyes with air.

. . . .

That which is now a horse, even with a thought
The rack dislimns, and makes it indistinct
As water is in water.   (IV.xiv.2–7, 9–11)

Antony is describing the loss of his clear Roman identity, an unmanning
and an undoing, in the amniotic fluid of Egypt. Plutarch linked Antony to
two deities, Dionysus and Hercules (Hercules became a deity at his
death). This mythology can serve as a psychological shorthand, as astro-
logical signs do in Chaucer. Dionysus is the god of irrational energy, a
little like William Blake's Los, and Hercules is the strong man who was
brought low by a woman. Shakespeare plays down Dionysus, perhaps
because by his time Dionysus had degenerated into the comic, tipsy
Bacchus (who gets into the play as the pink-eyed,[30] Rubens-like god of
the drinking song at II.vii.114). But Hercules is a powerful, unseen presence. When Antony's fortune begins to slide, mysterious music is heard
under the earth and a soldier says, " 'Tis the god Hercules, whom Antony
loved, / Now leaves him" (IV.iii.16–17). In the old myth Hercules in the
house of Omphale was dressed in women's clothes and made to do
women's work, at the loom. This cross-dressing reappears in Shakespeare's
play when Cleopatra says,

                I drunk him to his bed;
Then put my tires and mantles on him, whilst
I wore his sword Philippan.   (II.v.21–23)

Antony is here "effeminate" in the old meaning of the word according to
which Samson was the most effeminate of men—"subdued and taken
over by a woman." For Antony as he both observes and feels the process it
is dissolution. Dissolution marked the vanishing death of Timon. Yet in
Antony and Cleopatra it entails neither reduction nor annihilation (though
death will come) but an immense expansion of being, an amplification.

The Antony we see in *Antony and Cleopatra* is historically the same man we saw in *Julius Caesar,* but he is now conceived quite differently by Shakespeare. The Antony of the earlier play is emphatically "man of the future" to Brutus's "doomed man of the past." The earlier Antony is a controlled figure who can manage his own deepest passions to political effect. His rhetoric, however, as we saw, is technically "Asiatic"—that is, swelling and exultant.[31] It is likely that Shakespeare knew this rhetorical use of the word "Asiatic" when he wrote *Julius Caesar.* It then becomes not likely perhaps but possible that further rumination on the word in connection with Antony gave him the idea of another play in which the frigidly linear structure of the Roman world could melt, not into nothingness, but into an *Asian* splendour, a sudden huge increase.

The Roman way of life seems, to those living it, to exhaust reality, to be all there is. To such a temperament the full experience of Egypt is very nearly unassimilable. It is a shock of a strangely fundamental kind. That is why I referred to "a reduplicated metaphysic." We saw something of the sort much earlier in Shakespeare's career when, in *A Midsummer Night's Dream,* he set the daylit world against a counter-world of moonlight and imagination. There Hippolyta, so much more intelligent than Theseus, saw a separate coherence in the events of the magical night, a coherence that naturally becomes a truth-claim. In *Antony and Cleopatra* the love-vision of the play, richly coloured though it is, is dreamlike when set beside the grey daylight of Roman politics. Cleopatra, like Hippolyta so many years before, philosophizes. Her metaphysical meditation follows the death of Antony just as Hippolyta's speech follows the passing of the enchanted night of love in the wood. Cleopatra is talking to Dolabella, a high-ranking soldier in the service of Octavius Caesar. As if he wants to remind us of the early comedy, Shakespeare starts the speech with the word "dream":

CLEOPATRA I dreamt there was an Emperor Antony.
  O such another sleep, that I might see
  But such another man!
DOLABELLA   If it might please ye—
CLEOPATRA His face was as the heavens, and therein stuck
  A sun and moon, which kept their course, and lighted
  This little O, th' earth.

DOLABELLA   Most sovereign creature—

CLEOPATRA His legs bestrid the ocean, his rear'd arm
  Crested the world, his voice was propertied
  As all the tuned spheres, and that to friends;
  But when he meant to quail and shake the orb,
  He was as rattling thunder. For his bounty,
  There was no winter in't; an autumn it was
  That grew the more by reaping. His delights
  Were dolphin-like, they show'd his back above
  The element they liv'd in. In his livery
  Walk'd crowns and crownets; realms and islands were
  As plates dropp'd from his pocket.

DOLABELLA   Cleopatra!

CLEOPATRA Think you there was or might be such a man
  As this I dreamt of?

DOLABELLA   Gentle madam, no.

CLEOPATRA You lie up to the hearing of the gods!
  But if there be, nor ever were one such,
  It's past the size of dreaming. Nature wants stuff
  To vie strange forms with fancy: yet t' imagine
  An Antony were nature's piece 'gainst fancy,
  Condemning shadows quite.   (V.ii.76–100)

"I dreamt" at the beginning is self-disparaging, skilfully aimed at Dolabella, who as a virile Roman can be expected to despise women's talk. But as soon as she thinks of Antony, Cleopatra is rapt; her vision takes over and her speech becomes a mounting wave that rolls irresistibly over the attempted interruptions of Dolabella. The energy in the speech is enormous. The "dream" of Antony assumes a colour and strength that will make it indeed a whole world in itself, as strong or stronger than Dolabella's.

As the amplification develops, much as a drowning man is said to see the whole of his past life flash before his eyes, the procession of Shakespeare's oeuvre can be glimpsed, half hidden in the texture of the language. The "dream" and the "moon" are *A Midsummer Night's Dream,* but the moon is no longer opposed to the sun, nor is it the thief of the sun's pale fire as in *Timon of Athens* (IV.iii.438). The moon is set with the sun in a single blazing cosmos. The "little O" is no longer as it was in *Henry V* the Globe Theatre mimicking the world but is instead the earthly element lit by Antony. The legs that "bestrid the ocean" recall the "huge legs" of Caesar in *Julius Caesar* (I.ii.137), but where Caesar was a frail colossus, Antony is entirely majestic. The glorious paradox of an autumn that *grew* (like the speech itself) by reaping may have started from etymology. Shakespeare would have been aware of the etymological link between the Latin *autumnus* or *auctumnus* and *augere,* "to increase." It is in accord with the logic of Cleopatra's speech that the *inner* nature of "autumn," increase, should prevail over and defeat the practical business of (destructive) harvesting. The killer Coriolanus went to work like a harvester (I.iii.36), and Antony has been cut down by the iron swords of Rome, but the inner essence of Antony is still brighter than anything that has happened in the Roman political sphere. The sexual essence of Cleopatra has the same inner fecundity: "She makes hungry / Where most she satisfies" (II.ii.236–37). The ever-growing autumn is followed by the "dolphin-like" delights. Here the subaudition is erotic. The reference to Antony's back, showing like a dolphin's above the wave, can take us to "the beast with two backs," signifying copulation, in *Othello* (I.i.116–17). A couple of years after *Antony and Cleopatra* the word "back" is linked, with sexual reference, to Hercules by Ben Jonson's Epicure Mammon, who desires a back as tough as that of Hercules "to encounter fifty a night" (*The Alchemist,* II.i.144). If there is indeed an erotic nuance in this line, the sea in which the dolphin plunges, over and over, is Cleopatra herself, not too wild a thought in view of the identification of Cleopatra throughout the play with the liquid element.

Cleopatra has social skills. She can see that her experience of splendour is something the honest soldier she is talking to has not experienced and probably never will. So she borrows from the men their minimizing talk of old wives' tales and dreams. But the content of her experience bursts through, as glory. In Hippolyta's corresponding speech the distinctively Shakespearean thing was the hesitation, "but howsoever, strange and admirable" (*A Midsummer Night's Dream,* V.i.27). Any other writer, having come up with an insight as profound as Hippolyta's, would have set about corroborating it. Shakespeare has her immediately question the scope of her own thought. Here in *Antony and Cleopatra* we have, again, a break in the movement of the thought. At first Cleopatra's speech is a crescendo that seems unstoppable as it overwhelms the attempted interventions of Dolabella. But then she stops, focuses on the man standing before her and asks him point-blank whether he thinks the person she has just described ever existed, or ever could. Very politely, Dolabella says, "No." This provokes an explosion from Cleopatra—"You lie!"—followed at once by a recovery of social amenity (almost as if she could agree with Dolabella): "But if there be, nor ever were one such . . . ." After giving him the strident lie direct Cleopatra reverts to the inoffensive mode of hypothesis. Where Hippolyta abruptly acknowledged that the experience of the night was clearly separate from ordinary experience and so a matter for wonder, Cleopatra, more emotionally, makes a last-ditch effort to see the whole thing from the outside, coolly. The word "nor" is especially interesting. We might have expected "or." The First Folio text, the sole authority for this play, gives "nor," but it was changed later to "or" in the Third Folio. I hope "nor" is right. It brilliantly communicates the way her half-embarrassed thought is tripping itself up, so that it falls into a momentary excess of negation.

But then comes, with a strange violence, the full philosophical counterblast. Though nature lacks the means to match the wild fictions of imagination, the mere imagining of an Antony would instantly turn the tables, so that the imagined thing would become "nature's piece," would assume the status of reality. When Hippolyta philosophized I suggested that she was working within an empiricist framework, subverting its associated prejudices from the inside. Your sturdy empiricist is usually clear that mental images are unreal. But Hume, the arch empiricist, was to discover that the only way he could distinguish percepts from images was by the greater "vivacity" of the percepts. Hippolyta, as we saw, placed the main weight of her case on coherence rather than vivacity. But in Cleopatra's speech vivacity, the Humean criterion, does all the work.

Empiricism is the philosophy of experience. If "experience" means "all the things we experience," materialism is not threatened. But if "experience" denotes a sort of private television screen, the perceptual *ideas* immediately before the mind, empiricism melts at once into idealism. This happened openly in the philosophy of George Berkeley. It is as if Shakespeare, long before these developments in "professional" philosophy, smelled out the latent idealism in notions like "coherence" and "vivacity" and became interested in making them the basis of an *objective* idealism. To those who are sure that "good" means more than "what I like," ethics is at once a promising field for objective idealism.

Yet we shiver when something we had thought merely ideal seems to turn real under our hand—and Shakespeare understands that shiver also. Anselm's celebrated ontological proof of the existence of God produces such a shiver.[32] First he obtains assent to the proposition "God is greater and better than we can conceive." Then he points out that a real thing is better than a painting of a thing (a real island, say, is obviously better than a merely notional island). Then he says, in effect, "That means that if God lacked real existence we could 'conceive him greater than he is' by mentally attributing real existence to him. But you conceded at the outset that God is greater than anything we can conceive. Therefore he must already have this 'existence'—he exists." The rabbit jumps out of the hat.[33]

Of course philosophers have objected. Existence, they say, is not a virtue; it is absurd to say, for example, that Mr. Pickwick is a nicer person than Adolf Hitler but Hitler finally is the better man because *he* has real existence. Or they say that Anselm has only shown that if God were to satisfy the definition "greater than we can conceive" he *would have to be* (rather than *now is*) an existent God. Meanwhile many ordinary people find the proposition that a real island is better than a merely notional one oddly persuasive.

The logical hook in Anselm's argument is present in neither of the Shakespeare passages. But the flip-over from ideal to actual is there—and it feels weird—"strange and admirable." Note that Shakespeare, even while he is developing the astonishing thought of Cleopatra, retains sympathy with Dolabella and his "Gentle madam, no." The courteous firmness of his scepticism gives his counterposition its own quiet authority. Perhaps the final effect of this, in juxtaposition with Cleopatra's huge assertion, is to suggest a plural ontology, as happened in *A Midsummer Night's Dream*. Shakespeare, pretty consistently, avoids metaphysical theses beginning with the thrasonical word "All": "All reality is a social construction," "All primary motivation is contextual, not from the individual," and so on. He recoils from the presumptuousness of the unitary system. The world seen by Dolabella is consistent, fully real (*not* "subjective to Dolabella"), and respected by the playwright.

Cleopatra's praise of Antony is a feat of synthesis. We feel as we listen that the great antithesis, Rome versus Egypt, has become in the love-story a reciprocal relation. Cleopatra brings to her panegyric the rich colours of her Egyptian sensibility, but she is describing a great Roman imperialist, a soldier. We become aware that Shakespeare is subtly confounding Roman and Egyptian traits in the latter part of the play. Romans are supposed to be experts in suicide, but Antony bungles his and Egyptian Cleopatra is given the grandest suicide in all drama. "Let's do't," she says, "after the high Roman fashion" (IV.xv.87). Cleopatra, the incarnation of feminine inconstancy of mood, enters the inner sanctum of Roman male-dominated Stoicism with its strange drive to turn human beings into statues:[34]

I have nothing
Of woman in me; now from head to foot
I am marble-constant;   (V.ii.238–40)

But as she puts the Stoic case for despising life and death, she sexualizes it: "The stroke of death is as a lover's pinch, / Which hurts, and is desir'd" (V.ii.295–96). The snake as it bites her becomes the "baby at my breast, / That sucks the nurse asleep" (V.ii.309–10). This dizzy intertwining of male and female tropes might have resulted in humour, in a satirized Roman death. In fact the effect is symphonically powerful. The incongruities are synthesized.

N. K. Sugimura in a subtle essay offers a list of adjectives to describe the Egypt of the play: "the over-abundant," "the fluctuating," "the passionate," "the disorderly" and "the eternal."[35] The surprise word in her list is "eternal," but it is accurate. "Eternity was in our lips and eyes" (I.iii.35). We have already seen in the marriage endings of the comedies Shakespeare drawn to a quasi-Platonic sense of transcendence, marriage itself as a distant yet audible music, high in the air above the faulty persons of the play. The Sonnets that, taken as a sequence, exhibit an erotic life of tormented complexity and change, gesture at times towards the idea that love itself is timeless: "Love's not Time's fool, though rosy lips and cheeks / Within his binding sickle's compass come" (Sonnet 116). This looks more like Cleopatra's version, in that it discovers eternity in love rather than in marriage. But Shakespeare will never keep still. In the sonnet, lips, subject to physical decay, are contrasted with timeless love. In Cleopatra's speech, lips are the proper habitation of love's eternity. This means that the Shakespearean opposition to the Platonic *chorismos,* or separation of the Ideal Forms from the things of this world, is more emphatic in *Antony and Cleopatra* than it was in the sonnet. Similarly, where Plato associates rationality with the eternal Forms, Shakespeare turns rationality into low practical reason and locates it on the Roman side. It is now time-bound, a matter of endless competitive negotiation. Cleopatra is far from innocent, but there is something Arcadian and therefore timeless about their love, as she liberates Antony from the remorseless "and-then-and-then-and-then" of political machination. Spenser's phrase "eterne in mutabilitie" (*Faerie Queene,* III.vi.47) may seem to apply here, but Spenser may simply have meant "continually changing, forever." Cleopatra means more than that: that their love admits them to another order of reality, is in itself wholly independent of historical change. It is the Romans who are associated with clarity of form, with clear definition. That is why Antony feels himself to be melting when his Roman-ness slips from him. For Plato, the lover of geometry, such clarity is the essence of the transcendent form. He is drawn both by philosophic reasoning and, one suspects, by temperament to place the heady turbulence of the erotic life on the other side of the equation, with mere un-meaning flux. But, as Sugimura saw, Shakespeare has effected a profound transformation of Platonism, fusing it with the physical. The lips of the lovers are transfigured.

It might seem that in turning to Egypt Shakespeare found what was needed to expand and enrich a world starved and shrunk by narrowly masculine Roman culture. Certainly Egypt supplies passion and colour in abundance. But something is missing still. What is missing is goodness. Cleopatra's court is a place of dazzling light, entirely destitute of moral warmth. Marilyn French in an early feminist essay argued that Cleopatra represented real moral values, feminine values of warmth and fertility.[36] There is no doubt that imagery of fertility permeates the representation of Egypt in the play. Usually however we find within it a hint of the disgusting: creatures form like maggots in the slime of the fertile Nile (II.vii.24); the primary sexual image of the play is the phallic serpent, a death-bearer. Cleopatra's son by Julius Caesar, Caesarion, is referred to in a curiously remote fashion at III.xiii.162; the union of Antony and Cleopatra, meanwhile, is childless. Here Shakespeare departs from Plutarch—I believe, deliberately.[37] He wanted—not sterility—but a certain blankness to surround this spectacular case of *égoisme à deux*.

If we think for a moment of *Romeo and Juliet* the ethical poverty of the later play will leap out. Early in the twentieth century L. C. Knights persuaded everyone that it was logically absurd to to speculate on the previous lives of persons in drama (he was wrong: all dramatists implicitly rely on such speculation in the audience).[38] I propose now to do something that Knights would have thought even more scandalous, to speculate on the possible alternative *later* lives of two dramatic persons who actually die before our eyes. Romeo and Juliet, had they lived, would have had children and would thereby have helped to heal the dynastic wound that racks Verona. Romeo and Juliet are moral beings. Their death is far sadder than that of Antony and Cleopatra because of this simple fact. In comparison with the young lovers Antony and Cleopatra suddenly seem to be *all* splendour, *all* style.

In the earlier plays we saw a running tension between role-playing and a possible interiority, reaching a climax in *Hamlet*. In *Antony and Cleopatra* Antony feels the loss of public, Roman definition as a loss of identity but never discovers an inward self as Richard II did before he died. There is a strong sense in the play of performance. Antony and Cleopatra are putting on a show for the world to watch and wonder at. This indeed isolates them, and isolates the splendour of their love, but it leaves us with one more spectacle rather than any exciting disclosure of core identity. There is one faint trace in the play of Henry V's conference, incognito, with the common soldiers: "To-night we'll wander through the streets and note / The qualities of people" (I.i.53−54). In the darkness conferred both by night and his disguise Henry was thrown back upon himself and his responsibility. Antony and Cleopatra go out into the dark streets, the public show suspended, but make no such moral discovery. Instead the theatrical dialectic is merely reversed: they become the audience, the people provide the show.

G. Wilson Knight was interested in those moments near the end of Shakespearean tragedy when the protagonist is allowed a glimpse of life beyond the grave.[39] When Lear, near death, was united with Cordelia he felt that they were both entering a site of mystery, were becoming the eyes of God (*King Lear,* V.iii.16–17). But for Antony and Cleopatra the equivalent moment is a pagan spectacle—"Where souls do couch on flowers, we'll hand in hand, / And with our sprightly port make the ghosts gaze" (IV.xiv.51–52). Not so much "We'll be together in heaven" as "We'll make 'em sit up in Elysium." They are playing still—to an audience of ghosts. The word "ghosts," with its alien northern register, falls across the glowing picture like a cold shadow. It is magnificent but it is not warmhearted. Marilyn French's claim for strong female values is unsustainable. W. K. Wimsatt, Jr., came nearer the truth when he argued that the love shown in the play is immoral (though that word is too strong) and that what triumphed was aesthetic.[40] Of course words like "love" and "transfiguration," words I have used, carry a natural charge of value, but Shakespeare seems to have made a point of draining from them everything but splendour. It is technically interesting that it should be possible to write a play in which the hero and heroine are repeatedly humiliated, morally, and are afterwards effortlessly glorified by an infusion of lyric power that would seem cynical were it not so overwhelming.

9 The Last Plays

Thought Suspended: *Pericles* and *Cymbeline*

With *Pericles, Prince of Tyre* we cross a threshold. The last four plays, *Pericles, Cymbeline, The Winter's Tale,* and *The Tempest* are so different from what has gone before that the editors of the *Riverside Shakespeare,* having followed the Folio division into comedies, histories, and tragedies, suddenly create a separate category, at the end of the volume. These are the plays that came to be called "the romances." In a way the move is unnecessary; all are clearly comedies. But they are a special kind of comedy, and that distinctness demands some kind of separate recognition.

Many scholars believe that the first two acts of *Pericles* are not by Shakespeare at all.[1] It is obvious, however, that the greater part of the play, including the brothel scene and the moving recognition scene—the sequence that haunted T. S. Eliot—are unmistakably his. It is possible that Shakespeare was recruited to intervene in the writing—to "save" a play begun by someone else. But it would still be a mistake to suppose that the first two acts, with their apparently primitive episodic movement, can simply be set aside. Obviously if Shakespeare took over the venture he could not have proceeded without a careful reading of what was already on paper. In fact the "cod-medieval" doggerel given to "moral Gower" must always have been in a certain sense sophisticated. In 1608 such writing, by whatever hand, must be consciously primitivist rather than primitive. The childlike character of the narration must have been registered and separately enjoyed. The whole enterprise reflects a mood of cultural nostalgia, but for Shakespeare the nostalgia may have had an extra, personal sting.

At the beginning of his career he had written a romance comedy about children lost at sea but found again at last, a play that drew on the old, originally Greek tale of Apollonius of Tyre. The story of *Pericles* is drawn from the same source. *The Comedy of Errors,* though built on a Plautine model, is not consciously archaic in the manner of the later play. It is a young man's piece, explosive, fast-paced, gymnastically brilliant. But the haunting music of those Greek stories of children lost and found can be heard, and the presence of the sea is felt throughout. These are the deepest things in *The Comedy of Errors,* and it is to these that Shakespeare returns in *Pericles.*

We have seen in the histories and tragedies how Shakespeare gradually reduced the intelligence of the protagonist. Writing for a half-hysterical ironic consciousness like that of Richard II, Shakespeare could show off (young dramatists must be allowed to show off). Such writing provides abundant ammunition for one arguing for Shakespeare's powers as a thinker. When the less intellectual, more passionate figures came along, however, it turned out that there was still plenty of evidence of intellection on the part of the dramatist. But in *Pericles* the primitivist mode set by the opening, though highly conscious and, so far, formally clever, really does have the effect of cutting out exploratory thought. Lytton Strachey notoriously believed Shakespeare's late romances were the work of a man "bored with people, bored with real life, bored with drama, bored in fact with everything except poetry."[2] Strachey's presumption that one can be interested in poetry without being interested in people or real life is absurd. He is however responding, like the Bloomsbury intellectual he was, to a real and sudden suspension of cleverness in Shakespeare's final period. In the romances that follow *Pericles,* however, the liveliness of the poet's intellect starts to break through once more.

The wonder of sea-sorrow and sea-healing, the uncanny quality of these deaths that are no deaths, resembling Christian resurrection yet at the same time wholly natural (for neither the wife nor the daughter of Pericles actually dies in the story), remain in a luminous world of pure feeling. There is no diminution of power. What is going on in the recognition scene in *Pericles* is something better than thinking. Shakespeare's undiminished strength is evident in lines like the belching whale

And humming water must o'erwhelm thy corpse
Lying with simple shells. (III.i.62–64)

Here the adjectives are all good: the gross "belching," then "humming" that evokes vividly the sensation in the ears when one's head is immersed, and then, strangest of the three, "simple." Rough turbulence gives way first to an inhuman half-musical sound and then to the tranquil simplicity of shells at the bottom of the sea, pale, mindless, innocent, powerless, unchanging—a concentrated anti-type of the ghastly procession of incest, storm, and life-threatening childbirth in the world above. This is clearly the poet who will soon write, "Of his bones are coral made / Those are pearls that were his eyes" (*The Tempest,* I.ii.398–99). It will be said that I read too much into "simple." Not so. It is all there. There is intense activity of mind in such writing, and if all mental activity is thinking then Shakespeare is here thinking very hard. But ordinary usage allows us to say that the mind can feel, imagine, and explore echoes as well as think, as if these were different from one another. By that second use of terms, Shakespeare is not thinking here.

The brothel scenes are like a jig planted half-way through a symphony. We are transported back to the frowsy world of *Measure for Measure;* Marina single-handedly destroys the sex industry in Mytilene. Exhibited for sale, she converts one lecherous customer after another to higher thoughts. The bawd and the pander are close to despair. The episode makes excellent theatre. It has the rough hilarity one finds in the scenes carved on medieval misericords, but the hilarity is at the same time something more exalted, a wholly joyous Christian charity shining in a dark place. As in *Measure for Measure* (which could be seen as Shakespeare's play about AIDS), we are made aware of the link between brothels and sexually transmitted diseases:

PANDER We lost too much money this mart by being wenchless.
BAWD We were never so much out of creatures. We have but poor three, and they can do no more than they can do; and they with continual action are even as good as rotten.

PANDER Thou sayest true, there's two unwholesome a' conscience. The poor Transylvanian is dead that lay with the little baggage.

(IV.ii.4–9, 21–23)

There is social realism here mixed with a kind of horror. Boult, the pander's serving-man, is given an "island"[3] in which he challenges the pious form of the sequence: "What would you have me do? Go to the wars, would you? where a man may serve seven years for the loss of a leg and have not money enough in the end to buy him a wooden one?" (IV.vi.170–73). In earlier plays such moments of radical "otherness" are left hanging, unresolved by the surrounding action. When wool-gathering Holofernes told the smart people their mockery of the little play was unworthy of them, when Jack Cade said it was hunger that finally defeated him, the words retain their autonomy, so that we remember them, perhaps uneasily, when the play is over. But Boult is instantly steam-rollered by Marina. Do *anything*, she tells him, but this! The editors of the New Cambridge *Pericles* (1998) make much of the play's "conceptual" concern with good government. But if one thinks for a moment of the way the concept of government is racked in *Measure for Measure* one cannot help seeing that it is here entirely subservient to the easier logic of romance narrative.

Enter upon the squalid scene Lysimachus, Governor of Mitylene. He arrives at the brothel and expresses interest in Marina. She meets lust with virtue and Lysimachus has to back-pedal hard. He hastily explains that if he had been seeking sexual gratification Marina's words *would* have changed his mind (IV.vi.104–5). To say that the speech is unconvincing is to put it mildly. Some editors stoutly maintain that Lysimachus's off-colour chat in the early part of the scene is all a pretence. But one cannot help asking, "Why *did* you come to the brothel if not for sex?" One may clutch desperately at the idea that he is testing them all, but this sits very uneasily with the way he is welcomed on arrival, in familiar terms, by Boult. Clearly he is "known to the management." In *Measure for Measure* we have moments of discomfort that are superficially similar: Mariana's acceptance of Angelo, Isabella's apparent acceptance of the Duke's proposal. But in *Measure for Measure* the discomfort is authentically part of a crackling bonfire of stock conceptions; the collisions are so remorseless that we intuit that they are designed. All works to intensify and sharpen the fierce *thinking* in the play. The shifty Lysimachus, like Duke Vincentio, is to marry Marina at the end. Yet the discomfort of this later marriage is effortlessly absorbed by the romance. There is just one faint signal that Shakespeare knows (as he always knows) what we might be thinking. When Lysimachus tells Pericles that he intends to propose marriage to Marina, he uses, to describe his own planned conduct, the humorously self-deprecating word "sleight" (V.i.261).[4] Hiding somewhere in this word is a confession of the general dodginess of his character. When the Duke in *Measure for Measure* says in effect to Isabella, "And I've got good news for you, sweetheart, you're going to marry *me!*" the harsh incongruity is apparent. In *Pericles* the parallel incongruity is barely registered, still less forced on our attention. Lysimachus *is* good news for Marina because he is an important fellow. This is a comedy after all. The preposterously base behaviour of Lysimachus leads nowhere in the intellectual fabric of the play.

Fear no more the heat o' th' sun,
Nor the furious winter's rages,
Thou thy worldly task hast done,
Home art gone, and ta'en thy wages.
Golden lads and girls all must,
As chimney-sweepers, come to dust.   (*Cymbeline*, IV.ii.258–63)

I first heard these lines when I was about eight years old. They ravished me at once and have haunted me ever since. I knew nothing about Shakespeare. I suppose that if today someone were to ask me, "What is the finest lyric poem in the English language?" I would point to this. And yet I do not understand the lines. Why "chimney-sweepers"? It has been suggested that it is an old word for dandelions. I hope this explanation is wrong. If we think of the shock-headed golden flower the lines are at once more intelligible and more ordinary. I know that my childish mind conjured opposite images, glorious tall "lads and girls" and a grimy, desperate child-worker, Blake's "little black thing."[5] The force of the lyric was in the vertiginous space between the golden people and the sooty figures—all alike ending in death. The violence of the difference threatens the sense of the stanza, but coherence is achieved by the latent but easy association of chimney-sweepers with dust. The association carries the mind from shining life to the dust of the grave at the end. If the sense "dandelion" were proved right I would still want to fight a rearguard action, to say that calling the flower "chimney-sweeper," rather than the metrically identical "dandelion," briefly evokes counter-images of grimy darkness.

This is the dirge from *Cymbeline,* written soon after *Pericles.* It is spoken (not sung) by two brothers over someone believed to be dead but really alive, someone believed to be male but really female. This magnificent lamentation is therefore wasted, it might be thought, on a richly inappropriate object. It will by now be obvious that the old energies of earlier Shakespearean comedy are being reactivated. This in yet another form is the topos of defeated satire; that is, where we expect the incongruity of high imaginings and low, purblind human error to result in a satirical guying of those high imaginings, instead the mistakings on the part of the human agents seem to throw the exalted idea into purer relief. As the music of marriage soared above circumstance at the end of *All's Well That Ends Well,* so here the elegy for all the young people who must die soars above the conditions of its singing.

Pericles, as we saw, shares an important source with *The Comedy of Errors.* It at once goes out of its way to distance itself from the glittering cleverness of the youthful work. The result is a sudden simplicity of mind—stylistically sophisticated, but still simplicity of mind. In *Cymbeline* the "suspension of cleverness" we saw in *Pericles* is beginning to break up. The triple plot is as jazzily complex as was the plot of *The Comedy of Errors* (where Shakespeare doubled the twins of the Plautine source). In *Cymbeline* Shakespeare interweaves three plot-lines: first, the story of Cymbeline's clash with the Roman authorities, taken, freely altered, from Holinshed's Chronicle; second, the story of the wager on the chastity of Imogen, taken from Boccaccio; third, the story of the defence by the heroic few of the narrow pass (carried out in the play by Belarius, Guiderius, and Arviragus) taken again from Holinshed but from the Scottish section (the section he had used earlier for *Macbeth*). This chronological liberty goes some way towards accounting for the appearance in a single play of Roman soldiers under the emperor Augustus and Jachimo, a trendy Renaissance Italian with a strong interest in, first, works of art and, second, seduction. All three plots meet in the extraordinary dénouement. "Dénouement" originally meant "untying" or "disentangling." It is one term in the vocabulary of plotting, all based on the idea of first tying and then untying knots, brilliantly devised by Aristotle in his *Poetics*. In *Cymbeline* the "knot" is one unknown to Lord Robert Baden-Powell, almost crazily complex, so that the final scene of disentangling produces its own secondary hilarity, at a purely formal level. Cymbeline himself is left scratching his head. "I am amaz'd with matter," he says (IV.iii.28), little knowing that far worse is to come (later he says plaintively "New matter still?" V.v.243). The word "amaz'd" holds more clearly than it does today an allusion to mazes, labyrinths.

Reference is repeatedly made in *Cymbeline* to Augustus Caesar. This firmly historical figure is someone we have already met. Octavius Caesar, the cold "man of the future" in *Antony and Cleopatra,* will become Augustus. But the Plutarchian perspective is absent from *Cymbeline*. Instead of looking at Romans through the eyes of a highly educated Greek, we look through the eyes of British Holinshed and his predecessors. The war arises because Cymbeline has not been paying the required tribute to Rome. Modern audiences are puzzled, after watching "the Heroic Defeat of the Many by the Few" (V.ii.11−18, V.iii.18−52), to find that the Romans are not the bad guys in this play. Suddenly at the end it becomes apparent that the war was trivial and that all are friends:

Although the victor, we submit to Caesar,
And to the Roman empire, promising
To pay our wonted tribute, from the which
We were dissuaded by our wicked queen.   (V.v.460−63)

It is as if Oxford United had just beaten Real Madrid three nil but actually knows that it must have been a fluke. The subtext is that the Romans are family. In this very British history there is always a sense in the background of Brutus, the great-grandson of Roman Aeneas, who found his way to Britain and became its first king. Geoffrey of Monmouth, who died in 1155, says that Walter, archdeacon of Oxford, gave him "a certan, very ancient book" that told the history of the British kings from Brutus to Cadwallader.[6] Geoffrey explains that Britain, "best of islands," was virtually uninhabited when Brutus arrived, though rich in forests full of game and rivers teeming with fish (like the happy England with its forests and "plenteous" rivers Lear thought he would give to his daughters at the beginning of the play). There were a few giants, admittedly, but Brutus and his comrades drove them to take refuge in remote mountain caves.[7] Aeneas, the great-grandfather, is vivid to early modern people because of Virgil's *Aeneid,* a standard school textbook. There we are told that Aeneas, who founded the Roman nation, himself came from Troy, after that city was sacked by the Greeks. Michael Drayton re-tells the story in his *Polyolbion* and explains how Brutus repeated the adventures of Aeneas, since he too, though he returned to Troy, was forced in his turn to take to the seas; he found landfall not in Italy, as Aeneas had, but in Britain or Albion.[8] Brutus founded Troynovant, or New Troy, the city we know as London. From Brutus descended such mythically resonant figures as Vortigern, Lud, Arthur, Gorboduc (the king who, like Lear, divided his kingdom), and Cymbeline himself.

In London today the street that runs down from St. Paul's Cathedral is still called Ludgate. Gog and Magog, two giants who first appear in the Bible but who turn up in Geoffrey of Monmouth, conflated as "Gogmagog" and become heavily ancient-British, still stand in effigy in Guildhall. The name "Imogen" (perhaps properly "Innogen") is the name of Brutus's wife in Spenser's *Faerie Queene* (II.x.13). Shakespeare freely shifts names and events but makes sure meanwhile that the line of the old British kings is before our minds:

> So through Lud's-Town march,
> And in the temple of great Jupiter
> Our peace we'll ratify. (V.v.481–83)

Much earlier Cloten speaks of "the gates of Lud's-Town" (IV.ii.99). In this play Posthumus sees a prophetic vision in which Jupiter descends in thunder and lightning, sitting astride the imperial eagle. In the earlier comedies the assumed religion is a strangely innocent "old Christianity," a world in which the Reformation is scarcely visible, a society of kindly abbesses and benevolently ingenious friars. In his romance *Cymbeline,* while the restoration of those thought dead to life may naturally propel our minds to thoughts of Christian resurrection, the given religion is "Romano-British," with the accent on "Romano-." The "resurrections" in the four last plays are none of them truly miraculous raisings-from-the-dead. At no point in this play does Shakespeare seek to remind us of Lazarus as he does in *Henry V* (II.iii.9−10).

Where the atmosphere is not Roman it is Greek. The motif of apparent death is prominent in those Greek romances that had their heyday in the second century A.D. These clearly exert a modifying influence on Shakespeare. Usually we have to think of the Greek material as reaching him through the medium of an intervening Latin version (as with *Apollonius of Tyre*),[9] but Thomas Underdowne's English translation of the *Aethiopica* of Heliodorus had appeared, probably in 1569. Stephen Medcalf sees the sudden growth of apparent death in Greek prose romance and the Christian story of resurrection not as opposed but as allied phenomena. After all, as he points out, they arise together in the Mediterranean world; surely the obvious affinity is the most important thing. Medcalf concedes that there is one great difference: the historical reality of Christ's death on the cross is central to Christianity, but at the same time it is equally crucial to the tone and impact of the Greek stories that the deaths should prove to be unreal. Even if, however, we view the entire cultural phenomenon teleologically, as naturally ripening to the full Christian assertion, this scarcely helps the Christian allegorist's reading of Shakespearean romance. In these plays Shakespeare, from the heart of a fully Christianized culture, is clearly straining towards the Greek end of the spectrum. The movement of his mind is away from the tense engagement with Christian doctrine we saw in *King Lear* and *Measure for Measure* and towards a naturalized version. Resurrection becomes eucatastrophe. Life out of death becomes "We thought them dead but they live." *Cymbeline* is not Lazarus.

The "satire defeated" trope in *Cymbeline* is not the only element that looks like a revival of earlier concerns. The central comedies are notable for their contemptible men and glorious women. Posthumus belongs to the Bassanio-Claudio-Bertram line, and is perhaps the nastiest of the lot. His swift acceptance of the false report of Imogen's unchastity and his attempt to have her killed as a punishment are both disgusting. It may be said that early modern culture could approve of his reaction more readily than our culture can. But Othello took a lot more persuading. I am sure that Shakespeare intended our recoil and that it was always there (but indeed more muffled then than now). Near the end of the play, after Posthumus, having learned the truth about Imogen, has redeemed himself in the eyes of the audience by his abject repentance, he suddenly freezes our blood by striking Imogen (V.v.229). Of course Imogen is still disguised. He thinks he is striking Fidele, the male page. Imogen/Fidele has just broken in upon his speech of desperate contrition and is lovingly eager to set him right. Posthumus, not relishing interruption, strikes her so hard that she falls to the ground. Even when we have reminded ourselves that he does not know whom he is striking, the action is less than lovable. It is not too much to say that it reminds us, very effectively, of the unpleasant fellow we met earlier in the play. In the theatre the elementary fact that we see him hitting a woman has a great effect. The audience is always shocked.

Of course the moment is only a moment. It is swallowed up at once in the enormous happiness of recognition:

IMOGEN Why did you throw your wedded lady from you?
    Think that you are upon a rock, and now
    Throw me again.
POSTHUMUS   Hang there like fruit, my soul,
    Till the tree die.   (V.v.261–64)

Her head is still spinning from the horrible blow he gave her. Imogen's lines express pure joy. They are strongly sexual—the word "throw" may remind us of Rosalind in *As You Like It,* who said to Orlando, "Sir, you have wrastled well, and overthrown / More than your enemies" (I.ii.254–55).

At the same time there is a kind of vertigo in them. They are the last echo in Shakespeare of the "Dover Cliff" episode in *King Lear.* There Edgar, the devil-therapist, urged his blinded father to throw himself from the rock. Here Imogen urges her blind-till-now lover to throw her, his second self, from the rock, knowing that he will not be able to do it. The emotional effect is even greater than that of the blow, moments before. I remember watching Vanessa Redgrave play Imogen. Just after these lines I turned to look at a friend, sitting beside me in the theatre, a man I had always thought of as coldly detached. His face was wet with tears.

So the strand of unpleasantness in Posthumus is a fugitive, background affair. But it is nevertheless there. Naturally he is the anti-type of the disgusting Cloten and this is the dominant chord. But Shakespeare, having registered contrast, then enforces echo. Posthumus and Cloten are eerie doubles. In Act IV, Scene ii, Imogen awakes from her drug-induced trance to find herself lying beside the headless body of Cloten. He is wearing the garments of Posthumus, but Shakespeare seems to make a point of her going beyond the garments to *physical* details in her appalled (pseudo-)recognition of the dead man.

> A headless man? The garments of Posthumus?
> I know the shape of 's leg; this is his hand,
> His foot Mercurial, his Martial thigh,
> The brawns of Hercules;   (IV.ii.308–11)

Surely, we feel, she would have known what Posthumus's hand was like. In *Romeo and Juliet,* another play with a drug-induced trance in it, death changed places with Romeo in the dark. Now, in this late romance, a bizarre mangled double seems to have moved into and taken on the shape of the male lover.

When Posthumus is given his speech of vengeful hatred, believing Imogen unchaste, he says, thinking of their marriage,

> Me of my lawful pleasure she restrain'd,
> And pray'd me oft forbearance; did it with
> A pudency so rosy the sweet view on 't
> Might well have warm'd old Saturn; that I thought her
> As chaste as unsunn'd snow.   (II.v.9–13)

Much depends on whether these words have the status of generalized comment or whether they are "characterized," coloured by the distinctive nature of the individual speaker. I used to take them in the former way. Read thus, they seem to show that Shakespeare moved from the "sexually positive" women of the middle period to another kind of admired woman, a figure in whom purity is uncomfortably fused with something like frigidity. In *As You Like It* Rosalind, clearly loved by the dramatist, describes herself as "more giddy in my desires than a monkey" (IV.i.153–54). Yet Imogen's reluctance to have sexual relations with her husband is here seen as glorious. True, one of Shakespeare's earliest comedies is about the subjection of a resistant woman. *The Taming of the Shrew* may contain occasional hints of specifically sexual domination, but we are light-years away from what is suggested here in *Cymbeline.* In *The Taming of the Shrew* we have, clearly, consensual sex in the conclusion, to which all that went before was a preliminary *game.* Petruchio is not a rapist. Posthumus, we sense, would rather like to be one. It might be thought that the brothel scenes in *Pericles,* with their emphasis on Marina's abstinence, fall into line with this presumed development in Shakespeare. But Marina is in a brothel, an utterly horrible place, and Imogen is married to a husband she loves. Moreover in *The Winter's Tale,* written just after *Cymbeline,* Perdita speaks of Florizel's desire to "breed" by her with a frankness immediately reminiscent of Desdemona. No, the speech is characterized. This is Posthumus speaking, not Shakespeare. Note that when he conjures the memory of the blushing, reluctant Imogen he is sexually excited *by the reluctance.* "Might well have warm'd old Saturn" means "would have been a turn-on to any man, however old." If we listen we shall begin to think that we are learning as much about Posthumus as about Imogen. Later in the same speech vowing vengeance he imagines Jachimo taking Imogen:

> Perchance he spoke not, but
> Like a full-acorn'd boar, a German one,
> Cried "O!" and mounted; found no opposition
> But what he look'd for should oppose and she
> Should from encounter guard. (II.v.15–19)

The language is ugly, relishingly gross. "Full-acorn'd" means "with testicles surcharged with semen." We become uneasily aware that, as his imagination takes fire, Posthumus begins to identify with the hated rival. We have after all just been told that Posthumus was excited by female resistance. So when he says that Jachimo would find the act all the more pleasurable if it included some opposition from Imogen, we recognize the sexual taste and know to whom it properly belongs. It is surely no accident that this speech is reminiscent of a speech by Claudio, uttered in a similar situation, in *Much Ado about Nothing.* "I will write against it," says Claudio (IV.i.56). "I'll write against them," says Posthumus (II.v.32). The weak shrillness of the threat after the preceding violence comes very close to satirizing these two intermittently dreadful young men.

When Shakespeare reverted to myth in *Pericles* he stopped thinking in an explicitly philosophical manner. Of course myth has metaphysical presuppositions. These are the stories, as the Neoplatonist Sallustius observed, "of the things that never were and always are."[10]

But then all statements have metaphysical presuppositions, though we do not normally notice them. *Cymbeline* may seem at first to be as resolutely unreflective as *Pericles,* but there are emerging signs, in this second romance, that Shakespeare was indeed conscious of some of the presuppositions. The quasi-Platonism we detected in earlier comedies is coming through again, in a new form. There is a sense now, not that love or marriage is prior to the persons involved, but that the whole story is somehow there, before it is instantiated in a particular telling. If we stress this priority and make the transcendence absolute we shall find ourselves talking of Christian resurrection. In a way it is predictable that some will do this. But Shakespeare has in these plays interposed signals that direct our minds away from the Christian story to the Greek world of myth.

Arcadia Revisited: *The Winter's Tale*

The Winter's Tale belongs, identifiably, to the same genre as *Pericles.* But we can no longer say that Shakespeare is giving us mythically simplified persons as in *Pericles*—at least in the first half of the play. The opening scenes in which we see Polixenes about to part from his old friend Leontes but persuaded to stay longer by Leontes' wife are dramaturgically at an opposite pole to the rattling episodic narrative provided in the first part of *Pericles.* Suddenly Shakespeare is involved again in psychological complexity. The context is socio-sexual. The full subtlety of these scenes is available only to those who are of a suspicious nature, are ready to guess early in the play that all may not be as it seems. We need in short to be ready to think, "Are the feelings Leontes has for Polixenes partly homosexual?" Modern audiences rarely make the inference, but that is probably because Jacobean English has become difficult to follow. I suspect that if the dialogue were transposed into twenty-first-century idiom, audiences would catch on at once. As far as I know the first person in modern times to detect the substratum of sexual reference was J. I. M. Stewart in his *Character and Motive in Shakespeare* (1949). The first lines in the play are an exchange between two courtiers. They are talking about the beautiful friendship of Polixenes and Leontes, and one of them observes that there is absolutely nothing in the relationship for malice to seize on (I.i.33). The method here is analogous to that of the rhetorical *occultatio*, in which an idea is dropped into the listener's mind and then ostentatiously withdrawn or minimized. Malice is firmly denied any place in the happy scene by Archidamus, but malice has now registered in the mind of the audience. Already we have enough to get suspicion going.

In Act I, Scene ii, we watch Leontes fail in his efforts to detain his friend for a longer stay, after which Hermione succeeds. Before the scene is over Leontes will fall into fit of irrational jealousy and hatred, directed at Hermione. Readers of Freud will already have formed an explanation of this outburst. Leontes cannot bear to see Polixenes (who has almost forgotten anything that might have happened between them years before) responding to an attractive lady, to *his* wife when *he* had got nowhere. The only thing to do with this violent emotion, which cannot be expressed in its primary form, is to project it as guilt, onto Hermione. Leontes is unfaithful in his inmost heart to his own wife. He is angry, here and now, with that same wife. So he gives the infidelity to her. He wildly accuses her of a sexual liaison with Polixenes. But, to be sure, Shakespeare had not read Freud.

Consider now the following exchange:

HERMIONE   Come, I'll question you
Of my lord's tricks and yours when you were boys.
You were pretty lordings then?
POLIXENES   We were, fair queen,
Two lads that thought there was no more behind
But such a day to-morrow as to-day,
And to be boy eternal.

HERMIONE   Was not my lord
   The verier wag o' th' two?
POLIXENES We were as twinn'd lambs that did frisk i' th' sun,
   And bleat the one at th'other. What we chang'd
   Was innocence for innocence; we knew not
   The doctrine of ill-doing, nor dream'd
   That any did. Had we pursu'd that life,
   And our weak spirits ne'er been higher rear'd
   With stronger blood, we should have answer'd heaven
   Boldly, "Not guilty"; the imposition clear'd
   Hereditary ours.
HERMIONE   By this we gather
   You have tripp'd since.
POLIXENES   O my most sacred lady,
   Temptations have since then been born to 's: for
   In those unfledg'd days was my wife a girl;
   Your precious self had then not cross'd the eyes
   Of my young playfellow.   (I.ii.60–80)

The dominant chord here is innocence, the exact opposite of everything I have been insinuating. The timeless boys, the lambs look back to ancient pastoral even as they anticipate the a-sexual vision of Wordsworth's *Prelude*. But the passage is polyphonic. There are other strains to hear, of an opposite character. If we listen to Hermione we are admitted at once to an unexpected (but lively) train of thought. The situation is a little like that we saw earlier in *A Midsummer Night's Dream* where Theseus, in dialogue with Hippolyta, is given the big speech that will get into the anthologies but Hippolyta is given the subtle, exploratory lines. A good rule of Shakespearean criticism might be, "Always listen to the lady." Hermione's tone is teasing. In effect she is saying, "What did you two get up to when you were boys?" "Tricks" is a word of low register. "Pretty lordings" would have triggered homosexual thoughts in the author of *Dido Queen of Carthage* and perhaps in others too.

Polixenes first reacts by setting against Hermione's "low" register a tone, in his reply, both friendly and lyrically exalted. But Hermione refuses to be drawn onto the higher plane. "Verier wag" keeps up the implication of "tricks," earlier. In answer Polixenes offers a strikingly emphatic assertion of innocence. Obviously he feels the presence of a suggestion that requires strenuous denial. The language of the denial is authentically beautiful, but it very nearly ends in hysterical overstatement. "The imposition clear'd, / Hereditary ours" is virtually meaningless to modern audiences. Polixenes is claiming that if they had died in boyhood they could truly have described themselves as wholly without sin—free even of original sin, inherited from the fall of Adam. This is an extraordinary thing to say. It at once marks the speaker as off-balance. Hermione is obstinately unimpressed: "By this we gather / You have tripp'd since." Polixenes eagerly responds by pointing out that that of course they fell later—along came Hermione for Leontes and his own future wife. The reply makes it clear that Polixenes had been thinking about naughtiness (or sin) in relation to sex and that he assumed that Hermione had been thinking along similar lines. It is a relief for him, placed as he is, to be able to confess sexual sin now that the context is firmly heterosexual. A certain judge in a British court once commended a re-offending child molester for beginning to abuse little girls instead of little boys. It was, said the judge, "a move in the right direction." Polixenes, who evidently feels harassed, thinks he can make a move "in the right direc-tion." The result is the oddly discordant gallantry of "your precious self" and the rest. Hermione does not spare him. She immediately rebukes him (humorously) for his "compliment." What sort of a compliment is it to be described as a source of sin?

Polixenes is not like Leontes. For him whatever happened is a remote half-memory. For Leontes it is present crisis. There are further hints of a secret life attached to Leontes scattered through the play. When Leontes learns that Polixenes has fled the court by night, he asks, "How came the posterns / So easily open?" (II.i.52–53). The lord explains that the gates were opened after dark on Polixenes' authority, and adds that they have often been opened by night on Leontes' authority, also. Leontes' reply is interesting: "I know't too well" (II.i.55). The moment flashes past, but an audience used to the customs of walled cities has time to ask, "Why has Leontes had the gates opened by night?" Leontes' rueful response seems to suggest that the action was discreditable in some way. The moment is like that in *Measure for Measure* when Lucio starts gossiping wildly about the Duke's unofficial sex life, "He knew the service," and so on (III.ii.119–20), but in *The Winter's Tale* the effect is fainter.

What has happened here? Shakespeare is thinking again about pastoral, a genre he had explored in *As You Like It*. He is now joining the doctrine of pastoral to his comedic theme of same-sex bonding replaced by heterosexual marriage. He can make the link by way of the enormous stress on innocence and childhood that lies at the heart of traditional pastoral. The sheep-shearing scene is the big formal pastoral of the play, but Polixenes' reference to lambs places his speech as part of a pastoral pattern. Christianity has a story of a lost green place of innocence, the Garden of Eden. In most versions of the story (though not in Milton's) sexuality and sin enter together with the eating of the apple. This is the end of innocence. The Latin poet Virgil in his eighth pastoral Eclogue wrote about apple-picking: "In our orchard I saw you when you were small picking dewy apples with your mother (I showed you the way). I was thirteen and could now reach the fragile branches. As I saw, I died. Sin carried me away." Adolescent love is here both beautiful and disastrous—a kind of death. It too, in that other less famous orchard, is the end of innocence.

Polixenes' ill-judged compliment, "Well of course sin began when you delicious girls came along," is like a distorted echo of Virgil's wonderful lines. The presumption is that what preceded heterosexual love is itself luminously without sin. Shakespeare as we have seen has long been interested in the possible intensity of that same-sex bonding that marriage will later eclipse. What if heterosexual union is naturally preceded not by asexuality but by something that is sexual, but in a different way? Suddenly the deep retrospective comfort offered by the pastoral myth is withdrawn. Leontes gazes hungrily at the innocent blue eyes of his little son, hoping that the sight will cure the black thoughts "that would thick my blood" (I.ii.136, 171). As he seeks to lose himself in the child, he remembers himself when young, his "dagger muzzled, / Lest it should bite its master" (I.ii.155–56). "Dagger" may carry phallic overtones. If we accept these, the self Leontes imagines is a not asexual; rather sexual energy is present but impeded, so that the subject of that activity may avoid hurt. The blood-thickening thoughts are now appearing on the wrong side—the child's side—of the equation. There is no sense, I think, that children can be both sexual and innocent as there is in Longus's *Daphnis and Chloe*.

It may seem that Shakespeare has poisoned his pastoral myth at its root.

In the play taken as a whole the myth of love followed by loss and restoration prevails. The eucatastrophe transcends and erases the murky complexities of the play's first half. Leontes repents of his insane jealousy, and we forget its source in our joy that the wife he thought dead is alive and well. But he never got his son back. Mamillius, the little boy, really died (the casualties in this comedy are surprisingly numerous). But he does find Perdita, the daughter he had lost.

Indeed the structure of the play is broken-backed, or at least painfully double. Sixteen years elapse between the first action and the second. The violence of the division is uncomfortable, but in Shakespeare's hands the very awkwardness of the transition becomes a source of excitement. He does this by a technique of overlapping. The pivotal line of the play, the point at which we turn from the story of loss to the story of renewal, comes in Act III: "Thou met'st with things dying, I with things new-born" (III.iii.113–14). We are on the non-existent sea-coast of Bohemia and a storm is blowing itself out. As in the other romances, people are divided in storms at sea before they can come together at the end. A shepherd is talking to his rustic friend, the "clown." The clown tells of the horrors of the shipwreck he has just witnessed, but the shepherd has just found the infant Perdita, left behind by Antigonus, wrapped in a rich cloth. This is the beginning of the second, ascending movement of the play, the point at which grief gives place to joy. So far, so predictable. What, however, is distinctively Shakespearean is the overlapping of the comedic tone, laid over the still unfinished tragic business. The shipwreck and the death of Antigonus are unfolded in *comic* tempo: "Now the ship boring the moon with her mainmast, and anon swallow'd with yest and froth, as you'd thrust a cork into a hogshead. And then for the land-service, to see how the bear tore out his shoulder-bone, how he cried to me for help, and said his name was Antigonus, a nobleman. But to make an end of the ship, to see how the sea flap-dragon'd it; but, first, how the poor souls roar'd, and the sea mock'd them; and how the poor gentleman roar'd, and the bear mock'd him. . . . The men are not yet cold under water, nor the bear half-din'd on the gentleman" (III.iii.91–107).

Rationally this tone makes no sense. "Musically" it is electrifying. A lurching, earthy rustic dance, with a bear and a gentleman that seem to have stepped straight out of a nursery-rhyme book, is afoot before the ascent into happiness has properly begun. The storm has scarcely finished its work of killing, and yet we sense joy in the wind. "The red blood reigns in the winter's pale" (IV.iii.4).

In the great formal pastoral of Act IV Perdita, believing herself to be a simple country girl, is unconsciously noble, is "queen" of the feast. The sentence I have just written is already buzzing with the oxymoron endemic in pastoral, that genre that exalts nature above art but is itself irremediably artful. When Duke Senior in *As You Like It* praised the brute, prelinguistic truth of wind and rain in mannered language, he almost became a figure of fun. Here, in *The Winter's Tale,* Shakespeare is beginning to think again about nature and our images of nature. Perdita's simplicity is in a way belied by unseen circumstance, but she is in no sense ridiculous. The rustic game that requires her to play the part of queen may seem naive, untainted by "art" in the bad sense. In fact Shakespeare has transposed his own theatrical art to the far side of the glass screen that divides the simple people from the fallen, conscious, pastoral poet. Centuries before, Virgil, as we saw, invented a second self, Tityrus, who was a simple shepherd and yet a singer of songs, a player upon the pipe. As soon as Tityrus touches his flute, to "teach the woods to re-echo the name of fair Amaryllis" (Eclogue 1), we know that art has begun to interpenetrate nature, innocent till now. So with Perdita's "performance." If the myth of simplicity were to hold, Perdita's "queen" would be inept, unrealistic. But she is completely elegant, as linguistically adept as Duke Senior himself. To be sure Shakespeare avoids in the case of Perdita the outright collision between the overt disparagement and the simultaneous employment of art. Perdita's graceful language of queenly welcome is not offered as a specimen of artlessness but is on the contrary intentionally courteous. This only means, however, that the implied collision has moved to another place. "Court" is the natural antithesis of country, so "courtesy" is already implicitly anti-pastoral. In like manner the society proper to pastoral is egalitarian and communist. The people of the Golden Age took what they wanted from the common store.[11] Perdita herself enunciates the antimonarchical, anti-aristocratic principles of pastoral when she says,

The self-same sun that shines upon his court
Hides not his visage from our cottage, but
Looks on alike.   (IV.iv.444–46)

This speech follows the shattering of the idyll. Florizel began the scene by assuring Perdita that he would marry her despite the great difference in rank between them. But by this point Polixenes, Florizel's father, has condemned the match and stormed out. That is why Perdita's graceful courtesy is momentarily replaced by a direct assertion of pastoral values.

There is a remedy to hand, but it may not please everyone. Perdita is graceful in her performance as "queen" because she really is of noble birth, although she does not know it. The pretence reveals a truth. The comedy ending in which Perdita can after all marry Florizel would not feel satisfactory to the early modern audience—would not be a completely happy ending—if Perdita had not turned out to be a princess. The obvious courtliness of Duke Senior's language cast a shadow of mockery on his pastoral sentiments. Perhaps more deeply the fundamental nobility of Perdita—its obvious importance in the eyes of all—leaves the pastoral vision looking frail and insubstantial.

Yet, when all this is said, the lines about the same sun shining on palace and cottage can linger in the mind. It is as if, in another place and time, they might have carried more weight. We associate communism with Karl Marx and revolution. But communism—that is, the imagined abolition of private property—before the mid-seventeenth century, in More's *Utopia,* say, or in monastic institutions or in poetry about the lost Golden Age, isn't revolutionary at all. Auden was right to see the Arcadian as the reverse of political. The common store, the equality, are palpably impracticable, a retrospective dream. But the dream is beautiful and can beckon from afar. The effect of Perdita's words is more poignant than ridiculous.

The sheep-shearing scene is full of flowers:

> daffadils,
> That come before the swallow dares, and take
> The winds of March with beauty; (IV.iv. 118–20)

But all these flowers, Perdita explains, are absent from the scene, which is set not in spring but at the time when the warmth of summer is giving place to a growing coldness. This wealth of imagery, these armfuls of notional flowers, are all governed by an initial "Not." These, Perdita explains, are the flowers she *would have* lavished on them if she had been able to do what was fitting. Human language and human art are capable of referring by symbols to absent objects. The alarm calls of birds, say, may look like language but are not truly so, because they are emitted only when danger is present. Thus Perdita, in her verbal conjuration of these ravishing images, is engaged in something "deep" pastoral naturally shrinks from—re-presentation, "saying the thing that is not," art, not nature. As Tityrus in Virgil brought the taint of art with him when he taught the woods to re-echo the name of Amaryllis, so Perdita teaches the poor gillyvors she has in her hand to re-echo the flowers of spring. Yet the content of the pretence—flowers—is in itself pastoral! The actual country scene in which her speech occurs cannot, then, be itself a practical demonstration of simplicity. Indeed it is instinct with tension, with oxymoron (as written pastoral always is). This does not mean that the pastoral celebration of nature must necessarily die the death of a thousand qualifications.

It is fashionable today to treat pastoral as a spectacularly formalist genre, as utterly artificial. I insisted earlier that the landscape in Virgil's *Eclogues* glows, as mere form never could. In *The Winter's Tale* the flowers, the shepherds, and their flocks, however ironized by intruding art, glow in the mind afterwards. If the direct beauty of nature is eliminated from pastoral, the pathos arising from the tension of that beauty with art would instantly drain away. Good readers of poetry, remembering *The Winter's Tale* after an interval of time, always see Perdita as the flower-girl and the scene as full of sensuous splendour. They are not wrong. Something similar happens with reference to the politics of pastoral. Learned commentators heap up evidence for early modern approval of patriarchy, but it is immediately clear if one stands back and allows the plays to settle in one's mind that Shakespearean comedy is on the side of young lovers, against harsh fathers. *Before* the dénouement brings home to us the real high birth of Perdita we know that she, not the forbidding Polixenes, is the focus of sympathy in the sheep-shearing scene.

Suddenly Shakespeare is thinking hard:

PERDITA Sir, the year growing ancient,
   Not yet on summer's death, nor on the birth
   Of trembling winter, the fairest flowers o' th' season
   Are our carnations and streak'd gillyvors

(Which some call Nature's bastards). Of that kind
   Our rustic garden's barren, and I care not
   To get slips of them.
POLIXENES   Wherefore, gentle maiden,
   Do you neglect them?
PERDITA   For I have heard it said,
   There is an art which in their piedness shares
   With great creating Nature.
POLIXENES   Say there be;
   Yet Nature is made better by no mean
   But Nature makes that mean; so over that art
   Which you say adds to Nature, is an art
   That Nature makes. You see, sweet maid, we marry
   A gentler scion to the wildest stock,
   And make conceive a bark of baser kind
   By bud of nobler race. This is an art
   Which does mend Nature—change it rather; but
   The art itself is Nature.
PERDITA   So it is.
POLIXENES Then make your garden rich in gillyvors,
   And do not call them bastards.
PERDITA   I'll not put
   The dibble in earth to get one slip of them;
   No more than were I painted I would wish
   This youth should say 'twere well, and only therefore
   Desire to breed by me.   (IV.iv.79–103)

At first the sub-reference of this dialogue is social class, but before it is
over the argument has become metaphysical. The love of Florizel and
Perdita in her simple guise is threatened and will be blown apart before
the scene is over. Florizel is anxious from the start about Perdita's low
birth (as he supposes). He tries to deal with his distress and what he
imagines hers must be by Platonizing pastoral; that is, he gallantly turns
her into the Ideal Form of her role as distributor of flowers: "No shepherdess but Flora," the goddess of flowers (IV.iv.2). He is then given a
wonderful speech about the gods taking on the form of beasts in order to

have intercourse with mortal women—a speech that successfully captures the alien, august splendour of ancient religion—so that it is a shock to realize that he is trying to cheer Perdita up: "It's OK—if gods can descend so far for sex, surely I can do the same?" As with Polixenes' reply to Hermione earlier, the gallantry is off-key. Here, when Polixenes speaks of grafting one kind of plant upon another, the audience will at once begin to think of human mésalliance.

Optimistic persons, eager for the happy ending, may think, as Polixenes extols the mixing of stocks, that he will welcome the idea that his son should marry a shepherdess. Certainly, Polixenes is not arguing from hybrid vigour (mongrels are healthy, pure-bred bulldogs wheeze). Rather, he notices how the progeny from low and high stocks can take after the higher. That is what he sees as gain. At the same time, however, his readiness to consider cross-breeding at all is in marked and ironic contrast with his behaviour at the end of the scene. When Perdita resists his suggestion this is comically at odds with her interest, but it may well be that Shakespeare expects her allegiance to pure descent to register as instinctively, deeply virtuous (a little like her nobility showing through elsewhere). There is no escaping the fact that early modern people actually believed, 90 percent of the time, something hardly anyone believes today: that noble persons are actually better than ignoble. This is somehow compatible with complete and unembarrassed clarity on, for example, the contemptible characters of certain kings.[12]

Perdita says she is against gillyvors because they are duplicitous, as the streaks on their petals betray. Art, she says, has been admitted to work alongside nature. That, she thinks, is reason enough to reject them. Polixenes in reply, in effects, asks, "What is nature?" Now the dialogue becomes metaphysical. Nature, he suggests, simply means, "What really happens." We may say that trees grow naturally while houses are artificial constructions, but surely it comes *naturally* to *Homo sapiens* to be ingenious, to build and contrive? In which case, houses are nature too. We may contrast wild roses with horticultural blooms, but horticulture is also something human beings do—naturally. Polixenes cunningly suggests that although Perdita speaks reverently of "great creating Nature," she has underestimated the scope of nature's power: *everything* that actually happens is natural. It is a clever move on his part, and Perdita's first reaction is to submit to its force. But then, without fully articulating the ground of her dissent, she breaks out in direct rebellion: "I *won't* plant them," she says in effect, "anymore than I would wish Florizel to love me for my lipstick rather than my lips."

Her words forcibly remind us of a distinction we all usually accept, though it is not allowed by Polixenes' philosophy of nature. The implication of the reply might be unpacked by a modern philosopher in the following way: "You say art is nature too as if that abolished the distinction we all commonly employ. To make nature cover everything that happens is simply to empty the word of any useful content. Meaning thrives on difference and distinction. Everyone knows at once that rosy cheeks can be natural while rouged cheeks are not. My use of terms is vivid because it affords real purchase on things and people in the world." And if Polixenes persisted in his challenge, she might say, "Interference by conscious intellect counts as artifice, and the fact that conscious intellect may itself be the product of evolution need not dislodge this entirely useful distinction."

I am putting some very alien terminology into Perdita's mouth. But it is hard to account for the feeling that she has "won" without some such exercise. She is of course the voice of deep pastoral, in her insistence on the profoundly antithetical relation between nature and art. Polixenes, conversely, as might as have been predicted from his maleness and gravity, speaks with the voice of Stoicism. We noticed earlier that, for Stoics, to follow nature and to follow reason are one and the same, whereas for pastoral poets they are opposed.

The amazing climax of *The Winter's Tale* in the statue scene depicts a triumph of nature over art. The ingenious effigy from the hand of Julio Romano (V.ii.97) turns out to be the real, living Hermione, older, her face lined and entirely natural. Paulina, who is impresario of the episode, speaks at first in the accents of the mystagogue or even of the fairground huckster, pausing at one point to warn persons watching not to touch— the paint may not be dry (V.iii.46–47, 81). But as she speaks, her utterance is strangely transfigured: a serious natural beauty replaces the dexterous showmanship.

> Music! awake her! strike!
> 'Tis time: descend; be stone no more; approach;

Strike all that look upon with marvel. Come;
I'll fill your grave up. Stir; nay, come away;
Bequeath to death your numbness; for from him
Dear life redeems you.   (V.iii.98–103)

The new serious music begins with the word, "Come." The heady talk of dangerous magical powers (V.iii.91) is replaced by a poetry adequate to the far more moving fact of Hermione herself. *The Winter's Tale* belongs to the period of candlelit production in a more intimate theatre where the audience had come to expect wonders, transformations wrought by cunning devices. Shakespeare here throws the process into reverse. He denies the audience the miraculous resurrection they expect and gives them, simply, an older woman, a woman who never died but was alive all the time—and this, as it happens, is the greatest wonder of all.

Formalist literary thought in the late twentieth century liked to assert that realism was itself a tissue of conventions. Often the argument rested on no more than a demonstration of the conventional character of the means of representation. Language itself is a conventional system but it is meanwhile obvious that the system can convey reality. "Where is the post office?" says *A. B* answers, "Take the second turning on the right." *A* does so and finds the (real) post office. Of course the conventions of realist fiction exist and are historically variable. But it would be absurd to conclude that realism has nothing to do with reality. On the contrary, the realistic writer is obliged to consult the real world with a special care. Things that would not be there, would not occur, are excluded. *The Winter's Tale,* indeed, is not an ordinary realist text. It is "marvellous realist." The central drive of the play is to present a marvellous thing that could (just) happen. That is why the characters repeatedly exclaim that what they see happening is amazing, incredible, and so on (for example, V.iii.116). Such exclamations are read straight by naïve critics as plain information: "This actually *is* an incredible story—and must therefore be treated as pure caprice." In fact such exclamations are a trope of realism. In fairy-tales the ogres and the wizards are simply given, by the unrealistic narrative mode. No one in the story stops and scratches his head on being told that an ogre lives at the top of the beanstalk. It is the kind of thing *we* everyday people would do.

Of course the statue scene, within the play, is presented, aggressively, as utterly theatrical. But this very theatricality proves to be a mere paper screen, to be torn asunder by natural fact. Paulina says at V.iii.90–91 that it may seem that her (very theatrical) magic is diabolical—but denies that it is so. Jonathan Bate in his admirable analysis of the episode says that the play as a whole proclaims that the statue turning into Hermione is, in implicit contrast with the dubious arts of Prospero in *The Tempest,* wholly lawful magic, and seeks to identify it with the magic of the dramatist's art in making the play.[13] To this, I answer, "No, because it is not magic at all." I grant that immediately after "Bequeath to death your numbness" Paulina says, "You hear my spell is lawful" (V.iii.105). But she says it smiling because everything is now changed. After the earlier mystagogic thunder, "It is requir'd / You do awake your faith" (V.iii.94–95), and the authentic exultation of "You perceive she stirs," Paulina relaxes, and her words are now laced with humour (she rallies Leontes on his failure to embrace Hermione at once). "My spell is lawful" could almost be, in modern punctuation, "My 'spell' is lawful." Paulina is saying that now no one need have any worries about illicit magic because Hermione is here. Similarly Leontes'

O she's warm!
If this be magic, let it be an art
Lawful as eating.   (V.iii.109–11)

exorcizes the idea of magic with things as familiar as bread and butter.

In a way Bate knows all this. He says the art is lawful because it is "not really an animation or a resurrection."[14] But he continues to assert that the play as a whole is analogous to the art of the sculptor, Julio Romano, and to the theatrical art of Paulina. *The Winter's Tale* itself, then, is lawful magic. I suspect that he feels impelled to say this because of the pressure of formalist theory, which has trained him to notice that the work is itself a complex of artful conventions. Obviously *The Winter's Tale* is fiction; obviously the text is entirely composed of words. But the symbolic system can direct us to reality. *A* found his way to the post office. Theatrical fictions can direct the mind to real aspects of the world (as Aristotle put it, "the kinds of things that would happen," *Poetics,* 1451a37). *Romeo and Juliet* is not about "love"; it is about love. When Bate says that "Paulina's art . . . stands in for Shakespeare's" and that the final scene of the play "seems to offer an art like Pygmalion's, 'surpassing the perfection of Nature,'" he implicitly destroys Shakespeare's ending by loftily pointing out to the dramatist that his strong distinction between art and nature evaporates when we remember that *The Winter's Tale* is itself a play.[15] Shakespeare's art indeed makes all, but this is an art in express opposition to the arts depicted within the story. Poetry can do this too. It can point away from itself to things that could really be. Milton's dubious poet-magician acknowledged that poetry need not always be a sweet intoxication: "Such sober certainty of waking bliss / I never heard till now" (*A Masque*, 262–63).

We have reached a position in curious symmetry with that taken by Polixenes earlier. Where Polixenes said, "Surely everything is nature," the modern critic says, "Everything is art." Shakespeare in his early comedies saw at once how the formal character of utterance can usurp our attention, and produced a dazzling series of self-referential jokes on the subject. Such textual self-reference is treated with reverence by modern critics, as disclosing a deep "truth-against-truth." For Shakespeare it was something he soon outgrew. Of course he continues to emphasize theatricality, but over and over again, the theatricality is made to serve as a foil to something other than it.[16]

I have said that *The Winter's Tale* is in a way broken-backed: a psychologically fraught complication answered, on a wholly different level, by mythic eucatastrophe. But Shakespeare allows the dark anxieties of the first part to be felt in the midst of the happiness at the end. A shadow of perversity pursues Leontes to the end. *Quisque suos patimur manes.*[17] Leontes, reunited with his lost daughter, begins—or seems to begin—to be attracted by her *sexually*. He says to Florizel, the young and entirely appropriate lover of Perdita, that he wouldn't mind borrowing his girlfriend for the evening. He is at once sharply rebuked by Paulina (whose function it is to keep everyone in order): "Your eye hath too much youth in't" (V.i.225). She urges him to keep his mind on his lost wife, Hermione. Leontes answers that he thought of Hermione even as his eye strayed—and the audience can think, "How sweet!" But the relief is somehow incomplete. Ovid's story of Pygmalion lies behind the play. Pygmalion made an image of a woman, kissed it and caressed it, dressed and undressed it, and laid it in a bed (*Metamorphoses,* x.257–69). He made a sex doll. There is a trace of this in *The Winter's Tale* when Leontes wants to kiss what he believes is the hand of a statue (V.iii.46). Again Paulina cuts in to stop him. Boyhood homosexuality, incest, and agalmatophily are all different of course, but all would have been thought of as perversions in 1610. Shakespeare, with the lightest of touches, is merely keeping our anxiety alive.

Is the ending of *The Winter's Tale* in any sense religious? The Christian word "resurrection" arises in the mind of almost everyone who sees the play. When the statue moves, Paulina says, "Dear life redeems you" (V.iii.103). "Redeems" is charged with all the power of Christ's death and resurrection, saving sinners (people like Leontes). But, as "magic" is countered by ordinary "eating," so "redeems" is countered within the line by "life." Leontes is not, then, redeemed by a suffering God, but by life— not even "Life" with a capital "L" but ordinary life. People of strong faith will always see the hand of God in such sequences and will therefore wish to say that, on another level, Christ *is* redeeming Leontes; that is why, they urge, Shakespeare has chosen to use the religious word in this line. Per- haps, however, it makes better sense to say that Shakespeare used the word "redeems" because he wished to make it clear that he was moving the conception to a new location. The drive to lift the play from the expected supernatural frame of reference to a natural glory is consistent and strong. Is not the play concerned to teach us that redemption can come from a warm, living body?

Brave New World: *The Tempest*

In the television series *Star Trek* Captain Kirk of the starship *Enterprise* says, "Are you feeling emotion, Mr. Spock?" Spock, as his ears show, is not from our planet but from Vulcan. Captain Kirk has come to know and value his remorselessly logical approach to life. Hence his surprise at what looks, for the moment, like human emotion manifesting itself in the Vulcanian. In *The Tempest* Prospero says to Ariel,

Hast thou, which art but air, a touch, a feeling
Of their afflictions, and shall not myself,

One of their kind, that relish all as sharply
Passion as they, be kindlier mov'd than thou art?   (V.i.21–24)

Ariel is not of our world but is a mysterious electrical being. Prospero
thought he understood this inhuman creature but is brought up short by a
sense that Ariel might be feeling pity. The passage is reminiscent of the
point at which Hamlet, seeing a tear on an actor's cheek, is aghast at his
own lack of passion (II.ii.551–69), but the idea has now been transposed
to a systematically unfamiliar world. Shakespeare, in this, the last play
completely from his hand, is inventing science fiction. Nicholas Nayfack's
science fiction film *Forbidden Planet* (1956) is a version of *The Tempest*.
Classic science fiction, as written by H. G. Wells, gives us alternative
worlds in which things we have never experienced are imagined in cir-
cumstantial detail. When we watch *A Midsummer Night's Dream* we know
what Puck is at once. He is a tricksy sprite, the familiar Robin Goodfellow of folklore. Ariel is obviously in certain respects Puck rewritten,
but a fundamental change has taken place. We do not know what he is.
He is that thing that becomes normal in science fiction, a vividly imagined being for which no covering concept is readily available.

Other things contribute to our sense of incipient science fiction. Prospero is a magician, which may seem to link him to *A Midsummer Night's
Dream,* but Prospero is the new sort of magician, a fashionable, dangerous
figure, like the real-life Dr. John Dee (with a touch perhaps of the Italian
"natural magician" Giambattista della Porta). It is a matter of history that
in the course of the seventeenth century these magicians gradually turned
into scientists. Isolated eccentrics trying to turn base metals into gold
found themselves engaged in serious metallurgy and soon, encouraged by
Francis Bacon, formed committees and pooled results. Prospero in gaining control of Ariel is, as I have hinted, harnessing the power of electricity.
This sounds like nonsense, but there is a grain of truth in it. We are told
how Ariel "flam'd amazement" in the ship's rigging (I.ii.198). There is an
allusion here to the prose account of the wreck, in the Bermudas, of the
Sea Adventure and, in particular, to St. Elmo's fire, an electrical phenomenon associated with tropical storms. The magician-scientist Prospero has
made the spirit of air and fire his servant. If one begins from the other end
and works backwards from H. G. Wells, the genre of science fiction can

be shown to derive from earlier Utopias and Dystopias, such as the final voyage to the land of the Houyhnhnms of Swift's Gulliver. Shakespeare carefully plants a miniature Utopia in Act II, Scene i: Gonzalo's communist commonwealth (II.i.144–65). This facetiously offered ideal state is in some ways familiar to us. It has some of the characteristics of the pastoral Golden Age (no work, food abundant). We saw earlier[18] how the Golden Age is the Good Place for those who instinctively locate happiness in the past, while the New Jerusalem is the Good Place for those who place happiness in the future. W. H. Auden famously called the latter party Utopians;[19] the Utopians, unlike the Arcadians, are political activists, straining towards an as yet unrealized goal. In Gonzalo's speech we can watch the glowing Golden Age of Virgil take on a political character, as it is made the basis of a plan to colonize new territory.

Much—perhaps too much—has been made in recent criticism of reference to America in *The Tempest*. Certainly the island is placed firmly in the Mediterranean, somewhere off the north coast of Africa. But at the same time we have references to the Bermudas, and when Caliban is called an "Indian" we are surely to think of an American rather than an Asian Indian. The distances invoked are not Mediterranean. They are oceanic, super-Atlantic; the Queen of Tunis can have no word from Naples "till new-born chins / Be rough and razorable" (II.i.249–50). The play undoubtedly draws on accounts of Atlantic voyages, including one that Shakespeare read before publication.[20] Curiously, as Prospero's words to Ariel find an echo in Captain Kirk's to Spock, so Ariel's phrase, "the still-vex'd Bermoothes" (I.ii.229), finds an echo in a myth of our time, the Bermuda Triangle. *The Tempest* contains the most mysterious of all shipwrecks. The Bermuda Triangle is reputedly the place where vessels vanish. There is in the play a sense of the map of the Mediterranean overlaid by an imagined larger topography, the old world somehow instinct with a dream of the new. So we can extend our list of anticipations of science fiction. To the imagined aliens (not just Ariel but Caliban too), the magician scientist, and the Utopian alternative world we can add an indistinct intuition of a huge undiscovered environment.

When the American astronauts landed on the moon in the twentieth century they knew rather more about the place they had reached than the first settlers knew about America. America was as strange as that. The very phrase "brave new world" comes from *The Tempest* (V.i.183), but the words are deeply ironized by their context. When she says these words Miranda is not gazing from a peak in Darien, like Keats's Cortez, upon an unknown ocean; she is looking at the worst of the old world coming towards her in the shape of assorted courtly criminals. "How beauteous mankind is!" she says, "O brave new world / That has such people in't!" and her father answers, " 'Tis new to thee" (V.i.183–84). The phrase did not clearly acquire the meaning "territory in the western hemisphere" until the nineteenth century. It is likely, however, that when the use finally established itself, it owed something to this anticipatory verbal gesture on the part of Shakespeare. Given that he is thinking about America and the hopes it aroused in speculative would-be colonists, there is almost certainly a brilliant play on the whole notion of cultural relativism in the exchange between Miranda and Prospero. Miranda has grown up in a new world, with the result that to her it is tame, while the old world at first sight is entrancing. Prospero's reply is flattening, desolating. His is the relativism of a bleak levelling. It hangs somewhere between Marlowe's "For Christians do the like" (that is, Christians are no better than Jews, their anti-type) in *The Jew of Malta* (V.ii.116) and the ending of William Golding's *The Inheritors,* where the gentle, doomed Neanderthals, seen through the eyes of *Homo sapiens,* look bestial and frightening.

To call Caliban "an alien" is obviously chronologically scandalous, and some readers will reject the description forthwith. But the concept is, in a manner, grounded in the thought of Shakespeare's time. Giordano Bruno, who was in England in the 1580s, speculated that the American Indians were not descended from Adam but had an independent origin.[21] In other words, he was an early believer in the heretical doctrine of "polygenesis." Richard H. Popkin has suggested that Bruno might well have talked about these things in the group of free-thinkers around Sir Walter Ralegh (what used to be called "the School of Night").[22] This group included Marlowe and Thomas Hariot (or Harriot), the author of *A briefe and true Report of the new found Land of Virginia.* Hariot's account of Virginia includes the now-famous reference to the "invisible bullets" that caused sickness and death among those Indians who had contact with Europeans. This too finds an echo in the science fiction of a later age. Hariot is referring, we can see, to the microorganisms that cause disease. The very germs are assisting the already dominant invaders. In H. G. Wells's *War of the Worlds* the technologically superior Martians are at last *defeated* (not assisted) by microorganisms, by "the humblest things . . . put upon the earth . . . our microscopic allies." The chattering magpie Thomas Nashe refers in his *Pierce Pennilesse his Supplication to the Divell* to the notion that there may have been human beings before Adam and in his *Christes Teares over Jerusalem* to the reported fact that the American Indians can "shew antiquities" from long before Adam's time.[23] Curiously, in Hariot's account of Virginia, the Indians themselves say that they are not descended from a first man, like Adam, but from a first woman.[24] Shakespeare's Caliban had a mother, but we never learn of a father.

There have been two remarkable editions of *The Tempest:* one by Stephen Orgel (The World's Classics, Oxford, 1987) and one by Frank Kermode (the Arden edition, London, 1958). Orgel brought out vividly the relation of the play to colonization and Utopian ideals. Kermode, earlier, held that the play was clearly a pastoral. Just as in Gonzalo's miniature commonwealth we find the Utopian schemes of the colonist grounded in the retrospective dream of a Golden Age, so in the play at large we find pastoral eerily entwined with radical novelty. Kermode rightly observed that the relation of nature to art, central to pastoral, is at the heart of this play also. The narrative pattern of Shakespearean pastoral is clearly present. As in *As You Like It* we have a banished duke who takes refuge far from his court in a wild place; the courtiers are re-educated in the wild place, and in the end they return to civilization. Just as in the earlier play the usurped duke finds that he has ousted the deer (to whom the forest properly belongs, II.i.61), so Prospero, ejected from Milan, in his turn displaces the uncivil creature Caliban, who held the island by lineal succession (I.ii.331).

The nature-art debate, however, is now conducted in very different terms. In *The Winter's Tale* the talk was of gardening and cosmetics. Now it is of government, power relations, education, and civilization. "Civilization" comes from the Latin *civis,* "a citizen," and of course cities, like art, are antithetical to pastoral. *The Winter's Tale* is not obviously a political play, but *The Tempest* is. If we decide that the final "message" of the play is that Caliban is evil, *brute* nature unredeemed by civility, we are saying that one central impulse of the play is anti-pastoral. If we discern a haunting beauty within the savagery of Caliban and feel that this is destroyed forever by the morally tainted courtly intruders, we are asserting that the play is at bottom a true pastoral still.

If so, however, it must be acknowledged at once that it is a very strange specimen of the genre. As early as *A Midsummer Night's Dream* Shakespeare was alive to the possibilities of "transposed pastoral." There by the simple manoeuvre of darkening the forest and placing the trees closer together he produced his utterly original pastoral-of-the-night, a world ruled not by the sun but by the moon. In *The Tempest* the place to which the duke flees is more radically other. It is *epistemologically* wild. The central problem of epistemology is the differentiation of what we know to be real from the unreal. In *The Tempest* we are brought to a place-that-cannot-be-placed. The Mediterranean Sea is not huge. One can see North Africa from the southern coast of Sicily. But Shakespeare's oceanically remote Mediterranean island is utterly strange. The one thing that we know about the pastoral landscape is that it is green. Is the isle in *The Tempest* green? Gonzalo tells us that it is: "How lush and lusty the grass looks! How green!" But Antonio answers, "The ground indeed is tawny," and then Sebastian puts in a qualification, "With an eye of green in't" (II.i.54–56). The director who provides either a bright green or a brown setting destroys the extraordinary effect of these lines. The staging must be neutral. An audience that knows the early comedies would be propelled at once, by Gonzalo's "green," into an expectation of pastoral. But Antonio cannot see the grass. He is looking at a tawny landscape. The promise of straight pastoral is disconcertingly withdrawn. What kind of a place is this? We start to speculate wildly: Have they all died and gone to another world? Is Gonzalo seeing a rich landscape because he is good, Antonio a barren because he is wicked? . . . In *Hamlet* death is at one point conceived not in the usual terms of heaven and hell but as *an undiscovered country* (III.i.78). If the dialogue of the castaways in *The Tempest* is anticipated anywhere it is in the moment of Viola's arrival in Illyria, after the shipwreck. We saw how the chiming of "This is Illyria, lady" with "My brother, he is in Elysium" (*Twelfth Night*, I.ii.2–4) could start the thought, "She means that she should be dead—perhaps is dead."

Caliban, deformed, vindictive, is utterly unlike the shepherd of traditional pastoral. The usual "thesis" of pastoral is that the simple life of a shepherd is better than life at court, where flattery poisons all. At the same time, however, pastoral has traditionally included, within this thesis, an "ultra-pastoral" version of itself, according to which animals are the only truly good beings, genuinely at one with nature. The image of the stricken deer haunted the imagination of Virgil and finds its place in *As You Like It*. If Caliban is an animal he has, then, a deep pastoral precedent. Meanwhile there is pastoral precedent for the *monster* in Arcadia in the sixth Idyll of Theocritus. The singing match in this poem alludes to the love of the huge, one-eyed monster Polyphemus for Galatea.[25] If we remember satyrs (lustful half-human creatures that live in woods) and the "salvage men" (wild men) in Spenser's *Faerie Queene*, we shall find it easy to see that Caliban, profoundly strange though he is, does fit in with the earlier anti-civilization literature.

Caliban is certainly not a nice person. He attempted to rape Miranda (I.ii.347–48) and thinks with pleasure of knocking a nail into Prospero's head (III.ii.61). Prospero sees to it that Caliban is educated, and the pupil responds, "You taught me language, and my profit on't / Is, I know how to curse" (I.ii.363–64). Duke Senior, in "ultra-pastoral" mode, liked to suppose that the language-less simplicities of nature apprised him of his own humanity, but when Caliban is given his voice a torrent of hatred is released. At the same time we are given to understand that Prospero delegated the teaching of Caliban to his daughter, Miranda.[26] It is no great strain to imagine that from Caliban's point of view it all looks different. No one has told him that he must not have sexual relations when nature bids. Here is this vividly attractive female, set beside him for hours at a time. He does what his body tells him (remember Duke Senior's pastoral "sermon"—"these are counsellors / That feelingly persuade me what I am," *As You Like It*, II.i.10–11), and at once everything round him changes. From being the petted experiment in education he becomes the reviled serf, tormented by his technological superior with cramps and pinches. Caliban is sexually mature but culturally a child. Many years ago I argued that the imagery of the play places Caliban in a near-sighted child-world.[27] He is taught to speak, is stroked and made much of, is shown the man in the moon, is eager to show newcomers where birds' nests are, is given glimpses of inexplicable beauty, and cries to sleep and dream again (I.ii.363, I.ii.332–37, II.ii.141, III.ii.135–43). The innocent child is iconic in pastoral. But it will be said that Caliban is not innocent. Once again it is a matter of dominant and minor chords in the musical texture of the writing. The dominant effect is one of harsh collision—Caliban's attempted rape of Miranda is at the same time a violation of pastoral itself. In *As You Like It* the sudden appearance of the bloody napkin was a similar violation of genre—death in Arcadia. Now sex enters Arcadia, and the shock effect is obvious. But the minor chord, in the background, is more subtle. This carries a suggestion that Caliban's innocence of any educational influence *renders* even a violent sexual move on his part innocent too. The healing word "nature" helps this intuition (animals are the saints of pastoral, and animals have sex, don't they?).

Meanwhile the civilizing agents in the drama are a morally dubious lot. Stefano and Trinculo are vulgar as Caliban himself could never be, and even Prospero is in the grip of some moral distress that is never explained to the audience. Ferdinand is a moral blank. Gonzalo and Miranda emerge as the only manifestly good civilizers. Caliban's sexual violence is ironically mirrored in Ferdinand ("Mr. Right"). Remember, mirrors reverse. The two are explicitly paralleled in the log-bearing scenes (II.ii and III.i). When Prospero begins to fulminate against premarital sex, Ferdinand (who must be played by Hugh Grant) says, "The white cold virgin snow upon my heart / Abates the ardor of my liver" (IV.i.55–56). This means either "The coldly chaste nature of the love I feel has reduced physical desire" or else (if Prospero has just surprised the lovers embracing) "The cold purity of the girl I am pressing to my heart dispels thoughts of sex." Either way it is disconcerting. When Othello asserted the un-physical character of his love for Desdemona (I.iii.261–65), his language was distorted by social embarrassment, and meanwhile Desdemona stands in the play as an approved example of strong natural sexual desire. It is as if Ferdinand is saying to Prospero, "You really don't have to worry about me, sir; I'm not a bit like that frightful Caliban. Actually, I don't have much sexual feeling at all." Ferdinand is hardly a blazing anti-type to the baseness of Caliban. His virtue is almost comically limp.

What meanwhile of the sexuality of Prospero? It will be said that he has none or, what comes to the same thing with a fictitious person, none is attributed to him in the play. But Shakespeare has chosen to set us wondering, as the opening exchange of the courtiers in *The Winter's Tale* set us wondering. Prospero carries an obscure load of guilt. His speeches are systematically biased in a certain direction. Where one would expect a benevolent father overseeing a welcome marriage to speak with affectionate warmth to his prospective son-in-law, most of Prospero's energy goes into telling Ferdinand in the fiercest terms that he must not lay a finger on Miranda until they are married. Then we remember that the crisis in Prospero's relations with Caliban came when Caliban made a sexual move, attempted to take Miranda. The thought forms: "Prospero is not gaining a son; he is losing a female." The presentiment is assisted by the desert island setting (to this day cartoonists know that "desert island" means "sexually limited environment—only so many possibilities"). The nubile Miranda is alone on the island (until other parties come into view) with three males, Prospero, Caliban, and Ferdinand. Prospero is "out" because he is her father, Caliban is "out" because he may not be human, and Ferdinand is just perfect—except for the fact that he lacks a sex drive. The obvious explanation is that Prospero is fighting his own incestuous desire for his daughter. There is not a line in the play that supports this inference directly. But if we think of the other late romances, the thought may begin to seem less wild. *Pericles* begins with a full-blown tale of incest. Robert Greene's *Pandosto,* the principal source for *The Winter's Tale,* contains an incest episode, and as we have seen, there is in Shakespeare's play the oddly powerful moment when Leontes begins to respond sexually to his own daughter and is rebuked by Paulina (V.i.223–25). Incest is, one might say, never very far away in this half-Greek world of romance.

What, then, of Caliban? It will be said, "But rape is rape." Even if we are sure, however, that Caliban's act is wholly unforgivable, the model or models of civilized sexuality in the play hardly compose a satisfactory "correction from on high." They are too obviously tainted. But all this, in its turn, is predictable by the logic of pastoral, according to which the courtly, unnatural complex is the truly disgusting thing.

I have noted that "civilization" is etymologically antithetical to "pastoral." "Political," from the Greek *polis,* "a city," is antithetical in much the same way. The anti-Arcadian Utopian is a political animal. But in this play both the Arcadian dream of innocence and the Utopian dream of good government are subverted by radical uncertainty. This reaches a pitch not found elsewhere in Shakespeare—not even in *Hamlet*. D. G. James in *The Dream of Prospero* asked an interesting question: "What happened to the ship in *The Tempest?*"[28] The beginning of the play is a spectacular explosion in which we all witness the wreck of a ship. In Act V the Boatswain joyfully tells us that the ship supposed wrecked is in perfect condition, ready to sail (V.i.221–25). Ariel observes in an aside to Prospero, "Sir, all this service / Have I done since I went" (V.i.225–26). So what did happen to the ship? We have two possible sequences: first, the ship was really wrecked and was afterwards put together again, magically, by Ariel; second, the wreck was a delusion, the ship was never really broken up, and that is why it is ready to sail at a moment's notice. Most will say that Ariel's aside to Prospero settles the question, in favour of the first story. But Ariel could mean only that he led them to the (undamaged) ship. This is more in his line. Reconstituting a smashed sea-going vessel sounds like bigger magic than Ariel can command. Prospero could have done it, but he does not say he has. So some will continue to entertain the second possibility. Here we meet the truly extraordinary thing: we are now considering as possible something directly contradicted by our own experience. We know as clearly as we ever know anything within a drama that the ship broke up—"we split, we split!" (I.i.61, 62)—accompanied no doubt by a loud rending noise. To say that the ship was never smashed is to say that *we,* the audience, may have been deluded *by Prospero.* Miranda is certainly sure that she has seen a shipwreck, but Prospero, fascinatingly, says quietly to her, "There's no harm done . . . no harm" (I.ii.15). That Miranda should be benevolently deceived by her magician father (in line with the second hypothesis) is quite conceivable, but I know of no dramaturgical precedent for members of the audience being slowly brought, by the unfolding character of the play, to a point at which they wonder whether *they too* ought to believe their eyes.

We have reached a pitch of uncertainty more radical than anything we have seen before. Ever since Edward Dowden wrote that Shakespeare's final period was a time of "large, serene wisdom" in which the poet "had attained some high and luminous table-land of joy,"[29] it has been common practice to assume that *The Tempest* is like the other romances, a radiantly happy work, *deep* comedy. The pattern of the family smashed by a storm and afterwards reunited is obviously present. But where the endings of

Pericles, Cymbeline, and *The Winter's Tale* are simultaneously this-worldly and Paradisal, the ending of *The Tempest* seems somehow infected. The source of the contagion may be uncertainty.

The term "Paradisal" is mine. The other romances never mention Paradise. But it is almost as if Shakespeare in *The Tempest* decided to interrogate the idea of an earthly Paradise. He read Montaigne on noble savages. He politicizes and analyses a notion that had operated in the other romances with healing imaginative force. Early in the play the earthly Paradise is subjected to a process of comic diminution and caricature in Gonzalo's "ideal commonwealth." When Ferdinand and Miranda are "discovered" playing chess together (V.i.172), we have a curious late instance of the Shakespearean habit of establishing a stereotype and then working against its grain. Here the conventional form of the episode is that we expect the lovers to be caught in a sexually compromising action but find instead that they are behaving with perfect propriety. Meanwhile, however, the brief dialogue between the chess-players looks like the beginning of a quarrel. Miranda accuses Ferdinand of cheating, he says that of course he hasn't cheated, and she tells him that it's all right, she loves him just the same. If Ferdinand has cheated, his lying is disquieting. If he hasn't, Miranda's reply is utterly infuriating. The word "wrangle," Shakespeare's word for sour marital exchanges (*As You Like It,* V.iv.191), follows a line later. When Shakespeare wrote against the grain of stereotype in *2 Henry IV* it was to impart an unlooked-for beauty to the conversation of Falstaff with Doll Tearsheet, to make the seemingly disgraceful strangely graceful. But here he makes the seemingly virtuous a site of implied dissension. We have seen in earlier comedies many morally dubious persons in some way transfigured by the joyous fact of marriage. That feeling is perhaps less vivid in *The Tempest* than in any other play. The enervating uncertainty has got into those very quasi-Platonic comedic structures that elsewhere stand in splendid contrast to the human imperfection of the persons of the play. Our sense meanwhile of political resolution, of dynastic healing, as Prospero forgives his enemies, is weakened by the fact that Prospero's thoughts are now all on his own impending death (V.i.312). A good death, for which the dying man is thoroughly prepared, might be the surest way to heaven. But in Prospero's case (more uncertainty!) we are far from sure of his ultimate destination. A Faustian smell still hangs about the figure of the magician. We have seen how throughout the play

Prospero appears to be haunted by a consciousness of some sin that is never explained to us, the audience. The strangest thing of all, to one interested in the strength of early modern dramatic convention, is the intrusion into Prospero's Epilogue of a plea that the audience should pray for him. Prospero explains how he feels his powers draining out of him and adds, "My ending is despair / Unless I be reliev'd by prayer" (Epilogue, 15–16). It is almost embarrassing. Remember Puck's Epilogue at the end of *A Midsummer Night's Dream,* which so elegantly reassured the audience and, most important, told them when to applaud. As Prospero comes forward to speak our hands, perhaps, are already raised, prepared for clapping, but then, as he speaks of prayer, some will bring their hands together, not with a plosive sound but softly, in anxious assent to his bizarre request.

In the forgiveness of Antonio and Sebastian we have, again, a contrast between the sorry imperfections of the persons and the overriding fact of forgiveness itself nevertheless taking effect, a contrast we have seen before. But now, although the forgiveness certainly takes place, it seems "merely technical," as if inwardly weakened. When the appalling Bertram is married to the determined Helena at the end of *All's Well That Ends Well* the wedding is so incongruous as to be almost funny, but it is at the same time matter for joy. The audience smiles, and the smiling reflects both aspects of the scene. But the forgiveness of Antonio in *The Tempest* seems deliberately contrived to kill any smile that may be starting in the audience:

For you, most wicked sir, whom to call brother
Would even infect my mouth, I do forgive
Thy rankest fault—   (V.i.130–32)

Never did forgiveness sound more like continuing, unabated hatred. Antonio meanwhile is given no speech of contrition. It is as if they are stuck, frozen in the moral wasteland from which the act of forgiveness should be freeing them. Prospero looks at Antonio and loathing takes over, but somehow, he gets out the words "I do forgive." The strongest explicit image of constriction in the play is attached to Ariel. Ariel was confined for twelve years in a cloven pine (I.ii.277). Prospero freed him but retained him as a servant (with threats of future confinement if he were disobedient, I.ii.294–95). We are aware throughout the play that Ariel is still painfully enclosed by Prospero's power. The last thing Prospero does before his Epilogue is to set Ariel free—at last—"to the elements." Because Ariel is all air and fire it is no great step, given the linking in Jacobean psychology of the elements to certain aspects of the psyche, to associate him with one part of Prospero's mind, and also with the poetic imagination (Shakespeare has seen magic and poetry as near-allied since he wrote *A Midsummer Night's Dream*). The book of magic was to be surrendered to the waters ("I'll drown my book," V.i.57). If Ariel is in some sense Prospero's genius and Prospero is in some sense Shakespeare, after the strange constriction of moral efficacy in the grand eucatastrophe, the poetic gift is at last freed, but not to heal or reconcile human conflict—to vanish from our sight into the air, leaving "not a rack behind" (IV.i.156). When at the beginning of his writing career Shakespeare "froze" the expected comic ending of *Love's Labour's Lost* with news of a death, our trust in comedy itself was not damaged. The weddings, we could reasonably hope, would come later. But as we watch the full, resolving act of forgiveness performed in *The Tempest* and see *this* withered in the act of utterance, we can feel that comedy itself is dying. The sense of redemption so strong in the other romances is replaced by a kind of vertigo.

One obstinate uncertainty in the text of *The Tempest*, unlike the question whether the isle is green or tawny, must be resolved in performance, and that is the question, "What happens to Caliban at the end?" The plot summary of *The Tempest* in *The Oxford Companion to English Literature* says roundly, "Prospero . . . leaves Caliban once more alone on the island."[30] There is no textual support for this. Nor, it must be said, is there clear textual support for the alternative, that Caliban is taken back to Milan. Caliban's last speech in the play runs,

> I'll be wise hereafter
> And seek for grace. What a thrice-double ass
> Was I to take this drunkard for a god,
> And worship this dull fool! (V.i.295–98)

"Grace" can mean "the un-earned loving generosity of God" or "the favour of a (human) superior." It is most unlikely that Caliban has suddenly got religion. The tone of the rest of the speech is social. He means, "I'll be a good servant and get the favour of my master." It certainly looks as if Caliban thinks he is continuing in service, that is, going with them. It is entirely possible, however, that in the first production of *The Tempest,* Shakespeare made sure that Caliban was after all left behind, king of the island once more. The words on the page *settle* nothing. If they *suggest* anything, it is indeed that Caliban departs with the company. Natural Romantics want Caliban to be left behind. Politically minded people cynically incline to the alternative view. They imagine him transported to Milan, where he will become a one-man freak show, as happened to certain American Indians in the seventeenth century. The clown Trinculo swiftly decided that Caliban was marketable: "Were I in England now (as once I was) and had but this fish painted, not a holiday fool there but would give a piece of silver. There would this monster make a man. . . . When they will not give a doit to relieve a lame beggar, they will lay out ten to see a dead Indian" (II.ii.27–33).

Trinculo thinks of Caliban not as an ape-man as post-Darwinians expect but as a fish-man. His scheme of showing Caliban at a fair carries my mind back to the fair held in the streets of my native Hereford in my boyhood. There I once saw a booth with a garish sign, "Come and see the Mermaid!" I paid my sixpence, entered, and at once wished I hadn't. The poor woman got up in a shiny mermaid's tail had puffy stumps with exiguous fingers instead of arms and a bulbous forehead like a dolphin's. The country people were delighted: "Look! She's got fins!" Perhaps Shakespeare saw something similar in a Stratford fair. The ambiguity remains. Either Caliban at the end is alone, king of the isle, or he is hauled off, probably to become a sad freak show. But this any director must resolve, in performance, one way or the other.

In *A Midsummer Night's Dream* we were led to wonder whether the perceptions of lovers and dreamers might have their own separate claim to reality-status. In *Antony and Cleopatra* the vision of the lovers was allowed to break free from the disabling term "illusion" by its own warmth and vivacity. In the vertiginous world of *The Tempest* the tide is now flowing in a contrary direction. Unreality seems to be winning.

The betrothal masque laid on to celebrate the joining of Miranda to Ferdinand breaks up abruptly when the *thought* of rebellion suddenly enters Prospero's head, presumably disturbing his concentration on the matter in hand. It as though the entire performance by his spirit-actors is held in a forcefield, by an effort of intellectual exertion. All the plays-within-plays in Shakespeare abort, but this is the weirdest abortion of them all: "To a strange, hollow, and confused noise, they heavily vanish" (IV.i.138).[31] In the early comedies, plays-within-plays are laughed out of countenance. *The Mousetrap* in *Hamlet* is broken off by the hurried exit of a frightened king. But the betrothal masque gurgles away like water down a plughole or, more grandly, like astral matter drawn into a black hole. The whirling tempest that began the play has turned into a maelstrom of vanishing fictions. The comedic mythology of union, Juno, Ceres, rainbow Iris, and the reapers, is overtaken by an inexplicable downward-spiralling. The well-mannered Ferdinand asks Prospero whether everything is all right. Prospero's answer begins as reassurance, but as he keeps talking his words begin to express a still greater, more comprehensive vertigo:

> These our actors
> (As I foretold you) were all spirits, and
> Are melted into air, into thin air,
> And like the baseless fabric of this vision,
> The cloud-capp'd tow'rs, the gorgeous palaces,
> The solemn temples, the great globe itself,
> Yea, all which it inherit, shall dissolve,
> And like this insubstantial pageant faded,
> Leave not a rack behind. We are such stuff
> As dreams are made on; and our little life
> Is rounded with a sleep. (IV.i.148–58)

I denied earlier that *King Lear* was nihilist. This speech, however, comes very close to full nihilism. Shakespeare's imagination no longer works generously to find substance in our wilder perceptions. Instead the *absence* of substance spreads like a viral disease. In modern English the sequence runs: "Nothing to worry about, Ferdinand; the actors are insubstantial and have simply evaporated as spirits can—and moreover, like them, the palaces and churches will dissolve—even the terrestrial globe will vanish as the last smear of cloud vanishes in a clear sky; you and I, Ferdinand—indeed all of us—are no more than dreams and our destiny unconsciousness." The circle of unreality spreads and engulfs the audience. This is not the dual ontology of *A Midsummer Night's Dream*. It is monist—but monist-*un*realist.

Prospero, who had at first sought to cheer up his prospective son-in-law, is, we notice, profoundly upset. He has to go for a solitary walk "to still my beating mind" (IV.i.163). Politically minded persons in the audience tend to stick with the thought that it is the conspiracy of Caliban and the buffoons that has upset Prospero. But the speech about the dissolving revel and the dissolving universe has changed all that. Prospero's fear is of something that lies deeper than his own murder. It is the thought that he has never really been born at all.

But, it may be said, Prospero is not Shakespeare. The whole speech is what Aristotle called *ethike lexis,* "characterized language." Prospero's vision of un-being may be as much a matter of pathology as of philosophy. There is something wrong with him. Had Ferdinand been made of sterner stuff he might have said to Prospero, "The mere fact that you have *told* me this means that a *teller* must exist; you at least must exist." Such dogged common sense certainly plays a part in the general effect. Audiences, by and large, think of Prospero and his associates as existent (within the fiction). But the vision of the shaken magician is frightening. And the sense of values and irenic rituals *being eroded,* involving a special pathos and tension unavailable within a settled nihilism (in which such values have never existed), is strong.

Wilson Knight thought all the late plays were allegories of resurrection. "Resurrection" is conceived in Christian terms. But *The Tempest* gives us a picture of eternity that has nothing whatever to do with resurrection, Christianity, or life:

Full fadom five thy father lies,
  Of his bones are coral made:
Those are pearls that were his eyes:
  Nothing of him that doth fade,
But doth suffer a sea-change
Into something rich and strange.   (I.ii.397–402)

Instead of the enhanced consciousness central to the Christian afterlife we have the elimination of consciousness. Coral and pearl are beautiful, but their beauty is not like that of living men and women; it is the beauty of filigree, jewellery, sculpture, art. Paradise becomes heartless *ecphrasis,* eternal life eternal death.[32]

Although Prospero is not Shakespeare, the possibility of identification is stronger than with other characters. Nineteenth-century readers inferred at once that when Prospero promised to drown his book and give up magic, this, occurring as it does in the last of Shakespeare's plays, is the dramatist's farewell to play-making. For some reason I have never understood this is seen as sentimental nonsense today. We are allowed to say that *The Tempest* is all about art but not allowed to say that it is about the artist in question. Yet the masque-like character of the late plays makes such quasi-allegorical reference to real persons almost predictable. In Milton's *A Masque* "a lady and her two brothers" were played by—a lady and her two brothers.

Perhaps the clue to Prospero's embarrassing request for our prayers lies in the "Dover Cliff" episode of Shakespeare's greatest play, *King Lear.* There, as we saw, the dramatist may have been visited by a kind of nausea as he contemplated the obscene power of his own manipulative art. The devil conjured in Edgar's mendacious picture of Gloucester's fall is made to stand exactly where he, Edgar, had been standing, close at the ear of the blinded man, to trick him into repentance. And meanwhile the real puppet master was standing behind both—Shakespeare himself. The inexplicable guilt of Prospero may be the guilt of the dramatist. At the beginning of our story Berowne in *Love's Labour's Lost* had to repent of his verbal cleverness. I am suggesting that a wave of something like despair engulfs the play as the broadening circles of unreality engulfed the audience in Prospero's speech after the masque broke up. "Despair" is the shock word in Prospero's Epilogue. I hesitate to call this philosophy, although it is a kind of scepticism. *The Tempest* is not a happy play. That strange contrition we saw at the end of *Love's Labour's Lost* and glimpsed again in *Hamlet* and *King Lear* returns, with a special sharpness, at the end of his last play. It is not inconceivable that the author of this prodigious body of work, these plays for which the world has never ceased to feel grateful, was ashamed at what he had done.

Coda

On that summer night when I walked in the gathering darkness from Stratford to Shottery I was looking for the boy who would grow up to become the author of *Hamlet, King Lear, As You Like It,* and all the other amazing plays that bear his name. At the moment when I imagined that we stood side by side I became aware that he had eluded me, that I had to return to the words on the page. Perhaps he eludes me still. Yet the notion of a single personality, a literary intelligence behind the immensely varied writing, is something to which I adhere. I have assumed throughout this book that Shakespeare's plays are the product of a single remarkable mind, that Shakespeare wrote *Shakespeare.* There was much talk in the later twentieth century of "the death of the author." Literary works, it was maintained, are really the expression of the society of their time. Conventions determine the nature of the work and conventions are necessarily interpersonal, social. More recent years have seen a more modest echo of this grandly metaphysical theory, in the contention that the texts we refer to as "Shakespeare's" plays are cross-sections of a theatrical process that was never under the control of a single directing mind. The "text" would have changed from one day to the next; an actor might see the chance for some effective business; a bad reaction from the audience might lead to a crucial cut; and so on. Contemporaries, we are told, understood this rather better than modern, reverent readers, isolated in book-lined rooms; we would do better to think in terms of current television drama; we are enthusiastic about *The Sopranos,* but few can name *the* author of *The Sopranos;* thus the early quarto edition of *2 Henry VI* (1594) excitedly proclaims on its title page, "The First part of the Contention betwixt the Two Famous Houses of York and Lancaster, with the Death of the good Duke Humphrey," but says not a word about Shakespeare.

Scholars have known for centuries that any printed text of Shakespeare is a freezing, a cryogenic perpetuation of something in itself mobile. But this intuition is entirely compatible with the presumption that the plays have an author. Moreover, within the lifetime of Shakespeare, the public had certainly caught on to the fact that Shakespeare was the mind behind the plays. Of course the grand collected edition, the Folio of 1623, makes much of the author's genius, but that, we are told, is because it belongs to a later culture; Shakespeare himself had been dead for some seven years. But, although it is true that the very earliest quartos do not name Shakespeare as author, most do name him. The quartos of *The Taming of the Shrew* (1594), *2 Henry VI* (1594), *3 Henry VI* (1595), *Richard III* (1597), *Richard II* (1597), *Romeo and Juliet* (1597), *Henry V* (1600), and *Titus Andronicus* (1594) do not give the author's name. But the name is given on the title pages of *Love's Labour's Lost* (1598), the second quartos of *Richard III* (1598) and *1 Henry IV* (1599), *2 Henry IV* (1600), *A Midsummer Night's Dream* (1600), *Much Ado about Nothing* (1600), *The Merchant of Venice* (1600), *The Merry Wives of Windsor* (1602), the first and second quartos of *Hamlet* (1603 and 1604–5), *King Lear* (1608), the second quarto of *Richard II* (1598), *Pericles* (1609), *Troilus and Cressida* (1609), and *Othello* (1622). All but the last named fall within the life of the playwright. It is quite clear that the words "by William Shakespeare" were a selling point, in Shakespeare's own culture. They knew they had a *writer,* who could now be sold to *readers.*[1] There is an individual human being behind these plays, but the man himself is elusive, endlessly mobile.

Of course he is not a systematic philosopher; he is a dramatist. But the very avoidance of system may be shrewd—even, perhaps, philosophically shrewd. He shares with the major philosophers a knack of asking fundamental (sometimes very simple) questions. "How do you know," says David Hume, "that the sun will rise tomorrow?" "Are dreams real or unreal?" asks Shakespeare. This readiness to ask the simplest question takes a kind of courage. All the great philosophers have it, and that is why, when people write today about, say, the *Theaetetus* of Plato, they write not about social conditions in fourth-century Athens, but about the relation of knowledge to the flux of experience. Because Shakespeare will question anything, he treads on the toes of *later* theorists. Hamlet has as much to do with Existentialism as with Elizabethan neo-Stoicism. The patronizing assumption in current Historicist criticism, that poor Shakespeare was locked into an undeveloped, savagely hierarchical political philosophy by the period in which he lived, is absurd. Shakespeare, it emerges, often has the edge, intellectually, on those who go in for such premature simplifications (not to be confused with the initial simplicities of real philosophy). He is less "locked in" than they.

The elegant Lord Shaftesbury once observed that "the most ingenious way to become foolish" was "by a system."[2] It is a very English sentiment. One of our myths of national identity is founded on the presumption that intellectual systems are for Continental Europeans; the French may pride themselves on their Gallic lucidity, but this is the land of empiricism, piecemeal adjustment, and general "muddling through"—and *our way is better.* They have Leibniz and Descartes, we have Locke; they have Roman law, we are the happy inhabitants of the great forest of common law.[3] Shakespeare plays a part in this myth. Towards the end of the seventeenth century, when French culture was frighteningly stylish, Dryden sought to counter French neoclassical insistence on "rules" with the anarchic magnificence of Shakespeare, who so wantonly mingled tragedy with comedy, yet had of all men "the most comprehensive soul."[4] I am here dealing in clichés—stereotypes—but such things have their own (sometimes enormous) cultural efficacy. The old antagonism of France and England over the real status of the "rules" of art lives on today in a thinly disguised form: France is the land of Literary Theory, England or Britain its chaotic (but more truthful) obverse. Samuel Johnson, conscious of the scandal (to Continental eyes) of Shakespeare's disorderly plenitude, compared his works to a great forest[5]—the phrase that came to me a moment ago, as a way of describing the body of English common law. A forest, as both Dante and the author of *A Midsummer Night's Dream* knew very well, is a place to get lost in. It is properly the site of questions, not of answers—or rather, while it may supply immediate and local answers (that tree is an oak), it refuses to offer itself as an intelligible, organized whole. I have, with studied neutrality, presented the contrast between Continental system and British chaotic pluralism as myth. This myth, however, is not utterly without foundation in fact. The facts, indeed, do not always assist the British side. Descartes, with his prickly clarity, is a better philosopher than Locke, whose famous *Essay* perhaps dies the death of a thousand confused qualifications. But I would be less than honest if I did not add that, where pluralism means that the world in its real richness and complexity exceeds our pictures of it, I stand squarely with the British party. The universe is indefinitely recessive to the understanding. It will not provide the thing that philosophers cannot help pursuing: The Answer.

I began this book on Shakespeare as a thinker with an enormous concession: that we do not know what he thought—finally—about anything. Of course the word "finally" is important. We know *that* he thought. Moreover, the fiery track of his thinking can be followed, though never, it seems, to a settled terminus. If he is indeed the genius of "muddling through," this endlessly local use of the intelligence is suddenly a glorious thing. No sooner has he resolved some difficulty than he must add, implicitly or overtly, "But—wait a moment—something else might be going on here." We find ourselves wanting to explain to a resistant Ockham that actually the philosopher looks better with a full beard. It is a commonplace of modern criticism that Shakespeare delights in throwing out questions, not answers, and we find it easy to admire this long, glittering refusal to descend to the vulgarity of a unitary thesis. But there is something troubling in the picture.

Gilbert Ryle liked to remark that he had asked all his philosophical questions by the age of twelve—but that now he was actually answering them. Is it so discreditable to answer a question—finally? This it must be conceded is the hardest thing of all. What would we think of a poet who not only posed a fascinating philosophical problem but actually answered it? Has this ever happened? Both George Bernard Shaw and Bertolt Brecht, in their very different ways, wrote plays in which a Marxist answer in terms of underlying economic laws was deemed to emerge from behind the play of individual character, but as the years pass these plays seem less and less persuasive. When Shaw notoriously observed, "There is no eminent writer I can despise as heartily as I despise Shakespeare, when I measure my mind against his," he was probably thinking primarily of Shakespeare's palpable failure to be a good card-carrying socialist; to Shaw, Shakespeare was a political idiot.[6] I have meanwhile no doubt at all but that Shakespeare (who is not a card-carrying conservative, either) is far more intelligent, politically, than Shaw.

A better example of the problem-solving poet is John Milton. I began this book by offering Milton, that hero of daring political clarity, as a standing antithesis to Shakespeare. Milton engaged to answer what for Christians is the hardest question of all: *Unde malum,* "Whence comes evil?" If God is both all-powerful and all-good, how comes it that there is anything wrong in the world at all? Milton answered, "There is evil in the world because God in his generosity wished his creatures to be free; the obedience of a predetermined puppet, a creature that *cannot* sin, is wholly without moral life; the obedience of a free agent, exposed to darkness, danger, pain and sin is morally real because it is alive." It is an answer that persuades many but not all. I believe myself that in the end Milton himself came to think that it would not serve. But it is a very good try. It *may* indeed be that rare thing, a Final Answer. Is it not better to bring off a feat of this kind than to acquiesce in the altogether easier practice of asking interesting questions?

It is time to move from cliché to fact. Shakespeare would not be as impressive as he obviously is if he had done *nothing* but pose queries. He provides many answers, and sometimes these have a more than local efficacy. I have said that Shakespeare was a dramatist, not a systematic philosopher. "Systematic," here, is an important qualifier. The basic distinction between the making of great plays and profound thinking may be less absolute than we thought. Aristotle, as we saw, said that the poet tells us "the kinds of things that would happen" (*Poetics,* 1451a37). Shakespeare, the supreme dramatist, is strong both on what would happen and what could happen. He is the philosopher of human possibility. The epistemology of Karl Popper was very influential in twentieth-century Britain and America. This was a philosophy bearing many marks of what I saw earlier as an anti-Continental strain: he hated Heidegger and Hegel, he distrusted grand determinist theories of history such as that of Marx, he recommended piecemeal political reform, and, most important, he believed that the grand general propositions set out by science were never proved, they only survived disproof. You can never prove that all swans are always, have always been, will always be, white. You can advance the proposition as a hypothesis only. But you can disprove the hypothesis.

One black swan, once only, does the job. Popper is famous for insisting on a fundamental asymmetry between verification and falsification. We do not verify the hypotheses of science; instead, if we have any intellectual honour, we do our level best to disconfirm even our own theories. The process is Darwinian: the properly successful scientific theories are the ones that have survived, by a kind of logical natural selection. "Knowledge" is now a forest of flourishing but imperilled "might-be"s or a web of provisional essays. It all sounds like Shakespeare's dramatic universe (and quite unlike, say, Racine's).

But now I return to the notion of possibility. A philosopher friend once observed to me that Popper's famous law of asymmetry does not hold with regard to statements of possibility: just one snow-storm on Derby Day actually *proves* the truth of the statement, "Snow-storms are possible in an English June." Shakespeare is fascinated by what could (just) be the case. Motives *can* be (not are) constructed from outside the human subject (*Othello, Coriolanus*); the human subject, meanwhile, *can,* through behaviour and a kind of introverted rhetoric, create passions and desires, "from the outside in," in his or her own breast (*Hamlet*); hatred and fear, if given a simple sexual charge, *can* fuel sudden desire (*Richard III*); indiscriminate forgiveness *can,* given a certain social context, prove to be a kind of cruelty (the case put by the dark angel of *Measure for Measure*); words, if we attend only to their formal character and so make them elegantly opaque, *can* separate us from love and from reality itself (*Love's Labour's Lost*); words, when they become transparent once more, *can* engage reality (*Love's Labour's Lost* again); human identity *can* persist even when the public apparatus of function, conditioning, and negotiable relations is withdrawn (*Richard II, Coriolanus*). All these exercises at the edge of human possibility are *positive* additions to the stock of both wisdom and knowledge. They are much more like answers than questions. They alert us to the *range* both of public reality and of the human spirit in relation to that reality. The list of "can"s I have just given does not, however, include what I still believe to be the moments of major philosophical importance in the plays: the exploration of the ontological status of the imagination in *A Midsummer Night's Dream* and *Antony and Cleopatra* and the analysis of identity and the ethical subjectivism in *Troilus and Cressida*. Here indeed Shakespeare, though working with maximal intellectual power, finds no terminus to his thought. He was simply too intelligent to be able to persuade himself that the problems were completely solved, but it would be absurd to conclude that therefore nothing has been achieved; he gets further—much further—than anyone else I have ever read. And in his love of the "just-possible" he scores, over and over again, as a dramatist (as distinct from a sage). By this means he joins verisimilitude to wonder. Some years after the death of Shakespeare the young Milton wrote a poem (printed in the second Folio of 1632). In it he surveyed the work of the dead rival. He makes sure that the reader is made aware that Shakespeare is no scholar (this gives him, Milton, an opening, a chance to shine, later, in his turn). But then, addressing the dead poet, he says the really interesting thing: "dost make us marble with too much conceiving." For Milton, conscious of his destiny as England's poet, the blazing plays of Shakespeare were not a quickening agent; they turned him to stone. He meant, partly, that Shakespeare starts so many thoughts that the reader is paralyzed, like Hamlet, by excess of intellection. At another level, however, he was writing and thinking as a conscious competitor, one that knew, in his bones, that, with all his learning, he stood no chance against the boy from Stratford.

Notes

Introduction

1. See the record of the inquest in the National Archives, KB 9/650, pt. 2, m. 235.
2. E. A. Armstrong, *Shakespeare's Imagination,* rev. ed. (Lincoln, Nebr., 1963), 126.
3. The *Riverside Shakespeare* reads "askaunt the brook" at *Hamlet,* IV.vii.166, but other editions commonly read "aslant."
4. *Minutes and Accounts of the Corporation of Stratford-upon-Avon,* transcribed by Richard Savage with an Introduction by Edgar I. Fripp, vol. 3 (*1577–86*) (London, 1926), 50. See also Edgar I. Fripp, *Shakespeare Studies: Biographical and Literary* (London, 1930).
5. Clara Longworth de Chambrun, *Shakespeare: Actor-Poet* (New York, 1927), 26. Chambrun cites J. H. Pollen, "A Shakespeare Discovery: His Schoolmaster Afterwards a Jesuit," *The Month,* October 1917. She also draws on Carmichael Stopes, *Shakespeare's Warwickshire Contemporaries* (Stratford-on-Avon, 1907).
6. William Poole points out to me that this sentence in which the sliver breaks is an example of something in which I have long been interested: metamorphic syntax, as distinct from ambiguity of imagery; the preceding "clamb'ring" leads us to expect "she" as the subject of the main verb, but this is silently displaced by the impersonal "a sliver"; the syntactic shift subtly suggests (in a dream-like way) that the power of agency is passing from Ophelia.
7. Jacques Derrida, *De la grammatologie* (Paris, 1967), 227.
8. Christopher Norris, *Uncritical Theory: Postmodernism, Intellectuals and the Gulf War* (London, 1992), 51.
9. Horace, *Epistles,* I.x.24.
10. Late medieval Nominalists supposed the world to consist of an immense number of variously shaped concrete particulars and denied the substantial existence of universals: lovers exist but love does not.
11. Pierre Bourdieu, *The Rules of Art: Genesis and Structure of the Literary Field* (Cambridge, 1996), 104.
12. See Samuel Schoenbaum, *William Shakespeare: A Documentary Life* (New York, 1975), 79.

13. The description is Anthony Wood's. See ibid., 80.

14. See John Munro, ed., *The Shakespeare Allusion Book,* 2 vols. (London, 1909), 1:224. See also Richard Wilson, *Secret Shakespeare: Studies in Theatre, Religion and Resistance* (Manchester, 2004), 12.

15. Schoenbaum, *Shakespeare: A Documentary Life,* 42.

16. John Bearman, "John Shakespeare's 'Spiritual Testament': A Reappraisal," *Shakespeare Survey,* 56 (2003), 184–202, at 190.

17. John Donne, Preface to *Biathanatos,* ed. Ernest W. Sullivan II (London, 1988), 29.

18. Schoenbaum, *Shakespeare: A Documentary Life,* 234.

19. Ibid., 47.

20. T. W. Baldwin, *William Shakspere's Small Latine and Lesse Greeke,* 2 vols. (Urbana, Ill., 1944), 1:479, 486. Cf. Peter Milward, S.J., "Shakespeare's Jesuit Schoolmasters," in R. Dutton, A. Findlay, and R. Wilson, eds., *Theatre and Religion: Lancastrian Shakespeare* (Manchester, 2003), 58–70.

21. John Aubrey said that this story came from "Mr Beeston." See Schoenbaum, *Shakespeare: A Documentary Life,* 58 and 88.

22. By Oliver Baker in his *Shakespeare's Warwickshire and the Unknown Years* (London, 1937). See also E. K. Chambers, "William Shakeshafte," in his *Shakespearean Gleanings* (Oxford, 1944).

23. See Schoenbaum, *Shakespeare: A Documentary Life,* 114.

24. Both these arguments were put by Douglas Hamer in "Was William Shakespeare William Shakeshafte?" *Review of English Studies,* n.s., 21 (1970), 41–48. See also Robert Bearman's characteristically effective defence of Hamer's arguments against E. A. J. Honigmann's attempted rebuttal of them, "'Was William Shakespeare William Shakeshafte?' Revisited," *Shakespeare Quarterly,* 53, no. 1 (2002), 83–94.

25. Schoenbaum, *Shakespeare: A Documentary Life,* 115.

26. Ernst Honigmann, *Shakespeare: The Lost Years,* 2nd ed. (Manchester, 1998), 39.

27. Ernst Honigmann, *Shakespeare: The Lost Years* (Manchester, 1985).

28. *Records of the English Province of the Society of Jesus* (London, 1875), 159. This instrument was applied to Thomas Cottom. See John Hart's *Diarium Turris* in Nicholas Sanders, *De schismate anglicano* (Rome, 1586), I.i.5.

29. See David Crystal's letter in *The Tablet,* 24 September 2005, 21.

30. Schoenbaum, *Shakespeare: A Documentary Life,* 49.

31. Richard Wilson is readier than I am, however, to accept "John Shakespeare's Spiritual Testament" as genuine. Wilson, *Secret Shakespeare.*

32. See Stephen Greenblatt, *Will in the World: How Shakespeare Became Shakespeare* (London, 2004).

33. Wilson, *Secret Shakespeare,* 11.

34. Stephen Greenblatt, *Shakespearean Negotiations: The Circulation of Social Energy in Renaissance England* (Oxford, 1988), 119.

35. See C. S. Lewis, *The Allegory of Love* (New York, 1958), 322–23.

36. See Keith Thomas, *Religion and the Decline of Magic* (Harmondsworth, 1963), 729.

37. Goodwin Wharton (1653–1704) kept an extraordinary record of his life, including his fantasies or delusions. See Roy Porter's article on him in the new *Oxford Dictionary of National Biography* (Oxford, 2004).

38. Thomas Hobbes, *Leviathan,* xlvii.23, ed. E. Curley (Indianapolis, Ind., 1994), 483.

39. Thomas, *Religion and the Decline of Magic,* 67.

40. Richard Corbett, "The Faryes Farewell," in *The Poems of Richard Corbett* (Oxford, 1955), 51.

41. Gary Taylor, "The Cultural Politics of Maybe," in R. Dutton, A. Findlay, and R. Wilson, eds., *Theatre and Religion: Lancastrian Shakespeare* (Manchester, 2003), 242–58, at 255–56.

42. Richard Wilson, "Introduction: A Torturing Hour—Shakespeare and the Martyrs," in Dutton, Findlay, and Wilson, eds., *Theatre and Religion,* 1–39, at 4–5.

43. See Apuleius, *The Golden Ass,* x.22, *tam vastum genitale.* William Adlington's translation of 1566 bowdlerizes at this point; see *The Golden Ass of Apuleius,* trans. William Adlington (Tudor Translations), ed. W. E. Henley (London, 1893), 218.

44. Maurice Morgann, *An Essay on the Dramatic Character of Sir John Falstaff* (1777), in Daniel A. Fineman, ed., *Maurice Morgann: Shakespearean Criticism* (Oxford, 1972), 164.

Chapter 1: To the Death of Marlowe

1. The matter is uncertain. The precise order of the early plays—the three parts of *Henry VI, The Taming of the Shrew,* and *Two Gentlemen of Verona*—remains controversial.

2. Edward Burns in the Arden edition of *1 Henry VI* (London, 2000), 13, observes that in Act I, Scene iv (the Siege of Orleans), the dialogue is carefully informative, telling the audience that the English are in a turret at the end of a bridge, on the other side of the Loire from the French, while the gunner's boy is visible below. He infers that there is in consequence no need for cardboard props. I continue to think that a flimsy turret of some sort probably was constructed. Even if there were none, however, the dialogue itself exhibits the medieval readiness to contract spaces.

3. E. H. Gombrich, *Art and Illusion,* 5th ed. (Oxford, 1977), 76.

4. See L. A. Beaurline's new Cambridge edition of *King John* (Cambridge, 1999), 1, and E. A. J. Honigmann's Arden edition (London, 1954), esp. lvii.

5. Thomas Nashe, *Piers Penniless his Supplication to the Devil,* in *The Works of Thomas Nashe,* ed. R. B. McKerrow, rev. F. P. Wilson, 5 vols. (Oxford, 1958), 1:212–13.

6. See G. Lambrecht, "La Composition de la première partie de *Henri VI,*" *Bulletin de la Faculté des Lettres de Strasbourg,* 46, no. 3 (1967), 325–54; J. J. M. Tobin, "A Touch of Greene, Much Nashe, and All Shakespeare," in T. A. Pendleton, ed., *Henry VI: Critical Essays* (New York, 2001), 39–56; B. J. Sokol, "Manuscript Evidence for an Earliest Date of *Henry VI,* Part One," *Notes and Queries,* 26 (2000), 58–63; Edward Burns, introduction to his Arden edition of *1 Henry VI* (London, 2000), 73–103; and G. Taylor, "Shakespeare and Others: The Authorship of *Henry VI, Part One,*" *Medieval and Renaissance Drama in England,* 7 (1995), 145–205.

7. Tania Demetriou, "Out of the Silence Yet I Picked a Welcome" (M.Phil. diss., Oxford University, 2003).

8. Edward Hall (or Halle), *The Union of the Two Noble and Illustre Famelies of Lancastre and York* (London, 1550), the Scolar Press facsimile (Menston, 1970), "King Henry the vi," fol. 10v.

9. On the strange power in literature of seemingly random physical objects, see Guillaume Pigeard de Gurbert, *Le Mouchoir de Desdémone* (Arles, 2001).

10. Demetriou, "Out of the Silence," 36.

11. William James, *Principles of Psychology,* 2 vols. (London, 1890), 2:450.

12. See Edward Burns's Arden edition of *1 Henry VI,* 19–21.

13. In the Cambridge edition of *1 Henry VI* (Cambridge, 1991), 42–43.

14. Sigmund Freud, *Introductory Lectures on Psychoanalysis,* Lectures 2, 3, and 4, in *The Complete Psychological Works of Sigmund Freud,* trans. J. Strachey et al., 24 vols. (London, 1953–74), 15: esp. 38, 61.

15. Bertrand Russell, *Portraits from Memory and Other Essays* (London, 1958), 27.

16. Demetriou, "Out of the Silence," 35.

17. John Rous (Joannes Rossus), *Joannis Rossi antiquarii Warwicensis historia regum Angliae,* 2nd ed. (Oxford, 1745), 215. Translation from Alison Hanham, *Richard III and His Early Historians* (Oxford, 1975), 120.

18. *Holinshed's Chronicles of England, Scotland and Ireland,* 6 vols. (London, 1807–8), 3:413.

19. In G. Bullough, ed., *Narrative and Dramatic Sources of Shakespeare,* 8 vols. (London, 1957–85), 3:303.

20. Ibid., 346.

21. Hall, *Union of Two Noble Famelies,* "Kynge Edward iiii," fol. 50v. See Bullough, ed., *Narrative and Dramatic Sources,* 3:249.

22. In fact the Lady Anne of history was betrothed, not married, to Prince Edward. The "Milesian tale" of the widow of Ephesus has a similar, disquieting erotic logic: a certain widow, known for her virtue, is so overwhelmed by the death of her husband that she remains, day after day, with his body in its underground tomb, refusing all food and drink. Meanwhile a soldier guarding the bodies of certain crucified criminals hears the lady sobbing, leaves his post, and gives her food; he makes a sexual advance, and the widow suddenly yields. They have sex in the tomb beside the body of the dead husband. The soldier then finds himself in terrible danger because a body he had been set to guard has been removed. The widow ingeniously solves the problem by showing how her husband's body can be substituted for the one that is missing. The story is told in Petronius, *Satyricon,* Loeb Classical Library (London, 1969), 268–76. It is a curious mixture of *Richard III, Romeo and Juliet,* and *Measure for Measure.*

23. Ian McEwan, *Atonement* (London, 2001), 86 and 131f.

24. I have given the reading of the First Quarto. The *Riverside Shakespeare* prints "I am I" in place of "I and I."

25. In James Lull's edition of *Richard III* (Cambridge, 1999), 64.

26. Harold Bloom, *Shakespeare: The Invention of the Human* (New York, 1998), 67.

27. Interestingly, Marlowe may be behind this earlier passage too; see *Tamburlaine,* pt. 2, II.i.33–59.

28. Lull, Cambridge edition of *Richard III,* 12.

29. See Richard Rowland, ed., *Edward II,* vol. 3 of *The Complete Works of Christopher Marlowe,* 5 vols. to date (Oxford, 1987–), xvi.

30. Bloom, *Shakespeare: The Invention of the Human,* 36–40. Bloom does hesitate in the course of this essay to wonder whether something important might be afoot in the relationship of Valentine and Proteus.

31. We may compare this with the strong hint that Falstaff was going to cut in with a joke half-way through the new king's speech rejecting him (*2 Henry IV,* V.v.55).

32. M. C. Bradbrook, *Shakespeare and Elizabethan Poetry* (London, 1951), 151.

33. Quoted in Clifford Leech's Arden edition of *Two Gentlemen of Verona* (London, 1969), lxix.

34. A present-day falconer assures me that he can train a hawk in about three weeks without any competitive staying awake. The Elizabethans, however, seem to have thought it necessary (perhaps they required a higher standard of obedience from the bird). Cf. "I'll watch him tame" (*Othello,* III.iii.23).

35. Germaine Greer, *The Female Eunuch* (London, 1981), 209.

36. Ibid.

37. Semiramis is briefly mentioned in Shakespeare's favourite author, Ovid (*Metamorphoses,* iv.58), but the sensational material is in Diodorus Siculus (II.xiii.4).

38. *Rapuitque pudorem,* Ovid, *Metamorphoses,* i.588–600.

39. For example, Ann Thompson in her Cambridge edition of *The Taming of the Shrew* (Cambridge, 2003), 101. See also G. R. Hibbard's New Penguin *Taming of the Shrew* (Harmondsworth, 1968), 203–4.

40. Petronius, *Satyricon,* 66.

41. Harold C. Goddard, *The Meaning of Shakespeare,* 2 vols. (Chicago, 1951), 1:68f.

42. See Jonathan Bate's Arden edition of *Titus Andronicus* (London, 1995), 69–72.

43. A text (1604), in Christopher Marlowe, *Doctor Faustus,* ed. Roma Gill (Oxford, 1990), Scene xiii, 74–75.

44. A. D. Nuttall, *A New Mimesis* (London, 1983), 181.

45. See Hiram B. Haydn, ed., *The Portable Elizabethan Reader* (New York, 1946), 221–22.

46. *The Heroycall Epistles of Publius Ovidius Naso,* trans. George Turbervile [sic], ed. F. Boas (London, 1928), 5.

47. For those who enjoy labyrinths: Aeacus was the father of Peleus and of Telamon. Peleus was the father of Achilles and Telamon of Ajax. So both Achilles and Ajax were grandsons of Aeacus. The term "Aeacides" is applied by Ovid to Peleus at *Metamorphoses,* xi.227 and xii.365, and to Telamon, the father of Ajax, at *Metamorphoses,* viii.4. Ovid never refers, I think, to *Ajax* as "Aeacides" (unless in this one place, if Lucentio is right), but at *Metamorphoses,* xiii.25, he has Ajax explain that he is the grandson of Aeacus. Virgil calls Achilles "Aeacides" at *Aeneid,* i.99, and extended the patronymic as far as Pyrrhus, the son of Achilles, at *Aeneid,* iii.296. The only other

place where Shakespeare uses this patronymic—in the amphibologous oracle so deliciously apposite to the shimmering causal field of *2 Henry VI*—the reference is to Pyrrhus, the line of Achilles, not that of Ajax (I.iv.62).

48. John Lyly, *Euphues,* in *The Complete Works of John Lyly,* ed. R. Warwick Bond, 3 vols. (Oxford, 1902), 1:287–88.

49. See Lyly's prefatory letter to Lord Delaware, in ibid., 184–86.

Chapter 2: Learning Not to Run

1. See Jonathan Bate, *Shakespeare and Ovid* (Oxford, 1993), 116.

2. See Jonathan Bate's Arden edition of *Titus Andronicus* (London, 1995), 2.

3. See A. E. Housman's obituary for J. M. Image in the *Cambridge Review,* 28 November 1919, in Housman, *Selected Prose,* ed. John Carter (Cambridge, 1961), 152.

4. Henry Fielding, *Tom Jones,* xiii, 7, 2 vols. (Oxford, 1974), 2:715.

5. It can be argued that only three senses are involved: (1) "eye," (2) "enlightenment," (3) "eye" (again), and (4) "sight"—"The eye seeking enlightenment ingeniously robs *itself* of sight." The "four sense" interpretation gives weight to the fact that it is the mind rather than the physical eye that *seeks* enlightenment.

6. Ernst Cassirer, *The Platonic Renaissance in England,* trans. James P. Pettegrove (New York, 1970), 178.

7. Thomas Hobbes, *Human Nature,* ix.13, in *The English Works of Thomas Hobbes,* ed. Sir William Molesworth, 11 vols. (London, 1839–44), 4:46.

8. Thomas More, *Utopia,* trans. Paul Turner (Harmondsworth, 1965), 54.

9. *Ipse saepius quam dicta sua rideretur,* in *Utopia,* ed. Edward Surtz and J. H. Hexter, *Complete Works of St. Thomas More,* vol. 4 (New Haven, 1965), 80.

10. W. H. Auden, *The Dyer's Hand and Other Essays* (London, 1963), 177.

11. Thomas De Quincey, "Lord Carlisle on Pope," in *The Collected Works of Thomas De Quincey,* ed. David Masson, 14 vols. (Edinburgh, 1889–90), 11:119.

12. Jean-Jacques Rousseau, *Discourse on the Origin of Inequality,* in Rousseau, *The Social Contract and Discourses,* ed. G. D. H. Cole (London, 1973), esp. 58.

13. The *Oxford English Dictionary* does not give the sense "cat" for "tib" earlier than 1828, but it must be much older than that. The cat in Caxton's *Historye of Reynart the Fox* (1481) is called "Tybert."

14. Atypical, but not unprecedented. See Katherine M. Briggs, *The Anatomy of Puck* (London, 1959), 13, and Harold F. Brooks's Arden edition of *A Midsummer Night's Dream* (London, 1979), lxxi–lxxii.

15. Chrétien de Troyes, *Le Chevalier de la charette,* lines 4716–19, ed. Mario Roques (Paris, 1970), 144.

16. "Ratio quodammodo ligatur," Aquinas, *Summa theologiae,* 1a 2ae, 77.2, in the Blackfriars edition with an English translation, 61 vols. (London, 1953–80), 25:164–66.

17. Geoffrey Chaucer, *Troilus and Criseyde,* v.1835.

18. Graham Bradshaw, *Shakespeare's Scepticism* (Brighton, 1987), 44.

19. See Aristotle, *Metaphysics,* 1011b26–28, and Alfred Tarski, *Logic, Semantics, Mathematics* (Oxford, 1956), 155.

20. Gilbert Ryle, *Plato's Progress* (Bristol, 1994), 9.

21. Dorothy Emmett, *The Nature of Metaphysical Thinking* (London, 1945), 66.

22. On Bottom's speech, see Richard Scholar, *The "Je-Ne-Sais-Quoi" in Early Modern Europe* (Oxford, 2005), 282–88.

23. See my note, "Bottom's Dream," *Notes and Queries,* 246 (2001), 276.

24. Priscian, *Institutio grammatica,* iv.32, in H. Keil, *Grammatici Latini,* 7 vols. (Leipzig, 1857–80), 2:136.

25. *The Golden Ass of Apuleius,* trans. William Adlington (Tudor Translations), ed. W. E. Healey (London, 1893), 217–18.

26. Robert Kirk, *The Secret Commonwealth of Elves, Fauns and Fairies,* ed. Stewart Sanderson (Cambridge, 1976), 49.

27. For a fuller discussion, see my *"A Midsummer Night's Dream:* Comedy as Apotrope of Myth," *Shakespeare Survey,* 53 (2000), 49–59.

Chapter 3: The Major Histories

1. A. P. Rossiter, *Angel with Horns* (London, 1961), 29ff.

2. Henry de Bracton, "Rex . . . sub Deo et sub lege, quia lex facit regem," *On the Laws and Customs of England [De legibus et consuetudinibus Angliae],* ed. and trans. Samuel E. Thorne, 4 vols. (Cambridge, Mass., 1968–77), 2:33. Scholars now think that Bracton was more the editor than the author of this work.

3. Thomas Aquinas, in the Blackfriars edition of the *Summa theologiae,* 61 vols. (London, 1953–80), 36:78–82.

4. Richard Hooker, *Ecclesiastical Polity,* VIII.ii.3, VIII.iii.1, in the Folger edition of *The Works of Richard Hooker,* ed. W. Speed Hill, 7 vols. in 8 (Cambridge, Mass., 1977–93), 3:332, 337.

5. William Tyndale, *Obedience of a Christian Man,* Scolar Press facsimile (Menston, 1970) of the 1528 edition (described as having been printed at "Malborowe" but really Antwerp), fol. 32v.

6. *The Two Books of Homilies* (Oxford, 1859), 557, 555.

7. See *Holinshed's Chronicles, R II, 1398–1400, H IV and H V* (Oxford, 1923), 33.

8. See Peter Ure's Arden edition of *Richard II* (London, 1966), lix.

9. Sir Gelly Merrick testified under examination that "the play was of King Henry the Fourth, and of the killing of Richard the Second." It is overwhelmingly probable (but not certain) that the play performed was Shakespeare's *Richard II.* See *Calendar of State Papers (Domestic Series) Reign of Elizabeth, 1598–1601,* ed. M. A. E. Green, the Kraus Reprint (Nendeln, Liechtenstein, 1967), 575. For Devereux's identifying with Bullingbrook, see ibid., 555, 567. See also Andrew Gurr's updated edition of *Richard II* (Cambridge, 2003), 7.

10. *Richard III,* V.iii.183.

11. Walter Pater, *Appreciations* (London, 1910), 198.

12. E. H. Kantorowicz, *The King's Two Bodies: A Study in Mediaeval Political Theology* (Princeton, N.J., 1957).

13. Cf. Ovid, *Ars amatoria*, ii.313, *Si latet ars, prodest.*

14. I called him a "white Machiavel" in *A New Mimesis* (London, 1983), 147.

15. W. H. Auden, *The Dyer's Hand and Other Essays* (London, 1963), 205–6.

16. Niccolò Machiavelli, *Discorsi*, III.I, trans. Leslie J. Walker (Harmondsworth, 1970), 390–92. Near the end of *The Rape of Lucrece* Shakespeare tells how Brutus, at a crucial moment, threw off "the shallow habit / . . . wherein deep policy did him disguise" (lines 1814–15).

17. Tom McAlindon, "Perfect Answers: Religious Inquisition, Falstaffian Wit," *Shakespeare Survey*, 54 (2001), 100–107.

18. Maurice Morgann, *Essay on the Dramatic Character of Sir John Falstaff*, in Daniel A. Fineman, ed., *Maurice Morgann: Shakespearean Criticism* (Oxford, 1972), 192.

19. See pp. 9–10, above.

20. See Anselm's reply to Roscelin, canon of Compiègne, in J.- P. Migne, ed., *Patrologiae cursus completus; Series Latina*, 221 vols. (Paris, 1844–64), 158:col. 265.

21. Thomas More, *Utopia*, Book ii, in the edition by Edward Surtz and J. H. Hexter (New Haven, 1965), 158.

22. Morgann, *Essay on the Dramatic Character of Sir John Falstaff*, 182.

23. Stephen Greenblatt, *Shakespearean Negotiations: The Circulation of Social Energy in Renaissance England* (Oxford, 1988), 135ff.

24. Anne Barton, "The King Disguised," in Barton, *Essays, Mainly Shakespearean* (Cambridge, 1994), 207–33.

25. Niccolò Machiavelli, *The Prince*, trans. Harvey C. Mansfield (Chicago, 1998), 66.

26. Aristotle, *Politics*, 1253a.

27. "The well-being of the people is the highest law."

28. See B. de Locque, *Discourses of Warre and Single Combat*, trans. John Eliot (London, 1591), 33, and A. R. Humphreys's Arden edition of *2 Henry IV* (London, 1966), 33.

29. See Samuel Johnson's note to *2 Henry IV*, IV.ii.122, and A. C. Bradley, *Oxford Lectures on Poetry* (London, 1965), 256.

30. Hamlet has company, but it is not unambiguously welcome. He is haunted by a dead king.

Chapter 4: Stoics and Sceptics

1. See Walter Scott, *Life of Napoleon Bonaparte*, 9 vols. (London, 1827), 6:251.

2. See George Watson, *The English Ideology* (London, 1973), 11, and Watson, "How to Be an Ideologue," *Georgia Review*, 38 (1984), 731–46.

3. See G. Bullough, ed., *Narrative and Dramatic Sources of Shakespeare*, 8 vols. (London, 1957–85), 5:506.

4. Heather James, *Shakespeare's Troy* (Cambridge, 1997), 1.

5. Karl Popper, *The Open Society and Its Enemies,* 2 vols. (London, 1966), 1:123. See also Popper's *Conjectures and Refutations* (London, 1972), 351, and Plato, *Republic,* 565C–D.

6. Bullough, ed.,*Narrative and Dramatic Sources,* 5:90.

7. David Hume, *A Treatise of Human Nature,* II.iii.3, ed. L. A. Selby-Bigge (Oxford, 1888), 416.

8. Ibid., 415.

9. See, e.g., Seneca, *Ad Helviam de consolatione,* xi.7.

10. Epictetus, *Dissertatio,* III.ii.1–10.

11. Seneca, *De constantia,* iii.5.

12. William Poole, " 'Unpointed words': Shakespearean Syntax in Action," *Cambridge Quarterly,* 32, no. 1 (2003), 27–48.

13. Brian Vickers, *In Defence of Rhetoric* (Oxford, 1988), 263–64.

14. See W. K. C. Guthrie, *The Sophists* (Cambridge, 1971), 180.

15. John Locke, *An Essay Concerning Human Understanding,* III.x.34, ed. P. H. Nidditch (Oxford, 1979), 508; Immanuel Kant, *Critique of the Power of Judgment,* sec. 53, ed. Paul Guyer, trans. Paul Guyer and Eric Matthews (Cambridge, 2000), 204–5.

16. W. H. Auden, "In Memory of W. B. Yeats."

17. Hume, A *Treatise of Human Nature,* II.iii.3, p. 416.

18. Sir Philip Sidney, *A Defence of Poetry,* in *Miscellaneous Prose of Sir Philip Sidney,* ed. Katherine Duncan-Jones (Oxford, 1973), 85, 86.

19. It may be thought that Benet of Canfield's *Rule of Perfection* is a work of devotional piety rather than a treatise on the passions. In fact it is both at once. On all five writers, Wright, Benet, Charleton, Senault, and Reynolds, see Marion Müller, *These Savage Beasts Become Domestick* (Trier, 2004).

20. Steve Sohmer drew my attention to the passage in Suetonius in November 1994.

21. Cato, *Disticha,* i.4, in Taverner's translation of 1540.

22. Jean-Jacques Rousseau, "Confession of a Savoyard Vicar," in Rousseau, *Émile,* trans. Barbara Foxley (1911; reprint, London, 1982), 247.

23. Locke, *An Essay Concerning Human Understanding,* IV.i.1, ed. Nidditch, 525.

24. Hume, *A Treatise of Human Nature,* I.ii.6, pp. 67–68.

25. Saxo calls him "Amleth"; this is probably connected etymologically with *amlothi,* which in later Icelandic means "fool." See Saxo Grammaticus, *History of the Danes, Books i–ix,* ed. H. E. Davidson (Cambridge, 1980), pt. 2, 59, n. 63.

26. See William James, *The Principles of Psychology,* 2 vols. (London, 1890), 2:449.

27. Baron von Hügel, *Essays and Addresses on the Philosophy of Religion,* 1st ser. (London, 1928), 251.

28. Marriage to a deceased brother's widow was technically forbidden, but it was also a site of intense argument. Henry VIII obtained a papal dispensation to marry Catherine of Aragon, the widow of his brother, Arthur. See J. J. Scarisbrick's majestic chapter, "The Canon Law of the Divorce," in his *Henry VIII* (London, 1968), 163–97.

29. *The Collected Works of Samuel Taylor Coleridge,* gen. ed. Kathleen Coburn, 16 vols. (London, 1978–2001), 5:539.

30. G. E. M. Anscombe, *Intention,* 2nd ed. (Oxford, 1963), 52.

31. Georg Wilhelm Friedrich Hegel, *Aesthetics: Lectures on Fine Arts,* trans. T. M. Knox, 2 vols. (Oxford, 1975), 1:221.

32. Plato, *Republic,* 493E. Cf. 354B, "I have tasted many dishes without having discovered the nature of justice."

33. Ludwig Wittgenstein, *Tractatus logico-philosophicus,* 6.4311, German text with an English translation by C. K. Ogden (London, 1933), 184.

34. See Sir Richard Baker, *The Chronicle of the Kings of England* (London, 1643), 156.

35. Rabelais, *Oeuvres,* trans. Thomas Urquhart and P. A. Motteux, 2 vols. (New York, 1931), 1:419–21.

36. Although the phrase *in medias res* comes from the Latin poet Horace (*Ars poetica,* 148) the idea is clearly Greek and Homeric epic is the standard example. Aristotle praises Homer for seeing that artistic unity is not attained simply by narrating everything that happened to a given person from birth on (*Poetics,* 1451a16–34).

37. The word is used by an ancient scholiast commenting on Euripides' *Phoenissae,* 88; in *Scholia in Euripidem,* ed. E. Schwarz, 2 vols. (Berlin, 1887), 1:260.

38. Marco Girolamo Vida, *De arte poetica* (1517?), ii.299, text with a translation and commentary by Ralph G. Williams (New York, 1976), 62.

39. "Ecphrastic" here means "having the character of a work of art—say, a painting—presented within a literary work."

40. On Italian epic burlesque and Spanish parodic treatment of Homer, see W. R. Elton, *Shakespeare's "Troilus and Cressida" and the Inns of Court Revels* (Aldershot, 2000), 9.

41. First published in 1933, printed in L. C. Knights, *Explorations* (London, 1958), 1–39.

42. Sir Thomas Elyot, *Boke Named the Governour,* ed. H. S. Croft, 2 vols. (London, 1883), 1:3.

43. See, e.g., *The Catholic Encyclopaedia,* 17 vols. (New York, 1907–), vol. 1, s.v. "accident," sec. 2.

44. The word "subtle" is used in Robert Greene's *Euphues his Censure to Philautus* (1587), a work that clearly influenced Shakespeare's conception of the Greeks as they figure in the story of Troy: "Grecians, taught in their schools that that wisdom is honest that is profitable . . . their heads full of subtlety," *The Life and Works of Robert Greene,* ed. Alexander Grosart, 15 vols. (London, 1881–86), 6:162.

45. *Troilus and Cressida,* ed. Kenneth Palmer (London, 1981), 45.

46. G. E. Moore, *Principia Ethica* (Cambridge, 1962), 16.

Chapter 5: Strong Women, Weaker Men

1. See A. L. Rowse, *The Early Churchills* (London, 1956), 157. Rowse says "by verbal tradition." I think he means "by oral tradition."

2. See esp. Virgil, *Georgics,* i.121–46.

3. "There is no world outside the text": Jacques Derrida, *De la grammatologie* (Paris, 1967), 227.

4. Molière, *Oeuvres complètes,* 2 vols. (Paris, 1962), 2:848.

5. Some hold that the double time scheme is proved by Othello's words at V.i.209–11: "But yet Iago knows / That she with Cassio hath the act of shame / A thousand times committed." This, it is said, implies a very long time indeed, so long that it does not square with the likely period of the courtship; therefore we must simply grant that the time references really are irrationally inconsistent. But a brief glance at a Shakespeare concordance will confirm at once that "a thousand times" is commonly used as a loose intensive, meaning little more than "over and over again." Cf. esp. *Much Ado about Nothing,* IV.i.94.

6. Lady Caroline Lamb, who loved Lord Byron, is a possible counter-example, but Rosalind would say, "I said no men—Lady Caroline was a woman."

7. See Erwin Panofsky, "*Et in Arcadia Ego:* Poussin and the Elegiac Tradition," in Panofsky, *Meaning in the Visual Arts* (New York, 1955), 295–320.

8. See Laurence Lerner, *The Uses of Nostalgia* (London, 1972), 27.

9. Auden's poem "Vespers" (*Horae Canonicae,* 4), and essay, "Dingley Dell and the Fleet," in W. H. Auden, *The Dyer's Hand and Other Essays* (London, 1963), 407–28.

10. Malvolio himself ponders aloud on the imperfect anagram of his own name, in the letter left for him to find, at II.v.139–41.

11. John Whitgift, *An Answere to a certen Libel intituled an Admonition to the Parliament* (London, 1572), 18.

12. Lord Macaulay, *History of England,* chap. 2, in *The Works of Lord Macaulay,* ed. Lady Trevelyan, 11 vols. (London, 1866), 1:127.

13. Friedrich Nietzsche, *The Genealogy of Morals,* ii.16, in the translation by Francis Golffing, bound in one volume with *The Birth of Tragedy* (New York, 1956), 198.

14. Ernst Cassirer, *The Platonic Renaissance in England,* trans. James P. Pettegrove (New York, 1970), 217.

15. See above, p. 98.

16. Auden, *The Dyer's Hand,* 177.

17. Jonathan Bate, *Shakespeare and Ovid* (Oxford, 1997), 147.

18. *The Autobiography of Thomas Whythorne,* ed. James M. Osborne (London, 1961), 51–52.

19. The *Riverside Shakespeare* gives the Folio reading, "Hallow," but the sense is "halloo."

20. Elizabeth Story Donno, in her Cambridge Shakespeare edition of *Twelfth Night* (Cambridge, 2003), 24.

21. Henri Bergson, *Laughter: An Essay on the Meaning of the Comic,* trans. C. Brereton and F. Rothwell (London, 1911), 10, 57–58.

22. A. D. Nuttall, "*The Winter's Tale:* Ovid Transformed," in A. B. Taylor, ed., *Shakespeare's Ovid* (Cambridge, 2000), 135–49, at 148.

23. Bertolt Brecht, *Schriften zum Theater,* 7 vols. (Frankfurt, 1963–64), 5:177.

24. Søren Kierkegaard, *Either / Or,* trans. D. F. and L. M. Swenson, 2 vols. (Princeton, N.J., 1971), 1:14.

25. Ibid., 147.

Chapter 6: The Moralist

1. Today dictionaries define *usury* as "lending at *excessive* interest." In older texts the word is applicable to any lending for which interest is charged. It is interesting that society has had to make this lexical adjustment.

2. See Brian Pullan, *Rich and Poor in Renaissance Venice* (Oxford, 1971), 495.

3. See the preface to *A Critique of Political Economy,* in Karl Marx and Frederick Engels, *Collected Works,* 50 vols. (London, 1978–2004), 29:263.

4. See, e.g., *The Apocryphon of John* in Bentley Layton, *The Gnostic Scriptures* (London, 1987), 46, 49.

5. In the Pentateuch of 1530 (Antwerp), fol. iv.

6. See Augustine, *De haeresibus,* i.17, in J.-P. Migne, ed., *Patrologiae cursus completus; Series Latina,* 221 vols. (Paris, 1844–64), 42:28, and Epiphanius, *Panarion,* xxxviii, trans. F. Williams (London, 1987), 241, 242.

7. See, e.g., William Blake, *Vala, or the Four Zoas,* iv.38–39.

8. In David Erdman, ed., *The Poetry and Prose of William Blake* (New York, 1988), 565.

9. See *The Marriage of Heaven and Hell,* pl. 23, and *The Everlasting Gospel,* esp. f. 11–14, in Erdman, ed., *The Poetry and Prose of Blake,* 43, 521.

10. See Erasmus, *The Education of a Christian Prince* (1516), trans. L. K. Born (New York, 1936), 210. There is here no whiff of immoralism. On the other hand, Machiavelli's account of the manner in which Cesare Borgia first employed Messer Remiro d'Orco, "a cruel and energetic man," to tighten up the laws in the province and afterwards made himself universally popular by contriving a spectacular death for the hated officer is immediately shocking and must always have been so (*The Prince,* ed. Quentin Skinner and Russell Price [Cambridge, 1988]), 26).

11. See, e.g., Origen, *Commentaria in Matthaeum,* XIII.viii.9, in J.-P. Migne, *Patrologiae cursus completus; Series Graeca* 150 vols. (Paris, 1857–65), 13:1115.

12. Anselm, in *Cur Deus Homo?* in *Anselm of Canterbury,* ed. and trans. J. Hopkins and H. Richardson, 4 vols. (London, 1974–76), 3:56–57.

13. Roy W. Battenhouse, "*Measure for Measure* and the Doctrine of the Atonement," *Publications of the Modern Language Association* (*PMLA*), 61 (1946), 1029–59.

14. In *Luther's Works,* ed. J. Pelikan, 56 vols. (St. Louis, Mo., 1955–86), 26:279.

15. See *D. Martin Luthers Werke,* ed. J. K. F. Knaake et al. (Weimar, 1883–), 5:602.

16. See the marginal comment in the Geneva Bible on Epistle to the Hebrews, 9:8 (the context is the relation of Christ to the sacrifices described in Leviticus as proper to the Jewish Day of Atonement): "Christ is both high Priest . . . and sacrifice." See also J. G. Frazer on "the dying god" as scapegoat, *The Golden Bough,* pt. 6, *The Scapegoat* (London, 1913), 227.

17. Jorge Luis Borges, "The Three Versions of Judas," in Borges, *Ficciones* (Buenos Aires, 1962), 151–57.

18. R. Kasser, M. Meyer, and G. Wurst, eds., *The Gospel of Judas* (Washington, D.C., 2006), esp. 43. In about A.D. 180 Irenaeus, bishop of Lyons, wrote a hostile account of the

Gospel of Judas; he said that the author of this heretical work claimed that Judas was privy to secret truths and this was why he carried out his act of "betrayal" (*Adversus haereses*, I.xxxi.1, ed. A. Rousseau and L. Doutreleau, 5 vols. in 8 [Paris, 1965–82], 1:386). Irenaeus on heresy was widely read in the Renaissance period, but in 1978 the gospel itself was found (in a Coptic version) by Egyptian peasants. Irenaeus, it emerged, had not overplayed the heresy.

19. See Brian Pullen, "Charity and Usury: Christian and Jewish Lending in Renaissance and Early Modern Italy," *Proceedings of the British Academy*, 125 (2003), 19–40, at 26.

20. On a single page Anselm writes, first, "He offered Himself to Himself," and then "The Son freely offered Himself to the Father," in *Cur Deus Homo?* II.xviii (xix in Migne's numbering), in *Anselm of Canterbury*, ed. Hopkins and Richardson, 2:133. In Migne, *Patrologiae Latina*, 15:428.

21. William Poole, written communication to the author.

22. See Philip Brockbank, *Marlowe: Dr Faustus* (London, 1962), 10–11. On the "Baines note," see Millar MacLure, ed., *Marlowe: The Critical Heritage* (London, 1979), 36–38.

23. See his sermon preached on Easter Monday, 1622.

24. Most people know that there was a coin called an "angel" in Shakespeare's time. Fewer know that there was another coin (admittedly obsolete by Shakespeare's time) called an "angelot"—pronounced "angelo" (or, just possibly, with the final "t" sounded). Fiduciary coinage, "the medium of exchange," was itself still faintly mysterious in the early seventeenth century. Donne's phrase, "the king's reall, or his stamped, face" ("The Canonization"), with its slippage from authentic to vicarious efficacy, has its own relevance to Shakespeare's play. There is one path from *The Merchant of Venice* to *Measure for Measure* by way of the conception of mercy. Perhaps there was another, by way of *money*, so central to the earlier play. Perhaps Shakespeare started to think about coinage. My attention was drawn to the word "angelot" by William Poole.

Chapter 7: How Character May Be Formed

1. A. D. Nuttall, *A New Mimesis* (London, 1983), 134.

2. *The Collected Works of Samuel Taylor Coleridge,* gen. ed. Kathleen Coburn, 16 vols. (Princeton, N.J, 1978–2001), 5:315.

3. Fyodor Dostoevsky, *Crime and Punishment,* part 1, chap. 6, trans. Constance Garnett (London, 1914), 59–60.

4. Ibid., 60.

5. See A. W. Schlegel, *A Course of Lectures on Dramatic Art and Literature,* trans. John Black, 2 vols. (London, 1815), 2:192.

6. E. M. Forster, *Passage to India,* chap. 14 (London, 1947), 156.

7. Alan C. Dessen and Leslie Thomson point out that few stage directions seem to have emerged from "stage business" or to be have been inserted afterwards by editors; most were put in place by the authors of the plays. See their *Dictionary of Stage Directions in English Drama, 1580–1642* (Cambridge, 1999), ix.

8. Charles Dickens, *David Copperfield,* chap. 25.

9. In Tacitus's *Germania* (7) we are told that mothers and wives turned out to encourage the fighters when battles were fought, rather like fans at a football match. They exposed their breasts and *rejoiced* in the number of wounds sustained by their men. The coexistence of these two features makes it not improbable that the *Germania* should be included in the sources of *Coriolanus.* The snag is that although the writer is a Roman (with a Roman mindset), the behaviour described is German, not Roman. This objection is not as overwhelming as it first appears. The *Germania* is suffused with a cultural nostalgia: the war-loving Germans are seen as exemplars of primitive virtue— "the way we Romans used to be."

10. G. Bullough, ed., *Narrative and Dramatic Sources of Shakespeare,* 8 vols. (London, 1957– 85), 5:518.

11. *Aemilius Paulus,* xxi.5, in Sir Thomas North's translation, *The Lives of the Noble Grecians and Romanes,* 5 vols. (London, 1929–30), 2:31. Aemilius Paulus is gruffly reluctant when urged by the people to aspire to the consulship (2:9). There is a case for adding Plutarch's Life of this figure to the standard list of sources for Shakespeare's play.

12. Seneca, "Numerabit cicatrices," *De vita beata,* xv.5. See also Matthew Leigh, "Wounding and Popular Rhetoric at Rome," *Bulletin of the Institute of Classical Studies,* 40 (1995), 195–212.

13. Nutttall, *New Mimesis,* 120; Seneca, *Ad Helviam de consolatione,* xi.7, in *Seneca's Moral Essays,* ed. and trans. J. W. Basore, 3 vols. (London, 1958), 2:458.

14. Bullough, ed., *Narrative and Dramatic Sources,* 5:509.

15. Ibid.

16. See A. W. H. Adkins, *Merit and Responsibility* (Oxford, 1960), 37, 336f.

17. See George Herbert's poem "The Holdfast."

Chapter 8: Shrinking and Growing

1. Raphael Holinshed, I.xii, in *Holinshed's Chronicle as Used in Shakespeare's Plays,* ed. Allardyce and Josephine Nicholl (London, 1927), 225.

2. Geoffrey of Monmouth, *The History of the Kings of Britain,* trans. Lewis Thorpe (London, 1969), 61–62. Geoffrey explains how Bladud constructed a pair of wings and took to the air. Like Simon Magus, he fell and was dashed to pieces, on the Temple of Apollo at Trinovantum.

3. See David Willbern, "Shakespeare's Nothing," in *Representing Shakespeare: New Psychoanalytic Essays,* ed. Murray Schwartz and Coppélia Kahn (Baltimore, 1980), 244– 63, at 253.

4. My attention was drawn to this line by Sam Thompson in a dissertation he wrote for the Oxford M.Phil. examination in 2004.

5. See Kenneth Muir's Arden edition of *King Lear* (1952; reprint, London, 1959), 235.

6. See *Johnson on Shakespeare,* ed. Arthur Sherbo, 2 vols., being vols. 7 and 8 of the Yale

edition of *The Works of Samuel Johnson,* 17 vols. to date (New Haven, 1958–), 8:704, and *Tolstoy on Shakespeare* (London, 1907?), 43–44.

7. A. C. Bradley, *Shakespearean Tragedy* (New York, 1965), 231–75; J. F. Danby, *Shakespeare's Doctrine of Nature* (London, 1949), esp. 195; Barbara Everett, *Young Hamlet: Essays on Shakespeare's Tragedies* (Oxford, 1989), 59–82; John Holloway, *The Story of the Night: Studies in Shakespeare's Major Tragedies* (Lincoln, Nebr., 1961), esp. 79.

8. See R. A. Foakes's Arden edition of *King Lear* (Walton-on-Thames, 1997), 83.

9. See *The Works of Samuel Johnson,* 8:704.

10. Stephen Medcalf, "Dreaming, Looking, and Seeing: Shakespeare and the Myth of Resurrection," in *Thinking with Shakespeare,* ed. William Poole and Richard Scholar (Oxford, 2007).

11. Cf. Luke 2:49, "I must go about my father's business."

12. Bradley, *Shakespearean Tragedy,* 252.

13. Ibid., 241. Bradley contrasts pathos with tragic emotion at 232.

14. Ibid., 230.

15. Ibid., 263, 269.

16. Ibid., 262–63.

17. Ibid., 253.

18. This is the clear implication of the opening sentence of Johnson's 1757 review of Soame Jenyns, *A Free Inquiry into the Nature and Origin of Evil.* Johnson says the evil of the world will always be deeply puzzling as long as "we see but in part," in *The Works of Samuel Johnson,* 17 vols. (Oxford, 1958–2004), 17:397.

19. See Anne Atik, *How It Was: A Memoir of Samuel Beckett* (London, 2001), 25.

20. Marcel Mauss, *The Gift: Forms and Functions of Exchange in Archaic Societies* (London, 1954), 39.

21. See Francelia Butler, *The Strange Critical Fortunes of Shakespeare's "Timon of Athens"* (Ames, Iowa, 1966).

22. Although there is good reason to suppose that parts of *Timon of Athens* were written by Thomas Middleton, it remains clear in my opinion that the central ideas of the play and the thrust of its argument are Shakespeare's.

23. Alexander Pope, *An Essay on Criticism,* line 144 in *The Poems of Alexander Pope,* ed. John Butt (London, 1968), 149.

24. Yet Shakespeare shows that when Shylock withdraws from the public space of money-changing Venice to the private space of his own house he has a clear conception of "sentimental value"; it shows in his grief at the loss of the ring his wife gave him (III.i.120–23).

25. Some scholars attribute this scene to Middleton. I have argued that similar cannibalistic imagery in *King Lear* and elsewhere makes it likely that the scene is either Shakespearean or carefully revised by him. See my *Timon of Athens* (London, 1989), 34–36.

26. Albert Camus, "Avant-propos" to *L'Étranger,* ed. Ray Davison (London, 1988), vii.

27. See above, p. 204.

28. A C. Swinburne, "Hymn to Proserpine," line 35.

29. Thomas Mann, *Death in Venice,* trans. H. T. Lowe-Porter (Harmondsworth, 1955), 13, 9–10.

30. "Pink-eyed" may mean "half-closed" rather than "rosy."

31. See above, p. 187.

32. I first suggested a comparison with Anselm in my *Two Concepts of Allegory* (London, 1967), 133.

33. Anselm, *Proslogion,* chap. iii, in *Anselmi . . . Opera Omnia,* ed. F. S. Schmidt, 6 vols. (Edinburgh, 1940–51), 1:102–3. There is an English translation in *Anselm to Ockham,* vol. 10 of *The Library of Christian Classics,* 26 vols. (London, 1953–66), 74–75.

34. Compare the way Virgil moves, in connection with the figure of Dido, an earlier North African queen who tempted a Roman from the path of duty, from *Facile et mutabile semper / Femina,* "Woman was ever an easy, changeable thing," to Dido in death, as hard as Marpesian flint (*Aeneid,* iv.569, vi.471).

35. N. K. Sugimura, "Two Concepts of Reality in *Antony and Cleopatra,*" in *Thinking with Shakespeare,* ed. William Poole and Richard Scholar (Oxford, 2007).

36. Marilyn French, *Shakespeare's Division of Experience* (London, 1982), 251–64.

37. Plutarch explains that they had a son, Alexander, and a daughter, little Cleopatra, and how Antony nicknamed them "Sun" and "Moon." See G. Bullough, ed., *Narrative and Dramatic Sources of Shakespeare,* 8 vols. (London, 1957–85), 5:283.

38. L. C. Knights, "How Many Children Had Lady Macbeth?" (1933), in Knights, *Explorations* (London, 1958), 1–39.

39. G. Wilson Knight, *The Crown of Life* (London, 1948), 208.

40. W. K. Wimsatt, Jr., "Poetry and Morals: A Relation Reargued," in his *The Verbal Icon* (London, 1970), 85–100.

Chapter 9: The Last Plays

1. Many but by no means all. See Doreen del Vecchio and Antony Hammond, eds., the New Cambridge edition of *Pericles* (Cambridge, 1998), 8–15, for a highly intelligent questioning of the "scientific" evidence for dual authorship advanced in the Oxford Shakespeare and elsewhere. Del Vecchio and Hammond conclude that the whole play is probably by one person but then say that they do not care whether Shakespeare is that one person. I think that single authorship is probable but, unlike them, think that if we are to confine ourselves to one author Shakespeare alone fills the bill.

2. Lytton Strachey, *Books and Characters* (London, 1922), 60.

3. See above, pp. 43–f.

4. This is the Quarto reading that should be retained. The *Riverside Shakespeare,* following Malone, emends to "suit."

5. William Blake, "The Chimney Sweeper," from *Songs of Experience,* in *Blake: The Complete Poems,* ed. W. H. Stevenson, 2nd ed. (London 1989), 218–19.

6. Geoffrey of Monmouth, *The History of the Kings of Britain,* trans. Lewis Thorpe (London, 1969), 34.

7. Ibid., 35, 52–53.

8. Michael Drayton, *Polyolbion* (i.310–548), written before *Pericles* but published later (1612). Cf. Spenser, *The Faerie Queene,* II.x.9f.

9. Shakespeare got the story of Apollonius from Gower's English version in his *Confessio Amantis;* before Gower there were Latin versions, but the original is almost certainly a lost Greek novel.

10. Sallustius, *Concerning the Gods and the Universe,* iv, ed. with trans. by A. D. Nock (Cambridge, 1920), 8.

11. Virgil, *Georgics,* i.27.

12. When the disguised Henry V says that the King "is but a man as I am" (IV.i.101–2), modern audiences receive the proposition as a truth too obvious to need mention. To early modern audiences it would sound like a paradox. "As I am" wittily equivocates. It is one thing to say that one is no different from Williams or Bates, sitting over there; it is another to say that one is no different from the King of England.

13. Jonathan Bate, *Shakespeare and Ovid* (Oxford, 1993), 237.

14. Ibid.

15. Ibid.

16. It might be objected that if art can engage successfully with natural reality (as I have claimed), how can Shakespeare disparage art as woefully distinct from nature? Even successful naturalistic art is other than the nature it depicts (if it were not, no *engagement with* reality could have occurred). Shakespeare can with perfect consistency stress the distance between the artistic means and the nature so variably engaged thereby.

17. "We each of us suffer our own ghosts," Virgil, *Aeneid,* vi.743.

18. See above, p. 240.

19. W. H. Auden, "Dingley Dell and the Fleet," in his *The Dyer's Hand and Other Essays* (London, 1963), 407–28, and in his poem, "Horae Canonicae," 5 ("Vespers").

20. William Strachey, *A True Reportary of the Wrack,* first printed in *Purchas His Pilgrims* (1625) but accessible in manuscript from 1610.

21. See Giordano Bruno's philosophical poem *De immenso et innumerabilibus et universo,* v. 18, in *Jordani Bruni Nolani opera Latine conscripta,* ed. F. Fiorentino, 3 vols. in 8 (Naples, 1879–91), 1(2):282. In this work Bruno also argues for the existence of other worlds like ours, having intelligent inhabitants.

22. See Richard H. Popkin, *Isaac La Peyrère (1596–1676)* (London, 1987), 35–36, and Popkin, "The Pre-Adamite Theory in the Renaissance," in E. P. Mahoney, ed., *Philosophy and Humanism: Essays in Honour of Paul Oskar Kristeller* (Leiden, 1976), 50–69, at 57–58 and 61–62. See also Giuliano Gliozzi, *Adamo e il nuovo mondo* (Florence, 1976), esp. 269, 353.

23. Thomas Nashe, *Pierce Pennilesse his Supplication to the Divell,* and *Christes Teares over Jerusalem,* both in *The Works of Thomas Nashe,* ed. R. B. McKerrow, 5 vols. (London, 1910), 1:172, 2:116.

24. Thomas Hariot, *A briefe and true Report of the new found Land of Virginia* (London, 1588), E3r.

25. A. S. Gow in his commentary on Theocritus speculates that Polyphemus in the lost pre-Theocritean poem by Philoxenus was "a Caliban" (*Theocritus,* 3 vols. [Cambridge, 1950], 2:118).

26. That is if the Folio (the sole textual authority for the play) is correct in giving I.ii.351–62 to Miranda.

27. A. D. Nuttall, *Two Concepts of Allegory* (London, 1967), 140.

28. D. G. James, *The Dream of Prospero* (Oxford, 1967), 30.

29. Edward Dowden, *Shakspere: A Critical Study of His Mind and Art* (London, 1875), 403, 414.

30. Margaret Drabble, ed., *The Oxford Companion to English Literature,* 6th ed. rev. (Oxford, 2000), s.v. "The Tempest."

31. Most stage directions in Shakespeare are firmly professional, minimal instructions addressed by an insider to actors who understand their business. This one stands out. It presents the effect of the stage machinery and the noises involved as they would appear to a wondering outsider.

32. T. S. Eliot used "Those are pearls that were his eyes" in *The Waste Land* (i.48). Eliot's poem as a whole is all about the resurrection of *life,* but this allusion works as counterpoint to the central idea.

Coda

1. See Lukas Erne's cogently argued (against the wind of current fashion) *Shakespeare as Literary Dramatist* (Cambridge, 2003).

2. Anthony Ashley Cooper, *Characteristicks of Men, Manners, Opinions, Times,* ed. Philip Ayres, 2 vols. (Oxford, 1999), 1:151.

3. Here again I must stress that I am speaking in terms of myth, not of fact. There is plenty of Roman law in Bracton, and English prerogative courts used Roman law; meanwhile "customary law" figures prominently in French practice.

4. John Dryden, *Essay of Dramatic Poesy* (1668), in *Of Dramatic Poesy and Other Essays,* ed. George Watson, 2 vols. (London, 1962), 1:67.

5. Samuel Johnson, "Preface to Shakespeare," in the Yale edition of *The Works of Samuel Johnson,* 17 vols. to date (New Haven, 1958–), 7:84.

6. *Saturday Review,* 26 September 1896.

Index

Page numbers in italics indicate substantive discussion of a play

erosexual love in, 238–39; Touch-
stone and Audrey in, 69, 226–29, 253;
Touchstone as fool in, 227, 231, 232,
233; truth and honesty in, 227–28,
231, 232; unrequited lover described
in, 237
Aspinall, Alexander, 14
Atheist's Tragedy (Tourneur), 204
Atonement (McEwan), 52
Atonement doctrine, 268–70, 272–74
Aubrey, John, 386*n*21
Auden, W. H.: on Arcadians versus Uto-
pians, 240, 352, 362; on comedy, 98;
on *Henry IV,* 151; on poetry, 188; on
Twelfth Night, 242; writings by, 395*n*9,
401*n*19
Augustus Caesar, 339
Austen, Jane, 281
Austin, J. L., 91, 316

Bacchus, 323
Bacon, Francis, 83–84, 361
Baldwin, T. W., 14, 57
Bale, John, 26
Barrow, Henry, 20
Barton, Anne, 166, 224
Bate, Jonathan, 82, 88, 242, 358–59
Battenhouse, Roy W., 269
Bawdry, in *Romeo and Juliet,* 106
Bayley, John, 217
Beardsley, Aubrey, 244
Bearman, Robert, 13, 386*n*24
Beckett, Samuel, 312
Beeston, William, 15
Benet of Canfield, 189, 393*n*19
Bentham, Jeremy, 168
Bergson, Henri, 251
Berkeley, George, 327
Bible: Christ as priest and sacrifice in,
270, 396*n*16; Eden and Adam's Fall in,
229, 231, 240, 263–64, 349; Ephesus
in New Testament of, 58; Epistles in,
58, 127, 203, 264, 270, 396*n*1; on for-
giveness, 269; Gog and Magog in,
340; Gospels in, 24, 203, 241, 267,

269, 270, 318, 319, 396–97*n*18,
399*n*11; Judas's betrayal of Jesus in,
271; Last Supper in, 319; Lazarus in,
341; Lord's Prayer in, 318; on love in
New Testament, 49; on mercy, 267,
268–69; Ophite Gnostics' interpretation of, 263–65, 270–76; parable
of talents in, 24; Pharisees in, 241;
revenge prohibited by, 203–4; on
scapegoat, 270; scarlet sins and scarlet
woman in, 36; shepherd in New Tes-
tament of, 240. *See also specific books of
the Bible*
Black Prince, 40
Bladud, 398*n*2
Blair, Tony, 173
Blake, William, 264–65, 272, 323
Blood imagery: in *Coriolanus,* 291–92; in
Henry V and *Henry VI,* 293; in *Julius
Caesar,* 293–94; in *Macbeth,* 293; in
Titus Andronicus, 294
Bloom, Harold, 54, 64, 127, 389*n*30
Boar image, 47
Boas, G., 230
Boccaccio, Giovanni, 338
Boke Named the Governour (Elyot), 213–
14
Bolingbroke, 40, 41
Bonaparte. *See* Napoleon Bonaparte
Boniface, Pope, 37
Book of Martyrs (Foxe), 43
Borges, Jorge Luis, 270
Borgia, Cesare, 396*n*10
Borromeo, Cardinal Carlo, 13
Bourdieu, Pierre, 11
Bracton, Henry de, 140, 391*n*2, 402*n*3
Bradbrook, M. C., 67
Bradley, A. C., 46, 52, 168, 307–9,
312, 399*n*13
Bradshaw, Graham, 123, 216
Brecht, Bertolt, 253, 295, 380
*A briefe and true Report of the new
found Land of Virginia* (Hariot), 363,
364
Brooks, Harold, 67–68

Cicero, 85, 190

Cinthio, Giraldi, 267

Cleomenes, 168

Cleopatra, 400n37. See also *Antony and Cleopatra* (Shakespeare)

Clinton, Bill, 3

Coherence theory of truth, 123–24

Coleridge, Samuel Taylor, 200–202, 282

Collingbourne, William, 47

Comedic alienation, 253

Comedies: Bergson on, 251; Brechtian comedic alienation, 253; characteristics of, 100–102, 118; Christian *commedia,* 306–8; disquieting moments in, 58–59; Jonson's comedies, 98; and late romances by Shakespeare, 333, 334; marriage endings of, 237–38, 239, 252; mysterious-sadness-in-the-temporarily-frustrated in, 103–4, 105, 255–56; plays-within-plays in, 374; same-sex bonds versus heterosexual love in, 64–70, 100, 105–7, 130, 188–89, 221, 224–25, 238–39, 256, 281; Shakespeare's invention of laughing with rather than laughing at, 98, 242; and taboo subjects, 70–71; textual self-reference in, 359. *See also specific plays*

The Comedy of Errors (Shakespeare), *56–63:* Abbess and Egeon in, 59; Adriana in, 62; Antipholus of Syracuse in, 58, 61–62, 144–45; beating of servant in, 59; brothers Dromio and Dromio in, 60–61, 63, 245, 338; Catholicism in, 59; characterization in, 133; compared with *Pericles,* 61, 241, 334, 338; compared with *Richard II,* 144–45; compared with Shakespeare's late romances, 61, 241; compared with *Twelfth Night,* 241, 245; dating of composition of, 133; doubled self in, 133, 144, 145, 338; dramaturgical "islands" in, 61; kitchen wench in, 290; source of, 56–58, 61, 334; water imagery in, 61–62, 144

Commedia, 306–8

Constantine, Emperor, 273

Constructionism, 297–98

Cooper, Duff, 15

Cooper, Thomas, 57

Copland, Aaron, 186

Corbett, Richard, 20

Corinthians, Epistles to, 127, 264, 270

Coriolanus (Shakespeare), *290–99:* anachronism in, 172; Aufidius in, 295; banishment of Coriolanus in, 295; compared with *Henry VI,* 28; compared with *Julius Caesar,* 294–95; Coriolanus as figure of lesser intelligence in, 295; Coriolanus as harvester/killer in, 326; Coriolanus's recognition of truth in, 298–99, 322, 382; and corn riots in the Midlands, 9, 23; date of composition of, 290, 322; female/mother role in, 290–95, 297–99; guild-hall versus battle-field in, 28–29; Marcius in, 291, 294; Menenius's "fable of the belly" in, 295–96, 297; political rights in, 173; production of, and different historical contexts, 22; Roman politics in, 10, 23; sewing by women in, 290–91; sources of, 294, 322–23, 398n9, 398n11; stage directions in, 290–91, 298; Stoicism in, 295; theme of, 10; as tragedy, 297; Valeria in, 290, 291; Virgilia in, 290–92; Volumnia's conditioning of violence in Coriolanus in, 290–95, 297–99, 320, 322, 382; wealth of Coriolanus in, 296–97; wounds of Coriolanus in, 294

Correspondence theory of truth, 123–24

Così fan tutte (Mozart), 58

Cottom (or Cottam), John, 14, 15

Cottom (or Cottam), Thomas, 14, 386n28

Council of Trent, 17

Country life. *See* Pastoral

Courtly love, 224–25

Crashaw, Richard, 13, 88

Crime and Punishment (Dostoevsky), 284–85

Ephesians, Epistle to, 58

Epictetus, 178

Equality between men and women, 80, 82

Erasmus, 127, 212–13, 227

Eric of Auxerre, 157

Essay (Locke), 380

Essex, Earl of, 143

L'Être et le néant (Sartre), 134, 199

Euphues (Lyly), 85

Euphues his Censure to Philautus (Greene), 394*n*44

Euripides, 61, 145, 190, 394*n*37

Everett, Barbara, 307

Evil: Samuel Johnson on, 399*n*18; Milton on, 381. *See also specific plays*

Existentialism, 149, 199, 265, 379

Faerie Queene (Spenser), 10, 19, 108, 330, 340, 366

Fairies, 19–20, 108–9, 129

Falconry, 70, 113, 389*n*34

Falstaff. See *Henry IV* (Shakespeare)

Fawkes, Guy, 13–14

The Female Eunuch (Greer), 72, 79

Fielding, Henry, 91

Films. *See specific films*

The First Part of King Edward IV (Heywood), 166

Fool: in *All's Well That Ends Well*, 250–51; Armin on, 227; in *As You Like It*, 69, 226–29; in *Henry IV*, 227, 250; in *King Lear*, 250, 302; in *Much Ado about Nothing*, 227; in *Twelfth Night*, 246, 315

Fool upon Fool (Armin), 227

Forbidden Planet (film), 361

Forgiveness: Christian doctrine of, 67, 266, 267, 269–70; in *Measure for Measure*, 67, 266, 267, 274, 275, 317, 382; in *The Tempest*, 370–72; in *Two Gentlemen of Verona*, 65–66. *See also* Mercy

Formalist literary criticism, 357

Forster, E. M., 89, 104–5, 112, 288

Foucault, Michel, 44, 276

Foxe, John, 43

Frederick II, Emperor, 141

A Free Inquiry into the Nature and Origin of Evil (Jenyns), 399*n*18

French, Marilyn, 330, 332

Freud, Sigmund, 38, 74, 199–200, 207, 265, 287, 346

Friedrich, Caspar David, 103

Galatians, Epistle to, 270

"The Garden" (Marvell), 235

Gardner, Dame Helen, 53

Gawain and the Green Knight, 91, 214

Genesis, Book of, 229, 231, 263–64, 272

Geoffrey of Monmouth, 300, 339–40, 398*n*2

George a Greene, the Pinner of Wakefield (Greene), 166

George III, 300–301

Georgics (Virgil), 230

Germania (Tacitus), 398*n*9

Ghosts: in *Hamlet*, 11, 17, 205, 392*n*30; Protestantism on, 205; reference to, in *Antony and Cleopatra*, 332

Gibbon, Edward, 39

Gnosticism, 263–65, 270–76

Goddard, Harold C., 79, 80

The Godfather: Part II, 189

Goethe, Johann Wolfgang von, 193

Gog and Magog, 340

The Golden Ass (Apuleius), 23, 129

Golding, William, 363

Gombrich, E. H., 26

Goodfellas, 87

Gorboduc, 340

Gorboduc, 26–27

Gorgias, 185–86

The Goshawk (White), 70

Gosson, Stephen, 20

Gow, A. S., 402*n*25

Gower, John, 58, 401*n*8

Grace before meat, 317–19

Grace-gratitude nexus, 275, 313, 315–19, 372–73

Gratitude: grace-gratitude nexus, 275, 313, 315–19; ingratitude in *King Lear*, 312–13, 316, 317; ingratitude in *Timon of Athens*, 313–15

Greenblatt, Stephen, 11, 18–19, 21, 162

Greene, Robert, 166, 368, 394n44

Greer, Germaine, 72, 79

Grey, Lord, 10

Grimald, Nicholas, 306

Guercino, 240

Hall, Arthur, 209

Hall, Edward, 28, 30, 144

Hall, John, 14

Hamer, Douglas, 386n24

Hamlet (Shakespeare), *192–205:* authorship indicated on quarto of, 378; beginning of, 205; Catholicism in, 17, 18; Claudius in, 8, 179–80, 199–200, 203, 279–80; Coleridge on, 200–202; compared with *Henry V,* 196; compared with *Julius Caesar,* 180, 184, 192, 204; compared with Kyd's play on Hamlet, 196–97, 198, 205; compared with *Love's Labour's Lost,* 202; compared with *Macbeth,* 289; compared with *Richard II,* 196, 198; compared with *The Tempest,* 376; compared with *Troilus and Cressida,* 205–7, 210, 215; dating of composition of, 221; death as undiscovered country in, 365; death of Claudius in, 203; death of Hamlet's father in, 200; death of Ophelia in, 6–7, 8, 11–12, 108; Denmark as wicked kingdom in, 194, 196; dreams as nightmares in, 169, 194, 195–96; Empson on, 197–98, 201, 202; Freudian interpretation of, 199–200; Gertrude on Ophelia's death in, 6–7, 8, 11–12, 108; Gertrude's marriage to Claudius in, 199–200; ghost of dead king in, 11, 17, 205, 289, 392n30; grave-digger in, 205; Hamlet as player-avenger in, 196, 198; Hamlet as thinker in, 22, 200–202, 207, 215,

286, 383; Hamlet's decision not to kill praying Claudius in, 179–80, 279–80; Hamlet's failure to act in, 179–80, 196–98, 200–204, 279; Hamlet's isolation and darkness in, 168, 194, 198, 246, 282, 320; Hamlet's letter to Ophelia in, 198; Hamlet's rejection of Ophelia in, 194; Hamlet's soliloquy on death in, 204; Hamlet's "To be or not to be" soliloquy in, 8; Henry V compared with Hamlet, 168, 194; Horatio in, 8, 192, 193, 196; Laertes in, 192–93; law references in, 8, 11; Malvolio compared with Hamlet, 246; meaning of Hamlet's name, 196; metamorphic syntax in, 385n6; Ophelia's death in, 4–9, 11–12, 108, 385n6; Ophelia's songs in, 8; outside-in motivation in, 198–99, 277, 282, 382; play-within-play and actors in, 196–97, 198, 210, 374; Polonius in, 192–93, 200, 201, 207, 287; Purgatory in, 17, 18; real-life elements in, 4–9, 11, 12; retaliatory justice as God's work in, 260; and revenge as forbidden by Christianity, 202–4; Rosencrantz and Gildenstern in, 194; sexuality in, 199–200; stage directions in, 205; Stoicism in, 192–94, 196, 379; subjectivism in, 215; and unrequited lover described in *As You Like It,* 237

Hamlett, Katherine, drowning of, 4–8, 11, 12

Hammond, Antony, 400n1

Hariot, Thomas, 363, 364

Hathaway, Anne, 2, 15

Hattaway, Michael, 37

Hawk imagery, 70, 113, 116

Hebrews, Epistle to, 270, 396n16

Hecatommithi (Cinthio), 267

Hegel, G. W. F., 202, 381

Heidegger, Martin, 381

Helen of Troy, 185, 209, 215

Heliodorus, 58, 61, 341

Hamlet, 198; in *Henry V,* 152; in *Richard II,* 148–49; in *Richard III,* 54–56

Ideology, 171

Il Penseroso (Milton), 19, 103

Iliad (Homer), 209

Illyria. *See* Elysium/Illyria

Image-clusters, 5. *See also specific types of imagery, such as* Mirror imagery

Imagination: in *Antony and Cleopatra,* 382; Samuel Johnson on, 124; in *A Midsummer Night's Dream,* 121, 125, 132, 157, 372, 382; and Romanticism, 124–25

In Defence of Rhetoric (Vickers), 185

In medias res, 394*n*36

Incest, 359, 360, 368

Indians. *See* American Indians

Indulgences, 36

Inferno (Buffalmaccio), 37

Ingratitude. *See* Gratitude

The Inheritors (Golding), 363

Innocent, Pope, 272

Institutes (Calvin), 270

Institutio oratoria (Quintilian), 186

Introspection and interiority: in *Hamlet,* 22, 200–202, 207, 215, 286, 383; in *Richard II,* 22, 134, 144–49, 151, 251, 331; in *Richard III,* 53–56, 60, 85, 144, 151

Invisible acting, 150, 151, 168–69

Ion (Euripides), 61

Iraq war, 29

Irenaeus, 396–97*n*18

Isaiah, Book of, 36

Islands (dramaturgical), 43–45, 243

James, D. G., 369

James, Heather, 172

James, Henry, 31

James, William, 31

James-Lange theory of motivation, 31, 198–99

Jealousy: in *Othello,* 277–80, 281; in *The Winter's Tale,* 279, 346–50

Jenkins, Harold, 193, 194

Jenkins, Thomas, 14

Jenyns, Soame, 399*n*18

Jesuits, 13, 14, 18

Jesus Christ. *See* Bible; Christianity

The Jew of Malta (Marlowe), 54–55, 60, 82, 83, 84, 87, 260, 261, 363

Joan of Arc, 17, 28, 34–35

John, Gospel of, 267, 319

John Donne: Life, Mind and Art (Carey), 16

John of Gaunt, 40, 88, 134–35, 136

Johnson, Samuel: on evil, 399*n*18; on *Henry IV,* 168; and *Henry VI* stage directions, 33; on imagination, 124; on *King Lear,* 306, 307, 308; on optimism of Christianity, 309; *Rasselas* by, 124, 178; on Shakespeare's works compared to great forest, 379

Jonson, Ben, 56, 70, 98, 326

Judas, Gnostic Gospel of, 271, 396–97*n*18

Julius Caesar: assassination of, 172. *See also Julius Caesar* (Shakespeare)

Julius Caesar (Shakespeare), 171–91: anachronism in, 178; Antony and assassins in, 189–90; Antony's oration at Caesar's funeral, 150–51, 173–74, 186, 187, 188, 190, 324; assassination of Caesar in, 189–91, 293–94; blood imagery in, 293–94; Brutus and assassination of Caesar in, 189–90, 191, 293–94; Brutus as honourable man in, 184; Brutus's image in, 175–77; Brutus's justification for assassination of Caesar, 173–74; Brutus's oration at Caesar's funeral, 174–75, 186–87, 284; Brutus's soliloquy and his possible rationalization in, 179–84; Caesar as Colossus in, 178, 326; Caesar's dream in, 293; Caesar's fainting at refusal of crown in, 188, 190; Caesar's falling sickness in, 178; Casca in, 188, 190; Cassius in, 175–78, 190, 212, 277, 281, 288, 294; compared with

A Midsummer Night's Dream (continued)
compared with As You Like It, 128,
247; compared with Romeo and Juliet,
108–9, 116, 119–21, 125–26, 130;
compared with The Taming of the
Shrew, 73; compared with The Tempest, 361, 373, 375; dating of composition of, 119, 120; Demetrius in,
131–32; Duke Theseus in, 108, 121–
26, 129–32, 157, 169, 236, 247, 324,
347; Epilogue in, 130–31, 371; fairies
in, 108, 129; Fairy Queen Titania and
Bottom in, 73, 129; Helena in, 132;
Hermia in, 132; Hippolyta in, 23,
122–26, 129, 130, 132, 236, 324, 326,
327, 347; imagination speech in, 121,
125, 132, 157, 372, 382; love in, 119–
21, 131–32, 373; Lysander in, 119–
20, 122; mocking of "mechanicals"
in, 242; moon and sun imagery in,
125; mythological groundwork of, 23,
108, 121–22, 128–29; Oberon in,
129; as pastoral, 128, 129, 365; Puck
in, 122, 129, 130–32, 361, 371; "Pyramus and Thisby" play in, 119, 120,
126, 247; Snug the joiner in, 126;
Theseus in, 23
Millais, John Everett, 7
Milton, John: on beheading of Charles I,
1; compared with Shakespeare, 25,
381; on divorce, 1; on doctrine of the
Trinity, 1; on evil, 381; and meritocracy, 81–82; and Protestantism,
19; on Shakespeare, 383
—works: Il Penseroso, 19, 103; A Masque,
109, 143, 359, 376; Paradise Lost, 30,
41, 55, 264–65, 349; Samson Agonistes,
320
Minotaur, 128, 129
The Mirror for Magistrates, 47, 138
Mirror imagery: in The Comedy of Errors,
60, 63, 144–45; gender differences in
use of mirrors, 176; in Henry V, 175;
in Julius Caesar, 175–76, 212; and
Narcissus myth, 60–63, 147, 213,

245–46; in Richard II, 145, 146, 147,
175, 176–77; in Richard III, 47–48; in
Troilus and Cressida, 211–12
Molière, 233–35
Monarchical absolutism, 140–42, 172–
73, 180–81
Money: coinage, 397n24; in Measure for
Measure, 397n24; in The Merchant of
Venice, 255, 261–62, 272, 295,
397n24; and usury, 255, 272, 396n1
Montaigne, Michel de, 18, 370
Moon imagery, 77–78, 125
Moore, G. E., 216
More, Thomas, 33, 98, 158, 171, 352
Morgann, Maurice, 24, 25, 26, 156, 161
Motherhood: in Coriolanus, 290–95,
297–99; in Macbeth, 292–93
Motivation: Coleridge on, 282; in Ham-
let, 198–99, 277, 282, 382; in Henry
VI, 31, 281; Iago's motivation in
Othello, 281–84, 285, 287; James-
Lange theory of, 31, 198–99; in Mac-
beth, 284; in Othello, 281, 382
Movies. See specific movies
Mozart, W. A., 58
Much Ado about Nothing (Shakespeare),
221–26: authorship indicated on
quarto of, 378; Beatrice and Benedick
in, 221–25, 243; Catholicism in, 17;
Claudio in, 67, 68, 222–25, 345;
compared with Love's Labour's Lost,
221–22, 225; compared with Romeo
and Juliet, 225; compared with Two
Gentlemen of Verona, 67, 68, 221, 222,
225; dating of composition of, 221;
Dogberry in, 226, 227; Don John in,
222, 225, 244; Friar Francis in, 17;
Hero and Claudio in, 222–25; impediment of wit in, 221–26; language in,
225–26; marriages at end of, 222;
overheard conversation in, 223; same-
sex bonds versus heterosexual love in,
70, 221–22, 224–25; Stratford production of, 223
Mythology: Actaeon myth, 242; and

Cymbeline, 340–41, 345; of Dionysus/Bacchus, 323; of Hercules, 323, 326, 343; of Jupiter, 340; in *A Midsummer Night's Dream,* 23, 108, 121–22, 128–29; Narcissus myth, 4, 60–63, 114, 213, 245–46; Pasiphae myth, 23, 128–29; and *Pericles,* 345; Proteus myth, 64; of Pygmalion, 38, 359–60; Tereus and Philomel myth, 87; Theseus myth, 23, 108, 121–22

Napoleon Bonaparte, 171

Narcissism: of Cassius in *Julius Caesar,* 175–76, 178, 188; and Narcissus myth, 4, 60–63, 114, 213, 245–46; in *Richard II* and *Richard III,* 147; in *Romeo and Juliet,* 114

Narcissus myth, 4, 60–63, 114, 213, 245–46

Narrative and Dramatic Sources of Shakespeare (Bullough), 191

Nashe, Thomas, 27, 37, 364

Native Americans. *See* American Indians

Nature: art versus, 356–59, 364–67, 401*n*16; Pastoral/Romantic tradition on, 96, 103, 177, 228–29, 356; and reason, 177–78; Stoics on, 177–78, 356; in *The Tempest,* 364–67; in *The Winter's Tale,* 352–59, 364. *See also* Pastoral

Nayfack, Nicholas, 361

Neoplatonism, 345

Nero, 141

New Historicism, 9–12, 18, 21, 22, 23–24, 38, 157, 379

A New Mimesis (Nuttall), 9, 155, 179, 180, 182, 295

New Testament. *See* Bible

Nietzsche, Friedrich, 242, 246

Nihilism, 307–9, 312, 374

Niven, David, 52

Nominalism, 9, 97, 99, 157–58, 160, 385*n*10

Norris, Christopher, 9

Norsa, Leon, 272

Oaths, 91

Obedience of a Christian Man (Tyndale), 141

Objective idealism, 327–28

Objectivism, 214–17

Occultatio, 187, 346

Ockham's razor, 83

Octavius Caesar, 339

Oedipus, 149, 202–3

Oedipus at Colonus (Sophocles), 320

Oedipus Rex (Sophocles), 226, 288–89

The Old Curiosity Shop (Dickens), 46–47

Old Testament. *See* Bible

Olivier, Sir Lawrence, 45–46

"On Our Crucified Lord, Naked and Bloody" (Crashaw), 88

Ophite Gnosticism, 263–65, 270–76

Orgel, Stephen, 364

Othello (Shakespeare), *277–84:* authorship indicated on quarto of, 378; compared with *Romeo and Juliet,* 281; compared with *The Taming of the Shrew,* 75; compared with *Troilus and Cressida,* 219; date of composition of, 286, 290; "delayed consummation" motif in, 75, 280; Desdemona's death in, 278; Desdemona's lost handkerchief in, 31, 278; double-time sequence in, 235; Emilia in, 278, 282, 283; ending of, 277–78; and homosexuality, 280–81; Iago compared with Prince Hal, 151; Iago's manipulation of Othello in, 225, 278–84, 287, 297, 298; Iago's motivation in, 281–84, 285, 287; Iago's suspicions of unfaithfulness of Emilia with Othello in, 281–84; marriage of Othello and Desdemona in, 279, 280, 281; Othello's belief in unfaithfulness of Desdemona with Cassio, 235, 395*n*5; Othello's death in, 278; Othello's gullibility and insecurity in, 279–80; Othello's jealousy in, 277–80, 281; Othello's military career in, 279–80; outside-in motivation in, 281, 382;

nature, 177–78, 356; philosophy of, 24, 177–78, 192, 194–95, 228; and Virgil, 208, 209

Strachey, Lytton, 334

Stratford-on-Avon: description of, 1, 2, 3; grammar school in, 14; religion in, 14, 16, 18

Structuralism, 149, 213, 265

Stubbes, Philip, 20

Subjectivism, 214–17

Suetonius, 190, 191

Sugimura, N. K., 329, 330

Sun imagery, 77–78, 125

Surgeon imagery, 164

Swift, Jonathan, 362

Swinburne, A. C., 322

Taboo, 203

Tacitus, 398*n*9

Tamburlaine (Marlowe), 82, 84, 389*n*27

The Taming of the Shrew (Shakespeare), *70–82:* allusion to Ovid in, 190; audience reactions to, 70–71; authorship indicated on quarto of, 378; Bianca in, 71, 72, 80, 84–85; cap episode in, 81; characterization in, 133; compared with *As You Like It,* 73; compared with *Cymbeline,* 344; compared with *Henry V,* 155; compared with *Love's Labour's Lost,* 74, 89–90; compared with *A Midsummer Night's Dream,* 73; compared with *Othello,* 75; compared with *Richard III,* 48–49; compared with *Twelfth Night,* 73; "delayed consummation" motif in, 75; as early play, 387*n*1; falconry imagery in, 70, 113; father of Kate and Bianca in, 71, 75, 81; Greer on, 72, 79; Kate on wifely role in, 79–81; Kate's anger in, 71–72, 73, 78; Kate's submission in, 72, 76–81; Latin language in, 84; love and kisses between Kate and Petruchio in, 73–77; Lucentio's and Hortensio's wives in, 81; Lucentio's wooing of Bianca in, 84–

85; *mens intacta* (mind virginally intact) referring to Kate in, 92; Petruchio as good for Kate in, 71–72; Petruchio's ignoring of Kate's distress in, 48–49, 249; sexuality in, 72–73, 344; sleep deprivation of Kate in, 70; Sly in, 72–73; on sun versus moon, 77–78; Tranio and Gremio in, 75; wedding of Kate and Petruchio in, 74–76

Tarski, Alfred, 124

Taylor, Gary, 21, 22, 27

Teichoskopia, 209

Television, 58, 60, 186, 360, 377

The Tempest (Shakespeare), *360–76:* America mentioned in, 362–64; Antonio in, 365, 371; Ariel in, 360–61, 369, 371–72; betrothal masque in, 373–75; Caliban in, 5, 362, 364–68, 372–73; Caliban's attempted rape of Miranda in, 366, 367, 368; compared with *As You Like It,* 364, 366, 367; compared with *The Comedy of Errors,* 61, 241; compared with *A Midsummer Night's Dream,* 361, 373, 375; compared with *Twelfth Night,* 241, 365; compared with *The Winter's Tale,* 358, 367; editions of, 364; ending of, 370; Ferdinand and Miranda in, 367, 368, 370, 373–74; film versions of, 361; forgiveness in, 370–72; Gonzalo in, 362, 364, 365, 367; Gonzalo's communist commonwealth in, 362, 364, 370; grace in, 372–73; magic and Prospero in, 358, 361–62, 369, 372, 376; Miranda in, 363, 366–70, 373; nature-art debate in, 364–67; as pastoral, 364, 365–67; Prospero and Ariel in, 360–61, 371–72; Prospero and betrothal masque in, 374–75; Prospero and Caliban in, 366, 368; Prospero as impresario-figure in, 237, 281; Prospero's banishment from Milan in, 364; Prospero's Epilogue in, 371, 376; Prospero's guilt in, 367–68, 370, 371,